BAD SEED

THE BIOGRAPHY OF NICK CAVE

IAN JOHNSTON

LITTLE, BROWN AND COMPANY
Boston New York Toronto London

ISBN 0–316–90833–9

10 9 8 7 6 5 4 3 2

Printed in England

As a freelance writer Ian Johnston has contributed numerous articles on film and music to various publications. He has also worked on several music videos. His first book, an account of the turbulent career of the cult American group The Cramps, entitled *The Wild, Wild World of The Cramps*, was published in 1991 and has been described as 'simply one of the best and most diligently researched music books of all time'.

Bad Seed is his second book.

'Gripping and well-written . . . an impressively pukka examination' *Q*

'Remarkably frank' *Select*

'Nick Cave has found the biographer that his fascinating and often painful life deserves . . . An important piece of rock history deftly handled' *Melbourne Age*

CONTENTS

PHOTO CREDITS

ACKNOWLEDGEMENTS

━━━━━━━━━━━

Without the participation of the following, the book that I instigated could never have been written in the style that I wished. The story could have been told in at least half a dozen ways, from as many perspectives. This is the way I chose, right or wrong.

I am indebted to those named below for agreeing to be interviewed and quoted. Thank you for your memories, patience, frankness and generosity throughout the time that it has taken to write this book. I naively embarked on this project without any conception of the scale of the task I had set myself and you helped guide me through. However, I alone stand responsible for writing the story related here and any errors, omissions and misguided interpretations are my sole responsibility. Experience tells me there are bound to be some, so please accept my apologies in advance:

Barry Adamson, Blixa Bargeld, Bingo, Trevor Block, Edzard 'Eddie' Blum, Chris Bohn, Bleddyn Butcher, Jessamy Calkin, Chris Carr, Tony Cohen, Christoph Dreher, Evan English, Mick Geyer, Mick Harvey, Screamin' Jay Hawkins, John Hillcoat, Rowland S. Howard, Anita Lane, Lydia Lunch, Shane MacGowan, Daniel Miller, Peter Milne, Simon Pettifar, Kid Congo Powers, Peter Sempel, Mat Snow, Jim Thirlwell a.k.a. Clint Ruin, Ivo Watts-Russell, Thomas Wydler, Victor Van Vugt.

Many thanks are also due to Nick Cave, without whom there would be no story. All the quotes in this book are from interviews conducted with the author, apart from those attributed to Nick Cave, the sources of which are indicated in the text. Many thanks are again due to Mick Harvey, who is blessed with an incredible memory.

Also thank you to: Katy Beale, Beate, Polly Borland, Viviane Carneiro, Martyn P. Casey, Shaun Connon, Rayner Jesson, Marina Lutz, Mac McKenzie, Tex Perkins, Prudence, Conway Savage, Jeffrey Lee Pierce, Jo and Jackie at Mute, Tony at 4AD.

Thanks to Andrew and Lynn Trute for freely contributing a wealth of press interviews/articles, radio interviews, tapes and videos to add to my own, from their inexhaustible 'Cave archives', and for helping to compile this book's discography.

Thanks to the following for also contributing research material: Mark Isted, Damon Wise, Trish Scorgie, David Arnoff, Jane Giles, Paul Belchamber at the Vintage Magazine Company, staff at the BFI Library, Pete Martin, Rocky at Supermags. Thank you David Dix for translating certain material and Cathi Unsworth for freely providing an interview she conducted with Marc Almond.

Thanks to Benjamin Lefevre for providing accommodation while research was conducted in New York, to Peter Price, Pamps and Simone in São Paulo, Nora Natali, Simon Lubert and David Cook in Los Angeles.

Last, but by no means least, many thanks to my agent, Mic Cheetham, and to my editor, Richard Beswick, for his unstinting encouragement, insight, patience and faith. You are a saint.

This book is dedicated to Caroline Wale, and to all the musicians featured within.

Introduction

London 1982

A CONCERT FOR TV AT
THE ACE
BRIXTON (NEXT TO TOWN HALL)
BRIXTON HILL

BIRTHDAY PARTY

plus **VIRGIN PRUNES**
THURSDAY 25 NOVEMBER
Doors Open 8.00 p.m. Show 8.45
TICKETS £2.50

The venue's sound system is turned down as The Birthday Party slowly file on to the stage. A smattering of applause, whistling and shouts of abuse greet their appearance. The capacity crowd is crammed against the front of the stage and sways as people elbow each other for a better view. A stocky youth with a pink mohican methodically barges his way to the very front of the stage, pushing all around him to clear his path. He grips the stage for support, securing his vantage point. Mick Harvey briskly takes up his position at the drum kit, a determined expression on his face. Gaunt guitarist Rowland S. Howard, cigarette dangling from his mouth, gazes at the floor. Tracy Pew, sporting a large black cowboy hat, white frilly shirt, necktie, leather trousers and an enormous studded leather belt, plucks at his bass, momentarily sending ominous vibrations throughout the venue. Lead singer Nick Cave cuts a striking figure: tall, thin, his long, jet-black dyed hair piled up into an unruly bouffant quiff, further exaggerating his considerable height. He wears pointed Cuban-heeled boots, leather trousers and a T-shirt which bears just one word – JESUS. He stares disdainfully at the audience for a moment, then talks into the microphone: 'We've got to wait till they get the cable down. You can entertain us while we wait.' Jeers, whistles and laughter greet his announcement. Cameramen with large portable video recorders on their shoulders stalk the stage acknowledging instructions into their headsets. 'Get on with it!' The crowd's impatience mounts.

'Hands up who wants to die!' shouts Cave. The crowd erupts, hands shooting upwards. Mick Harvey's pounding military per-cussion begins. Cave paces the stage, grunting, yelping, punc-tuating the hypnotic rhythm. 'Have you heard how Sonny's Burning?' yells Cave. At once Howard's fractured, distorted guitar and Pew's rumbling bass start propelling the song towards eruption. The band's exhilarating sound is compressed, abrasive, unrelenting in its momentum. 'Flame on! Flame on!' screams Cave into the faces of the now seething mob at the front of the stage. Cave's feet kick into the crowd, fists are shaken in return.

During the climax of the set's penultimate number, 'Fears of Gun', Cave, writhing on the floor, is brutally dragged into the crowd, kicking in all directions. 'Love! Love! Love . . .' The microphone has disappeared into the throng. In an instant the pink-haired mohican, who has been awaiting his chance all evening to strike at the singer, tears Cave's T-shirt from his back and with other members of the audience begins ripping it to shreds. He smiles at his friends: he has obtained his souvenir of the evening. The camera crew hover at a safe distance in the background, trying to locate Cave in their sights. An arm, a leg, then Cave's head appears as he tries to pull himself across the crowd's shoulders towards the band. Two roadies try to hoist him back on to the stage. Cave throws punches in their direction. Howard blasts feedback from his amplifier, Pew and Harvey maintain a thundering beat. Suddenly the three musicians' onslaught halts but Cave is still grappling with audience and roadies. Slowly he slides back on to the stage, over the heads of the audience, while the roadies try to locate the microphone in the mêlée. Feedback, screams, applause.

'They'd finished the set, there was time for an encore and the TV people were waiting,' recalls the band's publicist Chris Carr. 'The director asked me, "What's going to happen?" I said, "I don't know." We had fifteen minutes left. I climbed up the stairs at the side of the stage. Tracy and Rowland were sitting at the bottom. I reached the top, went into the dressing room and approached Mick and Nick. I said, "Are you going to go back on and do some more stuff?" Nick said, "What's the point?" I said, "The first four songs were new material, so let's do it." Mick said, "Why don't you go and fucking do it!" I said, "What, I go on and play the spoons?" Nick replied, "Yeah, why don't you go on and play the fucking spoons!"

'There was a heated row where Mick was the basic aggressor. Nick did his scorpion act, he was the stinger. He had decided this was fun so he was going to give it a go for all it was worth. Eventually we managed to sort it out and they came back down the stairs. They had a meeting with Rowland and Tracy and decided they were going to play. The first song of the encore was to be "Release the Bats", which they had played a number of times during their lifetime. The TV people were very happy and so was the audience.'

'More! More!' The band reluctantly returns to the stage. Cave looks distracted, bored. Pew seems particularly unsteady on his feet, unfocused. Mick Harvey appears to be exceedingly angry. The band stare vacantly at each other. 'More! More!' Pew reacquaints himself with his instrument and begins trying to play a bass line which sounds suspiciously like a song the group have played much earlier in the evening. 'We've heard that one!' hollers a female voice in the crowd. Pew stops playing, then tries again. The riff sounds exactly the same. The group exchange hesitant glances. 'Get on with it!' Mick Harvey takes charge of the situation and shouts out the rhythm of the song they have agreed to play: 'One, two, three, four!' He starts to pound his drum kit. Pew begins playing as if he has just realised that he has missed his cue; he is out of time and playing completely the wrong riff. Exasperated beyond endurance, Harvey throws down his drumsticks and glares furiously at the bass player.

'I watched from the side of the stage and saw what seemed to be a misunderstanding between Mr Pew and Mr Harvey,' Carr continues. 'Mr Pew went over to rectify it. I remember parts of the drum kit flying through the air and falling off the stage. A sheepish Mr Pew unplugged his bass, Rowland "I don't know where I am" Howard wandered around and Nick Cave stormed off. I asked Tracy what had happened; he replied, "It wasn't my fault, I couldn't remember how to play 'Release the Bats' and Mick wasn't too happy so he destroyed his drum kit. I'm sorry."'

Guitarist Rowland Howard nonchalantly walks to the microphone amid much yelling and shaking of fists from the audience. Nick Cave, who has returned to the stage, moves towards him, places one hand over the microphone and begins to whisper into his ear. Snatches of his conversation are audible: 'Yeah . . . look . . . no way . . . yeah, we're all right. Look, if you want to tell them, then tell them.' Cave walks off. Howard clears his throat and addresses the audience. 'If you want an encore from Nick Cave and Mr Harvey then I think you'd better yell because they don't seem to want to do one . . . I'm sorry.' Howard leaves the stage. Members of the audience continue to stomp their feet in unison, the clapping becomes louder. 'More! More!' After three minutes Nick Cave, Tracy Pew, Rowland S. Howard and Mick Harvey have still not reappeared and the clamouring mob are drowned out as the venue's sound system is turned up, spewing forth a vapid white funk track with a stoic dance beat: thud, thud, thud . . . The show is over.

The following week Steve Sutherland's review of the gig in the *Melody Maker* concluded with this prophetic paragraph: 'When a band returning for an encore, arguing over which number to play and storming back off stage unable to reach any consensus of opinion, is the evening's biggest talking point, when it gets to the stage where what a band *doesn't* do matters more than what they do, then maybe the ultimate thrill is to cease to exist?'

1

HMS Britain: This Ol' Tin Tub

'Coming to England was really the making and the breaking of the band,' surmises The Birthday Party's former lead guitarist Rowland S. Howard. 'We all started to get on each other's nerves so badly. It was never the same again on a personal level. Myself and Nick [Cave] in particular had been friends until that time. We both seemed to go our different ways.'

The Birthday Party arrived in the UK from Melbourne, Australia, in late February 1980. From the beginning the individual band members – vocalist Nick Cave, guitarist Rowland S. Howard, multi-instrumentalist Mick Harvey, bassist Tracy Pew and drummer Phill Calvert – found the whole experience exasperating and a bitter disappointment. For twelve months the band had looked forward to this moment with mounting anticipation but the bleak, grey landscape of London dampened their ardour and a lasting depression set in. For the young Australians a long period of disillusionment and grinding poverty was only just starting to unfold. The problems began from the moment the group checked into a hotel near Euston Station for the night. 'We had money when we came over,' says Howard, 'but I had all my money stolen from my suitcase by one of the chamber maids when I arrived. Tracy's ghetto blaster went missing too.' 'I remember that Rowland was always losing money,' recalls a quizzical Mick Harvey.

After a couple of nights in the hotel they moved into a small basement flat in Earls Court, west London, where they would stay for a month. The rented accommodation, consisting of one bedroom with two single beds and a small kitchen which also served as a living room, could barely contain the band members and the few possessions they had brought with them. 'In Australia we were pretty much on the poverty line but that was a very different affair compared to London,' recalls Mick Harvey. 'In Melbourne I had a flat with two bedrooms. It wasn't very well appointed or anything like that, but it was on The Esplanade above St Kilda beach. I'd come out in the morning, and there was the bay. I didn't even think about it until I'd been living in London for a while. You come to London, and everything is very squashed, you are living in very close proximity to other people.' Within two weeks the ever-practical Harvey had found himself temporary employment and moved out of the Earls Court flat into a bedsit in west Kensington, as his girlfriend Katy Beale was arriving shortly from Australia.

Any thoughts of announcing the band's very existence, or even taking positive steps towards trying to secure gigs in the metropolis, had to be shelved for an indefinite period. Practical issues were far more pressing if the group's members were ever going to be able to cope with living in London. The vague contingency plans that had been laid in Melbourne had completely underestimated the trials and tribulations of scraping together some form of day-to-day existence in the midst of a deep economic recession. 'We went through a bit of a shock there,' said Nick Cave, recounting their initial reaction to England at the end of 1980, 'and it took about four months to get any confidence back at all.'[1]

The opportunity to escape from Australia had seemed like a dream come true when it was initially suggested by the band's manager, Keith Glass, who also ran their record label, Missing Link. Glass, who had spent three weeks in London during the summer of 1979, thought that the group would stand more chance of gaining a receptive audience in the UK than if they remained in Melbourne. The trip itself was partially financed from an advance from Glass but the group had also spent a year playing gigs across Australia, receiving $5 each a night, to save up for the move. After that they would have to fend for themselves, since Missing Link was only a small independent label incapable of offering the group the support or the budget of a major record company. A number of venues in Melbourne were closing their doors to the band because of their reputation, and relocation was necessary for its survival. If the band members could have envisaged the squalor that awaited them in London, they might have thought twice about moving.

In early April the rest of the band moved into a small shared house, 39 Maxwell Road, Fulham, west London. They lived on the breadline, unaware that they were actually able to claim supplementary benefit because of a reciprocal arrangement between the UK and Australia. The household existed on a diet of cheap curry dishes purchased for £1 from a seedy Indian restaurant in Earls Court. Within a few weeks Rowland Howard began to suffer from malnutrition and had to write to his parents, who forwarded him £70 a fortnight so that he could survive. For months the daily curry dish would be Nick Cave's only form of nourishment, apart from whatever chocolate bars and crisps he and Tracy Pew were able to steal from the corner shop.

Mick Harvey and Katy Beale soon moved into the Fulham house, as the rest of the group were experiencing difficulties in paying the rent. 'I didn't have a very good time that year,' laughs Harvey. 'I went to the cinema a lot and looked around the place. I hadn't got sick of struggling to live in London at that stage. The others weren't enterprising enough to find out what was good about the place. There was a lot of lethargy.' Those members of the band who could face the prospect of menial work would go daily to the local employment agency to find out if there were any jobs available that day. Tracy Pew obtained part-time work cleaning at Heathrow Airport. The space he and his workmate for the day were required to clean was vast. After five hours Pew would eventually meet his partner in the middle of the complex, having started work at opposite sides of the building. Pew would often be discovered at the house asleep on the stairs, so physically exhausted after his daily toil he couldn't find the energy to walk any further to reach his bed. Howard recalls: 'Half the people in the house had to get up at 7 a.m. to go to work and the other half had gone to bed at 5 a.m. I don't think it was much fun for Mick Harvey.'

Most days Cave would make the effort to drag himself off his makeshift bed in the house's narrow hallway at 7 a.m., to arrive at the agency by 8. Frequently he would be informed that there was no work that day, and on occasion he would be reduced to stealing bicycles in a vain attempt to raise capital. When employment was available, Cave invariably found himself walking for miles to London Zoo to wash dishes in the cafeteria or pick up litter around the grounds, for which he would receive £10 a day. Compared to the lifestyle he had enjoyed in Melbourne, living in London came as a severe shock. The unfriendly and aggressive attitude of many of the English people with whom he came in contact, coupled with the inclement English weather and the somewhat oppressive atmosphere of London itself, would have a profound effect upon him. 'Before Nick left Australia he'd always lived at home, he'd always been comfortable,' says Howard. 'He'd come round to my house and try and talk me into spending the last of my money on getting drunk. I'd say, "How am I going to live for the rest of the week?" "Well, you can come to my mum and dad's house and have dinner every night." As if! He didn't have any idea what it was like in the real world. Going out and living in that world really changed him.'

Owing to their impoverished financial state, the band members could not satisfy their cravings for hard liquor, heroin or amphetamine sulphate, which led to a frantic desire to obliterate the senses in any manner they could possibly afford. Cave and Pew would regularly scour the house and neighbours' dustbins for empty bottles, which they would exchange for cash at the local off-licence. With the little money they received the pair would buy a couple of bottles of cider each.

'There were always a lot of arguments about money,' says Anita Lane, Nick Cave's former girlfriend, who arrived at 39 Maxwell Road in mid-April. 'It was almost like there were white lines on the floor defining people's individual spaces. I remember sleeping out in the hallway on more than one occasion. I didn't really care, because I was with Nick. At that time I didn't really have any ambitions of my own. We just enjoyed each other's company and appreciated the same things.' With the arrival of Rowland's girlfriend Genevieve McGuckin and Tracy's girlfriend Caitlan, the lodgings were becoming even more cramped and tolerance levels quickly began to drop.

The group did not possess a television and the only in-house entertainment was provided by a cheap portable record player. 'We only possessed two records,' says Howard, *'Metal Box* by Public Image Ltd. and *Buy the Contortions* by James Chance. Mick Harvey had other records but he kept them in his bedroom so they wouldn't be destroyed; I remember Tracy fell on top of the record player in a stupor a couple of times. We played those records all day in rotation, that's all we listened to for months. As far as those records influencing us musically in any way, I think they drove us away from anything remotely like that.'

On a business trip to London, Keith Glass paid a visit to the Fulham house to check on his investment and the band's progress. He was not pleased with what he saw. 'Keith wasn't prepared to put up with any unpleasant duties. He immediately called a band meeting and said that he was disgusted with people's behaviour,' laughs Howard. 'We just continued to struggle on in our disgusting fashion. I couldn't live like that now.'

For the most part the struggle to obtain gigs and establish tentative contacts with record companies fell on the shoulders of Mick Harvey and the amiable Phill Calvert. 'Phill was a very enthusiastic person,' says Howard. 'He loves music but he didn't have any idea of what was going on.' The process was laborious and unrewarding: tramping around the capital with tapes and test pressings; knocking on the doors of small venues enquiring if the band could play. Initially the group had compiled an album's worth of recordings on Missing Link with the intention of releasing the record on the Ralph label in the United States. Ralph, who had introduced to the world the anonymous neo-Situationist pranksters The Residents, were very excited by The Birthday Party's recordings but insisted that any record deal must be on a global basis. The Birthday Party argued that they needed their record company to be based in England, and so the deal fell through. The group had scored some success in distributing a single, 'Happy Birthday'/'Riddlehouse', directly to shops specialising in independent music. The record had been made initially as a free single, given away at the last Boys Next Door concert (before they changed their name to The Birthday Party), before departing for England, and spare copies came in useful in trying to raise awareness of the group. A copy sent to the *NME* gained The Birthday Party their first English press notice, in late February 1980. The review was generally positive, although the writer complained of 'the odd unfortunate stray poltergeist guitar throwing fits here and there' and patronisingly asked readers if they were ready for 'rock'n'droll'.

In England, responses from both promoters and record labels were mostly negative. The band soon realised that their limited success in Australia meant nothing at all in London, and because of their nationality many promoters and companies refused to take them seriously. It became clear that the London gig circuit that had been so virile during the punk explosion of the late seventies, with scores of new bands appearing almost every night, was in its death throes and the popularity of the emerging nightclub scene was superseding any demand for live music. Not only that, but the group's innovative style, firmly based in rock music, was completely out of step with what most English groups were producing.

The band was shocked that the capital was not thronging with daring groups of the calibre of The Fall or The Pop Group, as they had naively been led to believe in Australia. When they actually saw or heard for themselves the bands who were critically praised every week in the music press, they were outraged by the bland, herd-like mentality which seemed all too pre-eminent. *En masse* the group went to see a special package show at the Lyceum ballroom off the Strand, featuring the supposed *crème de la crème* of new English rock music: Echo and the Bunnymen, A Certain Ratio, The Teardrop Explodes and The Psychedelic Furs. The Birthday Party were appalled. 'They all just stood there and played their guitars and sang,' says Howard. 'It was lame, bland. No one seemed prepared to do anything that might embarrass themselves or put themselves on the line in any way.' 'The only band I saw when we arrived who I thought were a great live band were Joy Division,' adds Mick Harvey. 'Live, they generated something. That's what was missing from the other groups we saw.'

To the Australians, British groups were too self-conscious about their work and suffocated by the upheavals rendered by punk. During the punk years Britain had held the world's attention with a vehement blast of musical energy and innovation. Now there was little left but a hollow shell with the media still proclaiming the UK as the foremost exponent of new music. Punk, the catalyst for change, which questioned anything and everything, had been transformed into new wave/post-punk, which in turn had become as conservative as the rock music that had preceded it. A new set of rules had been established in a medium where there should be none. Strict adherence to leftist, politically correct ideology had inadvertently limited the horizons of musicians' imaginations. Any group daring to be provocative was ostracised. Consequently most British groups, ever-fearful of being branded sexist, careerist, or perhaps worst of all, rockist, produced vapid music.

Rockist, a term flippantly coined by Pete Wylie of Wah!, was seized upon by the music press and became the all-important buzz word of the period. The vague ideology behind this slogan was that rock music was now completely redundant, having been terminally savaged by punk, and that the only way forward was to incorporate ethnic elements of any description into your music to avoid sullying your hands with inherently unsound rock. Rock was a dirty word. A professed dislike for a musical style such as reggae was tantamount to admitting racist tendencies. Even the amplified electric guitar, once so essential in articulating pop and rock's cathartic release, was now viewed as an ungainly phallic symbol, an instrument synonymous with male oppression/aggression. The synthesiser was the favourite instrument of the day and the result was countless groups playing sterile, up-tempo pop funk. Pop was the future; taste, design and style were the touchstones.

Some groups began to embrace what would be termed as 'new romanticism', an insipid celebration of consumerism and neo-glamour, which allegedly carried an element of irony.

Others were content to return to the styles and sounds of rock/pop of ages past: ska, blue beat, glam, rockabilly and mod. The regurgitation of old styles seemed unending, fads appearing and disappearing within months.

In June the escalating tensions within 39 Maxwell Road finally proved too much to bear and Nick Cave, Anita Lane, Tracy Pew and Caitlan moved out of the Fulham house and into a squat that Nick had found in Walterton Road, adjacent to Harrow Road, Maida Vale, W9. 'They moved out because they couldn't afford the rent, so I was stuck there paying the rent after I had my own fucking place,' says Mick Harvey. The five-room squat was filthy and completely dilapidated. None of the toilets worked as the bowls and cisterns had been smashed in a vain attempt to deter all but the most desperate squatters. The electricity and hot water supply had been disconnected. Nick and Anita's room was completely bare, apart from a begrimed mattress and a door laid horizontally across a couple of tea-chests which served as a table. A portable gas heater provided the only warmth and the room was lit by candles. 'Nick had discovered Samuel Beckett just before we came to England,' says Howard. 'Beckett played a large part in his life while he was living in Maida Vale because he could relate to the subject matter.' While Nick and Anita did little to improve their living conditions, Pew gathered together whatever scraps of fabric and furniture he could find at a rubbish tip, decorating his room until it resembled a run-down bordello. The Walterton Road squat would serve as Cave's home for some time and would eventually attract other desperate expatriate Australians. 'There was no phone and so there was no way to find out if they'd be home. No, I didn't go there, I was working, and it didn't seem like the place to visit somehow,' says Harvey.

Eventually the band managed to obtain their first gig in England, on 29 June, at the Rock Garden in Covent Garden, where the audience was often made up of bewildered tourists vainly looking for a good time in the capital. Eight days later they would play at a better venue with an enlightened policy towards 'alternative' music, the Moonlight Club in West Hampstead. In the audience that night was Ivo Watts-Russell, managing director of the then small independent company 4AD. Watts-Russell began his music career in the late seventies behind the counter at the Beggars Banquet record shop. He was very excited by a stream of amateur recordings that were being produced by groups after punk and would often pester the Beggars Banquet record label with demos that young hopefuls had brought into the shop. Impressed by his enthusiasm, Beggars Banquet decided to back him to the tune of £2,000 in trying to set up his own label with the shop's manager, Peter Kent, on the condition that Beggars Banquet would eventually sign the most successful bands. When Kent left the label, Ivo decided that he was not going to act as Beggars Banquet's talent scout any longer. He recalls: 'I was living in that wonderful twilight world of being someone who was a fan of music and who was able to release records.'

Ivo was at the Moonlight Club that night to see another band, The Lines, but inadvertently got to witness The Birthday Party, who were supporting Deutsch Amerikanische Freundschaft. 'Somehow Daniel Miller at Mute had got them that gig because he was working with DAF,' says Watts-Russell. In 1978 Miller, responding to the energy of the punk explosion, had formed his own record label, Mute, initially to release his own influential electronic single 'T.V.O.D.'/'Warm Leatherette', inspired by J. G. Ballard's novel *Crash*. Since then Mute had enjoyed a successful series of independent singles by Fad Gadget and Silicon Teens. Miller had initially heard of The Birthday Party through an Australian acquaintance, and after seeing them live decided he wanted to sign them to his label. 'I remember thinking, that's an unusual name,' recalls Miller. 'They'd pressed up white label copies of their album and someone recommended that they come and see me to put it out. Live, I was struck by their intensity, the atonality but within the context of songs. I can't say I caught the lyrics but their presence . . . they looked like a gang, they've always looked like a gang. That's a really good thing about a group, if they have a menacing gang vibe about them. Because they were Australian everything had a non-Anglo-American edge to it, the music, the look. I wasn't particularly interested in US or English music. I was very interested in electronic music but I felt they were the first real rock line-up band that I liked since The Ramones, say. That was very important because I wasn't into the concept of a rock group. To me, they were just using those instruments to do what they needed to do, they weren't using them with any reference to the past.'

Much to Miller's disappointment, he was unable to sign the band because he was too busy working with the German expatriate group DAF. 'The label was just me working out of my home and DAF were all living at my place at the time,' Miller continues. 'I had no money, because I hadn't released any albums at that time, just singles. All the people I had worked with up to that point in time were individuals, the cost of looking after a band I hadn't thought about. Just at that moment when I had to make a decision about The Birthday Party, in terms of workload, it was a very difficult period. Even though DAF were a brilliant band and I knew they'd do well, to have a group from Australia as well, feeding them and housing them because they were moving over, just wasn't on.' Miller then recommended The Birthday Party to Ivo.

'I walked in and they were in the middle of their set,' recalls Ivo of the Moonlight Club gig. 'They weren't going down very well, in fact they weren't being well received at all. Out of all the people I went with I was the only person that liked them. There seemed to be a feeling that they were just funny "Aussies" at that gig.' Unbeknown to Watts-Russell the reason for The Birthday Party's shambolic performance was that for the first time the group had been supplied with a 'rider' of free alcohol which they had eagerly consumed ten minutes before taking to the stage. At one point during the gig Tracy Pew momentarily forgot that he was meant to be playing the bass guitar and stood at the side of the stage with his arms by his sides staring into the middle distance. 'The next day I got a phone number for them and called them up and they informed me that they were playing at the Rock Garden the following month. I went to see them there. The thing that struck me and that I enjoyed the most, it's great when that happens when you're seduced, was Mick Harvey's keyboard playing at that time. I loved that wonderful old organ sound they had, that's what struck me first. They were tight and very polished at that point in time. They seemed to explode the longer they stayed in England. They just became wilder and wilder.'

Ivo had spoken to Mick Harvey when he had rung the band house in Fulham and it was with Harvey that he would build a lasting friendship. 'When I saw them at the Rock Garden I went backstage and spoke to Phill Calvert, who was the friendliest on that initial meeting I suppose, and then I got talking to Mick. The song that I enjoyed the most was called "Mr Clarinet" and they informed me that they had recorded it and Mick said, "Why don't you put it out?" That's how it started.' Despite Ivo having made tentative contact with the band, a formal arrangement regarding the release of any of their material would not be finalised until late September.

The group had in fact already released the 'Mr Clarinet' single on Missing Link and had distributed it in the same manner as the 'Riddlehouse' 7". The record would be reviewed in the *New Musical Express* on 28 June but the tone of the review would reveal the xenophobic attitudes with which the band would have to contend: 'The Birthday Party are an *avant-garde* Australian group, no sniggering at the back please . . . Presumably there is a dark heart of the Australian psyche, up-river from their own particular Saigon; at any rate this group seem to want to reach it. I'm not sure they live up to these pretensions but they sound serious . . .'

Cave, in particular, had become increasingly frustrated by the band's inactivity. Since arriving in England in February they had played a grand total of four gigs. In Australia, they had sometimes played this number in a week. Cave began to question whether he was still in a band. Even more disturbing to him was the fact that he had not been writing while in England. The inspiration just did not seem to come, although he had written the lyrics to a couple of extremely bitter, self-loathing songs entitled 'Nick The Stripper' ('Nick the stripper, hideous to the eye, hideous to the eye') and 'King Ink' ('King Ink feels like a bug, And he hates his rotten shell').

On 18 September, the band played at the Hope and Anchor

pub venue to celebrate their hook-up to 4AD through Missing Link. 'It was a peculiar relationship,' says Ivo. 'We didn't actually sign The Birthday Party until "The Bad Seed" EP in 1982. The other records were through this peculiar licensing deal through Missing Link in Australia. I wouldn't dream of entering into a relationship like that now, it would be restrictive, to say the least.'

In October the first Birthday Party single was released through 4AD. Again, this comprised material previously recorded at Richmond Recorders in Melbourne in January that year. The three-track 7" featured a brooding Cave composition, 'The Friend Catcher', drenched in waves of feedback perfectly mirroring Cave's lyric, 'It's a prison of sound'. '"The Friend Catcher" was one of the funniest guitar overdubs I've ever seen in my life,' reminisces The Birthday Party's long-term collaborator, sound engineer Tony Cohen. 'Rowland had spent a long time setting it up. He had all these pedals, including a thing called a Blue Box which didn't work properly but made a great sound, a complete fluke. He also had a Space Echo which is a tape echo machine which repeats the sound, but Rowland being the sensitive fellow that he is turned every knob up to the max, which makes the thing feed back and make a constant noise. He didn't even have to touch the guitar 'cos this horrible noise was just going on. He just started bashing the foot pedals. I was watching him, frantically trying to figure out what pedal to hit next.' Also featured was a frantic interpretation of the classic Gene Vincent and the Blue Caps' number, 'Cat Man'. Covering the song was Keith Glass's idea. Glass had long been an ardent fan of Gene Vincent and fifties rock'n'roll in general and had played the track to Nick Cave, who saw possibilities for the song in the hands of the group.

To promote the record Ivo would enlist the aid of the ebullient freelance publicist Chris Carr. Having already heard of the band through his brother-in-law, Chris Bailey, lead singer of The Saints, and his other Australian contacts living in London, Carr was keen to meet the group. 'Ivo was reserved due to the financial implications,' recalls Carr. 'He thought as soon as I met them, he'd have to start paying me.' Carr initially met the group by accident in the Beggars Banquet record shop in Earls Court, then encountered them again at the tube station, where he suggested they should talk. While handling the publicity for much bigger acts, such as Siouxsie and the Banshees, Carr would ceaselessly champion the band for a nominal fee, and often for nothing. He had instinctively recognised the enormous potential of each member of the band and would play a key part in gaining them press recognition, nurturing their talent and offering them invaluable advice. It is possible that without Carr, The Birthday Party would not have enjoyed the success that they did in England.

'I was intrigued by them,' says Carr. 'Their artistic leanings were more developed than their rock'n'roll leanings, there was an intelligence there. With Tracy, Nick and Rowland you could talk to them about other things apart from the rock business and the latest record release. It was strange trying to introduce English people to a young Australian group called The Birthday Party. The name didn't fit the climate; in those days there were groups with names like Killing Joke. I really had to drag people along to see them. A lot was done in the very early days but it was unfocused PR-wise. There is a hierarchy within the British music press and there were very staid people looking after the papers. We had to wait for new writers to champion the band but The Birthday Party's audience would develop ahead of the press due to their live shows.

'Usually a lot of Australian groups who come to England have to rely on an Australian audience but in The Birthday Party's case the audience would soon be comprised of 70 per cent English and 30 per cent Australian. I don't think any Australian group has ever done that. The Birthday Party did something that other bands weren't prepared to do; come over to England and live here. Most come over on a major label's money and then fuck off again when the money runs out. They were brave. It was a fairly austere time, living from hand to mouth, a very grim existence.'

The weekly music papers in the UK, unlike any other country in the world, have, or rather had, an influence both in the industry and over their readership disproportionate to the actual number of copies they sold. This was primarily because of the very limited number of radio stations broadcasting 'alternative' music; consequently music buffs had little chance of hearing the releases that were pontificated upon in the press. 'The band had no real affinity with anything that was going on in Britain,' says Chris Bohn, who wrote for the weekly music papers during this period. 'The British music scene would have been quite content to keep them isolated so they wouldn't affect anything that was going on. Echo and the Bunnymen, The Teardrop Explodes; cute pop was the flavour of the moment. British pop at every level seemed to take the easy option and was clearly not making new music of any kind. I got the feeling, and perhaps this is false, that when Ian Curtis of Joy Division killed himself a lot of people subconsciously took fright from using music to go deeper into themselves, or make any exploration outside of some superficial comfortable melody.'

Though the music papers were initially uninterested in The Birthday Party, the group were instantly seized upon by the respected and influential Radio 1 DJ, John Peel. Always on the lookout for challenging new music, Peel had been immensely impressed with their second Missing Link single, 'Mr Clarinet', and their new 4AD release. Peel would regularly air 'The Friend Catcher' on his radio show, on more than one occasion playing the record twice in one night. The single's success in the Independent Singles Charts was largely due to Peel playing the record continuously, to the point where his listeners would criticise him for doing so. 'He was always saying very kind things about the group on the radio,' says Rowland Howard, 'and he was very helpful in bringing attention to us.' Peel would further boost the group's profile by inviting them to record the first of many sessions for his show. The group rose to the challenge of recording four songs – 'Cry', 'Yard', 'Figure of Fun' and 'King Ink' – on eight-track recording equipment, in eight hours at the BBC's studios in Maida Vale. Peel was very pleased with the session and played it several times.

The Birthday Party played their eighth and final gig in London that year on 3 November at the Moonlight Club before returning to Melbourne. Encouraged by Peel's response to their records, and knowing that the group were going to record an album which he wanted to release in the UK, Ivo advanced Glass £5,000 towards the recording costs. Before they left the UK the band were enraged by news from Australia that Glass was going to release on Missing Link the LP that they had compiled for Ralph in the United States. 'The Friend Catcher' single was already available in Australia on import and Glass's release, *The Birthday Party/The Boys Next Door*, contained only two previously unreleased tracks. A number of angry phone calls were made to Glass in a vain attempt to persuade him to abandon the project, or at least release the record as a mini album and omit the group's previous name from the title, but Glass was obdurate. 'While we were away in London he [Glass] lost contact with us,' says Harvey. 'Even during the first year he was getting paranoid about us linking up with record companies in the UK and he started doing strange things. We didn't have a cast-iron deal with him.' The band were further angered when they saw the black and white sleeve Glass had commissioned depicting a series of badly drawn cartoon 'stick men' walking naked across an abstract backdrop. From this point on their relationship with Glass would rapidly deteriorate.

Upon returning to Australia the band would embark on a brief tour before commencing recording in December. When they played the Crystal Ballroom in St Kilda, Melbourne, on 22 November, they were shocked to see a queue stretching from the venue's steps around the corner of the building. Only nine months previously they had left the country having been neglected by audiences and the media alike. 'It seems we had to go away before we were liked,' Nick Cave indignantly told a radio interviewer. 'It's ridiculous to find ourselves in *RAM* [premier Australian music paper]. To find half a page on us is quite a shock, we really had to fight for those things before. It just seems indicative of the press and media over here.'[2]

The band felt that at last their long-held uncompromising stance had been vindicated, in Australia at least. Now they would direct all their energies towards England. 'We snapped out of our lethargy when we got back to Australia,' says Mick Harvey. 'That's when the negative reaction really hit home. The attitude was that we were really going to kick them in the teeth now and that's what happened. We were prepared.'

NOTES

1 3RRR radio broadcast, Melbourne, November 1980.
2 Ibid.

2

Seeds Bloom

Nick Cave's career in music began at Caulfield Grammar School in Melbourne, during the early seventies. In his third-form year at Caulfield he would gradually become involved with his first group. Initially named Concrete Vulture, although the name would change five or six times a year, this comprised John Cochivera, Mick Harvey, Phill Calvert and Brett Purcell, on guitar, guitar, drums and bass respectively.

At this time there was a steady influx of English progressive rock groups touring the country as Australia was becoming firmly established as a new territory for record companies looking to expand their market. During the space of a year Cave, who had first been introduced to rock music by his eldest brother Tim, would attend concerts by Manfred Mann, Jethro Tull, Procol Harum, Deep Purple and The Moody Blues. John Cochivera had introduced Nick to his elder sister's boyfriend Barry, who would indoctrinate him with the fashionable music of the era. Barry worked in a record shop in Melbourne, possessed an impressively loud hi-fi system and methodically collected every conceivable progressive rock record released. He treated his record collection with the utmost reverence and only he was allowed to touch the LPs he owned, which were stored alphabetically in protective plastic covers. Under Barry's tutelage Nick would be encouraged to buy albums by the likes of The Moody Blues, Pink Floyd and Genesis. Nick's relationship with Barry steadily soured when he began to discover rock music according to his own developing tastes, such as Alice Cooper's *Love It To Death* LP (containing Cooper's enormous hit 'I'm Eighteen') and T. Rex's glam rock anthem 'Get It On'. Barry would simply mock these records as moronic and chide Cave for their supposed lack of lyrical sophistication compared with the 'master works' being produced in the progressive rock field.

'I started playing guitar when I joined the group,' says Mick Harvey. 'I didn't have any training, or anything. I had been playing with them before Nick arrived on the scene. They'd asked me to join and I just picked up a guitar and started working out songs. It was all a bit of a surprise to me.' At first Cave was not that interested in the band, not seeing eye to eye with the bassist, Brett Purcell. In the early stages Purcell was clearly the most influential member of the group in terms of musical direction though not in terms of musical ability, which was Cochivera's domain. Purcell liked the heavy rock band Blue Cheer, and seventies super group West, Bruce and Lang, while Cave had long since begun to tire of the hard rock style. After much cajoling from the others, and a few shots of vodka from a hip flask that he carried around with him, Cave tunelessly howled his way through very ramshackle versions of The Animals' 'House of the Rising Sun' and Alice Cooper's 'I'm Eighteen'. The other band members began to ask themselves why they had asked him to sing in the first place, but as none of them wanted the chore, Cave became the lead singer by default. 'He became the singer because he had the biggest ego,' recalled Harvey in 1989. 'I mean, he couldn't really sing at the time.'[1] Though he could barely sing in tune or hold a note, Cave did possess an undeniably arrogant swagger which impressed most of the other members. In any case, apart from Cochivera, the group did not take themselves seriously; it was purely a social activity. The general idea was to have fun and inject some life into the regimented existence at school.

Cave and friends became infatuated with the Scottish group The Sensational Alex Harvey Band. Lead singer Alex Harvey once dubbed himself 'The Last of the Teenage Idols' after winning a competition in the mid-fifties imitating Tommy Steele. He formed a group that acted as a backing band to visiting American luminaries, including John Lee Hooker and Gene Vincent, but it was only during the early seventies that he himself rose to prominence. Despite his overtly theatrical stage shows, Harvey's energetic renditions of Jacques Brel's 'Next', Tom Jones's hit 'Delilah' and his own composition 'Framed' anticipated the emergence of English punk rock. Cave in particular was very taken with the group and Alex Harvey's rousing vocal style, delivered in his broad Glaswegian accent. The school group's repertoire would soon include a large selection of Alex Harvey songs. 'Alex Harvey was everyone's favourite and we used to do maybe eight or nine of his songs,' Cave would tell *Record Mirror* in 1986. 'We did just about everything off the first album, we did "Framed", "Midnight Moses", "Isobel Gaudie".' Whenever Alex Harvey subsequently released a record, Cave would always be among the first to buy it. 'We also played a few Alice Cooper songs, Lou Reed/Velvet Underground songs and strange originals which were usually influenced by the latest record that somebody had bought. David Bowie . . . Oh my God!' laughs Mick Harvey.

With the advent of glam rock, Cave and his friends began adopting the trappings of the glam style as sported by David Bowie and other performers of the era, dyeing their 'feather cut' hairstyles, wearing brightly coloured socks and platform shoes. Their mode of dress clashed with the strict school uniform policy at Caulfield and caused endless problems, in particular for Cave's close friend Tracy Pew, whose parents lived in the outer suburb of Mount Waverley. Pew wore his hair long and was repeatedly told by various teachers to have it cut. He would take no notice whatsoever, to the increasing annoyance of the staff. The final straw came when he dyed his hair green, whereupon he was informed that if he did not have it cut immediately he would be suspended. The following day he arrived with his head shaved. For his insolence he was rewarded with a three-week suspension and a warning of expulsion if this behaviour was to occur again. 'Tracy was very much the school character,' says Harvey. 'I was quite the opposite. I kept to myself because I didn't like the whole environment. I didn't try and buck the system because there was no way to do it. I was just waiting to get out of there, basically.'

Nick shared several classes with Tracy and was endlessly amused by his robust sense of humour. Through timing, coupled with his sardonic wit, Pew could read aloud to the class a set passage from Shakespeare and by the end of his recital have the entire room, including the teacher, weeping with laughter.

Although he was in no sense a loner, throughout his adolescence Nick felt ostracised from everyone around him. He felt unable to communicate other than with a handful of friends, and envied those who could engage readily in social conversation without being overanalytical about what was being discussed. Small talk was not his forte. Over many years this tendency in his character would become more ingrained. Being at a boys' school, his contact with the opposite sex was limited to school dances, and when he did meet a girl he would be awkward and shy. He would look at himself in the mirror and feel unhappy with his reflection. He thought his facial appearance was unappealing; his nose was too large and his chin too small and the acne blotches that covered his face did nothing to alter his opinion. He also felt that he was generally disliked by his friends' parents. Apart from Tracy's mother, Nancy, of whom he was fond, he got the distinct impression that the parents felt he was a corrupting influence, though he could never see any justification for their suppressed hostility towards him.

When asked by the school's career officer about his future plans, Cave would reply that he wanted to become a painter. Although he excelled at writing, painting seemed the only viable means of expression open to him. The bohemian lifestyle of the artist appealed to him and the work of his favourite painter at that time, Brett Whiteley, seemed to offer some focus for his rebellious attitude towards moribund suburban existence in Melbourne. Cave was intrigued by the intensity and diversity of the themes that the Sydney-based painter included in his landscapes. When he read interviews with Whiteley recalling his background as being 'Longueville, middle-class, overlooking yachts, tranquil, little squabbles about money'[2] and describing as a child pacing around 'in a Napoleonic rage', these emotions immediately struck a chord with him. Cave would often hanker for the freedom and undisciplined way of life he had enjoyed growing up in the countryside of Victoria.

Nicholas Edward Cave was the third child of Dawn and Colin Frank Cave. He was born on 22 September 1957 in Warracknabeal, a small country town 180 miles north-west of Melbourne. Dawn was a librarian, and Colin was employed at the local school teaching English literature and mathematics. Nicholas's older brothers, Tim and Peter, were respectively five and three years his senior. In 1959 the middle-class family was completed with the birth of sister Julie. Shortly after Julie's birth, when Nicholas was two years old, his parents sold up their small property in Warracknabeal and moved due east across Victoria to the much larger country town of Wangaratta to work at the local high school. Wangaratta, the county capital of Victoria, is 125 miles north-east of Melbourne on the Hume Highway, with the High Country and its rich vineyards to the north. Intersected by Ovens River and a railway junction, it is primarily an agricultural town, a commercial centre in the livestock trade, dotted with towering flour and woollen mills.

Glenrowan, the nearest small town, less than fifteen miles from Wangaratta is shrouded in the legends surrounding the final stand of one of Australia's most enduring folk heroes, 'the last bushranger', Ned Kelly, of whom the young Nick Cave was very much enamoured. Kelly and his outlaw gang dominated Victoria's north-eastern ranges for three years in the late 1870s, exacerbating the tensions between the small settlers and wealthy landowners in the region. They took every opportunity to flout the law by stealing horses, 'duffing' (rustling) cattle, robbing banks, killing policemen and occupying towns. In 1880 Kelly's bushrangers were finally trapped in Glenrowan. After the rest of the gang had been killed, the twenty-five-year-old Kelly, clad in heavy armour, stepped out of a pub and into a hail of police gunfire and immortality. Shot in the legs and captured, he was sentenced to death in Melbourne. On the gallows he reportedly muttered, 'Such is life' moments before his neck was broken. The era of the anarchic individualist standing beyond the law was over but a symbol of Australian anti-authoritarianism was born. During the late 1960s Colin Cave would write a foreword and book jacket notes for a volume examining the continuing fascination surrounding the Kelly legend, entitled *Ned Kelly – Man or Myth*.

After attending junior school, Nick Cave was enrolled at Wangaratta High School where both his parents were still employed. During the vacations he would often be sent to stay with both his paternal and his maternal grandparents, who lived in the suburbs of Melbourne. Throughout the 1940s his grandfather, Frank Cave, had worked in radio producing *The Shell Programme*, so named because it was sponsored by the petroleum company. Nick would always look forward to seeing his aged, chain-smoking grandfather and revelled in his cynical, ill-humoured temperament.

At the age of eight Nick joined the choir at the Wangaratta Cathedral, his parents' local church, which enjoyed a good reputation in the region due to the exacting discipline exerted by the choirmaster Father Harvey (no relation to Mick!). Cave took his role as a chorister seriously, although he never rose through the ranks of the choir's hierarchy, as he would humorously recall many years later, in 1987. 'There was a certain pecking order in the choir, you started off in a black cassock and ended up in a purple one, but unfortunately I never got to wear the purple cassock. So I remained getting taller and taller in the black cassock at the end of the line. It had something to do with the fact that I couldn't sing solos particularly well, not really having a natural singing voice. Little did the choirmaster know I would become in later years a world-famous vocalist.'[3]

Due to Father Harvey's perseverance the choir one year recorded a Christmas single, 'Silent Night'/'Oh, Little Town of Bethlehem', Nick Cave's very first appearance on vinyl. Despite the choirmaster's growing exasperation with his limited vocal range, Nick would dutifully sing with the Wangaratta choir for many years. He loved the solemn ritual involved in the Anglican religious services, and listened attentively during the extra-curricular religious instruction classes which were a formal requirement for the choristers in the parish. While many of his fellow choristers were completely uninterested and would make elaborate excuses to skip the religious studies groups, Nick would remain enthralled by the parables charting Christ's teachings and miracles.

As Nick grew older he would be increasingly drawn towards his eldest brother, Tim. While Peter's recreational activities centred around motorcycles and motorcycle racing, Tim was a devotee of rock music. In the late sixties he had become captivated by hippie culture. He wore his hair long and joined demonstrations in Melbourne against the conscription of young, voteless Australian men (the voting age in Australia was only reduced from twenty-one to eighteen in 1973) to fight against the North Vietnamese. As in America, the reverberations of the Vietnam War escalated the great divide between young 'free spirits' and the older conservative generation who supported the Liberal Party and their view that the war was necessary to stem the perceived tide of communism from sweeping through South-East Asia.

Tim would always bring back from Melbourne the latest rock albums he had purchased by artists such as Cream, Jimi Hendrix and Australia's The Loved Ones. Of all Tim's records Nick was most strongly drawn to The Loved Ones, in particular their songs 'Everlovin' Man' and 'Sad Dark Eyes' and thought that lead singer Gerry Humphries possessed a great emotive voice. He would while away many hours listening to his brother's records, which seemed to offer some form of liberation from the dreary day-to-day realities of school life in the remote country town and a link with the distant outside world.

Despite gaining above-average grades in English and art, Nick began to develop a reputation at the high school as a disruptive influence. Any misdemeanour he committed, no matter how petty, would immediately be reported to his mother and father. During the family's evening meal there would often be a long silence, followed by admonishments detailing whatever mischievous activities he had been involved in during the school day. Nick's incessant misbehaviour, from his openly hostile attitude towards his teachers to being caught by the headmistress, Miss Harris, smoking down by the creek, proved very embarrassing for his parents. No punishment administered by either themselves or the school seemed to stem the tide. For his part, Nick found the whole atmosphere oppressive; there seemed to be no respite from school, not even at home.

Nick's rebelliousness would begin to strain his relationship with his father. They would see each other only infrequently at school, as Nick would be allocated to classes where Colin was not teaching, and during the long evenings Colin would increasingly immerse himself in organising a highly successful adult education programme in the region. During the little spare time left to himself, Cave senior would be involved in amateur theatre production workshops. Nick began to feel that his father was shutting him out of his life, and he persisted in trying to gain his attention through any means possible. This would be the basic pattern of his antagonistic relationship with his father until Colin Cave's death.

At the age of twelve Nick's best friend was Eddie Baumgarten. The pair were inseparable. Together they formed a society called The Triple A Club, or Anti Alcoholics Anonymous, the first club that would boast Nick Cave as a member. Members used to meet in a friend's parents' garage in Wangaratta where they would contribute what little money they had towards buying a few bottles of cheap cream sherry. The money was handed over to a local taxi driver who purchased the liquor for them, as they were far too young to buy the alcohol themselves. After long sessions at the garage the pre-teen club members would furtively stagger back to their respective homes, drunk and sick. The resourceful Baumgarten actually built his own still in his father's back yard. It consisted of a little beaker on a tripod, into which potato peel and sugar was poured. When heated, steam would flow down an attached coiled pipe and supposedly the alcohol would collect in a bucket. More often than not the concoction Eddie produced tasted disgusting but the two boys enjoyed the illicit thrill of this extra-curricular science experiment.

At the weekends Mr Baumgarten would loan Nick and Eddie two shotguns and drive them to the ranges surrounding Wangaratta to indulge in their favourite pastime of shooting rabbits infected with myxomatosis. Unbeknown to Mr Baumgarten, the boys would smuggle cans of beer along for the trip.

Nick's other great friend during this period was Brian Wellington, whose family lived on a farm on the outskirts of Wangaratta. Brian's family owned horses and lent them to the boys to ride wherever they pleased. The Wellingtons would often invite Nick to join them hunting in the countryside, which he enjoyed immensely. During these excursions Brian would teach him about the intricacies of setting traps.

In order to try to keep abreast of contemporary fashions, Nick would have to shop at a clothing store in the centre of Wangaratta called Hattums, the only shop which stocked vaguely fashionable late-sixties clothes specially delivered from Melbourne. His two most treasured items of clothing purchased from the store were an orange button-down shirt and a pair of woollen flared trousers. Despite the constant itching and extreme discomfort that the fabric caused his very sensitive skin, he would wear the garments with pride at every available opportunity.

In 1970 the continuing problems with Nick's behaviour finally reached breaking point with both the school and his parents. His own recollections of the events that led to him leaving Wangaratta High School at the age of thirteen are as follows: 'Being an inquisitive twelve-year-old boy, me and my friend attempted to pull down the knickers of a sixteen-year-old girl, and twice the size of us put together. We were seen by an old maid, Miss Harris [the headmistress], and she decided that we were lost in some orgy of sexual degeneracy. The parents of the young girl tried to press charges of attempted rape, which didn't really stick because I was only twelve years old at the time. I was forced to leave the school in shame . . .'[4] Colin and Dawn, exasperated by his behaviour, and reminded of it every day by their colleagues, felt that Nick needed to have some discipline and responsibility instilled into him. They believed that a private boarding school in Melbourne, Caulfield Grammar, was the ideal establishment for this. In fact, it was to have the opposite effect.

Nick's first term at Caulfield began in the winter of 1971. From the very start he loathed the school, its teachers, the rules and regulations of the boarding house and most of his fellow pupils. Coming from an academically inclined background, he felt he was intellectually superior to his classmates, whom he perceived as the spoilt sons of rich farmers and bureaucrats. The modernist architecture of the school, with its red-brick walls, was like a prison to him. He felt alienated, and was obstreperous and aggressive towards the other pupils. On his very first day at school, he took it into his head to pick a fight with one Beaver Mills. Mills, despite his small stature, was the scourge of the boarders and was constantly fighting. Nick repeatedly goaded him, and when Mills retaliated physically, Nick beat him up. From now on he would be the natural target for anyone wishing to prove themselves a 'hard case' and would be frequently involved in mindless scuffles and brawls which he would invariably win. The boarders were united in their hatred of the pupils who attended the school on a daily basis, whom they branded 'day scabs' and upon whom Nick would often vent his pent-up aggression.

'The first time I saw Nick he was having a fight with somebody on the oval, Warwick Harrison, if I remember correctly,' recollects Mick Harvey. 'I thought he was really scary because he won. He was quite an extrovert at school, everyone knew him and he made a show of himself.' Michael John Harvey was born in the Victoria countryside but moved with his family at the age of four to the Melbourne suburbs. His father was a Church of England vicar in the parish of Ashburton where Mick was raised in a strict religious environment in a small house adjacent to the church. In the early seventies his parents enrolled him as a day boy at Caulfield. 'The boarders were quite separate from us, but I knew that he [Nick] was a new boarder. My association with Nick would grow very slowly.'

At Caulfield Nick did begin to pay more attention to his academic studies, especially the subjects that had always interested him the most, English literature and art. In these areas he would find release from the oppressive atmosphere of the school, and he would endeavour to read as much as he could rather than relying on the required set texts. Consequently his grades steadily improved. He liked and respected both his fine art and English literature teachers, and was particularly influenced by the latter. He began to read Russian novelists, especially Dostoevsky: *Crime and Punishment* made an indelible impression on him, as he was attracted to the concept contained within the novel that the world is divided into the ordinary and the extraordinary and that the extraordinary should not have to live under the dictate of the ordinary majority.

Nick would remain a boarder for only a year. In 1972, through his work on the adult education programme, Colin Cave was promoted and appointed director of a similar project in Melbourne. He bought a large two-storey, five-bedroom house covering half an acre on the tree-lined Airdry Road in the affluent suburb of Caulfield. The house had been previously owned by Mario Malano, a successful Italian-Australian wrestler. Nick rejoined his family on Airdry Road and continued to attend Caulfield Grammar as a day boy. Although he was initially relieved to be out of the boarding house, he soon discovered that he had made many enemies amongst the 'day scabs' whose ranks he had now joined and with whom he would have to mix on a daily basis. He would also have to endure the taunts of the boarders he had left behind, who had disliked him in the first place. School seemed more oppressive than ever and he longed to escape.

NOTES

1 Mick Harvey to Karen Schoemer, 'Get Your Wings', *Option* magazine. May/June 1989.
2 Brett Whiteley, quoted in John Rickard, *Australia: A Cultural History*, Longman, 1988.
3 VPRO, Dutch television documentary, *Stranger in a Strange Land*, March 1987.
4 Ibid.

3

The Boys Next Door

Throughout his last months at Caulfield, from 1974 until leaving in 1975, Cave would spend most of his free time with his friends David 'Dud' Green and Tracy Pew in a small building adjacent to the school purchased by Caulfield's art department. The 'art house', as it was known, was also the meeting place for the band members, Harvey, Calvert, Cochivera and Purcell. It was here that a lot of the group's ideas were initially formed, between bouts of drinking alcohol and smoking dope, the effects of which Cave disliked intensely.

Because of the friends' mutual interest in the arts, coupled with their unconventional appearance and unwillingness to socialise, the group would be branded a bunch of 'pretentious poofters' by their fellow pupils. Matters came to a head one lunchtime when a first-year was cajoled by a bunch of older boys to run into the art house and yell 'Faggots!' at the top of his voice. This he promptly did, but while fleeing the building he collided with Cave. The group then grabbed the terrified youth, threw him over a table and proceeded to pull his trousers down, taunting him mercilessly and informing him in no uncertain terms that they had been waiting for months for a young boy like himself to come and visit them and now they were going to introduce him to the joys of anal intercourse. After they had succeeded in scaring him half to death, they finally released him, crying his eyes out. The boy's story of how he had narrowly escaped being 'raped' in the art house during lunch hour soon swept throughout the school. The friends were now without doubt 'poofters' and Cave in particular could no longer appear in public without being verbally abused.

The band struggled on, playing gigs twice a year, at school socials and at dances at Shelford, Caulfield's sister school, 'We did quite a few shows playing schools when we didn't know any more than about four songs and played "Johnny B. Goode" in every key you could possibly imagine,' recalled Cave in 1979. 'They were complete fiascos but we went down quite well. Phill could drum OK but the rest of us were totally incompetent. I was a terrible singer.'[1] Within the band, animosity between Cave and Purcell continued to escalate. Not only were they at loggerheads musically, but Purcell thought the band was carrying dead wood by having Cave as the singer. After one abortive rehearsal, Purcell stormed up to Cave and told him he was the least musical member of the band. Cave could not have cared less: Purcell's opinions and the group were of no consequence to him anyway.

During 1975 the all-important HSC exams loomed on the horizon for the sixth-formers at Caulfield. Cave and friends continued to behave in the same manner that they had done throughout their schooling, undeterred by numerous warnings that their futures were at stake if they did not pass the exams. 'I was just amazed talking to people at the bus stop who were doing five hours' homework a night,' says Harvey. 'I was doing maybe fifteen minutes a night and absolutely nothing on the weekends. It's incredible to think of it now. It was matriculation, sixth form, a big year, you really had to pass. Other people were becoming more intense and working really hard.'

Cave continued to be preoccupied by literature and to read as much as he could concerning the history of art. Attaining good grades was not important to him, just so long as he got sufficient marks to enable him to attend art school. Tracy Pew, perhaps the most academically gifted of the group, did no work at all. 'I just wanted to pass,' says Harvey, 'and I made damn sure I did! I'm proud of it because I didn't do any fucking work at all.'

At one point it was extremely doubtful whether Cave and his friends would even be sitting the exams with the rest of their class. 'We got caught doing something or other,' recalls Harvey. 'Smoking, I think. They tried to suspend us from school for a certain number of weeks, which would have meant we would have been unable to sit the exams. It was ridiculous, just the culmination of years of being sick to death of us for not having the right attitude to life. I think there were a couple of us they really wanted to get. I knew what it meant at the time and I was shocked but they didn't get away with it.' The boys' parents vigorously contested the impending suspension which, if it had been enacted, would have meant their sons having to attend Caulfield for another year. 'It was an expensive school!' laughs Harvey.

When the exam results were eventually announced, the marks were surprisingly good considering the input the friends had contributed. Despite attending only two English literature classes throughout the year, as the lessons clashed with his French tuition at Shelford, Tracy Pew scored an A, as did Cave. Pew also received an A for French. The average mark for the group, however, was C.

On their last day at Caulfield the friends decided there were old scores to settle. The entire gang dressed in the most outrageous garb they could find, donning full make-up and women's high-heeled shoes. Phill Calvert carried a handbag, within which was concealed a brick. They proceeded to spend the day walking around the grounds of the school, and anyone who dared insult them was promptly and repeatedly hit with the handbag.

During 1976 the old Caulfield Grammar group, now renamed The Boys Next Door, became fragmented. Purcell left the band, Cave, who was still living at his parents' house in Caulfield, had enrolled at Caulfield Technical College to study fine art, while Harvey obtained employment in a tax office for a year. 'I told my parents that I was deferring university for a year and proceeded to never go there of course, which is exactly what I wanted to do,' he recalls. 'I had done my matriculation, which is what they really wanted from me.' Harvey actually stopped playing with the group, as he was no longer interested in continuing unless the band started to write more of their own compositions rather than relying purely on cover material. There were also problems with the lead guitarist, John Cochivera. 'His parents sent him to America to stay with his uncle so he'd be away from our bad influence, particularly Nick's bad influence,' says Harvey.

Cochivera came from a very strict, wealthy family of Italian descent and for some time his father had taken a dim view of the company that his son was keeping. The final straw came when John was persuaded to take LSD for the first time with Cave, David Green and Tracy Pew. He had an unpleasant experience from the moment he took it and for months afterwards maintained that he was affected by recurring hallucinations and 'flashbacks'. He would complain that a smoky film clouded his peripheral vision, and a distinct change seemed to occur in his personality as he became remote and uncommunicative.

Before Cochivera departed for America, where he would undergo psychiatric treatment, the band rehearsed briefly with new member Tracy Pew. To the group's complete surprise Pew had been learning to play the bass guitar under the tutelage of his best friend Chris Walsh. Walsh and Pew had known each other since they were twelve. They lived a couple of streets apart in Mount Waverley, and shared a similar sense of mischievous humour and a passionate interest in music. Throughout the years Walsh had amassed a sizeable record collection, often obtaining import LPs by mail order from England and America. His collection would prove to be very influential for the group. His taste was expansive, stretching from the raw nihilistic rock music produced by the now legendary late-sixties Detroit bands The Stooges and The MC5, through the proto-punk thrash of The New York Dolls, to the outlaw figures of country and western music, Hank Williams, Merle Haggard and Johnny Cash. Cave and Pew were particularly enamoured of these overtly masculine, larger-than-life figures from the annals of country and western music history. Their existential, alcohol-sodden tales of good and evil, sorrow, unfaithful women, murder and redemption immediately struck a chord with them: 'I shot a man in Reno, just to watch him die,' sings Johnny Cash in 'Fulson Prison Blues'.

The friends would often gather at Walsh's house for long

drinking and music sessions, repeatedly playing the first three Stooges' albums, The New York Dolls' first album and an LP Chris had purchased in April by a group called The Ramones. Cave was excited and intrigued by The Ramones. Their minimalist, mercurial riffs with their anthem-like choruses seemed at once to condense the entire history of popular music. Dee Dee's bass thundered in the left-hand speaker, while Johnny's guitar roared in the right. Songs seemed to, and on occasion did, blend into one another, the beginning of a new song often heralded by Dee Dee shouting, 'One, two, three, four!' completely out of time. Lead singer Joey's nasal whine and peculiar phrasing were unique and his lyrics were simultaneously brilliant in their simplicity, hilariously funny and supremely delinquent: 'Beat on the brat, beat on the brat, beat on the brat with a baseball bat'. The Ramones revelled in and celebrated everything that the hippy generation loathed and despised: fast food, violence, trash culture, the CIA. They even antagonistically flirted with Nazi imagery in some of their songs. With their uniform dress code of black leather jackets, T-shirts, ripped jeans and dilapidated sneakers, The Ramones seemed to be ushering in a new sensibility and attitude to pop music which had previously been glimpsed only in The New York Dolls.

To begin with, Nick Cave enjoyed his first year on the fine art course at Caulfield Technical College, despite the fact that in his opinion the lecturers and the facilities available left a lot to be desired. After the stifling environment of Caulfield Grammar, the atmosphere was positively liberating. He was surrounded by young, potentially creative people who wanted to develop their own ideas and style in relation to fine art painting. 'Nick did a lot of self-portraits at Caulfield Tech,' says Anita Lane. 'They were very unflattering, expressionistic paintings, figurative in style. He was a great painter, I still think he is. The art school teachers didn't like him very much at all.'

A typical day for Cave at Caulfield Tech would begin at around midday in a local pub near the college. Together with a group of third-year students who adopted him and admired his work, he would start drinking heavily and would continue throughout the afternoon. They would stagger back to the college and proceed to paint until the early evening in a drunken stupor. His third-year friends were wild hedonists, a motley collection of alcoholics, homosexuals and models who were dabbling in the fine arts and who, in their spare time, frequented the more seedy bars and clubs in the red-light district of St Kilda. Technically they might not have possessed the ability of the more conventionally gifted and sober students on the course, but Cave thought their wilful abandon laid bare on the canvas contained a conviction and emotional charge that the others did not express.

Cave struck up a short-lived friendship with a lesbian painter named Karen. He thought her figurative paintings were the most inspirational work he had ever seen. They gained her much attention and she was congratulated on the standard of her work by members of staff, who would award her the highest marks. Then, in front of the teachers who moments before had been singing her praises, she would dip her paintbrush into a pot of black paint and draw a large phallus across her canvas. This repetitive, wilful obliteration of her work mortified her teachers and would eventually lead to her expulsion from the course. Cave was profoundly impressed by her irreverent attitude towards her own talent and art in general. Throughout his two years at Caulfield Tech, he would increasingly apply Karen's sensibility to his own creative endeavours on canvas, to the mounting annoyance of his teachers. His attitude to his fine art painting would later be reflected in his approach to music and his work as a lyricist.

Unlike most of the other students, Cave paid a great deal of attention to the art history lectures, receiving high marks for his essays and continuing to conduct his own studies around the subject. His main interest lay in Renaissance and Gothic religious paintings by the old masters Titian, Mattias Grunewald (*The Crucifixion from the Isenheim Altar* being especially favoured), El Greco and Diego Velazquez. He seemed to have little interest in twentieth-century artists. Students were encouraged to decorate their workspace with prints by their favourite painters, and Nick's choices from the sixteenth and seventeenth centuries were always criticised. He would argue that he was more interested in the iconography of religious paintings and that they were created from an overwhelming sense of faith and passion, in sharp contrast to many modernist painters whom he felt were coolly illustrating intellectual debates about perception and the nature of art itself.

Despite his views on modern art, Cave's own painting style owed much to German expressionism. Notwithstanding his differences with his teachers, his work was seen as extremely promising throughout his first year at tech. During the last four months of 1976, and into 1977, his attitude towards his art became more adversarial, his grades fell steadily and his position on the course became untenable. In his first year Cave's painting style was influenced by Brett Whiteley almost to the point of imitation, but at the beginning of the second year he started to change direction. In 1984 he would describe his first painting of the second year as 'A bit of a dirty picture with lots of . . . it was a pretty stupid painting now that I think of it . . . lots of penises and that sort of thing floating around.'[2] He would continue to paint in this vein, primarily to antagonise a female tutor who found his work particularly distasteful. 'She said she couldn't relate to sleazy art and could no longer talk to me. I think this could run as a parallel to the way The Birthday Party developed, to a certain extent. Just the thrill that ran through me when I heard her say that, the joy of displeasing somebody, was such that she was responsible for the entire direction that my painting went in from that day.'[3]

During his last two terms at Caulfield Tech in 1977 the impulse to irritate his teacher had become all-encompassing and his work became progressively more infantile. By the end of the second year, he began painting over the same canvas again and again, primarily because he had become so disenchanted with the school and its teachers that he could not be bothered to stretch new canvases. 'I think it was my two very unrewarding years at art college that were my training in hatred for all critics,' he would recall in 1987.[4]

The only painting he would submit for his final second-year exams was an obscene portrait of a circus muscleman gazing up a ballerina's dress. An assessment was made of his course work and it was unanimously decided that he should be failed. Thoroughly disillusioned, Cave left Caulfield Tech, his education prematurely curtailed. Though in some respects he was probably glad to leave and had been subconsciously sabotaging his own chances, he was bitter that he had not received any positive encouragement which might have tempered his negative impulses.

'My adolescence was pretty hideous but I think it probably would have been anywhere,' replied Cave to a question posed to him concerning his formative years in Melbourne. 'When we fought the "Big One" in 1976 or '77 my life seemed to open up a bit.'[5] During the last two months of 1976, news of the reverberations emanating from the New York underground rock scene at Max's Kansas City and CBGB's and the punk rock movement in London spearheaded by The Sex Pistols began to filter through to Australia. Chris Walsh had immediately obtained import copies of The Damned's 'New Rose' and The Sex Pistols' 'Anarchy in the UK', frenetic recordings which seemed to emulate the feelings of boredom, frustration and anger that were shared by The Boys Next Door in suburban Melbourne. Punk rock provided the perfect soundtrack for their attitudes and the manner in which they were living their lives. The Sex Pistols in particular, with their libertarian nihilism, appeared to be calling everything into question and offered seemingly unlimited possibilities for those who dared to follow: 'Be somebody, Be someone,' screamed Johnny Rotten with venomous urgency on 'I Wanna Be Me'.

'We were excited by the, for want of a better word, philosophy that John Lydon was espousing; individualism, anger and that fuck-everybody attitude. We found that quite stimulating!' laughs Mick Harvey. Already long-term aficionados of The Stooges and The New York Dolls, 'punk' came as no surprise to Cave and his friends, but now that the sensibility had been labelled it offered some legitimacy to their anti-authoritarianism. 'Certain people in Melbourne were influenced by punk to the extent that it gave a licence to be as unpleasant as possible,' recalls Rowland Howard, who during this period was studying fine art painting at Prahran Art College. 'That was the extent of it really. When the punk thing happened in England there were a number of bands all over the world that had reached the same conclusions in different ways; like The Saints in Australia and American groups like Suicide. That was the path that those groups were following anyway. It wasn't the case that people suddenly saw the light and started approaching things in a different way, it just made you feel that you weren't so alone in Australia. It validated it, in a way. To an extent it was an advantage to be in Australia and so far away from what was happening in London because all it was was a piece of knowledge. There was nothing tainted about it, you could take it seriously or not.'

During 1976 through till 1977 and 1978, however, the rock scene in Melbourne, both in the inner city and the suburbs, was dominated by a seemingly endless succession of uninspiring 'pub rock' bands: The Leisure Masters, The Sharks, The Sports, and Jo Jo Zep and The Falcons. The members of these bands were mostly in their late twenties and early thirties and had been playing on the circuit for many years. Their music was uniformly loud rhythm and blues and covers of TV themes laced with witless attempts at humour. Their primary function for the places that hired them was to provide the soundtrack to encourage punters to consume as much beer as possible. The airwaves were cluttered with mainstream rock bands like Sherbet, Skyhooks, Air Supply and The Little River Band. These groups were specifically designed to break the American market by merely imitating established English and American hard rock bands, content to entertain rather than to provoke or challenge the listener. Australia's mass media, including the major music papers, *Juke* and *RAM*, ignored the country's emerging new groups, perhaps – from the punks' point of view – in the hope that they would eventually disappear. 'When we lived in Melbourne nothing happened,' recalled Cave in 1983. 'It was very much the same situation I guess that happened in London, perhaps on a smaller scale. It was a very dead period and The Saints, who were a Brisbane group, came to Melbourne and really shook things up considerably. They were a very strange group. It seemed to me they had arrived at this particular sound entirely independently. They lived in Brisbane, which is in Queensland, probably the most conservative state in Australia, and when they used to play their concerts would frequently be stopped by the police. I would say they inspired a movement in general.'[6]

In the first week of August 1977, The Boys Next Door played their first gig as a punk group. The venue for the band's baptism by fire was Mick Harvey's father's parish hall. Despite his intense dislike of the group, their music and everything they represented, Mick's father had always allowed them to rehearse at the hall and had given his permission for the performance. Among the various local gangs drawn by curiosity fuelled by media images of English punk rock gigs was a small contingent of Ashburton skinheads, whose decision to attend had predictable results. Nick and Tracy had already run into trouble with skinheads in Caulfield, who used to beat the pair up with monotonous regularity because of their appearance. On one occasion they had been pelted with eggs by a group of Caulfield skins who used to congregate daily inside a local fish and chip shop. Later, the same group began to circle the pair in their van as they walked back to Nick's parents' house. Cave finally lost his temper and threw a rock at the van, leaving a large dent in its side. The vehicle immediately skidded to a halt and the skinheads piled out, ready for a physical altercation. When Cave and Pew held their ground and threatened to take them on, the skinheads backed down, climbed back into their vehicle and left.

Also in attendance at the Ashburton church hall were Chris Walsh, who had temporarily become The Boys Next Door's manager, Cave's sister Julie, and Gary Gray, who with Walsh had formed a Stooges-inspired punk band called The Reals. Cave had written a song called 'I'm So Ugly', which he felt was more applicable to Gray, with his long, greasy hair and severe acne, and gave it to The Reals to perform. In exchange he took the title of a Reals' number, 'Masturbation Generation', and wrote his own song around it. Despite the fact that Gray's voice left a lot to be desired and that the band were tuneless in the extreme, belting out titles like 'Hard On For Love' and 'Hitler Wasn't So Bad', The Reals would become an important live act on the Melbourne scene.

The Ashburton gig quickly descended into chaotic farce. A few songs into The Boys Next Door set, the skinheads started chanting in unison, 'Are you punks?' Cave and Pew immediately retaliated by spitting at them as if to affirm that they were. Within minutes the microphone was wrenched from Cave's hands and he promptly jumped into the small gathering to retrieve it. A protracted brawl ensued, during which Gray, Walsh and Cave were badly beaten up as the rest of the band continued with the set. In the centre of the mêlée Walsh fell to the floor where a skinhead stomped the sole of his boot on his face; for a week his cheek bore a perfect bootprint. Throughout the heated skirmish, Julie Cave valiantly braved the flying fists and feet, shouting to whoever would listen, 'Save my brother!' while trying to drag Nick to safety. The gig and the fight only stopped with the arrival of the police. The hall's power supply was shut off and the skinheads were arrested, as the officers saw them as the main aggressors. The Boys Next Door were given a firm warning and Nick Cave was bluntly informed by one officer that if he had allowed his daughter to attend the gig, he would have arrested all of them, taken them down to the police station and beaten them up.

A couple of weeks later, on 19 August 1977, The Boys Next Door, together with The Reals and Melbourne's answer to The Ramones with a political conscience, The Babeez, played their first major gig, at Swinburne Technical College, to an audience of around fifty people. Despite the small attendance, the gig marked the beginning of the slow emergence on the Melbourne scene of the teenage underground bands who had been energised by punk and by seeing the Sydney-based group Radio Birdman play live. Radio Birdman had taken their name from a line in a Stooges song entitled '1970', featured on their seminal album *Fun House*, and were essentially a Stooges cover band. The group's lead guitarist, Deniz Tek, was an American raised in Detroit, who had witnessed first-hand apocalyptic performances by The Stooges and had tried to recreate the experience in Australia. Though Cave despised Radio Birdman's lead singer Rob Younger, who used to cut himself with glass in the middle of their version of The Stooges' 'TV Eye', he regularly attended their gigs. In March he had gone to see the group's third performance in Melbourne, in the lounge of the Beverly Crest Hotel in St Kilda, and had made his presence felt, as journalist Richard Guilliatt would recall six years later. 'Down in the front where the real mayhem is happening, the familiar call-to-arms chanting and fist-shaking is being interrupted by the antics of a gangly adolescent who's had a bit too much of everything tonight. Oblivious to everything but the crunching volume of Birdman's attack, his body crashes around, his elbows dig into people's ribs, he pogos and lands on someone's foot. A drunk punk looking just dangerous enough for everyone to stay out of his way. His name is Nick Cave.'[7]

The Boys Next Door were completely unprepared for their performance at Swinburne. Many of their own compositions had been written with John Cochivera and featured two guitar parts. Cochivera had returned briefly to Australia earlier in the year and had written some more songs with the group, but he soon discovered that his style of guitar playing, which was heavily influenced by Dave Gilmore of Pink Floyd, was simply unsuited to the band's sound. After he had departed for America once again, the group had not bothered to rearrange their material, so much of their set for the Swinburne gig would consist of irreverent cover versions: The Ramones' 'Blitzkrieg Bop' and 'Commando', Them's 'Gloria', Alice Cooper's 'I'm Eighteen' and a Stooges-style rendition of Richard Berry's 'Louie, Louie'.

Listening to an edited tape of the Swinburne gig today, it was clearly a highly charged, chaotic event. Cave's screamed vocals are at the forefront of the group's abrasive punk thrash propelled by Mick Harvey's crashing guitar. Between songs Cave constantly harangues the audience. He changes the lyrics of Screamin' Jay Hawkins' 'I Put a Spell On You' ('You're stinkin' of whisky, You're stinkin' of gin, If I ever see you again, I'm goin' to punch your pretty face in') and The Who's 'My Generation'. 'Here's a song that I wrote,' he announces in deadpan fashion before the group play their interpretation of Lee Hazlewood's 'These Boots Are Made For Walking'. 'Nancy Sinatra helped me.' The Boys Next Door's own songs are archetypal teen punk anthems, ranging from seemingly New York Dolls-influenced numbers like 'Masturbation Generation' and 'Who Needs You' to 'World Panic', which carries echoes of sixties surf music in its chorus. The overall impression left by the recording is of a group relishing the sheer exhilaration of playing live, struggling to overcome their lack of technical ability and the apathy of the audience. The Boys Next Door are captured slowly fumbling their way towards an identity of their own, but there is virtually no indication of what would bloom five years later, either lyrically or musically.

Peter Milne, then a young teenage punk fan, attended the Swinburne gig. 'I'd actually met Nick, Tracy, Chris Walsh and Ollie Olsen at a party that Janet Austin [a mutual friend] had given sometime before the Swinburne gig,' recalls Milne. 'At first I thought they were really stupid because they were really drunk and they danced through this party in this conga line with their pants down around their ankles, just being typical private school yobbos. They're the worst yob of all. "Hooray Henrys" I think you call them in England. Then I saw The Boys Next Door play and immediately it was obvious that they had something. Nick was a consummate performer. When he was a vandal he was a consummate vandal. He took it to the limit but with so much finesse and style. From the earliest days that I saw them it was obvious that Tracy was a very talented bass player and Mick Harvey was talented on every instrument that he could put his hands on. The Boys Next Door were compelling, catchy, entertaining and funny.' From this date on Milne would attend every Boys Next Door gig, slowly becoming friends with the band.

'We fitted in with what people's idea of a punk group was like,' says Harvey. 'There were precious few of them around and suddenly we were one of them, almost by accident, because we were already playing things along those lines. We were very young and impressionable. We'd get overtly influenced at different times by things that we'd hear. That was probably a good thing because we were able to get all that out of our system, not in the glare of the public eye.'

In the audience at Swinburne was Rowland S. Howard, who had first met Cave at a party in April. 'He just came up to me and slammed me up against the wall,' recalls Howard. 'He was on acid and had just ripped a sink off the wall. He demanded to know whether I was a punk or not but eventually I got away from him. The next night I was at a gig and he apologised profusely and gave me a little hand-drawn map of how to get to a party. I went there and the same thing happened again. Tracy was there as well and I thought that he was a complete psychopath.' After his first group, The Obsessions, broke up, Howard formed a band named The Young Charlatans with singer Ian 'Ollie' Olsen. The Obsessions were due to play at Swinburne but had had problems with their drummer, who had decided to leave the group days before the engagement. Consequently, their début performance would be postponed until January 1978.

Unlike Cave and the other members of The Boys Next Door, Howard had attended a very progressive, liberal state-run school, Swinburne Community School, in Melbourne. 'I lived in the suburbs in a beach house which was designed for the beach but had ended up in the suburbs,' says Howard. As a young boy he was encouraged to study the piano for two years by his musically inclined middle-class parents, who played recorder and guitar in a folk group. From the piano he graduated to the guitar. At the age of sixteen he left home to attend Prahran Art College in the hope of meeting like-minded creative individuals, but he soon became bitterly disappointed with both the students and the college. His interest in fine art waned considerably halfway through his first year, at the end of which he was firmly advised by his teachers not to return despite having passed his exams. His musical ambitions only really began to take shape when he met Olsen in 1977. 'He was the first person I ever met who assumed that he was naturally superior to everybody else,' recalls Howard. 'He remains to this day one of the best self-publicists I have ever met. Ollie had the ability to make you think he was a complete genius and he gave me the ability to take myself seriously as a guitarist. The Young Charlatans was one of those bands where people said they'd seen us before we'd actually played. It all seemed so easy.'

A couple of days after the Swinburne gig, Howard introduced Cave to Anita Lane at a party. He had met Anita at Prahran and they had been good friends for some time. She had been one of the few applicants accepted to study fine art at the prestigious Victorian College of the Arts, The Gallery School. She was actually too young to attend the course and had lied about her age to gain admission. She would be thrown off the course three months after meeting Cave, because of her virtually nonexistent attendance record, and would always feel guilty that she had not grasped the opportunity that others would have appreciated. 'Well, you see, once you realise there are other possibilities, that there are things wrong with the world and your own little society or even with the people who are teaching you, with adults, you lose the kind of respect you need in order to learn,' commented Lane in 1988. 'I'd always been precocious at school but after I began to think I became more disruptive. I don't think I had any reason to be, I just couldn't help it.'[8]

At this time Anita had no notion of where the future would lead and was not in the least perturbed by this. Although she was not as fanatical about music as her male friends, she found the Melbourne scene liberating and exciting. 'I guess everyone came to life out of punk rock, all that feeling that was going around at that time. It was funny for us because we weren't poor, working class or very upset. What were we? I don't know. I never cared what anyone was doing or what the fashion was. The tastes I had then happened to be in fashion and that's probably the case with Nick too. We were accidentally in time.'

From the very moment Cave laid eyes on Anita, he was entranced. He thought she was the most beautiful girl he had ever seen. With her long, flowing red hair and pale complexion, coupled with her beguilingly innocent looks and demure demeanour, she seemed to have emerged from his dreams. She started to engage him in conversation but the music blaring from the record player's speakers was so loud that he could hardly understand a word she was saying. For an hour he just stood transfixed while she talked, grinning and nodding his head in agreement with whatever she said. When she finally leant over and whispered in his ear that she loved him, he could hardly believe it was happening. 'When we met I was seventeen and he was nineteen,' says Anita. 'You haven't decided on anything at that age. You're all open and you want the world to show you everything, having rejected what your parents had planned for you. That was the springboard: rebelliousness. You just jump into the arms of whatever comes along and so we did.'

NOTES

1 Nick Cave to John Stapleton, 'The Boys Next Door', *RAM*, 1979.
2 Nick Cave to Josh Pollock, *BOT* magazine, 1984.
3 Ibid.
4 Don Watson, 'Trials of the Singer', *NME*, January 1987.
5 VPRO, Dutch television documentary, *Stranger in a Strange Land*, March 1987.
6 Live-to-air Dutch FM Radio interview with Nick Cave and Tracy Pew, 18 January 1983.
7 Richard Guilliatt, 'The Birthday Party, The Return and Revenge', *RAM*, 9 February 1982.
8 The Stud Brothers, 'Daydream Deceiver', *Melody Maker*, 25 June 1988.

4

The First Recordings

After Swinburne a slow momentum began to develop in The Boys Next Door's career as they were offered numerous gigs in pubs and clubs. The Melbourne punk scene in general received a boost of morale with news of The Saints' success in England, scoring a Top 30 hit in August with their frantic 'This Perfect Day' single which secured them an appearance on *Top of the Pops* in the same week as The Sex Pistols' 'Pretty Vacant'. The Saints had highlighted just how out of touch the Australian music industry was with the talent that was emerging on its very doorstep. After years of playing in isolation in Brisbane, it took the clout of EMI in the UK to secure the group a recording contract with the Australian division of the label, prompted by one ecstatic review of their first independent single 'I'm Stranded' in the British music press during November 1976. Not only were the record companies uninterested in the emerging new groups, but so was the majority of Australia's rock audience itself. 'The Australian public moves too slowly to pick up on new trends or groups for any kind of punk explosion to have occurred,' says Mick Harvey. 'All the groups just shuddered into action. It was a very underground scene and would remain so for years.'

The Boys Next Door secured their third date through supporting The Keith Glass Band, more commonly known as the KGB, in a pub venue. Glass represented the old school of Melbourne rock music. He had played a small part in the previous generation of Melbourne musicians, having been a member of a beat group during the sixties. In the seventies he had written songs for country and western singers in Nashville, and with his wife, Helena, ran Missing Link, acknowledged as the best record shop in Melbourne, specialising in imported LP releases. Originally named Archie and Jugheads, and based in a cellar, the Missing Link shop would eventually move to Flinders Lane, in the process becoming the leading shop for rock fans looking for new music. Glass was interested in the punk scene and saw potential in The Boys Next Door in particular, but was initially loath to become involved. His attitude would change as the group achieved more prominence.

By November 1977 The Boys Next Door had improved considerably through incessant gigging, as had the number and standard of songs in their repertoire. 'They made great music and they had great songs, as much as they might try and disown that stuff now,' says Peter Milne. 'Every time they played it was like a gathering of the clan. It's where you went and your name would be on the door. Of course being seventeen the fact that you didn't have to pay the $4.50 cover charge was important. They'd always come up with new songs, or reinvent old ones, there'd always be a development. I used to go and see them rehearse as well, it was interesting to watch them work on new material. That's why I became a photographer, so I could be a fly on the wall and watch things go on. Mick Harvey was always working on the music, making it more interesting.' Cave in particular had been writing prolifically, new songs such as 'Can't Do It', 'Maybe Zone' and 'Sex Crimes', spurred on by encouragement from Anita Lane and the prospect that now there was no alternative for him but to follow a career in music.

The Boys Next Door were now seen as the best band in Melbourne. Rowland Howard, who had been contributing album reviews to *RAM*, began writing for a fanzine called *Pulp*, published by Peter Milne's elder brother Bruce, which also featured illustrations by Anita Lane. Howard wrote a review of the group's appearance at a club called Bananas in Melbourne on 18 November 1977: 'Apart from the music the first thing you notice is Nick, black hair cut in a very Sid

Vicious fashion, green shirt with large polka dots, stovepipe trousers and a highly unsuitable tie. He appears to be in a state of constant hyperactivity; dancing, shaking, straining. His voice isn't the usual new wave vocal . . .'

As punk rock had not been widely publicised in the Australian media, dressing in a punk style caused a sensation in the streets, bars and clubs. 'I reckon there were thirty people in the scene who knew each other and maybe twenty or thirty who were loosely involved,' says Peter Milne. 'We were a bunch of middle-class kids trying to shock. One of the great things about it was it was so easy to shock in those days. All you had to do was wear something a little bit courageous. Pointy-toed boots for instance! My brother Bruce bought a pair and it was like a major trauma for people if he wore them on public transport. It was partly because Melbourne was a very conservative place, but it wasn't just Melbourne. I think the whole world was a very conservative place in '76, '77.' Cave enjoyed immensely the reaction he could provoke in a crowded club. Patrons would actually scuttle out of his way as he strode towards the bar, intimidated by his clothes and haircut. The fear that his presence could create titillated him no end. As he was now in a group, women appeared to become more interested in him, and he wasted no time in taking full advantage of the propositions made to him. The adolescent vandalism that Nick and Tracy had indulged in during their later years at Caulfield continued unabated as they steadily graduated from spraying graffiti and smashing telephone boxes to stealing cars and joy-riding.

The Boys Next Door played their last gig of 1977 on New Year's Eve. They were due to appear at a small club in St Kilda but the other punk groups on the bill overran, leaving them with no opportunity to perform. Annoyed but undeterred, the group travelled north across Melbourne to the Carlton area where they had heard there was a party where bands were playing in the street. When they arrived with all their equipment they drunkenly announced that they, too, wanted to play. 'It was ridiculous,' laughs Peter Milne. 'The audience were standing in the middle of the street and the band was on the footpath. Every now and again a car would drive past and interrupt the proceedings.' Unbeknown to Cave, his father, who had intended to see his son perform at the club, also made his way to the street party. Nick, who spent most of The Boys Next Door's open-air performance crawling in the gutter, screaming, momentarily caught a glimpse of his bemused father in the crowd. Mid-verse he muttered an apologetic greeting before he recommenced 'singing'. At last he had succeeded in attracting his father's attention, even if the only reaction he had managed to elicit from him was bewilderment.

'Sometimes The Boys Next Door would play at parties, just set up in someone's living room and start playing,' recalls Jim Thirlwell, who in late 1977 was studying at Melbourne State College. 'They were really exciting and they had a great set. Nick was completely wild, he was very intense. The scene that was happening in Sydney was distinct from what was going on in Melbourne, which was more art school orientated, more skinny ties than leather jackets. A lot of the influence that I could see, particularly with The Boys Next Door, was coming from England rather than Detroit.'

As the punk/new wave scene gathered momentum through the beginning of 1978 it could no longer be ignored by the Australian music industry. In an ill-conceived attempt to try and cash in on the movement, Barry Earl at the major Australian label Mushroom instigated the formation of a subsidiary label, Suicide, which would sign 'new wave' acts. The bands would be introduced to the record-buying public by way of a sampler album featuring the leading practitioners of the new music, with Suicide having the option of releasing a subsequent album's worth of material by any of the artists signed to the label.

'Some groups made a political stance and wouldn't have anything to do with him [Earl], while others thought it was a good opportunity to record,' says Mick Harvey. 'A lot of other bands didn't get to record for another two years, some really good groups never had the opportunity to record at all. There weren't any independent labels around at that stage. We saw it as a chance to make a start. You make mistakes . . .' Along with The Teenage Radio Stars, JAB, Wasted Daze, X-Ray-Z, Survivors and The Negatives, The Boys Next Door signed to Suicide, in the process gaining Barry Earl as their manager. 'Barry Earl used to sit us in his office and tell us what stars we were going to be,' recalled an amused Nick Cave in 1979. 'He was a very convincing talker.'[1] It soon became clear to the band that the label had no comprehension of the objectives or aesthetics of the new groups they had just signed. 'They just swooped down on all these bands and neatly packaged them,' says Jim Thirlwell. 'It was a finite "market" in Australia at that time and to put out your own record just wasn't going to be profitable. That option wasn't there.' The Boys Next Door would now also have to contend with open hostility towards the label and those directing it from the media and other bands who perceived the whole enterprise as a purely exploitative endeavour.

Even before the group went into the Media Sound Studio to record three tracks for the Suicide sampler LP, *Lethal Weapons*, there were problems. The band were adamant that they wanted to record their newer songs such as 'Sex Crimes' and 'Secret Life', but the record company insisted that they record their cover version of 'These Boots Are Made For Walking' and 'Masturbation Generation', older material that the group now found embarrassing and which gave no indication of their rapid development. Faced with Suicide's intransigence, the band reluctantly relented and agreed to record the songs the label wanted. They produced a five-track demo with which they were pleased, but Suicide were unhappy about the group's evident lack of 'professional polish'. 'They complained about what bad musicians we were,' laughs Harvey, 'and they wanted recordings that would make us sound like we could play.' Suicide promptly hired Greg Macainsh, to work with the band. The end result was simply horrifying. Not only were two of the three tracks the worst songs in the group's entire repertoire, but their abrasive roaring sound had been completely sanitised and as a result the songs sounded merely like polite pop. Only Harvey's newer composition, 'Boy Hero', was remotely indicative of their potential, but even this song was flattened out by totally unsympathetic production. 'We were young and stupid and as a result it was just a bit bland,' commented Harvey in 1979. 'I think that was very much a contributing factor for us spending the next year trying to be taken seriously; which was even worse for us than what we did on *Lethal Weapons*.'[2] When the LP was released in March the reviews were uniformly bad, although the music critics blamed the label rather than the groups and cited 'Boy Hero' as one of *Lethal Weapons*' more inspired moments.

A national package tour of the groups featured on the Suicide label was arranged and The Boys Next Door found themselves billed between headliners Teenage Radio Stars and X-Ray-Z, a situation that Cave in particular found extremely irksome. 'There's so much concentration on Suicide and not on the bands,' he complained to a fanzine. 'We're never treated as individuals. People even think that JAB and The Boys Next Door play the same music.'[3] The band were already becoming disillusioned with the straitjacket of the punk tag and were eager to explore other musical avenues. Visually they had begun to poke fun at the rigidity of the punk style. 'I remember seeing shows where Tracy would be wearing a purple polyester suit with big flares and platform shoes,' laughs Jim Thirlwell.

The Suicide label, which had invested in excess of $20,000 in the *Lethal Weapons* project, would soon flounder and fold, but not before taking up their option on an album from The Boys Next Door. In June the band began recording with Les Karsky in the producer's chair, but they were becoming increasingly confused about their musical direction and how to achieve their objectives in the studio. They would only begin to resolve this situation a year later. Harvey and Cave in particular viewed the *Lethal Weapons* recordings as embarrassing and moronic. They desperately wanted to exorcise the bad memory of the record by taking a more serious and experimental approach to their writing and recording. Their songs' arrangements would become complicated, Cave's lyrical style more abstract. 'Anita was responsible for Nick doing certain things creatively,' says Rowland S. Howard. 'I knew that when he first met her he felt that the lyrics he was writing were outrageously stupid and he almost started to be articulate to show that he could be.'

The band's general lack of confidence was not bolstered by the presence of Les Karsky. 'I remember Mick, who was staying at my house at the time, coming back from the studio very depressed,' recalls Howard. 'He had been playing pool with the guy who was producing the record [Karsky] who played in Supercharge who were an R&B disco band. He was, of course, an eminently suitable choice for the job. He'd let slip that his two most hated bands in the world were The Velvet Underground and Roxy Music and that his musical love of the moment was reggae! It was farcical that he should be doing the record.

'While they were recording I went in to see them. We ran out of alcohol and so we went to get some more. This involved Tracy stealing a car. It looked like some primary school teacher's car and had all these children's drawings in the back seat of elephants. Off we drove but we were frustrated in our attempts to get alcohol. Driving back to the studio Tracy said, "Let's crash the car." Nick said, "All right," and I'm going, "No! No!" All of a sudden . . . bang! Tracy went straight off the road into a lamppost. We got out and Tracy and Nick stood there pelting the car with bricks in a matter-of-fact fashion, as if this was expected of them. Then we had to walk back to the studio. Tracy had hit his head on the steering wheel and was bleeding profusely. Les Karsky was suitably impressed. I didn't know them that well at that time and to me the idea of driving along with somebody, in a stolen car, saying "Let's crash the car" was just not within my sphere of social reference.' Only half of the material recorded during these sessions would ever be released, as the band was so unhappy with the results.

Demoralised but unbowed, the group continued gigging incessantly. While still playing in his own band, The Young Charlatans, Rowland Howard would always attend The Boys Next Door's gigs, occasionally performing with them. 'I'd seen Rowland do backing vocals with them when Tracy was too drunk to perform,' says Jim Thirlwell. 'Even then, people were saying that was going to be their next step.' Howard had become a friend of Cave's, regularly socialising with him and the band around Melbourne. 'Nick was a real tearaway,' says Howard. 'He would regularly climb on top of the roof of Tracy's car as we were travelling at 80 m.p.h. down the highway. One time Nick and I were in this bar and we met this thirty-five-year-old dentist, whom we bullied into driving us somewhere. We were drunk out of our minds and Nick climbed on the roof of the car. I, for some reason, thought it would be a good idea if this dentist slammed the brakes on as hard as possible, which he promptly did because he was so scared of us. Nick went flying off the roof of the car and he's still got this enormous scar running down his back. This wasn't unusual behaviour.

'The first time I went round to Tracy's house there were *Playboy* magazines on the floor, he was drinking a beer and reading Plato's *Republic*. That sums up Tracy. He was really intelligent but didn't feel the need to display it to anyone. Tracy delighted in being seen as stupid, everything was a private joke to him and only he knew the punchline.'

The scene in Melbourne was steadily becoming more fractured. North of the River Yarra in Carlton things were more progressive and student-orientated, whilst to the south, clustering around St Kilda lying on the edge of Port Phillip Bay, the city's main centre for drugs and prostitution, the groups were of a more rock'n'roll orientation in both music and lifestyle. Whilst Ollie Olsen became a leading light on the Carlton scene, Cave gravitated towards St Kilda, where he soon developed a taste for heroin which was always in plentiful supply for $50 a bag. After experimenting with sniffing and smoking the drug, Cave quickly started to take it intravenously. Having experienced the overwhelming sensation that injecting the drug could induce, numbing the senses, alleviating all stress and bolstering confidence, Cave would continue to shoot up heroin and on occasion amphetamine sulphate, as he now considered any other form of ingestion a complete waste of time.

October 1978 was a very bleak month for Cave, who had only recently turned twenty-one. On the evening of the 11th he was being held at St Kilda police station charged with vandalism and being drunk and disorderly. Upon his arrest he was instructed to make a statement to the arresting officer. When asked his occupation he replied that he was a musician. The policeman dutifully recorded this on the charge sheet, writing 'muskian'. When Cave had the temerity to point out that he could not spell, he was promptly threatened with a beating. Allowed to make one phone call, Cave rang his mother, who hurried to the station to bail him out as she had done on many other occasions. When she arrived, she sat with her son whilst the police finished filing their report.

About a quarter of an hour later mother and son saw Anita Lane and Nick's sister Julie entering the station, looking extremely distressed. Dawn immediately demanded to know what was wrong but her enquiries were met with silence. Eventually a policeman came to the interview room and she was asked to step outside while Nick was told to stay put. When he was finally allowed to see his mother she told him that Colin Cave had been killed in a car accident. Through her tears Dawn implored Nick to ring her sister. While phoning, he heard two policemen next to his mother jokingly discussing the rape of a prostitute. He snapped and began to rail at them that his father had just died and his grieving mother was sitting within earshot of their conversation. They merely ignored him and carried on regardless. 'It was terrible,' says Anita Lane. 'I was with Julie at Nick's parents' house when the police came round looking for his mother. They told us what had happened and we went with them to the station where he was being questioned.

'Nick's got this incredible drive that's got him through everything. He's a workaholic. When we were younger I thought it was something that he'd grow out of and get over. He really wanted to impress his father and wanted him to think he was clever. His father would just laugh at him, he wouldn't take any notice. When his father died I wondered what was going to happen to Nick's drive, but it just got stronger.'

Towards the end of the year Rowland S. Howard officially joined The Boys Next Door, who for some months had been playing in performance his composition 'Shivers', a number heavily featured in The Young Charlatans' set. Although The Young Charlatans had attracted a sizeable following, the band broke up after playing only thirteen gigs in Melbourne, because of the volatile personalities involved, each pushing in different musical directions at the same time. 'I thought everything about the group should be recognisably unique,' says Howard, 'but it wasn't a case of sitting down and working it out. It just happened.'

Despite Suicide's collapse, the parent label Mushroom, headed by Michael Gudinski, still wanted to release the recordings that The Boys Next Door had made under contract in June 1978. The band were dismayed at the prospect of the album being released. 'When you're that age a year is a really long time in your artistic development,' says Howard. 'By the time I joined it seemed ridiculous that the record should come out as it was. The record company [Mushroom] magnanimously agreed that if we paid for the recording costs we could record some more songs.' After their dismal experiences working with producers, the band were adamant that this time they would produce themselves.

The sessions commenced in January 1979 and marked the group's first collaboration with the then Richmond Recorders sound engineer, Tony Cohen. 'They'd already done Side 1 of the LP with Karsky. Apparently they hadn't got along all that well,' recalls Cohen with much understatement and a mischievous smile. 'He'd stopped Nick while he was singing and told him, "No, no, your punctuation's all wrong there and you're not singing the words correctly." You can imagine how well that went down! Nick was horrified. So they'd come into Richmond Recorders and I was a little bit late. Very unusual. I must have been off trying to do something I shouldn't have. So I arrived and there were all these desperate-looking punks there, and I had hair down to my knees, no shoes and eyes as red as traffic lights from bonging on for breakfast. I saw the grand piano was stuffed full of metal; mike stands, paper clips, any metallic object they could find. They were all rubbing their hands together in glee waiting for the engineer to show up and say, "*Wow, you can't do that!*" but I just said, "Oh, that should sound interesting." I later found out that Mick had looked over at Nick and said, "He should do." So we started recording away. Around this time I'd had a couple of pop records going, a couple of Number Ones and all that. I met these guys and that was the end of it. No more pop records for me!

'We got on really well during that session. I can't really remember a lot of detail, it's going back a fair way. I can remember we started experimenting quite a lot, Rowland with his guitar in particular. My only trouble with Nick's singing was that he'd jump around so much he'd rip the plug out of the bloody headphones until we had none left! I'd never seen anything like it. At one stage I started mixing, and Tracy had collapsed dead drunk in the studio and someone decided to make a sculpture of mike stands over his carcass. Of course it got out of hand and everything that wasn't nailed down in the studio was piled up over poor old Tracy until he woke up and had to fight his way out of it. I was watching all this through the window, pissing myself. I didn't know these people, I'd never met them. They were just another band and I was going in to record but I thought this is a bit more fun than the average, stock-standard, eighteen tom-toms, bloody whatnot.

'I'd never really been interested in listening to music, I've been more interested in recording it. I never followed trends, The Sex Pistols were fascinating, I loved their records, but this was a totally new thing to me. I still don't follow anything, I stumble blindly through it. I think that's a good way because you don't copy things if you don't know what they are. I was very influenced by the group [The Boys Next Door] after I started working for them. I got my hair cut and bought a pair of shoes. A big change for me.'

In Cohen the band had finally found an engineer who was considerably younger than those with whom they had previously worked and who empathised wholeheartedly with their ideas and aspirations. Though they would enjoy an artistically fruitful, creative partnership with Cohen for many years, on this occasion their collaboration would be unsuccessful. '*Door, Door* I don't even count,' admits Cohen. 'It was just warming up, getting a working relationship and then learning what's possible in the studio and what isn't. I mean, they were all pretty young.'

'I'd never been in a recording studio before, only to watch them record bits and pieces,' says Howard. 'There was a general lack of confidence on how anything was to be done. Although we used Tony Cohen, it was like everyone was walking on ice. When the band played live it was powerful because of the fact we had Nick as a singer, but unfortunately none of that aggression actually made it on to vinyl. The second half of the record wasn't recorded with the band playing live because we just assumed you had to do everything in the most difficult way.' 'We were frustrated and naively tried to be experimental about what we were doing, and we fell over our own feet in the process,' admits Mick Harvey.

The Boys Next Door's first album, now entitled *Door Door*, was finally released by Mushroom in May 1979, an amalgamation of tracks recorded in 1978 and four comparatively new tracks featuring Howard, 'After a Fashion', 'Dive Position', 'I Mistake Myself' and 'Shivers'. 'Mushroom was our sole contact with the record industry proper, being told what tracks to record, being censored,' says Howard. 'Nick and I were given the task of putting together a little ad for the album and out of sheer desperation we came up with this phrase, "Drunk On the Pope's Blood", to attract people's attention. Of course it was vetoed very swiftly but it lurked in our minds for a later date. It wasn't applicable to the record in any way but we were trying to regain our character through the slogan.'

Mushroom desperately wanted a single from the group, who bluntly ruled out any selection from the tracks recorded the previous year. For want of a better song, Howard's commercial slow ballad 'Shivers', sung by Cave, was chosen. 'It's the only song people ever come up to me and talk about,' complains Howard, 'like it's the only song I've ever written, particularly in Australia. They tell me some anecdote about how it saved their lives. It was larger than life in its melodrama to affect people like that. One of the things you have to remember is the group did have a pop sensibility in those days.'

'I disagree with that,' says Mick Harvey. 'From Rowland's angle there may have been a pop sensibility but not from me, and certainly not from Nick. This is where the clash came with Rowland's songwriting maybe after a while. He came in with his style of songs which were very pop-orientated, which were really good in the way we'd handled them. Somehow the competition inspired Nick to greater heights and his writing just took off.' It is undeniable, however, that Howard's innovative guitar playing and arrangements had now broadened the scope of the band's sound, highlighting the enormous gap between the two sets of material. Although the album received generally good notices in Australia, the group were totally dissatisfied with *Door Door*, as it gave no indication of their true potential.

'*Door Door*' didn't go 10 per cent towards capturing what they were really like,' says Jim Thirlwell, who had been eagerly awaiting the album's release on import in England. 'The production was really awful. They sounded a lot more abrasive than that, there was an angularity to their material even then.' In trying to control the sound of their live performances, coupled with a bad choice of songs, the group sounded dissipated and vapid on record. Though the album captured their leaning towards English post-punk groups such as Magazine, it did illustrate that they were steadily trying to forge their own Australian cultural identity.

A promotional video for 'Shivers' and another track from the album, 'After a Fashion', was quickly made by two film students, director Paul Goldman and producer Evan English, while studying at Swinburne College. 'Paul was a music aficionado,' says Evan English. 'He liked a lot of English music but he was a major fan of The Boys Next Door and he brought them into the TV studios at Swinburne. Paul recognised Nick's qualities early on and he put his own money into filming them. It was an exciting period then, quite dynamic. The scene in Melbourne combined imported English culture with an idiosyncratic Australian vision. Melbourne is quite small, small enough in that the art school community are interrelated, so that film school people were on the same circuit and it really was a circuit. There were places, venues and so on and you'd see the same people every night: musicians, photographers, painters.' Director/screenwriter John Hillcoat, who was also studying at Swinburne during the late seventies, claims that the 'Shivers' video was Goldman and English's big break: 'It was shown on television and suddenly it seemed possible for the media to get involved as well. The film school was not in favour of us making videos as they were still a very new form.'

'By the time we'd finished *Door Door* we'd had all our bad experiences and we went on with a very fixed purpose of mind that there was nothing going to sway us from our path,' says Mick Harvey. 'That formed our bloody-minded attitude that followed. The whole thing with Mushroom was a very good experience for us to have. We were able to make our mistakes and still be able to carry on and not to be weakened by them because we were out of the public eye; no one was paying any attention to Australia. I don't want to say too many bad things about Mushroom, they were just acting like any big record company. We soon learnt that it didn't suit us to work with people like that.' At the time the band showed no reticence in slating both Michael Gudinski and Mushroom records in interviews, further ostracising themselves from the Australian music business.

After the release of *Door Door* Mushroom lost all interest in The Boys Next Door but the group had already been approached early in 1979 by Keith Glass, who now wished to manage them and sign them to his small Missing Link label. 'He saw we were having so many difficulties and that we weren't getting anywhere,' says Harvey. 'He just thought we were too good a group to let die. He told us that it was obvious that we needed help, so he'd sort us out.' Throughout 1979 the group had finally begun to define their increasingly left-field sound, in the process assimilating the work of the experimental Cleveland band Pere Ubu, whose LP *Dub Housing* had a profound effect on Cave and Howard, and the Bristol-based Pop Group, who were successfully fusing the energy of punk with avant-garde funk. 'They had a very big influence because they were breaking down musical structures and starting again,' says Harvey, 'especially on their first LP, *Y*. At a couple of points early on we copied certain elements, which I didn't really like, and then I rejected The Pop Group out of hand because it was having too much effect on what we were doing.'

In July 1979 the band re-entered Richmond Recorders with Tony Cohen to record an EP for Missing Link which would be titled 'Hee Haw'. 'That was the first time we'd allowed our sense of humour and mischievousness to be part of the music as well,' comments Rowland Howard. 'That was really a conscious effort on our part to produce something that was really different from everything else in Melbourne, although there are obvious reference points on it.' The group now felt less self-conscious in the studio and their new-found confidence was reflected in the recordings; the mistakes of *Lethal Weapons* and *Door Door* were not going to be repeated. Howard's composition, 'Death By Drowning', with its discordant clarinet, and Cave's frantic and undisciplined 'The Hairshirt' instantly propelled the group towards new, uncharted territory. 'Now that's when things got really, really interesting,' says Tony Cohen. 'For "The Hairshirt" Nick sang through a telephone. He wanted a squeaky little voice underneath the lead vocal. He sang into the phone downstairs at the studio and I put a microphone upstairs to the office and miked up the other end of the phone. The sound . . . aah, it was so piercing. If you turned it up it bloody blew your bloody head off. Frightening.'

Coupled with Cave's abstract, neo-absurdist lyrics, the band was successfully escaping the constraints of the basic rock structures, while retaining a powerful simplicity based around improvised embellishments. These recording sessions, which lasted four or five days, would provide a blueprint for their subsequent releases. '"Hee Haw" was an extreme reaction against what had been released before, those recordings do represent what we were doing in '79. In '78 it was all more related to rock somehow,' says Harvey.

During 1979 it became evident, to both the band and Keith Glass, that they had long since reached a plateau in Australia. They now had a hard-core following of around 600 people but the only way forward would be to travel to England, where it was perceived that a larger audience might prove more responsive. Glass began to organise the group, giving them $5 from each gig they played, and saving the rest for their relocation in the new year. They would regularly perform at the Crystal Ballroom on Fitzroy Street, St Kilda. Run by a local entrepreneur, Laurie Richards, the venue was a large, shabby, two-storey Victorian hotel, which would present as many as eight bands on one night. Nevertheless, the camaraderie which had been evident on the Melbourne scene during late 1977 was rapidly changing into open acrimony and hostility between groups. 'In Melbourne if anybody tried to do anything everyone would be bitching about them straightaway, especially if you were a girl,' says Anita Lane. 'It was very sexist in Melbourne. You were in a group of people who were meant to be liberated in their art concepts, revolutionary and cynical, and you didn't expect this sexism, you didn't expect any "ism" at all. We didn't really know that was happening but I know now when I look back . . .'

The Boys Next Door's obstreperous reputation was also proving to be a problem on the insular Melbourne scene. Within two years they had recorded for three different labels, been ridiculed by other musicians, and ignored by mainstream radio and the press. When opportunities did arise they were seldom able to take advantage of them. Earlier in the year the band had a very embarrassing evening at a Pyramid Agency showcase at Melbourne's Bombay Rock Club in front of many influential music industry figures, due to the late arrival of Mick Harvey. When they did eventually get to play they discovered that their equipment had been set up incorrectly, and they left the stage after only three songs uttering dire threats and accusations of sabotage. 'We were given opportunities, like supporting The Stranglers, but with each thing like that we always fucked up in one way or another, drinking before the gig or just playing badly,' recalled Nick Cave in 1981.[4]

The group also found themselves banned from many venues, including the Bombay Rock, because of their behaviour. At the same time, the number of arrests they were accumulating was rising at an alarming rate. 'We were driving to Canberra while on tour supporting this band called Skyhooks, and Nick and Tracy had to go with the equipment. Myself, Mick and Phill arrived at the venue in our car. Hours later Nick and Tracy still hadn't turned up. They'd been arrested. They'd been urinating out of the back of the van and unfortunately the car behind was being driven by the local policeman's wife who was convinced that they had been masturbating for several miles,' laughs Rowland Howard. When the band missed the gig entirely, Skyhooks were far from amused and proceeded to lecture them about their unprofessional attitude.

Cave also ran into trouble with the police during a tour of Tasmania while the band were playing a brief residency at the Red Lion, a pub venue in Hobart. 'Nick got quite drunk and decided he could drive and told this girl he could, which he couldn't,' says Harvey. 'It was probably an automatic which was why he could drive it at all. Nick turned up at the bottle shop at three a.m. to continue the party, bought some liquor, got back into the car and reversed straight into a police car. Nick burned off down the street and they set about chasing him. Nick stopped somewhere and quickly hid behind a rubbish tip. The cops stopped there too, looked around and said loudly, "Oh well, I guess he's gone," and pretended to leave and at that moment Nick waltzed out. He spent the night in the lock-up. The next morning we were getting ready to drive to Launceston to play the next show of the tour. Where's Nick? Rowland told us that he had been driving a car round Hobart, so we immediately assumed something terrible had happened.'

It was definitely time for The Boys Next Door to leave for England. 'We've gone about as far as we can here,' said Cave two months before their departure. 'We want to move on, to progress. I'm looking forward to it. And hopefully there will be a bigger audience there for our type of music. But sink or swim, it should be a really exciting experience.'[5] It seemed an opportune moment to change the band's name, which had long since ceased to be amusing in Cave's eyes. A new name would indicate that the band wished to make a fresh start. The scene in Dostoevsky's *Crime and Punishment* where the deranged and consumptive Katerina Ivanovna throws an inebriated dinner party to commemorate her late husband had always been one of Cave's favourite passages in the novel. For some reason he always mistakenly remembered the scene occurring at a birthday party, hence the group's new name.

NOTES

1 3RRR radio broadcast, Melbourne, interview with Rowland Howard and Nick Cave, November 1979.
2 David Leslie, interview with Mick Harvey, *Distant Violins* fanzine.
3 Jillian Burt, 'The Boys Next Door's Battle', *Road Runner*, November 1979.
4 Andy Gill, 'Abbo – The Album', *New Musical Express*, 13 June 1982.
5 The Boys Next Door interviewed by John Stapleton, *Road Runner*, November 1979.

5

Prayers On Fire

In November 1980 The Birthday Party came home to Melbourne after their first dismal ten-month stay in the UK with any illusions they might have had about post punk-music and UK groups in particular irrevocably shattered. 'As far as I'm concerned, leaving Australia was the best thing they did, they were a band when they came back,' says Tony Cohen, who had remained in Melbourne. 'They lived in squats, in squalor, all sorts of trouble, and had nothing, but they stuck with it. It was good for them. I know it's a corny thing to "suffer for your art" but it's actually very true. They were very determined, but then again, that determination was always there. When they came back they were really a band as compared to a ramshackle outfit that could put a good recording together with some effort. They could play together. I thought, "Shit, this is slotting into place quite nicely." I went to one or two gigs and usually stood outside 'cos it was killing my ears. It was bloody frightening. It was like putting a jumbo jet in a little room and turning all the engines on full blast, except the bottom end had been taken out and all the treble was on. Really scary stuff.'

Looking back at their experiences in London, Cave realised how complacent and lazy the band had been. There was now some urgency in trying to rectify the situation, and a desire to distance themselves from the UK groups they detested because of the disturbing realisation that they shared many of the same faults. 'I mean, we used to hate all those groups, but when we really examined ourselves we couldn't really see much difference between us and them anyway,' Cave later commented. 'There was almost a conscious decision that our music should be more assertive, because we witnessed so many groups who just seemed so insipid on stage, and their music seemed to lack any kind of energy or humour.'[1]

On New Year's Eve The Birthday Party played a special show at the Crystal Ballroom. 'A couple of people started stage-diving but there was one guy who stayed on the stage and Tracy Pew kicked him in the small of the back and he just went flying off the stage really hard,' says Trevor Block, then a member of a local Melbourne group, Precious Little, who attended the gig. 'Afterwards I was in the band's dressing room trying to nick some beer and this guy who Tracy had kicked came in. He'd been hurt, he was really uptight, staring at the band. Someone said, "What do you want?" This guy was so angry: "I think you've broken my fucking ribs!" The band couldn't give a fuck, or if they did they didn't show it. Cruel, but if you got on stage while they were playing, what did you expect. You didn't fuck with Tracy Pew. Nick was really sarcastic and just said, "Tough shit." This guy hobbled out of the room and there was some uneasy laughter. Tracy said, "If I've broken those ribs, at least he'll never wash them again," like they'd been broken by a star or something.'

In late December through till January 1981, The Birthday Party were ensconced in Studio 2 of Armstrong's Audio Visual Studios, Melbourne, recording their album *Prayers On Fire*. 'Each song was written separately, each has a different atmosphere and thought behind it,' commented Cave towards the end of 1981 on the tracks that were recorded in January. 'I write a hell of a lot of lyrics when I'm really drunk. When we were recording *Prayers On Fire* I was fairly drunk the whole time . . . take that song "Just You and Me", for instance. I opened up my song book and found that song there. I gather I had written it the night before but I really can't remember writing that song. I know I wrote it because it's written in my handwriting. Anyone's interpretation of "Just You and Me" is as correct as mine.'[2] In Cave's humorous and scrambled lyrics, delivered with fervent urgency, echoes could be detected of the nonsense poetry of the French absurdist dramatist Alfred Jarry, who strived to confront himself and his audience with the horror of their own complacency and ugliness: 'Wake up – what's in that house? Express thyself, Say something loudly' ('King Ink'). 'I don't think the abstract lyric style was something that Nick was ever really happy with. It didn't last that long,' says Rowland Howard. 'I think he felt that he should be doing it. There was always a problem with the lyrics when it came to anything I wrote. They had to be impersonal enough so that Nick felt he was able to sing them without feeling he was crawling into somebody else's skin.'

The *Prayers On Fire* sessions marked the first credited recorded lyrical collaboration between Cave and Anita Lane, on 'A Dead Song', a track that John Peel would play incessantly upon the album's release. 'Her [Anita Lane's] lyrics lie around our room on pieces of paper accumulating coffee rings until they become grubby and get thrown away,' commented Cave, 'but "A Dead Song" – that has been immortalised.'[3] Lane recalls: 'One time I wrote some lyrics for him and he just took one look at them and screwed up the paper they were written on and threw it in the bin.'

The atmosphere in the studio was more akin to a party than a working environment, with many of the group's friends wandering casually in and out. Three of the many visitors to the studio were Philip Jackson, Mick Hunter and Stephen Ewart, from the Melbourne group Equal Local, who would provide the brass section for 'Nick The Stripper' and the frantic, rhythmically charged 'Zoo Music Girl'. 'Equal Local were an avant-garde outfit,' says Howard. 'They'd all stand in a line and tap their feet frantically all at the same time.' While The Birthday Party were recording, the New Zealand new wave pop group Split Enz were working in Studio 1 on the follow-up LP to their massive hit *True Colours*. On occasion a member of Split Enz would wander uninvited into Studio 2 and proclaim that the music The Birthday Party were making was uncommercial and would never reach the higher echelons of the Top Ten. 'They were working with David Tickle, a big producer,' says Cohen. 'He [Tickle] had every piece of effects equipment imaginable piled up to the roof, cables everywhere. I thought he was a complete dickhead about it. We had basically nothing, so I had to beg, borrow one of the lousiest reverb machines that he had; at night when he'd finished, and it had to be put back with all the settings the way they were.

'Of course we worked over Christmas and Split Enz didn't. Now, on Christmas Eve, Tracy had run out of booze and wandered up to Studio 1 and found twelve bottles of very expensive Moët champagne lined up along the mixing desk, all gift-wrapped in Christmas paper with baubles and everything, individually addressed to each member of the band and crew from their record company. The funny thing was, Tracy opened one of them and the wrappings and baubles were all along the corridor, and finally there were twelve empty bottles in our studio. I remember Tracy drinking, saying, "Ahhh, this is fuckin' horrible!" He still drank it though. I just loved the way he left the wrappings all the way along the floor to our studio and didn't make any effort to conceal that he'd scoffed the lot. Serves them right for not working over Christmas. Tracy was a lovely person and a fucking great musician. For someone who probably never owned a bass guitar, let alone practised, he was just magic. An absolute natural. He was terrific to work with because he never needed a drop-in or a retake, he just played and that was it. He liked to drink, though . . .'

As 'Nick The Stripper' was going to be released as a single in Australia, it was decided by Glass that an accompanying video would be required. Goldman and English, who now worked together under the name The Rich Kids, and who had previously collaborated with the band for the 'Shivers' video, would produce the promotional clip, while fellow Swinburne student John Hillcoat would serve as editor. Cave had met Hillcoat through Goldman and English. 'We recognised we had mutual interests,' says Hillcoat. 'I was heavily into the blues. Nick would come round and make tapes as I was a fanatical record collector, actually I'd go out and steal them.' Cave had also seen the director's short Swinburne degree film, *Frankie and Johnny*. The plot of the film was based upon the ballad of the same name, written by Mammy Lou, a singer at Babe Conner's cabaret, New Orleans, in which she related the *crime passionnel* of Allen Britt's shooting of Frankie Baker in St Louis in 1899. 'Nick really liked it,' says Hillcoat. 'It was a sick film and I must admit I was unhappy with it. It was taking the Western genre and using the plot from the song as the basis for a "punk" Western. It was very raw, it was like the raw energy and violence that The Birthday Party started developing.'

Frankie and Johnny was also very heavily influenced by *The Collected Works of Billy The Kid* by the Canadian author Michael Ondaatje. In the novel Ondaatje creates a vivid portrayal of the famous outlaw and the brutal environment in which he lived, through a seamless blending of poetry and prose, fact and fiction, and utilising actual photographs from the era. 'Nick and I both liked his writing, it's very passionate. Nick particularly liked the poetic side to the book. He also really liked William Faulkner and Flannery O'Connor.' Cave was particularly enamoured of a story from Ondaatje's novel that Hillcoat had adapted for *Frankie and Johnny* concerning a character named Livingstone who creates a race of forty mad dogs through inbreeding and malnourishment, only to be eaten by his creations.

Various ideas were discussed between the band and the film-makers for the video. Someone knew a tow-truck driver who was frequently called out to car accidents, and Cave suggested that Goldman and the group drive around with him to a crash site where the band would perform with a recent accident acting as the backdrop. Another idea involved Cave riding an elephant in a circus big top tent. Eventually Cave and Goldman decided that the song would be best presented visually as a carnival vision of hell, with strong allusions to the work of Fellini, on a budget of around £1,000. The location chosen for filming was a garbage pit yet to be filled with rubbish, in the suburb of Camberwell, Melbourne.

Shooting commenced the night before The Birthday Party were due to return to England. 'It turned into a party, a farewell party for The Birthday Party. It was insane, we're talking about a lot of drink and drugs,' says Evan English. In order to create the right atmosphere for a carnival of the obscene and the absurd, the shoot had been publicised around Melbourne, and about a thousand people took up the open invitation to attend dressed in the most ridiculous garb they could muster, as if they were about to descend into hell. As well as the group's friends, a large number of Melbourne's down-and-outs, alcoholics and drug casualties were in attendance. Among the motley throng was an old hippie, crazed on LSD and robed as Jesus Christ, who stuck a cross in the ground and hung himself on it for the duration of the shoot. A hideous fat man who had recently been released from a mental asylum was dressed as an Egyptian eunuch. He sat himself at the top of the gallows that had been erected for Cave and spent the evening crying and howling at the moon.

All night the band walked through the crowd, miming the song, with Cave leading the procession clad only in a loincloth. 'It was shot in reverse sequence so the opening shot was filmed at eight in the morning and everyone was completely dilapidated,' says Rowland Howard. 'The whole thing was just dust and mud. Mick had to spend the whole time blindfolded, with all these maniacs loose.' For the video, Tracy Pew borrowed Chris Walsh's cowboy hat, which became synonymous with Pew's developing persona as a debauched urban cowboy. 'A lot of Tracy's sense of humour and the running jokes that he'd have were often instigated by Chris, actually,' says Mick Harvey. 'From then on Tracy just wore a cowboy hat. Chris, of course, had to stop wearing one because Tracy had worn one in the video.'

'Nick tried to get up on this rock and he couldn't because he was so drunk and out of it. It was appalling,' says Evan English. 'Some of the guys, being the rock star characters they are, were screwing some girl in the garbage in all this putrid shit. You could never find them when it was time to shoot another sequence.'

At the end of the shoot English was dismayed to discover that the generator he had 'borrowed' from the college to power the lighting equipment had disappeared. 'The film school called the cops, thinking I'd stolen it, and they turned up at my place at eight o'clock in the morning,' says English. 'They did their process of investigation and hassled me. They took me to Paul Goldman's place and turned it upside down, then they came into the room where we were editing on the Steinbeck. They saw this can of film and said, '"Nick The Stripper"? What's this!' They thought they'd stumbled across a porn racket because there was another film there called "Porn Star Spasm". Another guy who lived in the house had been making a film, but we won't go into that! So we had to put "Nick The Stripper" on the Steinbeck and show it to them. These fucking dumb cops had to watch the whole thing and afterwards some smart arse said, "What did you think?" and this cop replied, "Well, it was all right until you introduced the goon in the nappy."'

The Birthday Party returned to London in early March, playing a gig at the Rock Garden on the 18th of that month. Cave moved back into the Walterton Road squat with Anita, while Mick Harvey and Katy Beale shared accommodation with Jim Thirlwell in Maida Vale. During their stay in London the previous year the band had struck up a friendship with Thirlwell, who always attended their London gigs. While working as a singles buyer for the Virgin Megastore chain, Thirlwell was beginning to forge his own musical career, playing live with Matt Johnson's The The, and producing, as a one-man band, a succession of startling records under the name Foetus. 'I couldn't stand the democratic way of working in a band,' says Thirlwell.

The day after the Rock Garden gig The Birthday Party played their first date at the Venue in Victoria Street, SW1, supporting former Wire member Colin Newman for his début solo performance. 'I went to see Colin Newman and they were the first band on and within seconds I was completely bowled over. I immediately turned round and looked at the stage. I thought, what is this!' says laconic Australian photographer Bleddyn Butcher. Butcher had been living in London for several years, selling his work to the weekly music papers, and his experience of London had been similar to The Birthday Party's. 'When you're in Australia everywhere else seems so sophisticated, but when you come here it's such a class-ridden, squalid, sordid place.' An avid music fan, Butcher had become bored with the UK scene. 'In Australia a lot of bands learn their "craft" in pubs and clubs and don't expect to receive any attention for years, whereas over here a band who can barely remember two chords can get on the cover of a paper and start thinking that they're millionaires and an artist to boot. The Birthday Party had something to distinguish themselves against, a large negative force with which they didn't want to be identified. They had an immensely refreshing attitude to witness.' After their performance Butcher introduced himself to the band. In his professional relationship with them he would repeatedly capture and mould their striking visual presence, as well as developing a close personal friendship with Cave.

Also in attendance at the Venue gig was the former bassist with the Mancunian group Magazine, Barry Adamson. During a tour of Australia with Magazine in 1980, Adamson had heard The Boys Next Door's 'The Hairshirt'. 'I was knocked out by the power of it and the direction things seemed to be going in. I really clocked it as something of importance,' he says. 'When they came to England I was working as a "celebrity" DJ at the Venue. The Birthday Party were in town, they got invited along and I met them all there. They played at the Venue at the beginning of 1981 to a handful of people but within six months there were queues of thousands of people down the street. It was a very exciting time, I started hanging out with them.

'Magazine was a different kettle of fish from the punk thing and this was another whole bucket. They may have used punk as a vehicle to get out of Australia, come over here and rip it apart, that's what it seemed like to me. I liked all the elements that were combined together. The electric guitar of Rowland, the rock star amplified tenfold in Nick, the musical director in Mick Harvey, the solid, big, low bass sound of Tracy and the precision of Phill. It was all there.'

Slowly a few critics in the music press began to respond positively to the group's increasingly abandoned performances. 'They were superb,' wrote Terri Sanai in her *Sounds* review of the group's performance at the Moonlight Club supporting DAF on 31 March, 'a mixture of paranoia, demented self-parody and neurotic inebriated passion . . .' 'The first time I saw them Cave was wearing a check shirt, and there was something Huck Finn-like about his appearance. It wasn't the crow's-nest hair, black-clad look that got locked in the imagination. There was something of the depraved farmer's boy about him,' says music critic Mat Snow. 'I'd first heard of The Birthday Party in late 1980. My friend Barney Hoskyns had left Oxford University and was writing for *Melody Maker*, then quickly went to the *NME* and he had been adopted by Chris Carr, who was very good at spotting young talent. He pointed Barney in the direction of The Birthday Party. I began seeing The Birthday Party every few months after that with Barney, usually in a state of psychotropic disorder. I remember seeing Bleddyn [Butcher], his attachment to the band added to their strange, predatory glamour.' Hoskyns would play an important part in championing the band in print. 'Barney Hoskyns was young and intelligent but under the influence of what he thought rock'n'roll was meant to be,' says Carr. 'Barney was an integral part of Nick's development. He gave weight to certain things.'

Life in London was no better for Cave than it had been the previous year. The residents of Walterton Road made their animosity towards the squatters very plain, and Anita would sometimes be spat at in the street and pelted with rubbish by disgruntled neighbours who thought the pair were lowering the tone of the locality. As in Australia, Cave would also experience violent encounters with skinheads. One evening, while he was having a drink in a Maida Vale pub with Nick 'S.' Seferi, an old friend from the Melbourne scene, violence suddenly flared up with a group of skins. While Nick S. was ordering drinks at the bar Cave sat down at a table next to a skinhead girl. Her boyfriend told him that the seat was his and Cave moved to another seat. Another skinhead told him to move again and he sat back down next to the girl that he had been sitting with in the first place. Stoned and very drunk, Cave began talking to the girl, while Nick S. looked on from the bar in dismay. The skinhead who had initially told him to move ordered him to leave the pub. When Cave refused, the skinheads turned on him, punching him and throwing him to the ground. Cave slid under the table to avoid further blows. Nick S. charged from the bar headlong into the mêlée and had his head split open when a skinhead hit him with a chair. Cave managed to carry Nick S. out of the pub and headed towards the nearest hospital.

Despite the fact that *Prayers On Fire*, released in April, received universally laudatory reviews in all of the leading music papers in the UK, The Birthday Party would still experience difficulty securing feature pieces and interviews in the press. When they finally received their first full-page interview, with Lynden Barber in *Melody Maker* in May, Cave would bitterly complain about the constant comparisons with Pere Ubu and Captain Beefheart that were being levelled at the band by the music critics. 'The Beefheart categorisation caused a lot of bad blood,' says Carr. 'They said they'd never heard of him, how true that is I don't know.' Cave would later claim that he only listened to Captain Beefheart after comparisons had been drawn in the press. 'The Birthday Party didn't fit in with how it was meant to be categorised,' says Mick Harvey. 'The music's just odd, playing different time signatures at the same time, for instance. From the beginning we always wanted to make music that was very different somehow from anything else.'

Cave would also bemoan at length, in this and subsequent interviews, what he perceived as London's apathetic response to the band, saying that in his opinion English audiences were a mindless herd of sheep, a statement he would soon regret. 'British audiences were a bit taken aback by the band,' says Bingo, a former marine and ardent music fan. 'It was a time of self-discovery for me when I left the marines. Friends told me about this band called The Birthday Party but I'd missed many of their gigs because I was working night shifts. Eventually I got to see them and there was Nick, bashing people across the head with the microphone. The power of that group, produced by this sprawl of characters across the stage, was awesome. I thought, I love this band, love this sound. It was total chaos but there was some unknown strength there.

'The next day I read in the music press that Nick thought British audiences were like sheep acting under one mind. I thought, wait a minute! The next gig I went to I immediately went down the front and when he hit me with his drumstick I broke it into three pieces and handed it back to him. He just laughed when he held it in his hand. I used to go crazy at their gigs. I only wanted to enjoy myself and express myself, my ego was being fed through their band. I could hear it in his songs, he'd shout, "Express yourself, express yourself!" and you'd try and give it your all because he certainly was. The state he'd get into . . . He had no fear or regard for his own personal safety. He was demanding a lot of the audience. I think that's where his frustration came from. He wanted people to communicate and be individuals, but they couldn't because they didn't really understand what was going on at all.'

Bingo's attempts to challenge Cave during Birthday Party performances would steadily become more extreme. During subsequent gigs he would bite through microphone leads, and repeatedly grab Cave by his legs and throw him to the ground, holding him in a vice-like grip. Cave would only be freed when he gave way to Bingo's demand to beg for his release. Bingo's confrontations with Cave became compelling moments in Birthday Party gigs, exemplifying the physicality of the group's assault.

'When we did *Prayers On Fire* people still had difficulty in knowing how to interpret us,' says Rowland Howard. 'We were viewed as five quaint boys from the outback. The Australian thing was really annoying. We were not coming across as we would like so we decided we would do everything in a larger-than-life way. The reason we could get away with it was the songs themselves stood up. I don't think the songs are parodies. The ideas snowballed out of our hands because it was something the press could feed upon. It was one of the few conscious decisions we ever made, to just force ourselves upon people and be totally overpowering.'

In the majority of the press coverage that the band would receive during 1981 it became all too clear that the critics had no conception of the country The Birthday Party were from. They wanted to draw some spurious connection between the group and the current 'tribal' music fad in the UK, personified by Malcolm McLaren's protégés Bow Wow Wow and Adam and the Ants, who were plundering the ethnic drumbeats of Africa. 'Journalists just kept asking us about aboriginal culture influencing our music, I mean, come on, aboriginals in Melbourne!' laughs Mick Harvey. 'You just don't hear it in Australia, but they didn't want to hear that.' Despite the group's strenuous denials that they had no connection with their country's indigenous culture, half an *NME* interview entitled 'Abbo – The Album' would be devoted to the subject, with a quote from Cave ('Aboriginal culture's been razed to the ground') taken completely out of context and placed as an introduction to the piece.

On 21 April The Birthday Party recorded their second session for the John Peel show. This one was distinctly more assured than their previous recording for Peel, or the *Prayers On Fire* LP, and indicated the more aggressive path they were now pursuing. Their spirited, irreverent reinterpretation of The Stooges' 'Loose', which became a staple encore song in their live set, graphically showed that they were now ardently embracing the most nihilistic manifestation of rock music, laced with self-deprecating black humour. 'A big thing with Australians,' says Howard, 'is that you mustn't take yourself too seriously, that there must be an element of humour in what you do. That played a big part in The Birthday Party as well, and that's where it stems from.' The sheer emotional charge that the band would invest in the song was stunning and marked the beginning of the confrontational course that The Birthday Party would follow until their demise two years later.

As ever, the group had reacted against all prevailing trends with a ferocity that would plunge them headlong towards oblivion. 'They felt out on a limb, with London, England, everything. They felt like complete outsiders,' says Ivo Watts-Russell. The band's frenzied, rhythmic attack, coupled with Howard's discordant guitar feedback and Cave's seemingly possessed howling vocal, pushed 'Loose' to the limits of collapse and visceral parody. A new composition, 'Sometimes Pleasure Heads Must Burn', was similarly an intense assault on the senses. The song's title perfectly encapsulated the music's intoxicating passion and rage: 'I feel a little low, you know what I mean? Buried neck high in British snow'. The Birthday Party seemed to be issuing a declaration of destructive intent which would reflect the increasing turmoil of their personal lives and their utter disgust with England and all things English. 'They were living very hard and difficult lives on the edge of extreme poverty,'

reflects journalist Chris Bohn. 'That black-hole nihilistic effect
that the group had was great because it kept open options
that were being closed down all the time within music, within
popular culture, as it became more rigidly codified around social
issues or entertainment.'

The Birthday Party embarked on their first national tour of
the UK on 17 June in Newcastle, supporting Subway Sect and
another group at that time signed to 4AD, the humourless 'art'
rock band Bauhaus. Although a superficial display of camaraderie was adopted during the eight-date tour, The Birthday
Party detested Bauhaus's music, it being the manifestation of
everything they loathed. Peter Murphy, Bauhaus's lead singer,
presented a performance which in the band's eyes was little
more than a pale impersonation of David Bowie's creation Ziggy
Stardust, clumsily utilising elements of mime with the aid of
an offstage mirror and amateur theatrics. Bauhaus cultivated
an image based upon horror films, and their most successful
independent hit, 'Bela Lugosi's Dead', became the blueprint for
a succession of diabolical groups whom the music press would
label 'Gothic'.

Throughout the tour Cave became increasingly exasperated as
his attempts to incite a reaction from the crowd failed. Night after
night he grew obsessed with certain members of the audience
who were either mocking or ignoring him, until he was directing
his entire performance towards them, screaming into their faces
and lashing out in all directions.

'Bauhaus's bass player asked me if I was into William
Burroughs!' exclaims an indignant Rowland Howard. 'It was
horrible. We couldn't believe how bad they were. After the
last date of the tour at the Lyceum [London, 25 June], Nick
went back to the members of Subway Sect's house and they got
extremely drunk. Suddenly they got it into their heads that they
were going to blow up a car. They went into a car park across the
street, took a car's petrol cap off, stuck a sock in the hole and set
fire to it . . . and nothing happened. Disgruntled, they went back
inside to watch TV. Twenty minutes later the car exploded. "What
was that!" By this time they'd forgotten what was going on.'

During August, 4AD issued a single by the band that had been recorded in April in London. Entitled 'Release The Bats', it would firmly establish The Birthday Party as a leading independent group operating on the UK scene. Barry Adamson witnessed the recording session: 'They just went hell for leather about their work and they seemed to cut through all the bullshit and politesse. Their whole experience was so different from mine and I wanted to be part of it. They seemed to be expressing stuff that was inside me that I didn't have a clue how to get out.'

During rehearsals before recording the single, the personality clashes that had always existed between Phill Calvert and the rest of the group were exacerbated, and complaints about his rhythmic timekeeping grew louder as Mick Harvey increasingly had to work out more of his drum parts for him. 'When we learnt "Release The Bats" Phill said he had this fabulous idea that we do a cover of a Beatles song,' says Howard. 'Nick and I just walked out of the door into the courtyard of the rehearsal studio and looked at the ground in despair. When I first joined the group I was amazed how cruel they were to Phill and I was always nice and polite to him but then he started being rude to me, so I started being rude back. Then he was nice to me! I never had much in common with him. He was always such a willing target. If he'd stopped to think, he would have realised he was just goading Nick and Tracy on. When Nick was gobbing all over the inside of Phill's car, he'd say, "Come on, Nick, this isn't even my car, it's borrowed." That just made it better as far as Nick was concerned.'

Typically, The Birthday Party's most popular single was their least challenging. 'Release The Bats' would become something of a millstone around their necks as elements of its exuberant celebration of violent physical desire would soon be appropriated by a number of Gothic groups who completely misunderstood the band. 'It was conceived as a comedy number actually,' laughs Mick Harvey. 'When we first learnt it we just fell over laughing because it was so ridiculous, and why the hell not? We recorded it because it happened, almost by accident. We rejected it pretty quickly as a result. Since the dawn of time we had been sending up particular musical styles and I don't know if people ever even noticed. A lot of songs, just little snippets, were send-ups of some particular stylisation and "Release The Bats" was a complete send-up which stopped being funny after the first few times we played it. It was just too obvious . . .'

'The party favourite,' says Rowland Howard drily. 'It was an important song in England at that time because it was so incredibly energetic and it sounded like rock music. There wasn't anything particularly adventurous musically about it but the spirit of the band came across so well just in terms of sheer force of character.'

Despite the fact that *Prayers On Fire* was only available in America on a very small independent label based in San Francisco, and 'Release The Bats' had not even been released in the country, The Birthday Party agreed to undertake a short tour of the USA, with dates in New York, Washington DC, Boston, Philadelphia and Chicago. The ill-fated tour only further accelerated the group's self-destructive attitude and their open hostility towards any audience.

The US tour began in New York on 23 September with a supposedly low-key, unadvertised gig at an upmarket rock disco, the Underground in Union Square. 'We were still jet-lagged and I'd had too many gins,' says Mick Harvey. 'I was very drunk and could hardly stand up, so we were late going on stage. There were only ten people there and they didn't want to see us anyway. Then we started playing our obscene racket, which was probably even more obscene because I was a bar behind everyone else. I remember thinking that I couldn't keep up.' Having bludgeoned the small crowd of preppie executives in the disco with an uninhibited rendition of one of their new songs, 'Big Jesus Trash Can', Mick Harvey began repeatedly screaming, 'What's the matter with you bastards?' when the audience failed to respond in any way to the thundering assault. After their third number the band were told by the management that they could play one more song. They performed a fifteen-minute version of 'King Ink', during which Cave walked into the dwindling audience and wrapped the microphone lead around the throat of a woman seated at a table. 'Express yourself!' he screamed into her face. 'Express yourself!' 'The management were totally appalled at what they were seeing and hearing, and the ten people who were there started leaving,' says Harvey. 'For the town that can take anything it was too much. It was just a small incident but it turned into a big deal.'

As a result, The Birthday Party's advertised gig two days later at the Ritz, supporting the insipid English pop funk band The Au Pairs, began to look extremely doubtful. A riot had occurred at the Ritz six months previously when Public Image Ltd. had played, causing extensive damage, and the venue's management were beginning to have second thoughts about booking The Birthday Party. Ruth Polski, who had organised the tour, was becoming very agitated. 'She kept telling Nick, "Nobody gets drunk, play the show, get off and get paid," which of course was completely the wrong thing to say to him,' says Harvey. 'So Nick got totally drunk but we played a really great show.

'The Ritz were expecting a big crowd and this horrible, filthy group who were going to come on stage and do horrible things. They were ready for us. They had twelve security guys in red T-shirts lining the front of the stage. Nick was moving back and forth across the stage as usual and they moved like a little army, following his every move for the whole show. There was this one guy in the audience with horrible tattoos all over his face, who spent the entire gig screaming his head off. Nick was so out of it, he just grabbed this guy by the throat. I just went, "Oh, my God!" The security guys didn't do anything about it as they thought it would sort itself out, because if he wanted to this guy could have ripped Nick limb from limb.

'We were performing "King Ink" and I was playing the snare drum and Nick lurched over in a very overexcited state and started throwing his head up and down like he used to do. Then he just pushed me out of the way and began beating his head on the snare drum really hard. He didn't even know he was doing it. The snare drum was soon covered in his blood. This disturbed the security and the management and they quickly decided that this was really unsavoury entertainment and not fit for public consumption. They pulled the plugs on us. The curtain was lowered and they started dismantling the microphones and we were standing there thinking, "Oh, my God, it's happening again, we've been thrown off, we've really done it now!" It was a good show, and from my experience not an abnormal one. We got through most of the set, there were only two songs to go.'

After the Ritz gig, Cave told Barney Hoskyns, who was covering The Birthday Party's first US tour for the *NME*, 'When the history of rock music is written – which, since it's practically dead, will be soon – it'll just be remembered as a sordid interruption of normality.' Tracy Pew punctuated Cave's statement: 'Rock music will be remembered as the anus of culture. Not Del Shannon but Iggy Pop.'[4]

The Birthday Party had been an unknown group in America until these two performances, but thereafter they had a considerable reputation on the underground scene. In the wake of the Underground and Ritz shows a number of gigs, both in New York and across the country, were cancelled as promoters swiftly changed their minds about booking the band.

On 3 October the group played their third New York gig, at Chase Park, off Broadway. Among the thirty-odd members of the audience was Lydia Lunch. During the late seventies she and her discordant band, Teenage Jesus and the Jerks, had achieved prominence on the nihilistic New York scene which became labelled 'no wave'. In order to avoid the stigma of being simply labelled as a no wave rock singer, Lunch subsequently made a series of albums either with groups Beirut Slump and Eight Eyed Spy, or as a solo artist, each recording defiantly different in style from the last. Always at one remove from rock music, Lunch had begun to tire of the format by 1981. 'I was living in LA and I wasn't paying much attention to contemporary music,' she says, 'but a friend gave me a copy of *Prayers On Fire* which I thought was fantastic. Two weeks later I was in New York and they happened to be playing so I immediately rushed backstage and confessed my love for Rowland S. Howard.' Howard, who had been particularly enamoured of Lunch's seminal LP *The Queen of Siam*, responds: 'It was the first time

I'd met someone I'd previously admired from afar, or had any musical rapport with.'

Lunch's first meeting with Cave was more problematic. 'Well, Nick and I did not agree on anything. During our first full-length conversation we disagreed on every point, aesthetics, politics, everything,' laughs Lunch. 'The problem I had with him is the problem I have with most men on initial meeting, that they probably don't come into contact with someone as potent, forthright and powerful as I am. Most of the Australian women I've met are more demure and I was just thrashing and thrusting around in my own little reality. Nick was quite shy, so was Rowland, and I'm about as far away as you can get from that. Sometimes that intimidates these people who appear to have a great deal of self-confidence on stage, which is often the antithesis of how they are off stage. Often it's the manifestation of their exhibitionism that they can't convey in their everyday life. I think that's the case with Nick. He was quite charming, witty and amusing. I always respected his humour, which was at the forefront of his personality, even though it didn't manifest itself in the most obvious fashion at that point.'

After the gig Tracy Pew ran into trouble. 'The only time I think Tracy was ever in awe and fear was after they played that show,' says Chris Carr. 'They were leaving the club and Tracy was carrying his gear outside, walking down an alley, when he was confronted by this guy who had a gun. There had been a shooting going on moments before. Tracy said he'd never hit the ground so fast and he tried to just bury himself. He said, "I was wearing the cowboy hat, the boots and the string vest and there I was spitting gravel."

'Tracy liked Jon Voight's character in *Midnight Cowboy*. He had a great sense of humour and loved the Village People. Tracy was in your face. He was a gent but he also knew how to work space. We used to call him "The Boss Shitkicker". He was one person who could liven up anything, anywhere. Tracy was the first member of the group to come out of himself and he started to get loud and carried it off better than anyone I've ever seen. Tracy and Nick were the emotional heart and soul of that band.

They contributed to its public face. When Tracy was having fun there wasn't a lot of space for other people. Tracy took Nick along with him, and then Rowland.'

The last gig of the tour took place on 10 October in Chicago at COD. This date had been added to the band's schedule in order to try to recoup some of the money they had lost. A series of cancellations meant they had been left kicking their heels in New York for a week after their final New York gig at the Peppermint Lounge on the 4th, and they were now desperately in need of cash. 'The gig in Chicago was really wild,' says Mick Harvey. 'There were about six hundred people there and they were all throwing things at the stage. Rowland said, "Throw money," and so nickels and dimes started raining down on the stage. Then Nick said, "Don't throw money, throw drugs." So, sure enough, a little plastic bottle landed on the stage full of strange-looking pills.'

The following day, on the flight from Chicago to London, Cave and Howard decided that they would sample the mysterious pills, washing them down with all the duty-free alcohol they had purchased. Mid-flight Cave asked if he could eat his dinner late because he was beginning to feel seriously ill and kept passing out. He was completely unconscious when his dinner was later placed in front of him. Abruptly awaking from his stupor because he needed to relieve himself, he stood bolt upright, pulling himself up by the headrest in front of him, in the process spilling his food across the floor and other passengers. This did not endear him to the airline staff.

'When we got to Customs at Heathrow they looked through my bag and then started getting really serious with us because Nick had passed out on the baggage inspection table,' Harvey continues. 'He'd just sat down on it and collapsed, so it was immediate strip-search for everyone. When they couldn't find anything they reluctantly had to allow us back into the country. They were out of it for days afterwards. Rowland was sleeping for twenty-three hours a day. Genevieve had to take him to a restaurant to make him eat something and he'd just sit there throwing things in the air. They didn't remember anything that had happened.'

NOTES

1 Richard Guilliat, 'The Birthday Party, The Return And Revenge', *RAM*, 9 February 1982.
2 Nick Cave to an unnamed interviewer, in the pilot issue of *Allez Oop!*, December 1981.
3 Johnny Waller, 'Screamers with Streamers' *Sounds*, 8 August 1981.
4 Barney Hoskyns, 'Sometimes Pleasure Heads Must Burn' *NME*, 17 October 1981.

6

Junkyard

The Birthday Party's first gig upon arriving back in the UK took place on 16 October at Brixton Town Hall, in front of an audience of over 1,000 people, the largest crowd that the group had yet played to in London. 'I remember it was almost a bit too perfect, which was kind of scary,' says Mick Harvey. 'Our material seemed too streamlined. The gig was a big success, everything was going great and after that, of course, we started writing some really slow songs. It was almost like professional entertainment. It's so easy to fall into that trap once people have the idea that you're marketable and people love you; just to do the things you're meant to do, play music that you're meant to play. We could have become very popular, very quickly, but it wasn't in us somehow, it wasn't interesting. One gig was fun, we could play like a professional group and then that was the end of it. Maybe no one was too drunk that night.'

'I saw one of their concerts at the Moonlight Club and after about two songs I thought they were one of the best bands I'd ever seen,' says journalist Jessamy Calkin, who would manage to secure The Birthday Party's only interview piece in *The Face*, the magazine which more than any other symbolised the era of style over content. 'Their music was the antithesis of *The Face*, but I managed to get them in because everyone was talking about them and they were receiving rave reviews.

'The Birthday Party interview was the first I'd done with musicians and I was really nervous because I thought the band was so good. So I went along to 4AD's offices and it was a nightmare, the first and the worst interview I've ever done. Nick was really late and later I found out that he'd been busted on the way there. There was a lot of trouble then, Nick and Chris Carr whispering in the back room. I was totally in awe of them and didn't know what to say, they were really unhelpful. If I asked a normal straightforward question, Nick would say, "What?!" as if it was the most ridiculous question that he'd ever been asked. The only one who was nice to me, who was the only one I didn't end up becoming friends with, was Phill Calvert.' In the interview Cave described the Ritz gig as 'really sober and conservative'[1] and complained that having previously thought British audiences were terribly cold and frigid, they now reacted equally badly by flinging themselves into a frenzy the moment the group started to play. 'We set ourselves up in The Birthday Party,' reflects Rowland Howard, 'because we told people what they should do and were then disappointed when they did it. I don't blame Nick for this. It was almost like we wanted to be entertained by each member of the audience, in their own startling and original way.'

The issue of *The Face* in which The Birthday Party interview appeared carried a long cover piece on Blue Rondo à la Turk, a terribly inept English attempt at appropriating Latin music, dressed up in zoot suits, berets and goatee beards; a sign of the times. On the evening of the interview, 27 October, Calkin travelled again to the Moonlight Club to watch the band: 'That was the first time that they had performed "She's Hit", Nick had the lyrics in his hand.' The melancholy, slow blues-style ballad, co-written with Tracy Pew and first recorded during their third Peel session on 2 December, provided ample evidence that The Birthday Party were much more than a mere thrash band. 'She's Hit' also indicated that Cave's lyrical style was steadily becoming more narrative in form.

In early November, Lydia Lunch arrived in London and moved into an apartment in west Kensington, a darkly decorated flat furnished with a piano and with stuffed animals adorning the walls. 'I followed The Birthday Party to London,' says Lunch. 'I thought, this is something to pursue. Usually if I meet someone

I want to collaborate with, I make sure it comes to fruition. The minute I got to London, of course, they left for months, but, nonetheless, I carried on. I wasn't dependent on them for fun or creative output at that time.'

On 3 November The Birthday Party played the first date of their first European tour, at the Music Halle in Berlin. After playing four gigs in Holland, the band drove to Zurich in Switzerland in a rusting old British Rail bus which belched diesel fumes and had a top speed of 60 m.p.h. 'We played to the most surreal audience of all time,' says Mick Harvey of the crowd that witnessed the group's performance at Zurich's Kino Walche cinema on 9 November. 'We were totally exhausted because we hadn't been able to sleep on the bus. A nightmare. They were so conservative. We were so noisy and obnoxious in this totally clean environment. It was horrible, but of course that was perfect for us to be as obnoxious as possible.' As the bus had finally broken down in Zurich the band had to catch a train to Italy to continue that leg of the tour. From the railway station they were driven at breakneck speed cross-country to a small discothèque called Piropiro, outside Imola. 'We didn't have any of our equipment with us and we were meant to be on in ten minutes,' recalls Harvey. 'Not all the bags could fit in the car and Phill suddenly realised he didn't have any drumsticks, so he had to cut up a broom handle with which to play the drums. The equipment they had rented for us was terrible. I walked up to test the microphone and there was a blue explosion in my face! The whole PA was live. I didn't sing any backing vocals for the rest of the night, that's for sure. There was no time to explain to Nick what was going on, well we did but it didn't sink in.

'Nick was running around with the mike all the time but he was not earthed to anything, he kept going up to Rowland and giving him shocks. He didn't know what was going on. On the front of the stage were these steps that had metal edges on them, and when Nick went down into the audience he just went *zipp*! back on to the stage. There was a guy with metal-rimmed glasses in the audience and Nick put his finger on the centre of them and he got zapped. He must have thought

Nick was God or something. I bet he remembers that gig to this day.'

During the early eighties Italy was still relatively virgin territory for new independent groups, and the Italians' reaction to the band was often highly volatile. This leg of the tour was made more chaotic by clubs not paying the group their arranged fee and by delays in repairing the tour bus. A couple of days of intense activity would be followed by days spent on the Adriatic coast doing nothing, before a car was hired for yet another hectic dash cross-country for the next gig. The most extreme reaction to the group occurred when they performed in Certaldo. 'The promoter couldn't find the venue, which was a Big Top tent, and we arrived an hour after we were meant to be on stage,' recalls Harvey. 'There were one and a half thousand people inside and they were waiting. We just plugged in and started playing immediately. After two songs they started gobbing and Tracy walked up and kicked one of the audience. From then on it was . . . chairs, everything was coming up on the stage, people were trying to attack us. "*Fascisti, fascisti*!" It was a free gig organised by the communist party and the audience had decided we were fascists! The security were really beating the shit out of people who were trying to get on stage. We only managed to play eight songs.'

After the gig the band drove to Milan to catch a train, all attempts to repair the bus having failed, to travel to Cologne to play the final date of the tour. When they arrived at the venue, they discovered that the gig had been subtly advertised as featuring 'The Most Violent Band In Britain'. 'These old hippies who ran the place pleaded with our tour manager, "Is everything all right, please don't let them beat us up",' laughs Rowland Howard. During the frantic gig, fights erupted in the crowd and one inebriated member of the mob stumbled on to the stage, where he started to urinate down Tracy Pew's leg. Pew only became aware of what was happening when he felt a warm puddle filling up his cowboy boots. Spinning around Pew crashed the German across the skull with his bass.

During The Birthday Party's absence, Jessamy Calkin had become firm friends with Lydia Lunch. In the early evening of

26 November, before the band and Lunch played at the Venue, where both their sets were to be recorded by 4AD for a live mini-album, Jessamy met Cave again at Lunch's house in west Kensington. 'She'd invited me to dinner and Nick was there but he didn't remember me from the interview, which I was really glad about. He was very nervous and shy,' says Calkin. 'That night after the gig I met the rest of the band and all the girlfriends. The girlfriends were like a band in themselves. I thought it was incredible that they'd come all the way from Australia with them. All the girls looked so good together, Genevieve, Anita, Katy, and Tracy's girlfriend Kate Jarrett.' During The Birthday Party's first Australian tour, Pew had been reunited with Jarrett, who hailed from Auckland and with whom he had had a relationship in 1979. When she arrived in the UK in mid 1981, he broke up with Caitlan, who returned to Australia. Calkin continues, 'We later went on to this party, I think it may have been at Barney Hoskyns' place, where I overheard this conversation between Lydia and Nick talking about writing some plays and Nick's next record. I remember Nick saying, "I want to write songs that are so sad, the kind of sad where you take someone's little finger and break it in three places." That really stuck with me for ages.'

'Nick was living all over the place,' says Lydia Lunch. 'For him at that time that was the thing to do. I'm sure that it was a rebellion against all that is mom and dad. Nick always had his nose into a notebook, grinding away on something. At that time he was all vision. Although Nick and I had feverishly disagreed in the beginning, I'd heard that he'd been writing these one-act plays, and I cornered and cajoled him into writing forty more. I thought the spectacle of fifty one-act plays was something that had to be documented. I corralled him into my house for the two weeks that it took to write these plays. We sped them out, some we worked on together, some separately. Every play was different.'

Cave and Lunch's one-act plays, collectively entitled *The Theatre of Revenge*, were in part a pastiche of the surrealist dramatist and poet Antonin Artaud's 'Theatre of Cruelty'. 'The theatre will never find itself again,' wrote Artaud in *The Theatre and Its Double*, '. . . except by furnishing the spectator with the truthful precipitate of dreams, in which his taste for crime, his erotic obsessions, his savagery, his chimeras, his Utopian sense of life and matter, even his cannibalism pour out on a level not counterfeit and allusory, but interior.' However, rather than following Artaud's path towards a magical and mythic theatre that would bring liberation and release to the spectator, Cave's primary motivation was to pummel the audience into submission with a relentless series of extremely violent and profane tableaux. 'The reason I wrote them in the first place was because I found the theatre to be the most offensive thing around,' reflected Cave on the artistic medium with which his father had been actively involved. 'Theatre is dead and buried. One of the benefits of our plays was that they were new and exciting, if not a bit juvenile. It was to disgust people. It had no redeeming qualities whatsoever. Lydia dwelt on the sexual side of things, which was pretty vile. I tended towards boring or confusing the audience with violence.'[2]

As with Cave's relation to rock music in The Birthday Party and fine art painting at art school, he was drawn to theatre through a negative impulse, because its limitations produced a challenge to create something new. The plays themselves rejected psychological and narrative theatre and were instead based upon extreme violent action pushed beyond all limits. As in his lyrics, some of the plays he wrote were unconsciously incorporating elements of Americana with all the attendant clichés. Many of the plays were centred around speedway tracks, dragsters, their larger-than-life crazed drivers and girlfriends, addicted to the speed thrill of the circuit. The play that introduced the series was entitled 'Hells-Wheels-Called-Elvis', and was staged around a large racing car not unlike the creations Big Daddy Roth produced in the sixties. During the introduction a planted heckler interrupts the speech of Moose Kennedy, who is proclaiming with 'Shakespearian deliberation' that 'Hells-Wheels-Called-Elvis are a-coming.' The actor portraying Moose drops out of character and brawls with the heckler, who is beaten up and ejected from the building. The narrator announces that if any member of the audience has an opinion, they should write it on a piece of paper and put it in the comments box. This act is meant to unsettle the audience and set the scene for the unremitting assault of the other plays, beginning with 'Greasy-Hot-Rod-Cream', in which a man makes violent love to a girl in a hot rod to the sound of revving engines and a blaring radio.

The penultimate play of the series, called 'The Stoning of Ruby Von Monster' and co-written by Lunch and Cave, succinctly summed up the world view being espoused. Ruby Von Monster is a deformed hunchback who carries her affliction with dignity but is stoned by a drunken mob who consider her to be a witch. After the herd have killed her, heavenly angels descend singing songs of praise. Von Monster starts to rise into the air and the crowd who killed her begin to praise her as a saint. Suddenly her ascent is halted and she drops into the darkness offstage. The narrator takes to the stage: 'Did anyone really believe that we would allow anyone in these performances to rise above the muck? Man is allowed to rise . . . but only in order that he be flung down, even harder, into his eternal lot . . . the trash. Any fool knows that. Goodnight.'*

In order to break away from the traditional theatrical presentation from under the proscenium arch, the plays, each between two and three minutes in duration, were to be performed on four stages surrounding the audience, who would be held captive standing uncomfortably in a small, cramped central area. The collective effect that Cave wanted to generate within the audience was the sensation of being incessantly 'bombarded with a perpetual onslaught of pornography and violence'.[3]

'It was intense, we had to pound the plays out in a very short period of time, because we couldn't stand to be with each other probably,' says Lunch. 'We had deadlines because we had other things to do but we knew the genres we wanted to cover. I was always sad that we didn't work more . . . That was the closest period that I had working with Nick, because we never really worked on anything beyond that.'

---

* Both 'Hells-Wheels-Called-Elvis' and 'The Stoning of Ruby Von Monster', together with several other plays not included in Nick Cave's *King Ink* collection, were printed in an edition of the American rock magazine *Forced Exposure*.

Lydia Lunch's interest in Nick Cave was not purely confined to literary endeavour. 'Lydia's whole thing at that time was unadulterated sex,' says Jessamy Calkin. 'If she wanted to get involved with someone she'd ask them to work with her. She was very motivated by sex and The Birthday Party weren't. Lydia had this idea of Nick, she was often quoted as saying he was the perfect boy and he wasn't really that ideal. Nick is incredibly romantic and conventional in lots of ways and she visualised him as one of the characters in the plays they wrote who puts you up against a car and screws you. He's not like that, but that's what she wanted him to be like.

'I think Lydia was half in love with him but in many ways they weren't on the same wavelength. When they were writing those plays they had a poetical ideal that they shared, but their method of approach was really different. Lydia's very disciplined, she could never cope with the rock'n'roll aspects of his lifestyle, getting drunk, getting too out of it to do things.'

Lydia herself recalls: 'He overdosed three times when I was with him. I told him, you do that one more time and I won't be the one to save you. It was pathetic and awful. You can only take so much responsibility for someone's life, I won't nursemaid anybody. It was very disturbing to me. In my case I had an addiction to adrenalin and he had one to heroin. It's not that different. I was more interested in the drugs that the body could make under duress than what you could pump into your body. That's where my trouble lay: sex, fear, danger, death.

'He was a slush, but it never impeded what they were doing. The creativity did not suffer and that's the bottom line, OK, the rest of their lives were in complete collapse. They were living in squats, they were overdosing, whatever the story was it doesn't fucking matter, the bottom line is it didn't hurt ... but did it help? It did not hurt the creative process, it did not mar the output. Sometimes that's what it takes, burning your face into the bottom of the fucking scum bucket to come out with the gold, and if that's what it takes, so be it. I'm not here to criticise anyone's behaviour, so this is by no means criticism. It's just fact.'

After finishing the one-acters Cave's relationship with Lunch would quickly deteriorate and he would also lose interest in the plays themselves, though Lydia would endeavour to secure interest in the project.

On 11 December, before leaving for Melbourne, the band played a farewell gig at the Central London Poly. 'It was a cold day, six inches of snow outside,' says Chris Carr, 'but inside the narrow hall at the front of the stage it was hot, packed and sweaty. Both Tracy and Nick were loaded before the gig. I remember hearing a strange sound while they were playing. I went up on the mixing desk, from where I saw Sir Nicholas knighting people. It was like he was playing the drums, he was banging people on the head as hard as possible with the microphone, and it ended up with him just lashing out and kicking people.'

The band had arrived at the venue three hours early and had consumed all the alcohol that had been provided by the students. Ten minutes before they went on, Tracy Pew overdosed in the toilet and had to be given mouth-to-mouth resuscitation and injected with amphetamine sulphate in order to try to revive him. When they finally made it to the stage they were a complete shambles. At one point Pew fell flat on his face with a sickening thud as his bass hit the floorboards. 'The best thing about that night was when Nick took off his jacket while holding on to the microphone, then spent ages trying to work out why his jacket was strung, inside out, along the microphone lead like it was a washing line,' laughs Harvey. Five songs into the set the group struck up the slow, grinding riff of 'She's Hit', but Cave's attention was distracted by a full-blown fight he was having with someone who had insulted him at the front of the stage. The band kept playing the riff for two minutes but Cave had forgotten the music altogether and his only concern was trying to beat up the heckler.

The riff suddenly ground to a halt. Mick Harvey was so furious that he walked up to Cave and punched him in the mouth. Cave spent most of the rest of the gig bashing Bingo over the head with the microphone. Blood was streaming down his face. Backstage, after the gig, the buffet that the students had provided was scattered across the floor and walls. An intense altercation ensued, with each member of the band screaming dire recriminations at each other. A fan collecting autographs tapped Cave on the shoulder to attract his attention, and Cave swung round and punched him out cold. At the end of the evening Cave overdosed and collapsed unconscious on the floor. The tour manager was so appalled at his behaviour that he threw his share of the gig money on top of his prone body in disgust, and Howard and Genevieve McGuckin dipped in and helped themselves to what Cave owed them.

Years later, Cave would claim that the reason The Birthday Party were never offered a major record deal was because many record company executives had attended the gig to check out the group, and gave up any ideas about becoming involved with the band. 'It took me a long time to get over that gig,' says Harvey. 'That gig was a write-off to me. My reaction wasn't always positive because I always wanted us to play well. Sometimes I think it made us play badly. There was just no way of putting the music across at all, which was a waste. When the music was a secondary issue there wasn't much else left for me. It made you tense, the prospect of some disastrous, messy problem every night was nerve-racking. We fed off it but that's where a lot of violence came from, from hypertension.'

The Birthday Party arrived back in Melbourne in mid December to begin work on their new LP, *Junkyard*. The recording sessions again took place at the enormous four-studio, three-floor Armstrong's Audio Visual Studios complex, and were even more chaotic than the previous year's *Prayers On Fire* sessions, as the group careered further out of control. They were reunited with engineer Tony Cohen for arguably their most artistically successful collaboration. 'At the start of a session Nick would always come up to me and say, "I want the album to sound like this or that,"' recalls Cohen, 'I can't remember what words he used for *Prayers On Fire* but for *Junkyard* he said, "We want 'Trash', 'Junk' and a scratchy, ugly, trebly sound." He said, "We've got to get away from *Prayers On Fire*, it's too slick." At the time we thought we'd made a Little River Band-style record, horrible and slick. Now looking back, of course, it's not. Well, that's what we wanted, and that's what we got, great fucking fun to record. *Junkyard* was an experiment of sound and physical ability to cope with drugs. A general experiment in every direction. We were zombies by the time we'd finished. We went overboard, we were so determined to make something quite hideous. I think we succeeded.

'By this stage the studio had been taken over by a big corporation and had become quite ugly. On the first day there was only meant to be me and the band in the studio and all their friends and some punks were there. I'd been setting up all day, drums in cupboards, things in cupboards all over the joint. They just started the first take, I hit the record button, they did "Big Jesus Trash Can" and that was the take that was used, I might add. It was great, but as they were recording it this guy in a suit came in carrying a clipboard, saying, "Right, stop them! Stop them!" I thought, I'm not fucking stopping them, lucky I didn't or we wouldn't have had that take. He said, "There's too many people in this studio, there's only meant to be Nick Cave, Mick Harvey, blah, blah, blah." I said, "Look, I'm not stopping them. If you press the stop button it's not going to go down very well. Just wait!" So they did the track, came in, and this guy was about to go right off at them. Then Rowland and a couple of his friends started getting closer and closer to him and their eyes probably looked a little menacing. This guy went bright red and backed out of the studio. That was the last we ever heard of complaints, until they painted a big heart of blood up in the toilets when they were cleaning the syringes . . . The cleaners went on strike for two weeks. Oh, God, that went down really well.'

Cohen would mix tracks at maximum volume because he was partially deaf and could no longer hear certain frequencies. He would always endeavour to make the guitar sound as distorted and abrasive as possible. 'We made a tunnel out of corrugated iron around an amp and put mikes on the iron itself,' he relates with evident glee. 'The noise was so bad it made the fillings pop out of your mouth! A really vicious sound, which was perfect for the metallic sound we were after. We mistreated things very seriously. We put contact mikes on symbols. The things only last for three minutes before they're blasted to bits because it's so loud.' The LP's title track was recorded by accident,

Cohen managing to press the record button just as the band started playing, before he nodded out. When they'd finished the song, their enquiries as to the merit of the take were met with silence. Cohen would often be discovered flat on his back underneath the mixing desk, in a position that the group would describe as 'checking the wiring'. 'One time Tony said, "I'll be back in a minute," and we were left just sitting in the studio,' says Howard. 'We sat there, and sat there. Several hours later we tried to find him, rang people up. We eventually found him. He'd crawled into a ventilation duct and had gone to sleep for twelve hours and we were sitting there, paying $150 an hour. That was fairly typical. At one stage Tony lived under the piano in the studio.

'Tracy used to get so drunk during recording *Junkyard* that he'd only be able to parrot what you'd just said. His brain had ceased to function on any level. All he'd do all night is sit in a chair and mutter, "I am the producer, I am the producer," decimating the leather trim on the recording desk with his spurs, repeatedly grinding them into the upholstery. At the end of one session, at seven in the morning, he stumbled to his feet, walked out of the studio and there was a car outside, and he just stole it. How he got home, I don't know.'

Cohen confirms Howard's recollection: 'Tracy was running pretty wild on that one. A couple of wine casks before midday. Nick was wild, taking drugs everywhere, so was I, completely running amok. We were a complete mess, I don't know how Mick Harvey put up with it.'

The antagonistic sensibility that Cave had been embracing within the one-act plays, combined with his increasing use of juxtapositions of cultural references and characterisations, were becoming even more extreme in his lyrics for The Birthday Party. In 'Hamlet (Pow, Pow, Pow)' he recreated Shakespeare's Prince of Denmark as a modern-day psychopath, far from the battlements of Elsinore, pistol in hand, looking for vengeance and a Cadillac, while 'Big Jesus Trash Can' alluded to a grotesque vision of Elvis Presley, the quintessence of rock'n'roll music: 'Wears a suit of gold (got greasy hair), but God gave me sex appeal'. 'Dead Joe', a Cave composition featuring lyrics co-written by Anita Lane and describing a character's demise in an automobile accident, was based around just one chord.

In 'Six-Inch Gold Blade' Cave narrated a violent tale of extreme sexual jealousy, desire and hatred combined in the brutal murder of a girl not too dissimilar in appearance to Anita Lane. Although his obsession with Anita had manifested itself in a number of earlier songs, 'Six-Inch Gold Blade' marked her first obvious appearance as a narrative character. She would figure as a recurring motif in Cave's songs. When asked of her portrayal in his lyrics, Anita replied: 'I didn't know anything else. I didn't know my rights. I always felt fine about it. You live with what you know. To other people it may have been really shocking, but I liked the idea of how shocking it was. I didn't take it completely literally, that would be like believing in a soap opera in which a character had really died. It was like I was a character based in reality. I think Nick's writing is always one step removed from his true immediate feelings, it's always having a literary eye on yourself.'

Before and during recording, it became clear within the band that Phill Calvert was having problems with some of the band's newer material. 'It was getting tense because Phill couldn't play certain things they wanted,' says Cohen. 'They wanted animal drumming and Phill was a bit of a technician. They'd outgrown him, without being rude to Phill, he was a good drummer. It was to do with attitude. At the start of the session Phill found a syringe in his bass drum case, that Nick had possibly hidden in there, and he just flipped out! That was the last straw, which was amusing, at the time. They were writing songs in the studio, which was a new development, like "Hamlet" and "Dead Joe", which was about my girlfriend who was completely mad. Rather the title was about her, it was about a car crash. Charming. They wanted this jungle drumming and Phill couldn't do it. Mick would just jump on the drums and it was obvious that this was the way to go.'

More importantly, the main songwriting axis was shifting from Cave and Howard towards Cave and Harvey. When the LP was finally finished it would feature only two complete Howard compositions. 'As early on as *Junkyard* I realised that I couldn't write complete songs and expect him [Nick] to do them,' says Howard. 'I was just giving him music. I wrote a couple of lyrics but only if he was comfortable doing them. At the same time it was frustrating for me because I was writing complete songs and I couldn't do anything with them. Everyone was headstrong and didn't want to give an inch. The fights, no matter how trivial, were symbols of control. I felt I was missing out and usurped by Mick as the person who realised Nick's ideas. The reason I started playing guitar in the first place was I wanted to play songs.' The competitive clash between the three musicians, each with his own distinctive vision, would eventually tear the group apart. Cave no longer wished to be shackled to Howard's melodies and was unable to interpret his lyrics, of which he had never been very enamoured. As Cave was increasingly being perceived in the press as the group's leader, he wanted more control over the path they were taking.

At the end of the recording sessions the studio slapped a hefty surcharge on to the group's bill for the extensive damage they had caused, and for recording equipment that had 'disappeared' in order to fund certain band members' addictions. On Christmas Eve, Cave and Howard had discovered a large bag of prawns that had been delivered to the studio. They had unwrapped presents that had been laid at the foot of a large Christmas tree in the complex and placed the prawns inside them, and in the ventilator shafts all over the building, sending a foul odour drifting through the studios. The studio bosses were furious and The Birthday Party were promptly banned from AAV. 'There was a point when it felt like someone was losing it in terms of direction,' says Ivo Watts-Russell. 'They had to rerecord some tracks in England afterwards. The financial pressures were far greater then but they recorded quickly.'

Already Cave was considering the question of the album's cover artwork. He desperately wanted an image that was as far removed from the now typically tasteful 'new wave' sleeve art as possible. He remembered that his brother Tim used to wear a T-shirt emblazoned with an abominable creation of the American custom car manufacturer Ed 'Big Daddy' Roth. The shirt depicted 'Mother's Worry', a leather-capped deformity squatting at the wheel of an elongated, flame-belching hot rod, reaching with a taloned claw for a dice-shaped gear shift. Cave thought that the anarchic energy and humour in Roth's graphic art would be highly appropriate to illustrate the essence of The Birthday Party's recordings. Keith Glass happened to know the phone number of George Barris, a contemporary of Roth's who created the Batmobile, and through him contacted Roth. Roth told Glass that he felt guilty about lowering the moral standards of youth in the sixties with his artwork and that he did not wish to corrupt youth again in the eighties. However, he agreed to see Glass when he visited Los Angeles on business, to discuss the group's moral attitude and listen to the completed LP. Cave was understandably sceptical that he would ever agree to undertake the job.

Playing a series of dates to crowded venues in Sydney, Melbourne, Adelaide and Brisbane, it became apparent to The Birthday Party that the ecstatic applause they received before they had even played a note was false. As in England, Cave always revelled in the unpredictable response that the band could sometimes provoke, but already audience reaction was becoming regimented and safe. Music which was primarily designed to incite and taunt was being greeted with blind sycophancy. Cave was most irritated by the swelling Australian audience and the media, whom he perceived to be merely reacting in an exaggerated fashion to the accolades that had been showered upon the band overseas. This cycle would lead him to have grave doubts about The Birthday Party's ability to communicate with individuals rather than pandering to a mob. 'It's just hard for us, for a group that played for three or four years up against a brick wall to a couple of hundred people who genuinely liked us, or hated us, or whatever, to be playing to a thousand people who suddenly like us,' Cave complained to *RAM*, the music paper The Birthday Party loathed the most because of its claims that it had always championed the band. 'And you'd have to be an idiot to think they actually liked you because the music was good. To get 1,600 people at Sydney Uni was an insult to us, not flattery.'

Evan English comments: 'They came back and they were

big-time then. The shows were packed and wild. I think what happened with The Birthday Party is that they were reaching the physical extremity of rock'n'roll, verging on death. It had happened before with Iggy Pop. The point is that people are watching and saying, push the accelerator faster, for us! for us! It's voyeuristic watching these people destroy themselves and getting a thrill out of it. He was kind of manipulated by the audience in a very strong way. I've never seen anything like The Birthday Party performances at their peak. Absolutely sensational, nothing short of spine-tingling. You didn't know what was going to happen and there was a real sense of danger. When you get to that point, he's not going to be conscious of what's happening. I think that's what happened with Nick.'

On the evening of 16 January The Birthday Party, without Phill Calvert, under the name The Cavemen, supported by The Sunburnt Pharaohs and Precious Little, played at a special Missing Link party held at the Tiger Lounge in Richmond to celebrate ten years of the label. During the course of their set The Cavemen were joined by their good friends Robert Forster, Grant McLellan and Lindy Morrison of The Go-Betweens for a raucous rendition of Johnny Cash's 'Ring of Fire'. In the early hours of the morning, Tracy Pew was arrested for drunk driving, giving his name as Peter James Sutcliffe, one of Cave's oldest friends. As Peter Sutcliffe also happened to be the name of the Yorkshire Ripper, the police decided that he must be lying.

When the *Melbourne Truth* got hold of the story, it was splashed across the front cover in a banner headline: 'I AM THE RIPPER. DRUNK PUNK JAILED, THEN TOUR STOPS'. 'That impressed my dad, of course,' says a rueful Mick Harvey. When the case came before Messrs John Head and J. Austin, JPs, in Prahran Court, Pew pleaded guilty to his fourth drunk driving charge, as well as to stealing a sewing machine and clothes worth $450 from the National Theatre, St Kilda, on 1 December 1979, and stealing rice and frankfurters from a supermarket on 13 August of the same year. The court ordered that he be jailed for eight months. Pew was advised by his lawyer not to appeal against the sentence. His conviction disrupted not only the final dates of the band's tour of Australia, at which Chris Walsh took Tracy's place, but also three gigs in the San Francisco area, as well as some concerts in Germany.

By this time there had been a complete communication breakdown with Keith Glass, who had now ceased to be the group's manager, and with whom they had been in dispute over alleged non-payment of royalties. 'When we left Australia after *Junkyard* Keith came up to Nick and said, "I think you're getting out of town at just the right time. Everyone is so sick and tired of you,"' says Rowland Howard.

As Pew began his sentence at an open prison, the group was again thrown into turmoil. 'The jails in Victoria aren't that bad,' Pew would recall in 1983. 'I got sent to a nice little prison farm. The band was due to leave for America about a week after I was locked up, which was a little awkward. I often seem to be doing things like this to inconvenience the rest of them . . . it certainly cleansed my body. I was off the piss, exercised a lot, worked every day pruning pine trees, did weight lifting, that way you could sleep really well so time went a lot quicker.'[4] With a British tour imminent in March and *Junkyard* still not completed, the band contacted their old friend in the UK, Barry Adamson, who agreed to take Tracy's place until his release.

In the group's absence from the UK scene, 4AD released in February the live recordings made in November as a mini-LP package entitled *Drunk On the Pope's Blood*, the phrase originally coined by Cave and Howard to promote the first Boys Next Door LP. The title would again bring The Birthday Party into the pages of the Australian tabloids and distress Mick Harvey's father no end. As *Junkyard* was to be released a little later in the year, newer and better material was left off the record but the LP in many ways captured the essence of the band's irreverent attitude towards their own music, and music generally. 'We deliberately did pretty absurd mixes,' says Mick Harvey. 'A lot of the sense of humour and ideas behind the record get lost with time. Making a live record was a bit of a joke and the editing process was hilarious too. We were rolling around with laughter at the stupid things we were doing; the way we were mixing all the instruments, so extreme and unpleasant, making a cut-up of the audience cheering at the end. For us it was funny, but nobody else got the joke. It was almost a send-up of a live LP, just for us, not for anybody else. We could never do a live LP seriously. We left all the mistakes in and during mixing we were actually turning people up when they missed a key change.' The band would doubtless have been pleased by a negative review the record received in the *NME* entitled 'Bloody Awful Row'.

The Birthday Party, with Barry Adamson, played the first of four UK gigs on 5 March to a packed house at the Venue. Despite, or perhaps because of, Adamson's professional polish, neither he nor the other stand-in, Rowland's brother Harry Howard, could successfully fill the gaping void left by Pew's absence. Although Pew was just the group's bass player and never really contributed to the songwriting, he was an integral part of the band. 'When we came back without Tracy we were pretty much on collision course with the group folding,' recalls Harvey. 'We were becoming refined in what we were able to provoke, which is when Nick became uninterested in provoking a reaction. It became a show to do that, things were now expected of us. We had no objections to being popular, what we objected to was what would then be expected of us. The audience, especially in England, were becoming stronger than the band.'

NOTES

1 Jessamy Calkin, 'The Birthday Party: Release the Bats', *The Face*, No.20, December 1981.
2 Cave to an unnamed interviewer, 'The Art Anti-Christ Finds Resurrection?', *Film Reviews*, 1985.
3 Helen Fitzgerald, 'The Birthday Party', *Masterbag*, August 1982.
4 Chris Bohn, 'The Sound and the Fury', *NME*, 26 March 1983.

7

Berlin

Tracy Pew rejoined The Birthday Party in late May for two gigs at the Clarendon Ballroom in London after serving only three months of his prison sentence, due to good behaviour. To celebrate his return to the fold, Bingo attended the first Clarendon gig dressed as a clown. 'He was wearing full face paint and this big orange Afro!' exclaims Mick Harvey. 'I said, "Bingo, why are you dressed like that?" "Ah, special occasion, Tracy's back."' Shortly after Pew's return the band commenced their second tour of Europe in Eindhoven, Holland, on 3 June. This tour would prove to be equally as eventful as the first, and would be dubbed by Howard 'The Last Day of the Rest of Your Life Tour'.

The support band for the tour was the German group Die Haut, an instrumental outfit influenced by The Kinks, Quicksilver Messenger Service, The Stooges and The Velvet Underground. Although The Birthday Party and Die Haut would eventually strike up a lasting friendship, at first the atmosphere was strained, as Die Haut's Christoph Dreher relates: 'We went to the sound check for the first gig and it was a little strange for us to see the group because we had an entirely different idea of what this band might look like. We had a different idea of what a contemporary group should look like and there they were, wearing cowboy boots and, in one case, a cowboy hat. To say that we thought they were hillbillies would be going a little bit too far, but it was in that direction. We had an astonishingly arrogant attitude that made it easier for us to be the support group because we felt superior, for some reason.'

'I'd heard of the band before the tour,' says Die Haut's drummer, Thomas Wydler. 'Before I joined Die Haut me and a friend were the first people in Berlin to have singles by The Boys Next Door and The Birthday Party. You could only get their records at this one specialist store. My girlfriend arranged for us to tour with The Birthday Party. I think The Birthday Party quite liked our group because we were strange too with our music. We were much better live than on this one record we had out at the time. The Birthday Party were fantastic, they had this incredible explosive power on stage I'd never seen before, I must say. It was so aggressive on stage and in the audience. Most of the bands at that time weren't interesting at all. I didn't talk much because I couldn't speak English at all.'

After a couple of gigs in Holland the barriers between the two groups began to wear down. 'We all slept in this youth hostel in the same room, divided by walls just made of cardboard,' says Dreher. 'Nick started using Latin expressions in conversation with Tracy and then we discovered that half the people there knew Latin. I always thought that I was exceptional knowing Latin as a musician. They understood that we perceived them as hillbilly types, which was funny.' In Amsterdam the band discovered Dutch amphetamine sulphate, which proved to be a revelation for all concerned, and it was speed that would propel the whole tour. It amazed Die Haut to find Cave, the first man up at 6 o'clock, drinking Bloody Marys filled with raw eggs and scribbling away into his notebook, in the breakfast room of their hotel.

The concerts would also be augmented by brief improvised performances by Lydia Lunch and Rowland Howard. 'It was a ten-minute stab of white noise backed by satanic poetry,' says Lunch. 'I was experimenting with spontaneous combustion which most people shy away from. Everything else about that tour seems to be a blur. Nick was very antagonistic towards mine and Rowland's performance. It wasn't up his alley, that's fine, but I felt Nick, and Mick, never really got me. They never really knew where I was coming from. I was too arty and weird for them. I always wanted to work on different projects. I think they saw me as some arty hobo, flitting from one thing to the next. I just don't think they got me as a woman, as a person, or an artist, whereas Rowland understood me.'

Lunch's alignment with Howard for a cover version of Lee Hazlewood's 'Some Velvet Morning', with guest musicians Genevieve McGuckin, Barry Adamson and Mick Harvey, would further exacerbate the growing rift between Howard and Cave, 'The thing is, Nick doesn't open himself up very much,' says Howard. 'I was Nick's friend for a long time, for three years a good friend, but he would never tell you anything personal about himself; how he was feeling, if he was upset or anything. Things would occur where we would become friends for a while, then a tour would end and we'd part. He's a really difficult person to know.'

'Lydia is very important about what happened to the group in a way,' says Harvey, 'not to blame Lydia, but she did act as a distraction from a united vision which showed up the divisions which were forming about what people wanted to do. The competitive stuff between Nick and Rowland really started showing up, people were dissatisfied . . .' Lunch would argue that problems arose because Howard was not being used to the full extent of his abilities within the group. 'Rowland's contribution to The Birthday Party was immense,' says Lunch. 'I think that sometimes he wasn't recognised for the talent he was within that structure, because there were so many big egos in it. Mick Harvey's got an incredible ego and so has Nick, ego not being a dirty word, it's just a strong vision. I tried to keep away from that entanglement. I had enough problems maintaining my friendship with all of them anyway because of the difference between people who are doing drugs and those who are not. I had a hard-core, straight edge concerning a lot of things at the time. I wasn't completely drug- or alcohol-free but I wasn't experimenting in the same fashion.'

'It was all very uncontrolled, a real whirlpool of drink and drugs,' recalls Bingo, who accompanied the band on the tour. 'From what I saw of their lifestyle they ate when they could. They literally had to go on tour so they could eat. Most bands are controlled by a manipulator but no one had any control over The Birthday Party. They were complete nonconformists and individualists.' At the Hammersmith Palais in March, Bingo had finally gained the band's undivided attention by breathing fire at them, at the cost of burning the inside of his mouth. Thereafter, he had been adopted by them, often acting as Cave's bodyguard and, on occasion, handling press interviews for the singer. Cave had no interest in a third party expounding on his work, or trying to analyse it, as he felt it immediately diminished the very point of the group. His hatred of criticism and critics had only hardened since his years at art school. For a brief period he had lived with Bingo in his flat on the Isle of Dogs. 'I remember he liked the name,' says Bingo. 'He was like a travelling man, with his plastic bags full of papers, his lyrics . . . He was a chaotic character. Nick always had his nose in the Bible. He liked the Old Testament and he was obsessed with Jesus. He'd pick up on bits and pieces that would interest him, that were controversial in the sense that if he took them out into a different context it would be viewed differently; phrases, lines, words came from the Bible.

'Nick was always very difficult to communicate with at the best of times, very insecure, for whatever reason. He was sick a lot of the time. He'd say it was ill health but it was because heroin was destroying his natural immune system. He'd get really bad flu and he'd have difficulty in singing and then he'd have to take more drugs to get going, but no matter what he took he was always very articulate . . . I really wasn't into their drug culture scene. I don't like the feeling of being totally wiped out and insular. They'd have these heroin sessions and it did embarrass some people because I wasn't doing it. I saw some nasty characters trying to curry favour by offering them this, that, and the other, but they used to use and abuse people along the way. They'd get them running around and acting like little children. It became a necessity after a while.

'There were a lot of ego clashes, they were all battling against each other and that's where a lot of problems arose all the time. I saw a lot of them together on that tour, and there'd be a little bit of nasty humour going around, very dry poking fun at each other. The weaker one would be the whipping boy for the day.

Nick would have the last say in certain situations, just because everyone expected the singer to be the leader of the band, but Mick Harvey was the backbone, the organiser. He'd whip them into shape.' The task of trying to instil some semblance of order into a constantly chaotic situation, and even trying to communicate with the rest of the band while he was sober, would have an increasingly profound effect upon Mick Harvey's personality for many years. 'Mick was always organising and always angry,' says Anita Lane, who had returned to the UK earlier in the year to join Cave. 'We were often apart. He [Nick] started hanging out with Lydia and he wanted me to come back very quickly. He didn't like hanging out with her and I was kind of a way out, or maybe he was missing me.' Although they were often physically separated, or involved with other partners, the bond between the couple was unshakeable.

After their Amsterdam show at the Paradiso on 4 June, Cave was formally introduced to Blixa Bargeld, lead singer and untutored guitarist of the challenging Berlin group Einsturzende Neubauten, by another Berliner, Gudrun Gut of Malaria, whom Cave had met in Washington DC. 'Well, I knew nothing about The Birthday Party or their music but I instantly liked it,' says Bargeld. On their initial meeting Cave was first struck by Blixa's intimidating physical presence. He had never encountered any-one who looked so emaciated, Blixa's high cheekbones further emphasising his gaunt figure. 'Nick's a lot more innocent than he appears,' says Rowland Howard. 'He gets really impressed by things and people. He's almost a fan of certain people, particu-larly people who look slightly dilapidated, who look like they've lived. You can see that in the way Nick presents himself, too.' The following day, at the hotel where the band were staying, Cave became enthralled by a performance by Einsturzende Neubauten he happened to catch on Dutch television. Although the group played unconventional instruments, such as a 'drum kit' consisting mostly of sheets of metal, jackhammers, mallets, crowbars and a pneumatic drill, he instantly recognised Bargeld and the band to be kindred spirits. The group were totally unique, could not be placed in any convenient category, and embraced destruction as the premise for creation, hence their name, 'Collapsing New Buildings'. However, it was not their innovation which primarily excited Cave, rather their intention and savage conviction, so different from the majority of UK new wave bands who merely flirted with novelty for effect. 'They are a group which has developed its own language for one reason – to give voice to their souls,'[1] Cave would recollect years later in a piece recalling his initial ecstatic reaction to the band's performance. Almost inexorably Cave and Bargeld's paths would cross again a couple of months later.

The Birthday Party's one and only gig in France, on 8 June, nearly degenerated into a riot. When they arrived at the venue in Paris, a converted Turkish baths, they were outraged to discover that the management, who were well aware of the group's burgeoning reputation, would not allow them access to their rider before taking to the stage. They refused point blank to perform. As the packed house became increasingly restless at the delay, the management eventually capitulated. As an act of defiance the group managed to consume a couple of bottles of whisky five minutes before show time. Staggering on to the stage, Cave took immediate exception to three designer-clad Frenchmen who were yelling at him at the front of the stage, even though he could not understand a word they were saying. The hatred and tension that had been building up within him throughout the tour snapped, and before the band had played a note of their opening number, he had drop-kicked each one of the Frenchmen full in the face. 'Then Nick just leapt into the audience and started fighting, so I had to get out there with him,' says Bingo. 'Nick and I were back to back, fists flying with a crowd of people all around us. We were ready to take them all on but they wouldn't do it.' The usual pandemonium reigned backstage after the gig. 'There was a disagreement with the promoter so we "negotiated" the price. Minnou, the tour manager, was talking to this guy and we were backing her up, giving him some verbal. There were thick wedges of cash there and we were stealing as much as we could.'

After the rest of the group had left Paris, Nick and Anita would spend a further four days there holed up in the seedy Hotel Americana. Most of the time Cave was in bed sick because he was unable to obtain any drugs, and also having badly twisted his neck executing a back flip on stage. The couple would quarrel and Cave would go on to Berlin alone. In the interim Lydia Lunch had been offered an advance to make an album for Rip Off records, who would more than live up to their name. As the German leg of The Birthday Party's tour did not start for a week, Lunch initially put Howard, Genevieve McGuckin and Harvey to work on the LP in the intervening period. 'It was seriously conceived as a group, "Honeymoon In Red",' states Harvey, 'me, Rowland, Genevieve. Murray Mitchell was meant to play guitar as well. After a while we realised we didn't have a bass player. Murray didn't seem to play bass very well, which is fair enough, not everyone can. So Tracy got roped in, as did Nick to sing on a couple of duets. It was never put together as The Birthday Party all working with Lydia.' Lydia herself recalls: 'I wish I could say I recorded an album with The Birthday Party, but it wasn't even recorded with the whole band. There were complete problems doing it. Someone said they were going to pay for it and pulled out halfway through. Tracks were recorded at a number of different studios and the tapes were lost for a year afterwards.' A collection of songs from the sessions was eventually found by Lunch and remixed by Jim Thirlwell and Martin Bisi in May 1987, with a subsequent album, *Honeymoon In Red* released in April 1988. Very unhappy with the work that had been done in their absence, Cave and Harvey asked to have their names removed from the record.*

On 25 June the band began a seven-date tour of Germany, christened by Rowland Howard the 'Oops, I've Got Blood On the End of My Boot Tour', with tempers within the group becoming increasingly frayed. Within a few days Pew had punched Howard for taking his seat in the front of the tour bus which he, as a non-smoker, always occupied, having difficulty breathing in the ever-smoky vehicle. 'Rowland and I thought we'd stir him by getting in the front seat,' says Harvey, 'but he got incredibly angry, grabbing our hair and clawing at us. I was going to get out, it was only a joke, but Rowland took

* For further details, see Discography, p.318.

issue with it. Then he was in big trouble! That was the nature of that tour.'

The group's gig on 2 July at the Palazzoschokko, formerly a chocolate factory in Cologne, proved to be even more eventful than the previous year's concert at the same venue. 'There were all these punk rockers there,' recalls Bingo. 'Nick was in an obnoxious mood and there were all these people adoring him and he just wanted some reaction.' Cave spent most of the gig kicking people and hitting them with the microphone. Inadvertently he kicked one girl in the face, breaking her nose. 'Nick wanted to kick some skinhead who was getting on his nerves,' recalls Thomas Wydler, 'so he went to kick him but kicked this girl by mistake. At this moment the bouncers came on and tried to make something of it, but it didn't happen. Very dangerous bouncers.' As Cave tried to make his apologies, bedlam erupted. 'Some guy wanted to bash his head in with an iron bar,' remembers Bingo. 'Watching from the side of the stage, I saw this metal bar coming from the back, being passed through the air by some seedy punk rocker types and this character stuck it in his coat pocket. I timed it really well, just as he was reaching into his pocket for the bar, ready to hit him, I ran over, pulled it out and threw it to the back of the stage. Then three of them started having a go at me, they really wanted to get him.'

After the gig the band were informed that there was a problem. Another band had been booked to play at the venue that same day. The group in question happened to comprise members of the local chapter of the Hell's Angels. 'They were now asking if they could use our equipment,' says Howard. 'We blithely said no. The next minute we had Hell's Angels coming into the band room in an unhappy frame of mind.' Bingo was dispatched to defuse the situation: 'I went up to them and said, "Right, the story is . . ." and this big geezer nearly ripped my fucking shirt arms off, throwing me over. Then the band [The Birthday Party] were inspired by that moment because they'd hurt their friend and they were all there, even the girlfriends, ready to lay into these guys.' Bloodshed was narrowly avoided when Pew, who had been threatening mantra-fashion throughout the tour to bottle someone, had a bottle plucked from his hand just as he was about to hit one of the bikers. The next day, on the final date of the tour, in Frankfurt, Tracy finally achieved his goal when a skinhead poured a pint of beer over the head of the band's diminutive Balinese tour manager, Minnou. Silently, Cave and Pew, briskly followed by Mick Harvey, walked straight up to the skinhead, and Pew knocked him out cold with a bottle.

Junkyard was finally released in July, having been postponed awaiting Ed 'Big Daddy' Roth's sleeve artwork. The artist had eventually decided to undertake the project, despite his doubts about its moral content. Mick Harvey disliked the finished product but Cave thought that Roth's airbrush painting of a hideous salivating grotesque driving a hot rod made from a garbage can captured the spirit of the record. Roth's painting would become synonymous with the group, leading to misinterpretation from the press. '*Junkyard* and the whole rock'n'roll monster thing which we had put forth came out of our control, not just to the press but also in our personal lives,' recalls Howard. Whether Cave and the group were aware of it or not, there could be no path back after the extremity of the album, which was enjoying considerable success on the independent charts. After the innovation of *Prayers On Fire*, *Junkyard*'s all-out aural assault was viewed by some critics, who overlooked much of the record's overt black humour, as an exercise in self-parody: 'such wanton offence can only command brief attention and recorded revulsion soon subsides to neglect. Uneasy listening is no longer enough,' concluded Steve Sutherland's *Melody Maker* review. Cave in particular became increasingly irritated that journalists, having eavesdropped on the band's own dissatisfaction with their music, would appropriate their sentiments as their own. '*Junkyard* was our warped vision of rock,' says Harvey. 'It was very deliberately and consciously conceived that way. I remember some people saying that they didn't want to hear The Birthday Party doing their version of "Fun House", but that was kind of the idea. But it wasn't meant to be the end of the story. It was almost to make a record like that and have done with it but it didn't really work out like that because stagnation set in to a degree.'

Within a comparatively short period of time, key members of

The Birthday Party had become disillusioned with the band, the way it was generally perceived by the media and fans alike, and their London base. In order to maintain any conviction about their work they realised they would have to embrace change to avoid becoming merely a predictable rock band. Their first major decision was to move to Berlin, which everyone had found a ceaselessly stimulating environment, seemingly teeming with like-minded individuals involved in some kind of creative endeavour not necessarily connected with rock music. With their friends in Die Haut and Malaria, there would be no problem in finding accommodation in the city, and the cost of living would be considerably lower than London. More importantly, Berlin was a twenty-four-hour-a-day city which exuded an atmosphere of uninhibited freedom, whereas London appeared to the Australians to close at 11 o'clock when the pubs shut. 'In Berlin a beer cost 50 pfennigs and many flat rents were still frozen from after the war at around £10 a month,' says Howard. 'The main reason we went there was we met these people with whom we thought we shared a common ground, Malaria, Die Haut and Einsturzende Neubauten. For the first time since we left Australia we felt part of some sort of "scene". There was nothing like that in England; The Fall were the only group we felt any affinity to.'

The band approached Ivo with their plan and a request for the money they thought they would need for the relocation. 'It got to the point where they really needed money,' says Ivo. 'All bands for a while can exist on no money but all I could commit to was their recording costs and something towards them living there.' They would claim that they had not received any royalty payments, as Ivo was paying royalties directly to Keith Glass, assuming he would then send the band their share. 'Ivo felt bad about that,' says Chris Carr. 'Nick and I tried to get him to break his deal with Keith Glass but it just couldn't be done.'

Moving to Berlin also presented the perfect opportunity to get rid of Phill Calvert, who had long since outlived his usefulness in the group's eyes. 'We had wanted to chuck him out for a couple of years,' says Harvey, who would now become the group's permanent drummer. 'It had been talked about due to personal difficulties with him. We had to make a change to the set-up to inject new life and shake things up again. Getting rid of Phill deliberately put us in an awkward position again. I think the results speak for themselves. In the context of the group Phill had an outsider's perspective and as far as being able to cope creatively, I think it was very difficult for him. He was a very straight drummer in a way.' To begin with, the decision to drop Calvert was presented to the media as a mutual arrangement, but would soon degenerate into acrimony. Calvert understandably felt aggrieved, although he would initially present a brave face to the press. 'I'm happy in the sense that I can now do a lot of things that I've been wanting to do – but it's sad for me too,' he told journalist Helen Fitzgerald. 'I've been in this band a hell of a long time; I'm one of the original members. Me and Nick have known each other since we were ten or eleven. There's possibilities of me working on certain things, I suppose; they've got my number; it's awful . . . people are talking about me like I've died or something!'[2] Christoph Dreher felt that: 'Phill didn't take part in their attitude towards life or music. They thought he was a more typical rock'n'roll person. That was something The Birthday Party had in common with Die Haut in that we didn't consider it important to be professional musicians. It was based more around an artistic attitude towards life. Phill wanted to be a rock'n'roll star, a careerist.'

Before departing for Berlin, and with Phill Calvert still occupying the drum seat, the band commenced a brief five-day tour of the UK on 10 July at the short-lived Zig Zag club in Westbourne Park, London. The support group were the then little-known Leeds Gothic rock band The Sisters of Mercy, fronted by the enigmatic Andrew Eldritch. 'At the end of their set Mr Eldritch and friends wanted to know what The Birthday Party thought of them, and asked me to find out,' recalls Chris Carr with a wry grin. 'I asked them if they were sure about this, they were, so I went off to the dressing room. The only person who saw anything of their show was Mr Mick Harvey, who announced that The Sisters Of Mercy were the worst band to have ever supported The Birthday Party. I went back and recounted this to Mr Eldritch. The following Monday I got a call from The

Sisters of Mercy saying that the band had had a meeting and had decided to continue, and to wish The Birthday Party all the best in the future. They understood their criticism but thought that rather than break up, they'd carry on. It was all very dramatic,' Carr laughs. Within six years The Sisters of Mercy would become one of the UK's most successful rock groups.

The week after the Zig Zag gig, the group had their first truly disastrous interview, on this occasion with the then *NME* journalist Amrik Rai, a man who would become a particular *bête noire* for both Cave and Harvey for many years. Throughout the interview Rai deliberately antagonised the band by claiming that their music relegated sex and violence to the level of a Tom and Jerry cartoon, and that they were in effect a mock horror show. 'He knew nothing about the group, nothing about the recent record, he'd just got sent the records during the week and made notes on the lyrics and had taken the job on,' says Harvey. 'The fucking creep! We started talking very loudly about taking his cassette player and smashing it to bits.' The group tried to have the interview pulled from the paper, even though it was the largest article that they had yet received. Harvey adds: 'We'd rather have no article than an article by that guy.' Remarkably the interview would be reprinted in the *NME* in 1993 as part of a series entitled 'Classic *NME* Interviews'.

With a shared sense of optimism and release, The Birthday Party left the UK for Berlin in July. The first gig they played as a four-piece took place on 17 September at a music festival staged in Athens. With a line-up that included The Fall and New Order, the festival was a landmark event for Greek rock fans, giving them their first opportunity to experience first-hand post-punk music.

'We flew there from Berlin, via Budapest,' recalls Howard, 'and on the plane Nick befriended these two really repellent Australian hitchhiking girls who became his drinking buddies. That could be the only possible reason why he liked them, and the fact he was fatigued, his brain had probably shut down temporarily. When we got to the airport in Greece the promoter was so terrified that we were going to arrive in Athens with guitar cases full of heroin he had his cousin in Customs and Immigration whip us through on the sly. It was like what you'd imagine happened when The Rolling Stones went to Melbourne in 1968 or something: there were a dozen photographers there from the daily papers taking photographs of our every move as we pushed our baggage along. So we arrived at the hotel and everyone got their rooms and went upstairs, except apparently Nick, because an hour later the night clerk rang up Minnou, the tour manager, and said that Nick was downstairs demanding that his two Australian friends be allowed to share his hotel room. Minnou, in her typical fashion, rang up Mick Harvey, saying, "Oh Mick, you know, Nick is downstairs and he is making trouble." So Mick Harvey, in his pyjamas, marches downstairs and says, "OK, you stupid cunt, just get the fuck up to your bedroom and go to fuckin' sleep!" and Nick says, "OK, I'm leaving the band," picks up his little briefcase and marches off into the night.

'The following morning he was woken up by a policeman. He was asleep under a bush in a park and there were headlines in the papers saying, "Punk Rock Star Found Asleep Under Bush". Nick was convinced he was still in Berlin. He wandered around for a couple of hours trying to get on trams, trying to give them deutschmarks and finding it frustrating when they refused. Eventually he was sitting on this train station, forlorn and hungover, and then we were all coming out of the hotel, directly in front of him. An amazing piece of Nick's typical good luck.'

The festival would prove to be as eventful as the band's arrival in the country. Due to the crowd's mounting hysteria awaiting their performance, the concerned promoters insisted that The Birthday Party take the stage half an hour earlier than arranged. The stage itself towered above the audience, who were only just able to peer over its lip. Further obscuring their view was a line of six burly bouncers standing on the edge of the stage and separating the band from the crowd. Having tried to perform one song under these conditions, Cave rushed up behind each bouncer in turn, shoving them into the swelling throng, where they disappeared from view. This act of defiance prompted the audience to storm the stage. 'The audience went totally apeshit and stage diving,' says Jim Thirlwell, who accompanied the band on the trip and played saxophone during their rendition of The Stooges' 'Fun House'. 'Within the first ten seconds of the song a stage diver knocked my microphone over. At the end of the gig I remember Mark E. Smith of The Fall saying that he liked my saxophone playing because it was so minimal.'

With the exception of Mick Harvey, who found his own flat, the other members of the band would stay at various friends' flats in Berlin, the most frequent venue being Christoph Dreher's large apartment in a courtyard off Dresdener Strasse, with Cave the most regular visitor. 'My place was like a train station, people coming in and out often late at night,' recalls Dreher. 'A lot of groups lived at my place, Blixa Bargeld stayed for a while. The main drug in Berlin at that time was speed. We had this constant party situation, people sitting around a table and talking for hours and then going off to a club. At that time nobody thought it was that exciting, it was just happening, but if you look back it was quite liberating. A lot of projects were happening because people were meeting each other all the time. You didn't have to phone anyone up.'

The beginning of the eighties had seen Berlin emerge as a highly active centre across the spectrum of the arts, from the neo-expressionist 'Young Wild Painters' to a plethora of new groups who wished to develop their own sounds independent of US or UK bands. 'In the shadow of the Wall there were very special circumstances here,' continues Dreher. 'There wasn't much interest in the city, apart from a certain kind of youth from all over Germany. From the sixties onwards you could escape National Service here and you had much freer conditions to live, very different from the rest of West Germany. In Berlin clubs and bars stayed open all night, large flats could be rented cheap. It was a great luxury here, you could afford it without doing anything, you could live off social security. A lot of creative things could happen because people didn't have to worry too much about day-to-day living. Things had happened here in 1979 and 1980 that were very different to punk, they were influenced by the energy and the sensation that caused, but it was more complex.'

'Berlin was such a great relief after London, and everyone liked us,' says Anita Lane. 'It was very different for me because people were very encouraging about whatever I did. It was different because you didn't have to have any previous achievements attached to you. That was totally unimportant, it was whatever you said, or did, or thought about now. It wasn't competitive at all.' Cave also loved the city and Berlin would become his base for the rest of the decade. In a sense the city's tight-knit network of artists, film-makers and musicians reminded him of Melbourne. 'We were really broke but it was obvious to us we were making a big impact on Berlin,' says Howard. 'I think one of the reasons we were liked is that they couldn't believe how uncool we were. The fact that Nick would get drunk and fall off his stool. I remember we got accused of being "animals" because the Germans were so studied and cool and we made complete idiots of ourselves. It was a new experience for the Germans. Nick really thrived upon that atmosphere. Nick enjoys himself and likes to be with people but I don't think that's why he drank so much. I remember him telling me that if he woke up without a hangover he had a disturbing sense that something was wrong. Berlin was really lawless and Nick changed a lot living there.'

The Birthday Party soon discovered that their celebrity could reap unexpected rewards. The Sector, a new opulent nightclub reputedly run by two Turkish arms dealers, enticed both The Birthday Party and Einsturzende Neubauten to frequent the premises by offering them unlimited free drinks in order to attract customers. Blixa Bargeld had also secured gigs for the bands at the venue for a considerable amount of money, with a binding contract which was very advantageous for the musicians. 'It reached the stage where I could go behind the bar and get drinks for all my friends,' says Howard. 'I remember that at one point they tried to present me with a bill for 1,000 marks.' The club's owners slowly began to realise that the bands' expenses far outstripped the value of any custom they could attract. A week before The Birthday Party were due to play at the venue, the manager cancelled the gig after seeing a photograph of Cave and Howard hungover and in bed together which was going to be used to advertise the date. This was the final straw. 'Both gigs never happened but they still had to pay us,' Blixa Bargeld laughs. 'It was one of the best coups we ever had. They fired the manager for making a contract like that.' No one was surprised when the club closed shortly afterwards.

Cave had quickly become firm friends with Bargeld, perhaps seeing aspects of his own personality in the charismatic German singer, an uncompromising individual who saw no dividing line between his art and his life. While visiting a small studio in Kreuzberg, where Einsturzende Neubauten were recording with Rowland Howard, Cave had been deeply impressed by the sight of the band's muscular Mufti Einheit repeatedly pummelling out a rhythm track upon Blixa's miked-up chest. In the middle of the studio was a dog, also miked up, its face in a pile of meat.

The Birthday Party's incessant social life would increasingly revolve around a small bar named the Risiko on the border of Schoneberg and Kreuzberg. 'The Risiko was basically run by an alcoholic who put all his money into buying a bar. He opened it and renovated it. It was nothing more than a place to get drunk in,' recalls Bargeld, who regularly worked as the Risiko's barman, frequently dispensing drinks free of charge to a large proportion of the clientele. 'In the beginning it looked fantastic but then the walls were covered in blood, everything was broken and all the money had been spent on . . . other things rather than buying more alcohol.' Purchasing alcohol from nearby petrol stations and supermarkets, the Risiko and other bars in the area would be open virtually around the clock, with both bartenders and customers flitting from one bar to another as night passed imperceptibly into day. Located at the back of the Risiko were two storage rooms, the 'drug room' and the 'gambling room', from which Cave would repeatedly wander back and forth, sometimes for days on end, during marathon poker games held at the bar. In the course of a game, considerable amounts of money would change hands, more often than not to Cave's advantage, ensuring a reasonable standard of living for another week. Though the 'marks' were often celebrity-struck fans eager to lose money hand over fist to a rock star, the friends at the poker table would always honour their debts, paying up the following day no matter what the sum. After a long game Cave would often be found at Gudrun Gut's flat, nursing a crashing hangover, his face pressed against a large TV screen intently watching a video of Eisenstein's classic *Ivan The Terrible*.

During October The Birthday Party recorded four tracks for a 4AD EP entitled 'The Bad Seed', at Hansa Studios on Kothener Strasse, adjacent to the Berlin Wall, where both David Bowie and Iggy Pop had recorded several albums during the late seventies. The band would later inform the press that the reason they had recorded an EP rather than an album was because their music was far too intense for the longer format. While there was an element of truth in this statement, friction within the group was reaching breaking point and creative stagnation had set in. The collaborative axis was swinging from Cave and Howard towards Cave and Harvey. 'Nick had stopped writing music at that time,' says Harvey. 'He stopped wanting to write music with Rowland because there were arguments over songwriting credits, which I'm not going to comment on. We saw the same thing and Rowland saw something else.' Typically, the tense atmosphere within the band would be channelled into their creative endeavours, the end result being the most complete musical statement The Birthday Party would ever record. 'I think "The Bad Seed" is the best Birthday Party record and it doesn't even have anything I wrote on it but it's the record I think of when I think of The Birthday Party,' says Howard. 'At the time I was upset and it caused problems. It seems childish in retrospect, being in a group that great, but you are in a group to express yourself musically. It had always been four people who contributed and said what they wanted to say but then Nick started to get more of the attention than anyone else. Problems arose because there was very little communication between me and Nick, between anyone. People weren't spending a lot of time together socially . . . We reached a maturity all of a sudden on "The Bad Seed". Without Phill there wasn't a problem about what we wanted to do and Mick playing drums focused everything. Everything was reduced to the bare minimum, no one was playing just for the sake of it. The music was more muscular and lyrically stronger.'

After *Junkyard* Cave had originally intended to record an EP of cover versions of Walker Brothers songs, as well as The Loved Ones' 'Sad Dark Eyes', which the band had occasionally played live. Instead, the four songs featured on 'The Bad Seed' were original compositions and gave further evidence of Cave's rapid development as a lyricist and his increasing use of narrative. 'Wild World' evokes a tense scene of post-coital lamentation, while 'Fears Of Gun', set in a dingy hotel room, betrays the aftermath of violent domestic argument, with the alcoholic protagonist, racked with self-pity, wailing for his abused lover to return. As Gun becomes more aware of the passing of time his thoughts turn to violent retribution: 'Fingers down the throat of love'. 'Deep in the Woods' was yet another haunting blues-based song centred around a gruesome *crime passionnel* committed by a psychopath. The song, composed by Cave during an arduous journey through the Black Forest while on tour with the band, climaxes with a thunderous burst of feedback from Howard which accelerates the song while Cave's character exclaims over the body of his decomposing victim that 'love is for fools and all fools are lovers'. Even in one of the most grotesque songs The Birthday Party ever recorded, Cave's black humour shines through in the line, 'I took her from rags right through to stitches'.

'Hands up who wants to die!' screams Cave, introducing the frenetic 'Sonny's Burning', the most abstract song of the session which can be interpreted as a celebration of Rimbaudian disorientation of the senses, self-immolation as an act of hedonism. Initially Cave did not want to begin the song with the line but after much cajoling from Howard, who thought it was hilarious, he relented. 'It doesn't have anything to do with the song but it's in the spirit of the song, that's what I liked about The Birthday Party,' says Howard. 'There was a certain amount of truth in that statement,' recalled Cave in 1992. 'It was a very intense band. A lot of the members didn't really care about things. But in the end I think it was all showbusiness, certainly in the way the audience responded to us. I never got the feeling the audience was as serious about it as we were.'[3]

After recording, the band recommenced touring on 14 October in Rotterdam, and in November played a brief three-date tour of the UK, including the infamous televised Brixton Ace gig on the 25th. 'The shows were very physical,' says Bingo. 'Someone tried to kill me at that Brixton gig. The microphone cord was round my neck and some person behind me started really tugging it and nearly throttled me.' Although the streamlined Birthday Party were now an even more powerful spectacle in performance, two years of almost incessant touring, coupled with a debilitating heroin habit, had taken their toll on Cave. 'He was almost expected to be superhuman to an extent,' says Howard. 'It got to the point where we would get to the gig and Nick would be sitting backstage saying, "Oh my God, I just can't do it. I can't drag my shattered frame through another performance." You can't go on stage and do that sort of performance, night after night, when you're incredibly unhealthy, basically. When Nick cleaned up he said that before he had always felt eighty years old. I found it amazing how long he kept it up for. Nick has an incredible constitution, he's got away with things that not many people could have survived. Yet for a long time he looked relatively healthy.'

Cave was also becoming increasingly bored with the music The Birthday Party were creating, and the audiences' reaction to it. Throughout the band's existence he had virtually no interest in any post-punk music other groups were producing, which he considered to be without form or direction, wilfully obscuring their lyrical content. The type of music he wanted to create was rooted in much older, traditional genres such as country and western, blues, and epic sixties pop ballads. When he and Pew were invited to play three hours of their favourite music on a Dutch radio station on 18 January 1983, the DJ, Bram Van Splunteren, was taken aback not just by their behaviour but also by their selections, which included artists such as Hank Williams, The Walker Brothers, Van Morrison and Kris Kristofferson. 'That drunken interview,' exclaims Mick Harvey. 'Tracy ended up taking control of the station basically, and they started playing all this ridiculous stuff by the end. They were very rude to Bram. Tracy was just drinking and talking crap. The last hour was terrible because, as with most things generally, it wound up in excess. I was appalled. I was sitting in another room, shaking my head, muttering, "Stop! Get the security! Get them out of there!" It was a total gross-out.'

Cave's general disillusionment with The Birthday Party was exacerbated tenfold by a seemingly endless succession of English bands – Sex Gang Children, Southern Death Cult, The March Violets and The Inca Babies – who aped and parodied the most obvious aspects of the band. He was initially mortified when asked to write a piece for the 1982 Christmas edition of the *NME* on the new bands that he had supposedly inspired, but eventually relented and dictated his copy over the phone. Quoting Ezra Pound, he described the music press as 'the perverters of language'. He rejected outright 'the honorary title of forefathers to the New Superdeath Tribe', dismissing the bands as 'Paper Tigers all'. He further stated that 'a group that reflects anything other than their own idiosyncratic vision is not worth a pinch', concluding that 'The Birthday Party are in essence a slug, nomadic, and their journey is slow and painful and always forward, and their trail of slime is their art and so on, and they are barely conscious of its issue which bears little resemblance to anything bar ourselves and we make no excuses for that.'[4]

Unexpectedly, in January 1983 the band temporarily decided to augment their line-up with an additional member for a five-day tour of Holland. Brisbane drummer Jeffrey Wegener had previously played in The Laughing Clowns with former Saints guitarist Ed Kuepper. Although the band members knew Wegener before he joined the group, they soon realised that they had misjudged the extent of his alcoholism and mental stability. 'He was so unsure of himself,' says Howard. 'He was a very good drummer but he just didn't believe it. After every gig he'd immediately say, "Look, I know I was shit tonight."' Wegener would conduct himself in a straightforward, affable manner until he started drinking, whereupon he would suddenly challenge band members, or anyone else who happened to be present, to brawl with him. Initially his behaviour was deemed amusing and tolerated by the group, but upon their return to Berlin matters came to a head one bitterly cold night at a Neubauten recording session, where a drunk Wegener began to insult various members of the band. Cave left with Wegener, who was growing increasingly aggressive and abusive. After repeated attempts to 'lose' him, Cave, exasperated, punched him out cold. Waking up on the snow-covered ground, Wegener drunkenly staggered off into the night in the direction of Tracy Pew's apartment, where he was temporarily lodging. In the middle of the night Pew awoke to find Wegener leaning across his chest, nursing a black eye, brandishing a pair of garden shears inches from his face and demanding to know, 'Who's the cunt who punched me in the eye?' Pew calmly told him that he had no idea and that frankly he did not care, before managing to push Wegener aside. Later Pew would tell the rest of the band that he vaguely remembered Wegener stumbling out of the house wearing only a pair of jeans, mumbling that he was going to hitchhike to Hamburg. This was the last time any member of The Birthday Party would see Wegener for some time.

When 'The Bad Seed' EP was finally released, in February 1983, it received ecstatic acclaim in the music papers. 'If you prefer to take your love songs with coffee and notebooks, there's always Squeeze,' wrote Barney Hoskyns. 'The Birthday Party alone suggest the frenzy of desire given voice, of dread staged as ritual.' Predictably, controversy also surrounded the record's release. Not only were accusations of misogyny levelled at the track 'Deep in the Woods' but the EP's sleeve, featuring four photographic portraits of the band framed within a swastika, with a heart wrapped in thorns impaled by a flaming cross, painted by Cave, raised more than a few eyebrows. The image itself typified the band's irresponsibility, the extent of their nihilism and their naivety.

'It always amazed me that people didn't understand that,' says Harvey. 'It was just a belly laugh for us. It was pretty obvious why we did it. Hansa Studios, where we recorded it ["The Bad Seed"] was right near the Wall and used to be a Nazi ballroom, and here we were suddenly in this pretty horrendous historical environment, all around us. The ghost of the Nazi era was so powerful in Berlin in the early eighties. It was the centre of the hangover from World War II. Every week there was this programme on TV called *Forty Years Ago* with Hitler and Nazi propaganda footage. The swastika was an obvious reference to that, it just came in, rather than suppressing it like a lot of Germans would.'

In late February 1983 the band returned to the UK to play four provincial dates. During the tour they were interviewed by Chris Bohn for their first *New Musical Express* cover story, despite sections of the paper's staff having grave doubts about the group's 'morality'. 'They never actually won over the people in power at the time at the *NME*,' says Bleddyn Butcher. 'I stressed that this is a reported remark, I didn't hear it myself, but Neil Spencer, who was editor at that time, said to [journalist] Mat Snow that he thought Nick Cave was "promoting evil". A crass remark . . .' Initially Bohn tried to talk to the group together in a Soho restaurant, but the interview soon disintegrated with the arrival of the lead singer of the 'Gothic rock' band Sex Gang Children. 'It was going to be a casual affair and Chris [Carr] was trying to downplay their difficult reputation and present them as human beings rather than bats from hell,' says Bohn. 'Then this guy walked in wearing a grey mac tightly bound up, wearing mascara. "Scuse me, are you The Birthday Party? I'm Andi Sex Gang, we'd really like you to play at the Bat Cave. It would really do the movement a lot of good if you played there." They were, of course, very reluctant about this. The last way to get The Birthday Party to do anything was to try and co-opt them into a movement.'

Bohn later managed to interview each member of the band at their respective temporary homes after following the group to Brighton for a gig. It was a long-drawn-out process but the piece, published in March, accurately captured the band's mood, fragmented nature and transient situation at the time. 'Rowland said, "I sounded incredibly melancholic. I hope I wasn't as miserable as I sounded,"' laughs Bohn. 'They could be very charming. That was the thing about The Birthday Party, they always took interviews very seriously in those days. They were real gentlemen in a bizarre sort of way. Rowland had somewhere stable at the time in north London and when I arrived he was still in bed. Tracy was just moving out of a flat in Putney and going to stay with a couple of The Go-Betweens. I always found Nick the most difficult to interview, not because he wasn't trying or being evasive, but he tries so hard to answer a question it interferes with his ability to answer it. He was staying with Jim [Thirlwell]. He was sick when I arrived, lying on a sheetless bed in his clothes, covered with a crude rough blanket. He wasn't at all self-pitying or maudlin about it but he was sick. He was very hesitant in his answers but gradually, when it was pieced together, it was good.' During the interview Cave talked publicly for the first time about the rough outline for a narrative entitled 'Swampland', centred around the death of a character who is sinking in quicksand, listening to an approaching lynch mob seeking vengeance after he has attempted to murder an orphan girl. As he slowly sinks he is beset by visions and believes he is visited by an angel who absolves him of his crime. This tale would preoccupy Cave for the rest of the decade, materialising first in song then as an outline for a film script, before becoming the basis for the most ambitious undertaking of his career, his first novel. 'Nick came to stay with me in Hammersmith for a week or so,' says Thirlwell. 'He had started writing the book at that point and I remember him reading bits of it to me but the first draft I think he lost altogether. An incredible amount of stuff was lost, and great work too.'

NOTES

1 'Thistles in the Soul', in *King Ink*, collected lyrics, plays and other writings, Black Spring Press, 1988.
2 Helen Fitzgerald, 'The Birthday Party', *Masterbag*, August 1982.
3 David Cavanagh, 'The Saint of the Pit', *Select*, June 1992.
4 Initially published in *NME*, Christmas 1982; reprinted as a prose piece in *King Ink*, op.cit.

8

Mutiny

By March 1983 The Birthday Party were once again desperately short of money. They initially intended to record a double EP at Hansa Studios in Berlin, but such an undertaking would have placed an impossible financial strain on 4AD at that time. 'It was simply more than 4AD could afford,' says Ivo Watts-Russell. 'There was no anger about it, it was the most black and white situation there has ever been in the termination of a relationship with the label.' Initially Chris Carr, with The Fall's manager Kay Carol, tried to entice major label interest in The Birthday Party by presenting the band as a package deal with a number of other independent groups, such as The Fall, The Moodists and The Go-Betweens. The group, however, were keen to sign with Daniel Miller's Mute, with whom they had already signed a publishing deal for the 'Bad Seed' EP. 'As soon as there was any discussion about the next record Daniel was talking to us about doing it with Mute,' explains Mick Harvey. 'What Chris was doing was being appraised by us but we really wanted to go with Mute because of the way Daniel was. Chris would have to have come up with an amazing deal for us not to have gone with Mute because of what Daniel was offering, which was a fantastic option.'

Since initially seeing the band, Miller's company had grown considerably, as a consequence of the chart success of Depeche Mode, and could offer the band a 50–50 profit-sharing scheme on the record with total artistic control over their work. 'At that time there was no contract,' says Miller, 'it was record by record. There was just a piece of paper saying what the 50–50 deal was, where the money came from and where it went.' Chris Carr comments: 'Daniel is a great label boss. He is more than a benefactor because he has an artistic input, he has the ability to trust an artist by being who and what he is.'

Financially The Birthday Party had been resuscitated but relationships within the group, both creative and personal, continued to decline. Mick Harvey, who found himself increasingly held responsible for the running of the band, was the most dissatisfied with their direction and new material. 'The new songs we had, "The Six Strings That Drew Blood" [a Cave/Howard composition] and "Pleasure Avalanche", to me were not particularly inspired,' Harvey relates. 'The best thing I could do was ring people up and say I think we should break up. Rowland's first comment was, "I'm really surprised I didn't do it first." Everyone knew it was going down fast from what it had to be like. We had to stop or turn into something different, a successful rock band on tour that had this reputation for being wild. I didn't get any surprised reactions from anyone apart from Tracy, who was a good-time rock'n'roller basically. He was quite happy to keep going. Maybe he thought it was theoretically correct too, "then they get totally fucked up by success, that's the next stage", perhaps he was right. That was Tracy's attitude, let it roll. I always respected the way Tracy felt about it, it was very pure somehow. When it came to me explaining my position to Tracy, it was very difficult. Rowland knew what it was about, and so did Nick. Nick was kind of looking forward to it and he knew he had to have a change, but it took Nick a while to get out of some of his habits. He was being made more responsible for the group.'

Apart from recording a new EP, Harvey could see no point in the band continuing after completing a second tour of America. He was not in favour of a proposed tour of Australia in May but the US tour presented the band with a challenge as they were relatively unknown there. Their last US tour began in Boston at the Channel Club on 24 March and took them all over the country, even venturing down south to play in Dallas, Texas.

'Because the Americans weren't so press-saturated the reaction of the audience seemed to be far more genuine than in England, where it was like they'd read a rule book on how to behave at Birthday Party concerts,' says Howard. 'We were travelling in relative comfort for the first time. We had a tour manager who wasn't a friend of the band!' Jessamy Calkin, who had travelled to the States on holiday with Lydia Lunch, accompanied the band for much of the tour. 'It was quite incredible, the concerts I saw,' she recalls. 'That's when I got to know them quite well. Rowland was incredible, he was always very different on his own, really spunky and funny . . . and Tracy. It made me realise that they had such a great sense of humour. Tracy looked quite intimidating but I warmed to him the most because he was the easiest to get through to, he had a surreal sense of humour. He was so down-to-earth and he used to take the piss out of Nick the whole time, he deflated situations and looked after people. The others were really complicated . . .'

After playing Washington DC on 10 April, the band returned to Berlin to commence work on the aptly named 'Mutiny!' EP. 'The whole time everyone was really angry with me because I refused to go to Australia,' says Harvey. 'They decided they wanted the money and that's why I put my foot down because I could see they just wanted to keep going, they had started getting edgy about stopping, which I understood but I'd had enough. They kept pestering me about it. Eventually they said Ken West [the promoter] is ringing up all the time, he wants to know if we're going, what do we tell him? I said, "You tell him what you want to tell him." So Nick said, "Right." So they put the tour on. In their minds they thought I'd said yes, every time I said I didn't want to do it they wouldn't listen to me. It was very frustrating. I gave them a way out but they wouldn't believe it. I never intended to go but then it became this really bizarre game for a couple of weeks, they thought I was going because they'd never bring the subject up. Under these conditions we recorded the EP!'

Predictably, Howard's recollections of the dissolution of the group differ greatly from Harvey's: 'Mick says it would have been a cop-out to work together but it also would have been a real challenge because it was so difficult to work together. We were supposed to be having a break and if anyone was sufficiently interested we would get back together, but people became more upset and insulted. Nick, in particular, could not believe that Mick didn't want to work with him for a while.'

An unreleased twenty-minute video documentary of the Hansa sessions was made by Heiner Muhlenbrock, who was living in the same flat as Christoph Dreher at the time. The video, entitled *The City*, captures the tension and lack of communication bordering on open hostility between the band members. Throughout, Cave struggles through endless vocal takes of 'Jennifer's Veil', initially forgetting to put on his headphones which would enable him to hear the backing track. It becomes abundantly clear that he cannot, or has no inclination to, fit his vocal line to Howard's music. 'You look at that film and you think, these people are working together creatively? Look at the condition they're in,' says Harvey. 'At the sessions it finally dawned on them when the subject of the tickets came up and I said, "I'm not getting a ticket to Australia," and they all went, "*What!*" That was it. I did it for Nick as well because Nick needed to break away from being shackled to the group too. It wasn't working any more for him.' From the chaos Cave manages to deliver a compelling vocal track to 'Swampland', punctuated by chilling screams, the song in part being a metaphorical view of his own hounding by critics and fans alike. Set in a mythic Deep South/southern Australia of his own devising, his character is portrayed as the 'Patron Saint of the Bog' slowly sinking in quicksand as he awaits his executioners: 'Ya know ah cannot run no more!'

The 'Mutiny!' sessions ground to an inconclusive halt after a fraught, sleepless week, with seven tracks recorded and the band in complete turmoil. One of the tracks, a slow, atmospheric rendition of 'Wings Off Flies', the lyrics to which Cave had written many years before with his old friend from Melbourne, Peter Sutcliffe, was soon rejected. To their complete dismay, the group would soon discover that a German engineer had added his own creative touches to the remaining six tracks, levelling out the sound, which would necessitate the rerecording of much of the material and all of Cave's vocal tracks. In late April The Birthday Party returned, exhausted, to London to play their last gig with Mick Harvey in the line-up, at the Electric Ballroom, Camden Town. The tense and savage atmosphere of the gig was momentarily broken by Bingo: 'I got a female fan up on stage when they were doing a slow number and Nick and her did a little smooch together on stage. It was so crass and corny I thought, it's got to work.' After the gig the lead singer of an emerging Gothic rock group, Southern Death Cult, was impatient to meet his hero. 'A very young Mr Ian Astbury, who seemed to be rather intoxicated but knew what he was doing, asked me to introduce him to Nick Cave,' recalls Chris Carr. 'This I did at the rear of the ballroom, whereupon Mr Astbury got down on his knees. He announced to Nick that he lived in a squat, that he had few records, one of which was the "Bad Seed" EP, and that he played it with ever greater repetition. He said he was totally overwhelmed to be in the presence of such a master. Nick had no idea who he was. He just said, "Get him out," and we ushered him out of the room. Of course, he's now gone on to fame and fortune in The Cult.'

While in London, the news of Harvey's departure and the chaotic recording session had to be broken to Daniel Miller. 'I remember trying to get everybody to keep the band together,' says Carr. 'After only six weeks of being signed to Mute the band had split. Nick and I went to see Daniel and said there's no longer a band but there is a band without Mick Harvey. Daniel was very understanding and there was a certain amount of embarrassment within the band.'

Miller himself says: 'Because I'd been through the whole fucking thing before with Depeche Mode I wasn't particularly fazed by it. I used to feel that the band were on the verge of exploding anyway. You could see all that. I wasn't surprised but I was slightly miffed, thinking, Were they planning this? but I didn't really think that because neither of us had signed a contract, so it was my decision to carry on working with them. It wasn't like I was committed to releasing a lot of albums by them. Once I'd got over the fact they were going to split up, I was just interested in what they were going to do.'

Having agreed to regroup later in the year in London to complete 'Mutiny!', the remaining members of the band, Cave, Howard and Pew, flew to New Zealand to begin their Australasian tour, kicking off in Auckland at the Mainstreet Cabaret on 3 May. 'The reason why we went is Nick and I wanted to go back to Australia,' says Howard. 'The person who arranged the tour [Ken West] was a friend of ours. If it had just been contractual we'd have said no. Nick was the main protagonist of the tour. It was the first time we'd become sufficiently successful to act like prima donnas and get away with it, basically. So we demanded all these things from the promoter that he agreed to, so consequently the tour turned into an exercise in hedonism rather than an actual tour.'

Upon arriving in Auckland, the band met their drummer for the tour, Des Hefner of The Marching Girls, who had been recruited over the telephone and with whom they only had time for a rudimentary rehearsal lasting half an hour. For the entire Australasian tour The Birthday Party's set would consist largely of slow numbers, as they were the easiest songs for Hefner to learn. 'They couldn't play a lot of the songs without me,' says Harvey. 'The things I play aren't normal for a drummer to play because I'm not primarily a drummer.' The New Zealand leg of the tour was not a success and the band only managed to draw 1,600 people to the shows, prompting Ken West to comment that all the people who liked The Birthday Party had moved to Australia. 'It was incredibly boring,' says Howard. 'We were playing universities and we'd get the student union representatives coming up to us and saying you can't play "Six-Inch Gold Blade", you can't play "She's Hit". We'd just play them and say they were different songs, which infuriated them. It was like waving a red flag at a bull and for Nick and Tracy nothing could have been more delightful.'

After flying to Sydney, Cave gave a very revealing interview to Virginia Moncreiff on Radio JJJ. When asked if audiences had particularly high expectations of The Birthday Party he replied: 'Yes. This is the sort of pressure that makes you feel tired even before you go on stage but at the same time it's an exhilarating feeling being faced with a hungry audience rather than an audience who've come for a night out. I think it might have something to do with the fact that a lot of them have seen other performances of ours and know that we have the capacity to be the worst and best thing that they've ever seen. I think it's an essential fact for any performer or artist to fail as poignantly as they can succeed.'

The Australian leg of the tour was fraught with difficulties. 'The organisation was a bit of a disaster,' says Howard with much understatement. 'I don't remember a lot of the tour but the show in Perth was absolutely vile. We were in Sydney on the day of the show [18 May] and we had to fly there. The night before, the promoter said to our tour manager, "Make sure that you don't forget the tickets." Of course, when we got to the airport, he'd forgotten the tickets. Then we had to wait for the next flight, which got us in ten minutes before the show started. They had four amps for me and they were all terrible. After every song I had to get them changed. After I'd gone through all four it was a matter of deciding which was the best. We came across as really lame and unpowerful. We were trying to make the tour memorable but circumstances ganged up on us.' During the gig Cave was bitten on the leg by a hospital clerk named Sarah, and knocked to the ground by the former lead singer of The Shuffling Hungarians. Afterwards both professed to liking Cave a great deal.

The tour finally fell apart in Melbourne, where the band played three shows billed as 'The Last Birthday Party Concert'. Howard recalls: 'We'd done this tour and we'd grossed $80,000 but by the end we only had $700 each so we had to do another show to get back to fucking England! A lot of that was due to the fact that the money had been so badly mismanaged; there were about fifteen roadies and things like that. The whole tour was very strange because Nick and I were painfully aware that this would be the last time we'd be doing it and playing those songs.' The actual last Birthday Party gig took place on 9 June, fittingly enough at the Seaview Ballroom, whence the band had emerged years before. 'You get to the point where you can't go any further,' says Evan English, who was among the audience. 'When you get to that point you're not conscious of what's happening.

Nick went through all that. During the gig Nick turned his back on the audience and sang like that for thirty-five minutes then ended up saying, "Fuck you, I don't like this any more." Rowland sat in a chair completely fucked! That was the end of The Birthday Party. People demanded this ultimate expression from them and my God he [Cave] delivered. That's what it was about, sensation.'

The band, and Cave in particular, had reached the limit of physical and mental exhaustion and their energetic assault could simply no longer be sustained. The demise of The Birthday Party, so often prophesied by its highly strung, defiantly individual members, had finally come to pass, leaving all concerned a little stunned. 'It was the only group that Nick had ever been in and it had taken up a lot of time from 1974. It was a shock to him,' says Howard. In London a statement was issued to the music press: 'In view of the events of this year, it has become obvious that new challenges are needed to sustain our creative vitality. Rather than continue regardless of our better judgement (i.e., for money or through lack of daring) and diminishing the impact of our work, it has been decided to end The Birthday Party. Individual plans are not definite at this time but we hope this decision will prove as productive as is its intent.'

Cave retreated to his mother's house in Malvern East to recuperate. Apart from a determination to commit The Birthday Party's final statement to vinyl, his future plans were far from certain. He initially informed journalists that he wanted to forget about music for the time being and planned to concentrate on the staging of the fifty one-act plays he had co-written with Lydia Lunch, but this project would never reach fruition. He had a meeting with the head of a theatre company in Melbourne who wanted to stage the plays with the aid of government money, to which there was a lot of resistance. Cave insisted that real women should be used in the performance rather than showroom dummies, but it was the director who ultimately scuppered the project by trying to goad him to commit some outrageous act in a theatre bar to establish his reputation as the 'bad boy' of Australian theatre. Cave would achieve little during his two months in Australia, apart from steadily frittering away on drugs and alcohol the little money he had earned from the tour.

In August Cave, Howard and Pew returned to London to recommence work on 'Mutiny!' with Mick Harvey at Britannia Row Studios. 'I'd just sat around in London doing nothing for a few months. I didn't know what Nick wanted to do,' says Harvey. 'They were all still pretty pissed off with me.'

Cave and Anita Lane, desperately short of money as usual, stayed at music journalist Mat Snow's Brixton flat for a couple of weeks while they searched for their own accommodation. The shared domestic experience, arranged by Chris Carr before they returned to London, was not a happy one for either party and would later form the basis for one of Cave's most vitriolic songs. 'My two friends had moved out, leaving me with the difficulty of paying the rent,' recalls Snow, 'so I thought I could make a few bob and indulge my curiosity by having a rock star around the house. We went to a couple of gigs together, it was fun to go out with him because all the kids going in would point at him and say, "That's Nick Cave."

'I remember coming in one night and Mick and Katy [Beale] and Nick and Anita were sitting around listening to Van Morrison's *Astral Weeks*, Neil Young's *After the Gold Rush* and *Fun House*. Anita used to play "Fun House" all the time. I remember this because they treated my records very badly. He [Cave] was working on some manuscript, he never asked me if I wanted to look at it. Anita was very curious. I think she subsisted entirely on a diet of crackers, Dairylea cheese triangles and Haywards pickles, that's all she would ever eat during the entire time there. I always expected to find hideous evidence of drug-taking but I never found any at all. Maybe he'd stopped, or was being very discreet about it. I don't think I ever got back the £15 that I lent him, I suspect not.'

'I was living in Brixton at the time,' recalls Jessamy Calkin, 'and I was walking past the Oxfam shop one day and I saw Anita in there picking a dress. She was trying to get a suitable dress to impress a landlord. We had a cup of tea and I got on really well with her.' Cave and Lane, with money borrowed from Mute, moved into a small one-bedroomed flat in Brixton Hill, part of a circular block of upmarket private apartments surrounded by a fake Tudor façade with a garden and swimming pool at the centre. 'How they got it I don't know,' says Calkin. Everyone there was really bourgeois, middle class, and they didn't fit in at all. They were always staying at my flat because they were always getting thrown out of this place. I vividly remember one night, it was a Sunday, and the residents of these flats were having a barbecue round the pool, everyone was sitting there. Now, Nick had found this gun in the flat that belonged to this dodgy guy. He was completely out of his head and he lurched out of the flat with this gun in his back pocket holding a tub of pot noodles, his Sunday lunch. He was strolling around and everyone was just horrified, staring at him.' Throughout the summer of 1983 Cave would frequently be found by the other Tudor Court residents on their way to work in the morning slumped on a sun lounger by the swimming pool where he had collapsed the night before, clad only in leather trousers. As the couple were so short of money, they began depleting their landlord's collection of 1920s coins in the hope that they could pass them off as change on the tube.

Bingo was a frequent visitor to the Brixton flat: 'Every time I went round he was always asleep. He used to do a lot of writing in his own blood from jacking-up. Around the "Mutiny!" period there were all these drawings done in blood all over the flat.' Calkin adds: 'He did that once on the underground. He got the syringe out of his arm and he started writing this letter with the blood from his own vein. It mattered so little to him, Nick used to shock people in a way with all that. He was flaunting it in a way. When he was speeding he'd be constantly scraping away into his notebooks. All his lyrics have these marks on them where he'd nodded out . . . He was really forgetful because of the speed, there were always bits of paper everywhere. He always carried this carrier bag taped up with gaffer tape full of notes. One time at a friend's he picked up a carrier bag full of rubbish by mistake that happened to be in the kitchen.'

The London 'Mutiny!' sessions were as tense an affair as the previous Hansa sessions, with Howard again at odds with Cave and Harvey. 'Nick had figured out my position and he'd stopped being angry with me,' says Harvey. 'I mean, they'd had to teach Des the songs in an afternoon! During mixing Nick realised . . . well, he asked me to work on his next record.' Howard, however, still believed that after a year's sabbatical, during which time the band members would be engaged in solo projects, The Birthday Party could be rejuvenated. 'Maybe that's what he wishes had happened with hindsight,' states Harvey. 'At that time he wanted to stop the group. It was obvious to me from what Nick wanted to do that he didn't want to go back to a group like The Birthday Party. From his attitude at the time it was clear there was no way back.' Fittingly, matters came to a head during work on the track 'Mutiny in Heaven'. The backing track itself, recorded at Hansa, was only two minutes long, and comprised a brooding bass line from Pew which had been edited together four times and over which Cave had layered many vocal tracks of screams and commands. Howard complained incessantly that the track was too dense to add a guitar part and Cave had still not managed to complete a lyric for the song after many abortive weeks of writing.

The final straw for Howard came with the arrival of Blixa Bargeld at Britannia Row Studios. Cave had previously collaborated with Bargeld on an unreleased track called 'The Puppet', which had been recorded during three sleepless nights at a cheap studio in Berlin. 'He heard me playing guitar on that and said it was the loudest and most aggressive guitar that he'd ever heard,' says Bargeld. 'He told me that several times so he must have been impressed . . . I just happened to be in London at that time because, if I remember correctly, I was recording with Einsturzende Neubauten, so I came to see Nick and the others in the studio. At that time I think the break-up was already so, and it was manifestly obvious that Rowland and Nick didn't get on any more. Nick just wanted me to play guitar on Rowland's guitar and amp set up. After that Rowland packed his guitar and left. That's what I remember. I didn't delve into the psychological situation.' Howard's recollections differ radically from those of the rest of the group: 'The break-up of the band was a comedy of errors. I walked out of the studio on what I thought was the last day but there were four more days to go. It wasn't intentional, I didn't realise there was any more studio time. I find it amazing that no one rang me and told me that there was any more time.'

Though the music track was now complete with Bargeld's untutored and innovative guitar, Cave still could not provide a lyric to his satisfaction. Daniel Miller visited Britannia Row to discover Cave still feverishly slaving away over his notebook with only two days' studio time left. 'It was a very different way of doing things,' says Miller. 'It was something I wasn't used to but I wasn't fazed by it, I was just interested how it was going to turn out. I realised very early on that there was nothing I could do to give any real serious input.' That night Cave returned to the Brixton flat totally exhausted, sat down at his typewriter and wrote the entire lyric. Rich in the imagery of Catholicism, the multidimensional lyrics that appeared on the page seemed to him to encapsulate every aspect of his current predicament: the end of the group, his hatred of London ('Ah cain't tolerate this ol tin-tub/So fulla trash and rats!'), and his heroin addiction ('Ah yank the drip outa mah vein! *Utopiate*! Ah'm bailin out!'). When he added his searing vocal to the track it was evident to him that The Birthday Party had produced one of their greatest songs in the very throes of their ultimate demise.

With the 'Mutiny!' EP finally completed, Tracy Pew returned to Melbourne with no plans to pursue a career in music. 'I think Tracy's ultimate vocation in life was to be a writer,' says Chris Carr. 'He'd get his money and he'd be straight off to a second-hand book store to buy books. When he went, a certain self-editing process went out of Nick's life. Nick missed a soul mate.' Rowland Howard believes that: 'Tracy was very important in a number of ways. Just through his presence he changed the way Nick acted. Nick and Tracy would become this mischievous and absurd pair that didn't care what they said or did. In a lot of ways he was the heart and soul of the group. There was never any falling-out between Nick and Tracy. Tracy stayed out of band politics, he never tried to push himself within the band.'

During August the first post-Birthday Party recording featuring Cave as a vocalist was released. Months beforehand he had been invited by Christoph Dreher to be featured on an LP that his instrumental band, Die Haut, were making in Dreher's home town of Aachen. 'I really like Nick as a lyricist,' says Dreher. 'The only problem was we only had two days in the studio and Nick had to come over from England. We had a good deal on the studio but it was a bit of a rush.' Cave had travelled to Aachen by train with Anita Lane, with whose help he wrote the lyrics to four songs, 'Stow-A-Way', 'Truck Love'. 'Pleasure is the Boss' and 'Dumb Europe', during the long journey. Lyrically these songs echoed his work with The Birthday Party, giving little indication of the direction his solo career would eventually take. 'Truck Love' was essentially a comic song in a similar vein to 'Big-Jesus-Trash-Can' while 'Stow-A-Way' related a chilling tale of an overdose. Unusually for Cave, 'Dumb Europe' directly addressed, without his customary distancing devices of metaphorical imagery, characters or mythic locale, his current loathing of the Continent, his self-destructive lifestyle and his general disillusionment with his status as a rock star: 'And if I die tonight/Sell me as some prehistoric bone/A lump of junk-souvenir for Jap/To fob off on his friends back home'. Despite featuring *tour de force* performances from Die Haut and Cave, the record suffered from muddy sound. 'The mixing was wrong,' says Dreher, 'due to the lack of time available. The company distributing the LP went bankrupt three weeks after it came out.' Die Haut were never supplied with copies of the lyrics to the album, and misinterpreting a line in 'Truck Love', 'Burn my eyes', they called the album *Burning the Ice*.

Although in interviews Cave had intimated that he was considering giving up music, this was never really a serious proposition, and in September he began recruiting musicians for his first solo project, the intention at that time being to produce a three-track EP for Mute. The working title for the record was 'Nick Cave – Man or Myth', humorously echoing the title of the Ned Kelly biography for which Colin Cave had written the jacket notes. Ironically, the first person to join him was Mick Harvey, who had in effect split The Birthday Party. 'When I didn't go back to Australia with The Birthday Party I was all ready not to go back to music for years, or do something else entirely,' confesses Harvey. 'When Nick rang me up and asked me to go in and work on the first record I was really surprised. I don't know how long it took me to decide, but I thought, "It could be really great, I'll do it." I hadn't thought about it up until then. I knew Nick would do something but I didn't know whether he'd call me about it.' Throughout Cave's solo career Harvey would stoically act as a stabilising force, solidifying his ideas as his principal musical arranger. For many years he would work in the capacity of multi-instrumentalist, coordinator of the day-to-day running of the group and writer of some of the music accompanying Cave's lyrics, displaying his unerring ability to amalgamate diverse musical styles, focusing the direction in which Cave's musical career would eventually lead. His crucial contribution to the subsequent development of Cave's solo work cannot be underestimated.

Initially Cave and Harvey were joined at the Garden Studios in London by Blixa Bargeld and Jim Thirlwell to work on four new Cave compositions written on a small keyboard in the Brixton Hill flat, 'Saint Huck', 'Wings Off Flies', 'A Box For Black Paul' and 'From Her To Eternity', slower, more lyrically orientated songs than his work with The Birthday Party, and with a developed narrative style which would become the hallmark of all his subsequent writing. 'I perceived from Mick and Nick that they were very relieved that The Birthday Party had broken up because it had been coming for so long, they didn't want to take it further,' recalls Thirlwell. 'Nick and I had written the music to "Wings Off Flies" on a piano at Lydia's place; he'd written the lyrics many years before with Pierre [nickname for Peter Sutcliffe]. I played it to Mick, who then played it in the studio while I stomped my foot along to the beat. Then I played guitar on an early version of "From Her To Eternity" with Blixa.'

Cave's idea of having Bargeld playing lead guitar was inspired, bringing an avant-garde experimental sensibility to the slower, more conventional material he wanted to create. 'He just rang me up from London and asked me if I wanted to play on his solo record,' says Bargeld. 'It wasn't meant to be a band and was never conceived as being played live or anything. I thought it was a good decision to play guitar because I claimed my hatred for playing guitar in several interviews. I thought it was a good twist within the public view to do something with Nick because at that time nobody would have been able to fit it into my image. They would have put me together with something "industrial", which I don't like, rather than drawing the connection in intensity between Einsturzende Neubauten and The Birthday Party. It was so out of the way of what people thought I would do, or would be able to do. I did it because I like Nick and for public reasons. Nevertheless, it's probably good to play an instrument out of hatred of what other people do with it rather than play it conventionally. I hate the symbolism of guitars, the guitar hero, so I tried to do everything differently. I didn't have any effects pedals, apart from one somebody built me as a total anti-effect pedal, which cut on and off the signal. No reverb, no middle frequencies, no bass frequencies, only treble and a bottleneck slide.

'"From Her To Eternity" went through several versions. The version in the first session which Nick and I mixed in some sleepless night was an unforgettable document of total madness, a totally different song. It reminded me too much of "Ballroom Blitz" by The Sweet, so I hated it . . . I was still waging the war against sleep and a lot of the working process was totally unreasonable. I remember Nick and I slept under the piano in the studio and similar bizarre scenes.' During the long recording sessions Cave would repeatedly have to return to the Brixton Hill flat. According to Jessamy Calkin: 'They [Cave and Lane] were so broke that Anita couldn't afford to get a key cut to the flat. So she'd just stay in bed the whole time, and Nick kept saying, "Oh God, I'd better go back to feed Anita."'

Jim Thirlwell would soon leave the studio due to creative differences and his increasingly strained personal relationship with Cave during this period. 'Then I was really sick and dropped out, faded from the picture. Maybe there was some tension with the Lydia connection at that time . . . It was a turbulent time then,' he says. The friction between Cave and Thirlwell was probably exacerbated by a song the latter wrote entitled 'Sick Man', released the following year on the Scraping Foetus Off the Wheel LP *Hole*, in which he painted an unflattering portrayal of

Cave, unflinchingly citing what he thought was wrong with his attitude towards others around him and his lifestyle. 'That was inspired by being on the tube with Nick and we were talking about songwriting and I said to him, "What's your catalyst for writing songs?" and he replied, "Well, sometimes I'll take a character and say it through that character's viewpoint." He'd have a character like Dead Joe or whatever, and that's what prompted me to do it about Nick. He knew about it and when I first played it to him, I remember him listening to it with great scrutiny a couple of times, and he said, "That's really nasty!" I thought it was funny.'

With Thirlwell's departure Cave rang bassist and multi-instrumentalist Barry Adamson, who immediately travelled from Manchester to join the session. 'Nick approached me with this idea about going further without The Birthday Party and I wanted to be involved,' states Adamson. 'I'd tried to get two other groups off the ground and that wasn't very satisfying and this seemed so inevitable I said yes. I was attracted because I could see a little bit of myself in what was being said, but I was unable to express it. It was a role that was in me all the time and I wouldn't have entered into it unless I felt I had it in me. I felt I was able to get across in my playing exactly what was required. He [Cave] knew that and wanted to pull it out of me.'

The sessions ended inconclusively in October with much remixing still to be done. In the mean time Mute were repeatedly requesting the completed sleeve design for 'Mutiny!', which was due for imminent release. 'Anita was the muse, without a doubt,' says Jessamy Calkin. 'She was definitely his inspiration and I will always think of Nick and Anita as soul mates . . . they had a real understanding that I'd never really seen in other relationships of people that age. She also wrote a lot of lyrics but creatively there was a bit of friction between them too. I'll give you an example. A lot of cover ideas came from Anita. When they did the cover for "Mutiny!" Nick had eight deadlines and he had to finish it. He'd been up for five days speeding out of his head, didn't know what to do, sitting there with paints he'd bought at Brixton market. He couldn't think of anything and I had this wastepaper bin I'd bought from Woolworths which was black with roses on it, really tacky. Nick painted the basket quite quickly and that became the cover. I can't remember actually what Anita's input was but it was a lot. Then she got a credit on the cover. I remember saying to Anita. "You say he doesn't give you any credit, what about this?" and she said, "That's because he thinks it's not very good."'

Throughout the autumn Cave had been regularly socialising with Jim Thirlwell, Lydia Lunch and Marc Almond, who had recently left the highly successful electronic group, Soft Cell. Almond had been introduced to Cave and Lunch by Calkin, who had become good friends with him after interviewing him for a magazine. One evening in mid October the four musicians found themselves kicking their heels in a boring nightclub, whereupon Lunch suddenly proposed a joint performance. They would present three US shows at the 9.30 in Washington DC and the Danceteria in New York, under the banner of The Immaculate Consumptive. 'I just wanted to go to New York and do a Halloween presentation,' says Lunch. 'We were all associating with each other, it would be economical, fun, let's go do it. We did three shows. That was enough.' The shows were conceived as four interconnected solo performances, with musical accompaniment provided mostly by backing tapes, which were created during a hectic week in the studio with help from Bargeld, Adamson and Harvey: 'Which they made a lot of money from,' says an indignant Mick Harvey. For his solo segment of the shows, Cave decided to perform 'A Box For Black Paul', a long, haunting piano ballad in part a lamentation for the demise of The Birthday Party, and a cover of Elvis Presley's 'In The Ghetto'. 'Nick and me did that in some studio in London,' says Blixa Bargeld. 'Annie Hogan [multi-instrumentalist in Almond's solo group, and with whom Cave would collaborate on her solo record "Kickabye"] played the piano, Barry played drums. I tried to tune my guitar to the original key of the song. I did a little tape loop of the original string arrangement. It all happened very randomly.'

Cave had always admired Presley, but after reading Albert Goldman's biography and repeatedly watching on video the concert footage of Presley's pained performance of 'Are You

Lonesome Tonight' and 'My Way', recorded in Rapid City, South Dakota, on 21 June 1977, just months before Presley's death, he became increasingly obsessed with the singer's final 'Las Vegas' years. While rock critics deemed that Elvis was only ever of importance before being drafted into the US army in the late fifties, Cave, who was now embracing ever closer the ethos of mental and physical collapse as an artistic statement, took inspiration from the twilight of his career. Throughout Elvis's supposed artistic decline his repertoire consisted mainly of 'easy listening music' which displayed no innovation whatsoever, but this was not what primarily interested Cave. He believed that Presley on stage, in an advanced state of disintegration, finally presented the truth about himself and with such passion that his performance was totally uncontrived. 'Here's a man who's got everything and he's getting up on stage only to fall apart,' Cave would tell Chris Bohn. 'He fucks up "Are You Lonesome Tonight" completely. Sweat is forming on his face, his eyes are crazed with drugs and fear, like a trapped animal. He can't remember anything, so he tells bad jokes in the middle for which he has forgotten the punch lines. But then he concentrates and manages to sing "My Way". It was a truly inspired performance. That's what it's all about if you ask me . . . What is good is what affects me. There's no reason why a group should have to get up on stage and be "good", "youthful" or whatever. Why should it be that way?'[1]

This was the beginning of Cave's long retreat from the kinetic style of stage performance that he had presented in The Birthday Party, which he felt was all too often dictated by the audience. He told Richard Guilliatt: 'You'd be looking at the audience, they're all leering back at you, and you know they want you to do a back-flip. So you do one and feel like an idiot. That's when you begin to fail, when you start to recognise and attempt to satiate the appetite that's collected in the mass in front of you. It's just not a consideration with me as to what is relevant to anyone else any more . . . All of the great works of art, it seems to me, are the ones that have a total disregard for anything else; just a total egotistical self-indulgence.'[2]

'Nick had reached a peak when he was mentally and physically exhausted,' says Chris Carr. 'He was no longer the Nick he wanted to be and also what other people wanted him to be. People wanted him to be the stage character and take it further. There were votes on who was going to be the next dead rock star. It was a sick *NME* thing they'd run regarding Keith Richards and Nick Cave, who was the next guy going to go . . . He had very few friends. There were a few hangers-on. I'm not sure he'd even count myself as one of his friends. He has an intensely personal life, you can get in and out.'

Another figure who loomed large in Cave's consciousness during this period was the notorious Panamanian lightweight boxer Roberto Duran. Nicknamed 'Manos de Piedra' – 'Hands of Stone' – raised in the slums of Colón, Duran turned to professional boxing at the age of sixteen and rapidly reached the pinnacle of his profession. With his long, blue-black hair, moustache, goatee and scruffy sideburns, he cut a villainous figure with a reputation to match. His career peaked in June 1980 when he won the welterweight championship of the world, beating the then undefeated Sugar Ray Leonard. 'I'm not God,' announced Duran, 'but I'm something similar.' Later that year a rematch was staged between the sworn enemies and suddenly, during the eighth round of the fight, Duran put his arms down by his side and began shouting, '*No mas*' ('no more'). Rather than let Leonard possibly win on points, Duran had decided to capitulate during the fight, and was consequently vilified for his actions in Panama. Further defeats seemed to signal the end of his career but he would return in triumphant form, subsequently winning a further two title fights. 'We talked about Dylan, Van Morrison, Neil Young, writers, boxers,' says Chris Carr, who related the tale of Duran's career to Cave. 'Never long conversations but intense situations, a way for me to say to him there are others, without ever saying that. He [Cave] had a very natural sense of what boxing's about and is macho in the defined Latin way rather than . . . Tracy had that as well. I told Nick there was something heroic in the character, the whole country couldn't understand what he was doing.'

The Immaculate Consumptive tour went ahead, but there were problems. 'After the idea originated, Nick and Lydia really fell out. It was a bad vibe tour,' says Jessamy Calkin, who helped to organise the concerts. 'Lydia and Jim were really professional, Nick, Anita and I were drunk. Lydia didn't get on with Anita, although in a lot of ways I think that Lydia and Anita were the opposite sides of the same coin . . . Nick really admired the whole ethos of being destroyed by your lifestyle but still carrying on. He loved New York, I remember going on endless shopping trips around gold chain and crucifix shops.'

Chris Bohn also accompanied the quartet on the tour, about which he was writing a *New Musical Express* cover story. According to him: 'Nick was probably the least prepared in terms of what he wanted to do. It was a loose format of individuals, it was good but shambolic. There were strained relations between Nick and her [Lunch]. There were lots of really sharp, cutting remarks coming from Lydia but the bites didn't really take and Nick would respond in a seemingly amiable way. Lydia arranged an interview on cable TV and Nick was complaining that he only got ten minutes to Lydia's forty. Nick didn't really care, he was just trying to antagonise Lydia. "Well, I'm big in New York," said Lydia. "Well, so am I," replied Nick. "The only place you're big is in your head, dear," she replied. It would go on like this all the time. Jim would just sit there looking kind of awkward. Lydia was trying to keep the show on the road and it seemed like he was treating Lydia like a mother hen, which she wasn't. Marc wanted to keep everyone happy and together. Nick and Marc got on well at that point. Soft Cell didn't conform to what people expected them to be, like The Birthday Party, and he admired Nick. I have fond memories of Nick and Marc proposing a dirty tour of the Far East playing in the slooziest places in Singapore. I think he was surprised that he got on so well with Marc . . . They had something in common in that they had both just left groups that were very important to them and they were in a state of transit.'

The two shows at the Danceteria were the highlight of the tour. 'There was a piano upstairs at the Danceteria and we brought it down to make the stage look good,' laughs Jim Thirlwell. 'I smashed it, playing it with my feet Jerry Lee Lewis-style, except I had both my feet on the piano.' According to Bohn: 'These were Jim's biggest gigs up till that point and on the first night he got in a fight, started a fight, not really that serious but a tension relieving-exercise. Nick interfered and broke it up. He turned round to me with some dollars in his hand and said, "Hey, keep this out of the papers." I said, "No, it's OK, Nick." Then it hit me ten seconds later that he was joking, that's Nick's sense of humour.'

After the collective ensemble had performed a Thirlwell/Almond composition, 'Body Unknown', with Almond singing lead vocal, Cave screaming, Thirlwell on drums and Lunch on guitar, the shows would close with Cave's solo performances. The first night he could only perform 'In The Ghetto', due to Thirlwell's abuse of the piano. The second night he began 'A Box For Black Paul' before giving up halfway through and mid verse, much to Thirlwell's annoyance: 'He said, "Then it goes on like that for another five minutes," and just stopped! I thought it really broke the atmosphere and I was really pissed off about it. He'd just go, "You're a dick, you're a dick." It was a lot of fun.' Cave had managed to snatch defeat from the jaws of victory and cherished the occasion as his own private triumph; he would no longer be dictated to by his audience, or anyone else. 'It's one of those things that has become legend over the years, people have talked about it a lot,' says Marc Almond. 'It was only really the two shows, two really chaotic cabarets. I have a bootleg video of it but I've never watched it because I've always liked the memory. If I watched it, I'd probably think, Oh, my God! Each of us did duets with each other. But Nick came on and stole the entire show doing "In The Ghetto" and it ended up being his show really. It was brilliant, though, I think he's brilliant.'

NOTES

1 Chris Bohn, 'Love Amongst the Ruined', *NME*, 12 November 1983.
2 Richard Guilliatt, 'Nick Cave – Man or Mouth', *The Age*, 30 December 1983.

9

From Her To Eternity

After the last Immaculate Consumptive performance Cave, Anita Lane and Jessamy Calkin travelled to Los Angeles, from where Cave and Lane would fly back to Melbourne, primarily because Cave could not contemplate the prospect of another cold European winter. Though the plans to stage the fifty plays, about whose merit he now had grave doubts, had never reached fruition, he was still eager to pursue an artistic avenue outside the narrow confines of the music industry. An opportunity arose in November when he was approached by the video-makers The Rich Kids – Evan English and Paul Goldman – who enquired if he was interested in writing a screenplay for their first feature film production, in which he would also perform and provide the soundtrack. After due consideration he agreed, planning to use the narrative of the song 'Swampland' as the basis for his screenplay.

Though they had often temporarily broken up before during their turbulent relationship, Cave and Anita Lane separated permanently in November when she left to live with a political journalist, Nicholas Rothwell, in America. Initially Cave was devastated but slowly came to terms with Anita's decision. 'They realised that it wasn't a healthy relationship,' says Howard. 'Anita felt she was being squashed. If she was to live with Nick she had to keep up with his lifestyle. To be a part of his world she had to do the same sort of things he did. Anita's a fairly fragile sort of person and it took a far greater toll on her than it did on Nick.' Jessamy Calkin recalls: 'That whole time was very sick, horrible and destructive. He [Rothwell] was into going out with Nick Cave's girlfriend. Anita always handled things really well. If Nick had girlfriends she would make friends with them, she just seemed other-worldly about it all. I realise now in a way that was eating away at their relationship but she'd never show anything. Nick would show it, he was obvious about it.'

When Cave was interviewed by *Rolling Stone* in November he appeared to be adamant about the question of forming another band: 'I'm mainly interested in diversifying as much as possible. Doing projects. Being in a group and working to make that group successful is over.'[1] However, by December he was already assembling musicians to perform his first solo gigs. Mick Harvey, who had returned to Australia in October, would play drums and occasional piano, while Barry Adamson, conveniently on holiday in Melbourne with his Australian wife, played guitar and keyboards. As Blixa Bargeld was on tour with Einsturzende Neubauten, Cave recruited Hugo Race from the Melbourne group Plays With Marionettes to play guitar, while Tracy Pew, who was planning to study philosophy and politics as part of a general arts course at Melbourne's Monash University, played bass. 'There was never any question of whether we wanted him to play permanently or not,' says Harvey about Pew's presence in the line-up. 'Actually we might have if he'd been available, but that would have caused problems because Tracy wouldn't have put up with Nick's "self-indulgences", as it were, which is why he had such a big influence on the way The Birthday Party was. Nick would have felt awkward in that he was pushing himself to the fore, trying things that were risky while having Tracy put shit on him. Tracy's presence affected the way you approached anything, that's what he put into The Birthday Party. He was a very strong personality. He only wrote a couple of songs but a lot of songs were written because Tracy was there to play them.'

The group's first public performance was advertised as 'Nick Cave – Man or Myth?', which many people assumed incorrectly was the name of the band, and took place at the Seaview Ballroom to a packed house on New Year's Eve. The material aired by the group that night, and throughout a series of dates in Sydney and Melbourne in January 1984, acknowledged his past, with the performance of three tracks from 'Mutiny!', while the new songs indicated the direction of his future career. As well as 'A Box For Black Paul' and the humorous love song 'Wings Off Flies', the set included two cover versions: Screamin' Jay Hawkins' 'I Put a Spell On You', a radically different interpretation to that played by The Boys Next Door, incorporating key lines from John Lee Hooker's 'It Serves You Right To Suffer'; and Leonard Cohen's 'Avalanche', which Cave would record the following year. 'I really like it,' Cohen would tell Chris Bohn in 1985. 'He took it to the limit. I tried to take it just beyond the limit I contained – I mean, you always go as far out with a song as you can. But his idiom is a completely different idiom. He really goes out with it, makes the song alive. Not that I've ever abandoned it. I've always felt good about that song. Or bad. Whatever the feeling is. I often play it myself because I happen to like the guitar pattern that goes with it. And for a guy who reputedly can't play the guitar [Blixa Bargeld] I've never found a guitarist who can play that pattern.'[2] Cave, who had always admired Cohen, interpreted the song's lyrical content as an ironic comment on his own relationship with his audience and critics: 'I am on a pedestal, You did not raise me there.' 'Immediately it was different, one of the edges was gone,' says Harvey of the concerts. 'I was relieved, years of tension and worry . . . something had to give.'

In March 1984 Cave, Harvey, Race and Adamson returned to London to work at Trident Studios on what was now conceived as the A side of Cave's first solo LP, *From Her To Eternity*. The new material he had written continued the trend towards linear narrative songs, beginning and ending with a certain rhythm that would evoke the atmosphere he wanted to convey. Daniel Miller was very supportive of his new artistic direction: 'It didn't surprise me because they'd kind of talked about it, in a loose form. Maybe Chris [Carr] more than the band, really. He said that Nick wanted a more narrative style, epic kind of tales. I was fascinated how it was going to turn out. I just let them get on with it, I always have, almost more than any other band on Mute. All bands on Mute have artistic freedom to do what they want but I get involved in the actual making of some records more than others. I wasn't involved . . . Some of the stuff we do [at Mute] is really controlled, like electronic music which I really enjoy, and some of it is unfolding like some plot you have no control over. Ultimately, I suppose, you have some control but you choose not to. I try not to analyse it.'

In 'Saint Huck', Cave transposed Mark Twain's *Huckleberry Finn* into his own compelling tale of the corruption of an innocent in an urban jungle; in 'Cabin Fever!' he cast himself as Herman Melville's Captain Ahab in a thinly veiled account of his life with Anita Lane set on a ship drifting aimlessly on the high seas. 'A lot of the time I remember seeing Nick at the piano saying, "I've got this," and then it would be a case of adapting it to a working format,' recalls Adamson, 'The thing I found remarkable is we'd be in the studio doing a take and he'd be scrawling away at lyrics there. I've never seen anyone else work in the same way. He used all the elements around him and also remained in control of what he wanted to get across. He was like a driven conductor in some ways. I can remember playing "Cabin Fever!" and he'd say, "You know that thing you do when you move up the bass, a fretless bass?" Then he'd stand over me swaying and I imagined he was picturing a ship and he was there. He wanted to hear the ropes, feel the water coming over the side. On another level he wanted to get out the conflict that was in the group. He wanted to pin down the person who was suffering at that moment and get it across on the vinyl. That's how it came across to me. He would have his themes down in a narrative descriptive way. I was so concerned with getting them across I found I left myself behind somewhere.'

According to Jessamy Calkin: 'Nick was like a master of ceremonies in many ways, and at that time he was quite a controlling personality and if he could latch on to people and control them, he'd do it. He was sensitive to that. Rowland and Nick were always very overtly competitive but Blixa and Nick weren't. Nick and Blixa, a complete individual in his own right, got on really well because they didn't manipulate each other, but Nick could play the most incredible games and that was often a real cause of tension. In a way I think it was slightly like that musically . . . I think that was the problem between him and Barry in the end. It was head games and Barry was very vulnerable to that at that time. Nick could be incredibly destructive.'

Blixa Bargeld says of the album: 'Almost every song on *From Her To Eternity* is in C. Because C is called "the key of victory" I decided to tune the guitar to C only . . . I remember playing the guitar solo on "The Moon Is in the Gutter" with an electric shaver; I've done that on several songs. They recorded that while I was still fiddling around tuning up the guitar. I said, "I haven't even started playing yet!" The only thing you hear is the shaver running over the pickups and making this hum, in A flat I believe. That must be one of the most destroyed pieces of guitar-playing imaginable! That describes how the whole session happened for me.' Cave had chosen his players well. The abrasive guitar assault, mastered economically by Bargeld and Race, complemented perfectly the more musically adept but equally powerful contributions from Harvey and Adamson, leaving more space for Cave's melancholic voice and increasingly sprawling lyricism in the foreground than there had ever been in The Birthday Party. The frenetic rush that had been the hallmark of his former group had gone, but the musical range, extremity of emotion and overall coherence had increased tenfold. 'Well of Misery', a humorous death-knell lament featuring the group echoing in a call and response fashion Cave's lead vocal, gave a clear indication that he was becoming increasingly immersed in the blues and gospel traditions. 'There was this conscious attempt to make this really violent music but without relying on the usual clichés that violent music uses, like screeching guitars,' Cave would later state. 'I think that The Birthday Party were out looking for aggression and violence whereas on this particular record it's like what you're left with after a violent situation.'[3]

Arguably the LP's greatest achievement was the title track, 'From Her To Eternity', the lyrics to which had been co-written with Anita Lane six months previously late one night in the Brixton Hill flat. The song encapsulated Cave's continuing obsession with the limits of loss, love and desire, with Bargeld,

Harvey, Adamson and Race evoking the tense, claustrophobic atmosphere inherent in the lyrics. 'What I'm trying to say in that particular song, what I'm trying to say in a lot of my songs, is it's the actual desire of something that is ultimately pleasurable and once one attains what one desires it is therefore realised, and the desire is gone, and so is the pleasure,' declared Cave upon the album's release.[4]

Cave's first solo gig in the UK took place at the Fridge in Brixton on 10 April. Although the gig, and many others throughout the month, would be advertised under the humorous temporary name Nick Cave and the Cavemen, Cave had since decided that the group should be called Nick Cave and the Bad Seeds. The name alluded to the biblical concept of predetermined destiny as related in the Book of Psalms, Psalm 58, Verse 3: 'The wicked are estranged from the womb: they go astray as soon as they be born, speaking lies.'

The day after the Fridge gig Cave had his first meeting, in a pub in Brixton, with the then budding publisher Simon Pettifar, who had first heard of The Birthday Party while living in Brighton in 1981. 'I was living in a shared house and the girl next door put on a record very loud and this incredible sound came through the wall,' recalls Pettifar. 'I went straight in there and said, "What is this?" She said, "I don't know, it's a record someone gave me and I don't like it, it frightens me, you can have it if you like it." That was *Prayers On Fire*. It completely took me over . . . All those clichés were true, it was visceral, raw. I thought Nick's voice was wonderful, destructive and vicious and yet the lyrics were literate, incredibly poetic.' Pettifar was equally impressed when he saw the band perform in Brighton in 1982: 'It was one of those evenings, when the concert ended I didn't feel like going home. There were very few people there at two in the morning and in the end there was virtually only Tracy Pew and myself there dancing on this tiny dance floor. I just went up to him, I didn't know anything about the band or anything about Tracy and said, "That's a hell of a band you've got there." He just looked up at me from under this enormous hat with this great smug grin on his face and just nodded. He didn't really need to be told.'

In the autumn of 1983, having read interviews with Cave

where he mentioned the fifty-one-act plays, Pettifar decided to see if he could publish them. Cave was seldom in the UK and if he was he was always busy, but word came back that he was interested in talking about the proposal. In the interim Pettifar visited Lydia Lunch: 'She gave me the plays, which I read on the train back to Brighton. I've always had a higher opinion of those plays than Nick has. I thought some of them were fantastic but you could tell where each writer was writing and for my own personal tastes I was more interested in one than the other. I was still eager to do something but Nick wasn't very keen on writing something for publication. Then Richard Thomas [a mutual friend] introduced us and I said, "Nick, I'm really interested in you writing a novel." For me this was the most audacious suggestion, Nick had never heard of me, and here I was claiming I was a publisher. I was a fan, you know. I knew about publishing because I'd worked in it. What Nick said was that he was writing a film script, *Swampland*, but he said he had no idea how to write one and he'd been commissioned for his ideas on a story. He was writing it more as a novel but even if it was the same as the script he'd like to do it, but he was understandably very wary coming from a business that is rife with rip-offs.' Though Cave was now willing to write something for publication, the actual form and content were as yet undecided.

After the meeting Cave was involved in an altercation in the pub. Jessamy Calkin was there: 'Nick went downstairs to the toilet and this bouncer pulled him up the stairs by his jacket. "You've been taking drugs down there, get out of here, I'm not having drugs in my pub!" I was so embarrassed. As we walked out of the door the bouncer said, "I can smell pot anywhere." He'd just taken one look at Nick and assumed he took drugs. The last thing Nick would ever do is smoke pot! He'd been taking speed and the guy didn't even know . . . The speed he [Cave] was taking was really damaging, he was always hallucinating. They were so reckless about drugs, the Australians.'

The following day The Bad Seeds played their second London show, at the Electric Ballroom. It was a shambolic affair with the group frequently spiralling out of control and Cave forgetting his lyrics, distracted by disaffected barracking from the unruly crowd, who were expecting a repeat performance of The Birthday Party. Openly mocking the rapturous applause that greeted songs with which the audience could not possibly be familiar, Cave mercilessly goaded the crowd, promising to perform an encore of The Stooges 'No Fun' in reply to demands to 'Play a fast one!' and introducing the band's brooding cover of 'In The Ghetto' as 'a number you can really bang your heads to'. Throughout, a particularly irate, and quite possibly insane, heckler shouted at the band, 'You've sold out! You've sold out! You should have destroyed yourselves!' To which Cave laconically replied, 'We've tried, we've tried.'

The Bad Seeds interrupted their UK tour to play their first Continental date, supporting The Smiths, on 21 April at Meervaart, Amsterdam. As it was Easter weekend most hotels in the city were fully booked and the promoter reluctantly had to secure accommodation for the band in a luxurious five-star hotel. Cave and Hugo Race disappeared into the red-light district in order for Cave to try to score heroin. They were soon approached by a man who instructed them to follow him, and they eventually found themselves outside a houseboat near the main railway station. Race was suspicious but Cave was desperate and decided to go in. The moment he entered, the door was slammed shut but Race managed to barge through after him. The pair were led through a group of West Indians free-basing cocaine to a back room, where Cave sampled what was for sale. Satisfied with the product, he took the packet of heroin and furtively placed it under a large ring he happened to be wearing. After money had changed hands he was then informed in no uncertain terms that the heroin that was for sale was in two other packets. He refused to return the heroin and instantly a knife was drawn and held at his throat. Undeterred by repeated threats, with Race imploring him to return the packet, Cave stood firm. After frisking him the dealer holding the knife turned momentarily to talk to one of his colleagues and, seizing this opportunity, Cave and Race shoved him aside and ran headlong through the houseboat back on to the street.

Cave would have to spend more and more of his time while

on tour scouring red-light districts and low-life haunts trying to score in unfamiliar surroundings, often recklessly placing himself in physical danger, jeopardising entire tours. Through the years this never-ending cycle would have an increasingly debilitating effect on him, and also on Mick Harvey, who was constantly trying to keep the group on schedule. 'I was going through a hard time with all my other friends who were on drugs,' says Harvey. 'It was a confusing period for me . . . I didn't realise until recently how it affected me for years. I was very hardened by the whole experience, in a way that wasn't very constructive.'

Australian sound engineer and producer Victor Van Vugt, who worked for the group throughout their first European tour, says of the Meervaart concert: 'That was one of the best gigs I've ever seen The Bad Seeds do. They almost fell apart but they didn't. It was really emotional and powerful. No matter how fucked up he [Cave] was he could still get up in the morning and do it night after night. Even at the sound checks he'd be screaming away and performing, saying let's try this song, let's try that song. They'd never start with the bass drum, snare, floor tom, etc., like other bands, they'd just play their favourite cover versions.'

Whilst touring the Continent throughout May *From Her To Eternity* was released and greeted with universal critical acclaim. One of the most laudatory reviews, written by Mat Snow in the *New Musical Express*, began: 'Nick Cave's *From Her to Eternity* is one of the greatest rock albums ever made' . . . 'An opinion I have subsequently revised,' says Snow now. On the back cover of the LP were four Polaroid portraits of The Bad Seeds taken by Jessamy Calkin, with Anita Lane at the centre, leading many critics to assume that she had actually played on the record. 'One of the things Nick and I admired about Leonard Cohen was that he was impressively forthright about his personal life. It's important to be able to do that,' says Rowland Howard. 'Putting that picture of Anita on the back of the LP yet keeping the press at arm's length. I want to be able to do this, but only when I want to. It was a statement he wanted to make for a lot of reasons. He wanted to give something of himself away to particular people. When you write a record you have to write it for yourself.'

Anita Lane had as much influence on the shaping of *From Her To Eternity* as the musicians who played on the record. A single line from her would open up an entire idea for a song for Cave, encouraging him to adapt existing literary or non-fiction characters into the elaborate mythological locale in which his stories would unfold. As the characters were already established, carrying a wealth of associations, Cave could concentrate on his primary interest of charting their violent transgressions and inexorable decline. When questioned about his continuing fascination with his characters' disintegration, Cave sardonically replied: 'Well, there's something you're not taught in school. Ultimately . . . you learn about it in one way or another, and I can't see how any intelligent person can see life in a way that isn't ultimately tragic. I know it's a romantic, glorified stance to take, but it's basically the way I feel about things . . .'[5]

The Bad Seeds' first US tour, which commenced at Danceteria in New York City on 8 June, proved to be a tortuous ordeal for all concerned, not least for Jessamy Calkin, who had offered to act as tour manager for the fourteen-date trip. 'They knew I was completely disorganised and the complete opposite of how a tour manager should be but they thought that was funny,' says Calkin. 'I hadn't tour-managed before and at the time Nick had quite a bad habit, it was really out of control. Nick was really unhappy at that time, it was when he was at his most destructive. I couldn't get close to him, he was really alienated and just wanted to get money to score all the time. Afterwards he didn't even remember the things he'd done. Suddenly for the duration of the tour I was not a friend, I was in a position of authority and responsibility.'

While touring the west coast The Bad Seeds played a co-headlining show with The Cramps at Perkins Palace, Pasadena, on 22 June. Before the concert Cave had bumped into Evan English, who happened to be at the Tropicana Hotel on Santa Monica Boulevard. 'I was in the US to do with music videos,' says English, 'and I saw The Bad Seeds there by accident in the car park and I went with them to see the show in Pasadena. They were great and Nick and I got on well. Later that night he told me about an idea for a book he had. He'd never told anyone about it before so we went on talking till eight in the morning. I liked what he was saying as I questioned him about it.' English invited Cave to stay at a house he was renting with Paul Goldman on Melrose Avenue in West Hollywood, where they would work on a video for 'In The Ghetto', which was due for imminent release as a single, and on the film script *Swampland*. 'We thought it was commercial,' says English of the spartan 'In The Ghetto' video filmed in the house's garage, 'but we got these replies saying that it looked like an occult ceremony and the record company in the US said that it couldn't be played. The set was meant to be a chapel.'

On 25 June the tour recommenced in Kansas City, and closed five days later at the 688 Club in Atlanta, after which Hugo Race left The Bad Seeds to pursue his own solo career in The Wreckery and Cave returned to West Hollywood for three months to work on the *Swampland* script. 'He was quite dissolute at that stage, it's quite surprising he got anything done,' says English. 'His life was so fuckin' chaotic. If he'd written something, he'd lost it! It was hopeless. He just needed the support. Here he had a room in a free-standing house, there was food in the fridge. He'd grown up in a big house in Caulfield. It was a crazy time but by his standards it was quite domesticated.' In a vain attempt to try to instil some discipline into Cave's working day, English managed to persuade him to place whatever money he had in his bank account. Consequently he would have to approach English every day to try to obtain his own money to buy drugs in downtown LA. This would also involve borrowing English's car, which he would only relinquish under extreme duress, fearing that Cave would irrevocably damage it as his driving skills were barely adequate and he did not possess a Californian driving licence.

The scripts that Cave produced in longhand during the following months extended the song 'Swampland' and a short prose piece entitled 'The Black Pearl', printed on the inner sleeve of *From Her To Eternity*, into a narrative on an epic scale which would eventually form the basis for the writer's first novel. At the end of each day Cave would read aloud to English and Goldman what he had written as they were unable to decipher his illegible scrawl. As the days wore on it became increasingly obvious to

Cave, though the pair endeavoured to conceal it, that English and Goldman were beginning to have doubts about the feasibility of bringing to the screen his horrific and labyrinthine tale of an inbred mute, Euchrid Eucrow, recounting his wretched life story while sinking to his death in a swamp at the edge of an isolated township in a mythic south of the writer's imagination. Replete with lashings of black humour, religious imagery and ironic use of biblical allegory, the script's depiction of Eucrow's existence was unrelentingly hellish. Euchrid, one of twins, is born in an old Chevrolet in a junk pile. His first-born twin brother dies shortly after birth. In the novel that Cave eventually completed, in a passage laced with grim humour, Euchrid soon discovers his disability when demanding his first feed: '. . . in spite of all mah whoop and hollar – all mah howling and yowling – all mah bull-like bawling and shit-storming and caterwauling – in spite of it all – do you know what? Not a peep of sound did ah make – not from mah crate, not from mah cot.' He is raised by a foul-mouthed alcoholic mother, Jane 'Crow Jane' Crowley, and Ezra, his father, an animal trap maker and catcher, on the fringes of a bizarre fundamentalist sugar-cane community in Ukulore Valley, the setting for his slow descent into madness.

One of the influential sources for Cave's portrayal of Eucrow's twisted visions and maniacal delusions of grandeur was the biography by Flora Rheta Schreiber of the tormented psychotic murderer Joseph Kallinger, entitled *The Shoemaker*. The shocking account of Kallinger's cowardly, murderous activities, aided and abetted by his objectional thirteen-year-old son Michael, made an indelible impression on Cave. He rejected Schreiber's contention that Kallinger's later life was moulded entirely by his horrendous childhood upbringing, believing that one so evil was predestined to behave in such a manner from birth. Rather than the crimes he committed, what primarily interested Cave about a figure like Kallinger was the utter banality of his existence and his twisted thought processes, entirely logical to the killer, by which he justified his motives and actions. It was these characteristics which Cave invested in his central character.

'I've seen some fucking typical things with him living in LA,' says Evan English. 'It was a quiet life, hardly any of these sycophants coming round. Then one day he's giving a reading at this club and suddenly out of nowhere these people start arriving at two o'clock in the afternoon and each one was bearing gifts for the god, which were drugs, right, and here is this fucking guy sitting there and he's taking every piece of shit that comes through the door. "Fine, fine, gimme that." He's like a voodoo doll and here are these people, fat . . . they're putting needles into the guy, I mean like voodoo needles, literally as well, and they're pumping him up. I mean, fuck, what kind of life is that? "Here's an offering, I'll be your friend." He treated them like shit . . . these people need attention but are also repulsed by it. There was a song ["Swampland"] concerning "vulturehood" that he felt he was subjected to. The journalists and fans were picking the bones of an icon that he really wasn't. This is the nature of being in the gaze, these people create a persona that they need but are somewhat uncomfortable with, you are no longer who you are.'

On 31 August 1984 Cave gave only his second public reading of his prose, at the Lhasa Club in Los Angeles. 'I'm the one who spurred him on to do spoken word,' says Lydia Lunch. 'He only did the first spoken word performance at the Pyramid Club in New York because I forced him to. He was absolutely terrified of doing it. He thought it was a repellent idea. "Why would you want to get up there and do it by yourself?" It made him very nervous. I just told him to give it a go.' Cave read three excerpts from a work described as 'a novel and a film treatment tentatively called *King Euchrid*', and a thirteen-part short story entitled 'Bline Lemon Jefferson'. 'In that period Nick was getting quite genuinely interested in blues, gospel, black music in general,' says Blixa Bargeld. 'Maybe not so much the music but the mythology and symbolism of it . . . "Bline Lemon Jefferson" didn't really have anything to do with the actual person, Nick didn't, and doesn't, know anything about him. He just took the name because he liked the name.'

The imaginative first-person recreation of the legendary 1920s blues singer's life, owing more to Cave's invention than to reality, was originally conceived as part of a collection of similar stories based on famous figures including Jesus Christ, Roberto Duran,

Joseph Kallinger and Jerry Lee Lewis, the precedent for this type of book having been set by Bruno Schultz in *Imaginary Lives and Inspirations*. 'Meetings hadn't advanced things much,' says Simon Pettifar. 'Was it a screenplay he was writing or was it a novel? Then he sent me "Bline Lemon Jefferson" which I thought was fantastic. As a publisher it told me everything I wanted to know. I thought, yes, I'm not just imagining this, I definitely want to publish a novel because this guy's a real writer, he's got real talent. We ended up with this ridiculous idea that he was going to write a collection of pieces along the lines of "Bline Lemon Jefferson". It was a bit of a half-cocked idea because he didn't really want to do a whole book so I had to persuade him.'

From the script's pre-credit sequence, aerial tracking shot, Cave envisaged the film being centred around Euchrid Eucrow's actual field of vision, with much grand visual imagery mirroring the circular shape of the human eye. The script opened with a continuous sweeping shot across the valley with the camera capturing the entire town, the cane fields, women wailing lamentations in the street and flaming torches racing into the swamp, finally zooming into the mute's eyeball in the bog, at which moment he would commence his narration. Goldman and English would repeatedly shake their heads and try to explain the logistics required to produce such a shot but Cave would vehemently reject their reasoning, insisting it was integral to the film, that it could be created and that they lacked the commitment to realise it. Cave's obsessive intransigence over any changes to *Swampland*, bolstered by his large consumption of amphetamines, led to an impasse with English and Goldman concerning the project. 'Several months later we had a pretty good script but it would have cost $50 million, that put the script down from the beginning,' says English. 'A friend of mine was an agent, who was at ICM, showed it around town and got very good responses, but I just realised how improbable it was to make a film that size.'

'I didn't see the film script but I know that it was a big mess, it was overwritten,' says John Hillcoat. 'It was better as prose. At one stage he was plugging it as a film with me, then he wanted to do it himself, that's when he had no idea what film-making involved, but it all went sour that project, with Paul, Evan and Nick.' When Henry Rollins, at that time the lead singer with the Los Angeles hardcore band Black Flag, visited the house, Evan English's whole conception of the film script radically altered. 'Henry was taken by the whole Charles Manson myth, it's so important in LA culture even to this day,' says English. 'SST [Black Flag's record label] were going to put out an LP of Manson's songs. They'd smuggled a recording device into his cell . . . At times Manson says some insightful things, "I am what you want me to be." The tape had a personal quality, you could hear toilets flushing and people calling down the row. John [Hillcoat] in Australia was interested in prisons and I referred this tape to him.' Interviewing Manson and using his music was soon rejected because Hillcoat realised that the image Manson had created for the media would diminish the credibility of any film project.

Throughout July and August Hillcoat had been trying to ascertain whether the film rights had been sold to *In the Belly of the Beast, Letters From Prison*, Jack Henry Abbott's vivid account of the realities of long-term incarceration in an American maximum security penitentiary. Norman Mailer had been so profoundly impressed by Abbott's work that he successfully campaigned for his release from Marion penitentiary and helped publish his letters, but Abbott found it impossible to cope with his impending literary fame and society outside the prison system. While on parole in New York in July 1981 he stabbed a waiter to death after he was told that the men's lavatory was not available for customers. The victim, twenty-two-year-old Richard Adan, was himself a promising writer.

Initially Hillcoat had planned to make a film mixing fact and fiction, utilising taped monologues by Abbott and other state-raised prisoners, intercut with dramatic reconstructions based on passages from *In the Belly of the Beast*. Abbott replied to Hillcoat's letters in August. 'He was writing from Marion prison,' says Hillcoat. 'There were a couple of funny letters. He told me the rights had been sold and that he didn't want to be involved. Understandably, he'd had enough of media coverage.' Nevertheless, over the following twelve months both Hillcoat and English would gradually move towards planning to film a drama-based project centred around a maximum security prison, with which Nick Cave would be closely involved.

Before returning to his Berlin base, Cave visited Simon Pettifar in London in early October to finally sign a contract with the publisher. 'The more time that elapsed the more we realised we were talking about a proper novel,' says Pettifar. 'He'd kept me informed how *Swampland* was going and how he really wanted to write a novel. Trying to reach an agreement on signing the contract was a marathon. It was between Nick and me and it wasn't financial, it was him being very wary. He didn't want to commit himself, it took five years . . . The prospect of writing it filled him with dread and doing it for a company he didn't really know, who didn't seem to have much of a track record. We got on well but actually it took a lot of trust. It was quite a step for him to take, for someone in his position. For a lot of people he was a punk rock singer from Australia and if he was suddenly going to make a literary début then he was putting himself in a volatile position. If he was going to do that he had to have the best support and someone who was going to present the novel as a serious work. There were a lot of people waiting for him to fall flat on his face.'

Over the next few years the novel would consume more and more of Cave's time, the solitary existence of the novelist influencing and shaping his recording career and personal life in a way he could have not foreseen before he embarked on the project. He had underestimated the scale of the task which he had set himself and the enormous effort that would be required to maintain two careers. He was also very conscious of the fact that he was a rock musician attempting to write a novel. 'He thinks that people who play in rock groups are the lowest common denominator in the artistic world,' says Rowland Howard. 'Nick, who is someone capable of great artistic expression, felt he was doomed not to be recognised.'

Upon arriving in Berlin, Cave went to visit Elizabeth Recker, whom he had previously met only once, after The Bad Seeds had played at the Loft on 21 May. He had been instantly captivated by her long brown hair, beautiful eyes and smart appearance.

Though initially surprised to see Cave on her doorstep, Recker invited him to move into her flat. After only a week he awoke to find his bags packed at the foot of the bed. During the night he had undergone a violent fit, induced by the medication he had been prescribed in an attempt to reduce his drug consumption. Once again he found himself staying at Christoph Dreher's apartment, where he would write in the space of a week, on an old foot pump organ, many of the songs for the next Bad Seeds album, *The Firstborn Is Dead*. As the organ was damaged and could only be operated by pumping furiously to produce any sound at all, the new compositions were all the same tempo. Having written the album, Cave and Recker reached a reconciliation and he moved back to her apartment, marking the beginning of a tempestuous two-year relationship. 'Nick always goes for secretarial types,' says Jessamy Calkin, who frequently visited Cave and the rest of the group throughout the Berlin years. 'He likes people who are not self-conscious. Elizabeth was very straight and conventional, the opposite of Anita. He was amazed that he was going out with someone who was getting up and going out to work every morning. It was nice for him.'

'He just appeared one day in Berlin and I didn't really know who he was,' says the then 'entrepreneur' Edzard 'Eddie' Blum, a close friend of Cave's during the years he lived in Berlin. 'I met Anita Lane first, who had come to Berlin as well. Nick had a German girlfriend, Elizabeth. That was a pretty bizarre constellation anyway. Elizabeth suffered very hard because she couldn't cope with Nick's past and Nick's fame. It was heavy drug days at that time. She [Lane] brought me to him. I think we immediately liked each other. I had the aura of, how do you say, a criminal, and a well-respected but unliked person. I think this was attractive to Nick . . . I think one of the reasons he came to Germany was because here he didn't have to listen to what people were saying. In all the years he was here he learnt maybe two or three German words. I think that kept him away from having to deal with so many things because he just wouldn't understand, so he could concentrate much more on himself and his work.'

Now stripped down to an even more powerful four-piece unit,

The Bad Seeds began a ten-date European tour at the Discoteca in Turin on 31 October 1984. The tour provided an opportunity to play and rearrange the new blues-inspired material which made up most of the set before recording in Berlin. The slower tempo of the songs and the group's impassioned cover of Bob Dylan's 'Knockin' On Heaven's Door' indicated an even greater musical departure from the sound of The Birthday Party than had *From Her To Eternity*, further confusing sections of Cave's audience who had only ever responded to the group on a one-dimensional level. 'Sometimes it was very good,' says Blixa Bargeld of the four-piece Bad Seeds tour, 'but it was rather limited in that we couldn't play a lot of songs. We played "Saint Huck" with a backing tape. "Tupelo" was an improvisation that we did at a sound check in Madrid. Mick played the bass and turned around the "Saint Huck" melody which created "Tupelo".'

After playing a short set at the Electric Ballroom in London on 7 November, Cave was accosted by Antonella Black, an Australian music journalist who had been commissioned by the *NME* to review the gig and by *Zig Zag* magazine to interview him for a cover story. 'Nick didn't give a shit,' says Chris Carr. 'He was riding on the euphoria, and whatever else, from coming off stage. He told her to come along for the ride. He was given due warning. He was staying on a boat down in Chelsea, the infamous boathouse. Nick was in the land of nod.' When the interview finally began in the early hours of the following morning Cave became increasingly irritated by Black's highly personal line of questioning. Having endured questions enquiring how he felt when his father died and about the current state of his relationship with Anita Lane, Cave finally snapped and yelled a stream of abuse at Black, who fled the boathouse in tears. 'She worshipped Nick Cave,' says Mat Snow. 'Antonella and I were living together at the time in a flat in Marble Arch and she came in saying what a hideous state Cave had been in. She not only felt disappointed but personally affronted because he was her hero. I heard later that her piece, as one would expect, hadn't gone down terribly well with Nick Cave.' Black wrote a disdainful review of the gig, in which she described Cave's compelling performance as 'going

Previous page
**Cave on stage with
The Birthday Party**

Left
Cave sports an
Ed 'Big Daddy' Roth
T-Shirt, 1981

Right
The Birthday Party
London, Spring 1982
L-R Phil Calvert, Cave,
Mick Harvey,
Rowland S. Howard

Far right
The Birthday Party
during the 'Oops, I've
Got Blood on the End
of My Boot' tour.
Cologne, July 1982
L-R Mick Harvey, Cave,
Phil Calvert, Tracy Pew,
Rowland S. Howard

Left
Photo of Anita Lane used on the inner sleeve of *Junkyard*

Below
Birthday Party live Cologne, 2nd July 1982

Right
Tracy Pew

Below
**The Birthday Party
back stage, July 1982
L-R Cave, Harvey,
Tracy Pew,
Anita Lane**

The photograph of Cave and Rowland S. Howard that was to be used to advertise a gig at the Sector Berlin. After seeing it the manager cancelled the show. September 1982

The Birthday Party with temporary drummer Jeffrey Wegener, London, January 1983

Cave and Rowland S. Howard on stage at
The Roxy, Los Angeles, 30th March 1983

Cave with Lydia Lunch backstage at the
Roxy, Los Angeles, 30th March 1983

Nick Cave and Harpo Marx, Tropicana Motel, West Hollywood, California June 1984

Cave at work on
*And the Ass saw
the Angel* at
Thomas Wydler's
apartment, York
Strasse, Berlin,
July 1985

Cave and Shane MacGowan's first meeting at the *NME* summit,
Montague Arms, South London, September 1988

Cave and Mick Harvey, Melbourne, January 1992

Cave with his
mother Dawn

Nick Cave and the Bad Seeds
on stage at the Paradiso,
Amsterdam, 3rd June 1992,
Cave, Martyn P. Casey,
Mick Harvey

Far right
Nick Cave and the
Bad Seeds 1994
'Let Love In' tour
front row -
Thomas Wydler
L-R second row -
Jim Sclavunos,
percussionist
for the tour
Martin P. Casey,
Blixa Bargeld,
third row - Nick
Cave, Mick Harvey,
Conway Savage.

Left
Cave on stage at
the Reading Festival
1992

Below
Cave at Pedro's
Bar, São Paulo

Above Viviane Carneiro with Cave, Spring 1995   *Below* Cave with his son Luke in London

through the mandatory motions', and in her interview, entitled 'A Man Called Horse', published in January 1985, she portrayed her subject as a humourless, inarticulate, moribund junkie. The critical backlash against Cave and his band had started in earnest only seven months after they had produced 'one of the greatest rock albums ever made'.

NOTES

1 Peter Laurance, 'Nick Cave, After The Birthday Party', *Rolling Stone*, December 1983.
2 Chris Bohn, 'Tortoise-Shell', *NME*, 2 May 1985.
3 Jack Barron, 'Cave Man', *Sounds*, 12 May 1984.
4 Nick Cave to Josh Pollock, *BOT* magazine, 1984.
5 Ibid.

10

The Firstborn Is Dead

In Berlin work began on *The Firstborn Is Dead* in the last week of November and continued through December at Hansa Studios. 'Because of the way Hansa is built the recording process was similar to the last two records by The Birthday Party,' says Blixa Bargeld. 'We set up in the big room and then went upstairs to another studio and did a lot of overdubs and recording there. Even the LP's cover photo was done there . . . all the songs are in E or A which meant it was necessary for me to get a second guitar so I didn't have to retune all the time. I started playing a proper slide guitar. It was obvious what Nick wanted to do.'

The harsh, nightmarish landscape of Cave's mythic south depicted in the pages of his novel-in-progress filtered through into the lyrics and music of *The Firstborn Is Dead*: from the biblical flood that engulfed the inhabitants of 'Tupelo', heralding the birth of King Elvis Presley/the Messiah, to the final death-throe sensations of 'Blind Lemon Jefferson' in a ditch 'down the road of trials'. American critic Greil Marcus later observed in his book, *Dead Elvis*, that the identification of Presley with Christ in Cave's 'Tupelo' had existed in the collective consciousness even before Elvis's death. In reinventing the Elvis myth Cave's song took its formidable malevolence from the 'hoodoo' inherent in Mississippi Delta blues. Cave was not so much performing the song as possessed by it. Cave himself would later grow disillusioned with 'Tupelo': 'It inspired journalists over the next six years or so, in every interview I did, to ask me about Elvis Presley. That was one of the problems with it.'[1]

'Knockin' On Joe', the title taken from American prisoners' slang to describe an act of self-mutilation to avoid hard labour, portrays a prisoner racked with guilt pleading with a preacher to tell his lover not to visit him so he can 'die in the memory of her arms'. He admonishes his gaolers, for they too are incarcerated within the confines of their own mortality. In 'Train Long-Suffering', the protagonist hurtles towards oblivion on the 'rails of pain' with 'Memory', the engine driver, knowing his lover will never return: 'I'm missing you baby, And I just don't know what to do'. The new set also included lighter moments. Self-mockingly, Cave portrayed himself as 'The Black Crow King', a figure whose status has been diminished through imitation by his fans and other musicians. 'The King! The King!' he sang, echoing the egotistical chest-beating of *Junkyard*, before declaiming, 'I'm the King of nuthin' at all'. Paying tribute to both Bob Dylan, who wrote the song, and Johnny Cash, who sang it, The Bad Seeds covered 'Wanted Man'. Unhappy with some of the original lyrics Cave reworked them, then added a further fourteen verses while the group played the song at twice the speed of the original. The fugitive was now hunted across virtually every state in America. 'But there's one place I'm not wanted, Lord, it's the place I call home'.

'The difference between *From Her To Eternity* and *The Firstborn Is Dead* was we really got to know each other,' says Barry Adamson. 'We got to know the core of each other's personalities, that made it really touchy . . . in Berlin, in the snow, around Christmas, it was very emotional. We'd played dates in Athens and then we'd come back to this oppressive atmosphere, staying awake for days on end. The pressure was on. I myself could see I was heading for a nervous breakdown and I wasn't going to let this be seen by anybody. I tried to stay in there and the only way I could get it out was through what I played. I felt I couldn't talk to anybody about it.

'The use of conflict as creation, the use of negativity as power, all that seemed to me, from my angle, amplified by *The Firstborn Is Dead*. You can smell the tension on that record. Nick had been listening to a lot of blues stuff and he almost became, well, his various obsessions seemed to be heightened. The more he got involved with the book, the more he closed down, I felt. It was almost like I wanted to turn round and say "I don't know what you want any more". With the first LP everyone was in time, the second everyone was broken up within themselves . . . What I didn't get for a long time is that Nick's able to grab hold of the fact that it's his birthright to get out there and put his work out, whatever it costs. He wants the music in a certain way and so people are pulled together. I can think of me coming to blows with Blixa and his [Cave's] attitude would be, How can I sort this out? It was very important to him.

'Being in The Bad Seeds I was sometimes very threatened because I'd never addressed being black. I was brought up pretty much white, my mother was white, father black. Suddenly The Bad Seeds wanted to play the blues and I'm thinking, "Wait a second, guys, this is as far as I go," because I didn't want to address the fact that part of my nature is to have the blues because of a history of oppression of black people. Looking back it was good because I'm able to play that stuff and have some understanding, but "Knockin' On Joe" and "Blind Lemon Jefferson", I felt threatened by those songs. Nick was using those images to express himself and it pushed a lot of stuff up inside me. I took it on with an overblown guilt complex . . . Looking back it was pertinent that we played those songs because I was a suffering black man but I had to contain it. My health generally was deteriorating because the youngster in me was saying get out there and destroy thyself. I was up for that, but I was getting on a bit and things took their toll the way they do. Being physically unwell affects you mentally, emotionally and the way you relate to other people. I felt isolated. Mick would say, "Don't take things to heart."' Consumed by his own personal vision, Cave was totally unaware of Adamson's apprehension regarding the material and his precarious state of health. Even Harvey confesses: 'I was ignorant of the things that were eating at him, apart from the drug-related things that were going on and the psychosis connected with that, which everyone was going through. I didn't make any more of it than that.'

In February 1985 John Hillcoat and Evan English, who was still living in Los Angeles, paid for Cave to fly to Melbourne to begin working on a treatment for the prison film project, now entitled *Ghosts . . . of the Civil Dead*, an apt phrase coined by Jack Henry Abbott to describe the long-term prisoners' absence from the public's consciousness. Despite the problems experienced during the *Swampland* script, both English and Hillcoat had been very impressed by Cave's cogency and intuitive dramatic sense for narrative and, knowing his various preoccupations, thought he would be an ideal writer for the script. While Cave lived at his mother's house for an intensive nine-week period, the pair ceaselessly worked on the initial film treatment. 'Ideas went back and forth, Evan and I having input,' says Hillcoat. 'I wrote notes in point form and fed them to Nick. Nick had a very melodramatic story sense, that was his main contribution. I was very impressed by his natural sense of narrative, dramatic characters and wicked sense of humour. From these notes it branched out into other areas, stylistic devices, visual things that I wanted Nick to be aware of, thinking about the story, certain incidents. Nick had always been interested in crime, another mutual interest.'

A focal figure for Cave while developing the script was the American mass murderer Carl Panzram, described by the psychiatrist Karl Menninger as 'the logical product of our prison system'. Sent to a harsh reform school at the age of eleven, Panzram was treated extremely brutally, fuelling an intense hatred of society and humanity which was further exacerbated by his imprisonment in 1915 at the age of twenty-three for burglary. Panzram refused to be broken by the savage prison regime and escaped from the Oregon State Penitentiary in 1918. He embarked on a spree of sodomy and murder across the world, claiming twenty victims, crimes to which he freely confessed in his autobiography, written for a kindly warden when arrested again for burglary. At his trial he had shouted at the jury, 'I believe the whole human race should be exterminated. I'll do my best to do it every chance I get. Now, I've done my duty, you do yours.' Panzram killed his twenty-first victim, a prison foreman and Ku Klux Klan member, in 1929 while serving time for burglary at Leavenworth prison. Sentenced to death in 1930, he insisted that the sentence was carried out, chastising a penal reform group campaigning on his behalf for clemency: 'The only thanks that you and your kind will ever get from me is that I wish you all had one neck and that I had my hands on it . . . I hate the whole damned human race including myself. I preyed upon the weak, the harmless and the unsuspecting. This lesson I was taught by others: might makes right.' Even at the scaffold he was defiant, admonishing his hangman with the words, 'Hurry it up, you bastard! I could hang a dozen men while you're fooling around.'

Cave developed the central characters of the script, Wenzil, a young inmate recently incarcerated in the prison, Glover, a state-raised criminal based on Jack Henry Abbott who is locked in solitary confinement in the 'hole' for the duration of the film, and Maynard, a deranged homicidal maniac. 'We wanted a broad overview of a maximum security prison,' says Hillcoat, 'so there was the old-timer, the new boy, the psycho, all those ingredients. Nick worked on incorporating these elements, came up with some good narrative twists, Wenzil being attacked and the process of his degradation. Nick was interested in the horror of the situation and people who had crossed the line, delving into the imagination of a murderer.' Rather than the actual physical act of murder itself, Cave was beguiled by the loneliness of the murderer who had taken a conscious decision to become totally alienated from the rest of society through the premeditated act. One of the main scenes he created featured the violent sodomising of Wenzil for stealing a ghetto blaster and the forcible tattooing of the word 'cunt' on his forehead. 'The tattoo scene came out of research about the importance of tattoos in prison,' says Hillcoat. 'There was the story about Gary Gilmore doing a tattoo for a prisoner on his neck. Gilmore didn't do the tattoo the prisoner wanted but drew an erect penis, but this guy couldn't see it, a cruel joke.'

During March Cave read a review in the *NME* which left him seething with anger. While reviewing the latest Einsturzende Neubauten single 'U-Gung', Mat Snow commented in passing that Neubauten's record 'musters the psychodramatic edge disappointingly absent from Nick Cave's forthcoming LP'. The one-line criticism of the pre-released tape was relatively mild compared with other reviews Cave had received in the past, but he felt totally betrayed by a critic whom he had previously considered to be a supporter within his circle of acquaintances. That Snow could be so fickle was the final straw for Cave and marked a further deterioration in his relationship with the media. 'I found it disappointing because I liked the first solo Cave so much,' says Snow. 'It was just a throwaway comment to let the readers know, "Hey, I've heard the new Nick Cave album."'

'Nick is the one person I've ever met who really doesn't care what other people think of him,' says Jessamy Calkin. 'If he's got an idea, even if it's about clothes, he doesn't ask for opinions. He'll say something and really won't care what the reaction is. Yet, on the other hand, he'll get upset about something Mat Snow writes! . . . At this time Nick didn't think he had any friends. Mark E. Smith was a friend for a while but Mark was very judgemental. Blixa never criticised his behaviour, that's where their mutual respect came from. As soon as people started being judgemental of him, that's where trouble began, with Mark E. Smith, Lydia and Barney Hoskyns.' Hoskyns had been quoted as saying that he had only enjoyed The Birthday Party's music while he was on heroin, but since he had detoxed he could no longer listen to it. Despite the journalist's protestatations that he was being quoted out of context, Cave never forgave him.

Cave was not the only member of the band to feel affronted by Mat Snow's remark. 'It was that year, 1985, everyone thought they could get their pound of flesh,' says Mick Harvey. 'Mat Snow got the ball rolling, that's why he was the most hated one. He didn't actually do that much but his whole attitude about what the press was, what he was as a journalist, all this swagger about what they could do and how fucking important they were. That's why Nick hated him, because he started it. Then they all jumped on the bandwagon and started sticking the boot in.'

Rewriting the lyrics to Bob Dylan's 'Wanted Man' would cause much unforeseen inconvenience for Cave and the band, delaying the release of *The Firstborn Is Dead* for months and disrupting their nine-date British tour which was already booked to start at Coasters in Edinburgh on 16 April 1985. 'We didn't even know how the song went,' recalls Harvey. 'Nick had started singing it at a sound check and we put a two-chord arrangement into it and that became our version of the song. Originally it's a straight four-chord turnaround which we didn't use at all. So we wrote our own music to it, which we couldn't claim. So, Bob Dylan wrote six verses, Nick wrote fourteen, we wrote the music and Bob Dylan got all the money. That's a good one.' In Bob Dylan's contract it stipulated that Dylan himself would have to approve any alterations to his work, so a tape was duly sent for his inspection via his publisher. 'Of course, it wasn't very high on his list of priorities,' says Harvey. 'His representative in the States addresses him as Mr Dylan and he wasn't going to be very worried about the release schedule of Nick's album. I'm sure if it had been U2 or Queen it would have been a different matter. So we had to sit about waiting. Initially his representative said, "Well, I don't know, Mr Dylan hasn't approved one in years." Two months later he came back and said, "Congratulations! It's OK!" That was quite flattering, I guess, but a lot of damage had been done to our practical plans.'

Not only was there no record to promote, but a week before the tour commenced there was no band. 'There was just me and Nick,' Harvey continues. 'Barry didn't make it for the first rehearsal. So we started calling Manchester and tried to figure out if he'd left the band, which he hadn't, he'd just decided he couldn't face it and wasn't coming. Blixa was unavailable because of his commitments to Einsturzende Neubauten. Funny to look back on, but a total disaster at the time.' Bassist Christoph Dreher and drummer Thomas Wydler were hastily recruited from Die Haut while Harvey would play rhythm guitar and keyboards. 'I had to try and explain to Thomas what to do in German! His English was terrible and it was very hard communicating what had to be done. My German was' shaky in those days but fortunately we locked into these things. I've never given musical directions in German before . . . It was all a complete farce. We never felt confident. Christoph is a great bass player but he just wasn't right for our material.' With the lead guitarist slot still vacant, Cave and Harvey contacted their old friend Robert Forster from The Go-Betweens, who was eager to play and turned up for rehearsals, but on the fourth day was told by his booking agency that he could not back out of a short tour of Scandinavia. Cave and Harvey's other choice was Rowland S. Howard, who had been recording in London three months previously with Harvey's own group project Crime and the City Solution.

'It was almost insulting that I was asked,' says Howard. 'They seemed to have asked everyone that was humanly possible to fit the bill, like Robert Forster. He was so unsuitable it's absurd. I was told that Nick had to have a few drinks down the pub before he could ask me because he was so embarrassed. I was only asked twenty-four hours before the tour started so I only had an eight hour rehearsal with Nick and Mick in my bedroom while they showed me the songs. I'd only heard the LP once, it was still close enough to the break-up of The Birthday Party for me to be relatively ambivalent. It was a very odd tour. Nick always maintains it wasn't a proper Bad Seeds tour. Thomas was there but that was the first tour they'd done anything with him. There were a lot of songs we just couldn't do, there wasn't time. Some of it was good but tours of England are never the most enjoyable. If Nick could have pulled out he would have, he felt uncomfortable . . . On the tour I saw more of him [Cave] and he seemed more reserved, wary and weary. It wasn't to do with the group so much but the whole situation. I was just filling Blixa's shoes and I wasn't meant to be Rowland Howard. Someone in Leeds came up to me and said, "I thought you were dead." I hadn't done anything for a while. The main thing I remember about the tour was when we were playing at the Hacienda in Manchester, there was a gang of boys in the audience who every time a song would end would sing, "Rowland do a solo! Rowland do a solo!" [to the tune of "Aye, Aye, Conga"]. Nick was horrified. I don't think he thought it was funny.'

According to Harvey: 'Rowland has a very distinctive style which is fantastic but if he'd stayed it would have pushed the group back to The Birthday Party. I think he played true to his style, he couldn't really do anything else. We played "Jennifer's

Veil" and "Wild World" on that tour and I was very glad to have him along. It wasn't a last resort option at all. To a degree it was because we were under the hammer, but it was a very positive move. We feel positive about what Rowland does but we know that overall his style's not right for The Bad Seeds.'

The makeshift group at once plunged into the nine-date tour of the UK which they had only agreed to undertake as a special concession to Mute, with no record to promote. The British music critics, who were unfamiliar with the new material, savaged the under-rehearsed tour. Perhaps they sensed that Cave was vulnerable and the tour provided the perfect occasion to strike back at a performer who had openly treated them with disdain. 'Mostly the audience got what they came for. An ugly man with a lot of black hair rolling about on the stage. As dangerous as an assault with cotton wool, this was essentially a semi-comatose, masturbatory performance. These Bad Seeds remain unfertilised,' wrote Tom Morton in his *Melody Maker* review of the first gig of the tour.

Morton, in common with other critics, failed to realise that Cave was only appropriating the symbolism and mythology of the blues: 'Cave doesn't think he's Blind Lemon [*sic*], but another Delta blues master, Robert Johnson, who supposedly sold his soul to the devil for musical fame and fortune. Nick Cave may have sold his soul but he doesn't appear to have got much of a bargain for it.' Of the same Edinburgh concert, Andrea Miller of the *NME* wrote, 'Sometimes he sounds like a hardcore Tom Waits; sometimes he sounds like a Gothic Shirley Bassey', while Chris Manthorp mustered all his descriptive faculties to pen the following in *Sounds*: 'The music peaked in berserk stutterings and ebbed into a sound like cigarette ash being attacked with a cheese grater.' The picture that accompanied the review was captioned, 'Nick Cave: this man should carry a Government health warning.' 'Before *The Firstborn Is Dead* came out they were already stabbing Nick in the back,' says Harvey. 'They hadn't even heard the new material but they wanted to have a go at Nick because they'd built him up too high before. They decided to take a personal angle on him and give him a drubbing. It was like there was some policy decision taken in the press and there was no way he could get round it.'

In certain quarters Cave was perceived as a 'corrupter of youth', and many editors and staff writers working for the rock press began to adopt the extremely dubious stance of moral guardians concerning his perceived lifestyle, simply ignoring his work altogether. He found himself bearing the brunt of what journalist Chris Bohn would accurately term 'the new righteousness – a holy alliance of Liberal-Left attitudes and puritanical conservative muses'. 'Certain people didn't like the drugs they were associated with, but it was never something I went into because for me drugs are a private individual choice and not a point of issue,' asserts Bohn. 'You get into a situation where this drug is OK and this one's not. I hate that . . .' The sheer hypocrisy of the stance of 'the new righteousness' would be exposed three years later within the pages of the *NME*.

The Firstborn Is Dead was finally released in June and predictably the majority of the reviews were negative. 'There is a yawning distance between what Nick Cave aims for and what he actually achieves,' wrote Sean O'Hagan in the *NME*. 'It is one thing to transform suffering into an art and another to let that suffering intrude on your art. For the moment St Nick is too proficient at the latter.' Ted Mico's review in the *Melody Maker* opened with the line: 'Nick Cave has made a career out of disguising himself as a corpse, but lately this disguise has become a trifle too convincing.' Cave's distorted media image was now beginning to obscure his work completely. The complexity of the album, an altogether more fully realised project both lyrically and musically than the first solo album, was completely overlooked. The xenophobic reviews in the British music press that greeted an edited 7" single version of 'Tupelo' in July were even worse: 'There are those who would have you believe that this decrepit scuzzball and his infrequent record releases represent the zenith of the alternative pop scene'; 'A strange collection of howls and twangs that sounds a lot like Rolf Harris doing "Sun Arise". Perhaps Nick Cave should join up with Paul Hogan and cover Rolf's "Two Little Boys".'

During July, Chris Bohn travelled to Berlin with Bleddyn Butcher to interview Cave for the *NME*. 'He was very broke but he seemed in good spirits,' say Bohn. 'He was staying at Thomas Wydler's place on York Strasse. He had a tiny cubby-hole at the top of the place, we met there and talked casually. His mother rang while I was there to tell him that he'd been included in a prestigious Australian *Who's Who*. He seemed pleased. We went to America House to look for pictorial evidence for some kind of parallel area for the town in his novel and for pictures of frontier houses.'

'Nick was working all the time there, in his little room,' says Wydler. 'It still amazes me how small the room was. He'd hang outside a sign on the door, "Genius At Work". He'd just be in there and you'd hear this click, click, click of the typewriter. I'd pass him on the stairs sometimes. There was not only us living there, there was a family as well. Nick wasn't at the family table at breakfast, he was working. That went on for about half a year maybe, I can't remember, time went very fast anyway in those days.'

'He was very charming,' says Bleddyn Butcher of Cave. 'One evening he took me out drinking and we went to see the film *Witness* in German. Berlin was great ... He's very particular about photos but I wouldn't say he plays up to his image. He's very keen to be seen visually in a certain way, which is intensely fastidious from my point of view. I can empathise with the way he feels he's depicted in print. He has a robust sense of humour and it only rarely comes across. He's capable of being intensely charming. Generally speaking, when I've seen him interviewed he turns on the charm and that hardly ever filters through to the printed page. No matter whether it's turned on or not, it's still a facet of someone's personality and also the charm is highly amusing. It's surprising that people only see what they want to see. He's also a fairly intimidating character as well, if only because of his manifest intelligence which is enough to drive people back into their shells and make them make foolish mistakes in the way they relate to him, which is obviously the intended effect.'

With Wydler now firmly established as The Bad Seeds' drummer, the band recommenced touring Europe to promote *The Firstborn Is Dead*. Barry Adamson also rejoined the group as he felt that he had recuperated sufficiently from his breakdown to continue touring. According to Mick Harvey: 'Barry must have decided the best way to deal with it was to face it and get on with it, because a lot of it was in his mind. He was creating this situation that wasn't really there at all.'

In late October, before returning to Australia, Cave and the band played a four-date tour of Japan, the first concerts they had ever played in the country. 'When we were touring there,' says Adamson, who spent much of the tour in Cave's company, 'I don't think we stopped laughing for days. It was just because of where we were.' Much to Cave's bemusement, The Bad Seeds, like Einsturzende Neubauten, who had visited the country in May, were greeted with overwhelming adulation by a large contingent of Japanese teenage girls. After years of playing to predominantly male audiences, who at times seemed only interested in shouting abuse and wanting to beat him up, Cave was now being treated as a fully fledged teen pop idol. He was unable to leave his hotel without being mobbed by young girls, or reach for a cigarette in a restaurant without a lighter being eagerly thrust under his nose. 'It's the first time I've ever been in a band where the entire audience was made up of young females and there wasn't an ugly one amongst them,' he joked three weeks later in Australia, describing the tour as 'paradise'.[2] Unable to take drugs into the country, Cave spent the duration of the Japanese tour drinking heavily. Ever keen to confound an audience's expectations, he dressed down in jeans and never bothered combing his hair. The Japanese perceived the group to be very dark and mysterious but at many gigs Cave would have the band laughing hysterically as he ad libbed humorous lyrics the majority of the audience did not understand.

The 1985 Australian tour began on 8 November with two dates at Selina's in Sydney. Cave was shocked to discover that the rhythm and blues singer Screamin' Jay Hawkins, who had originally been booked to play on the same bill for a couple of gigs, was now co-headlining with The Bad Seeds for the entire tour. Though Cave had covered Hawkins' best-known song, 'I Put a Spell On You' throughout his career, he cared neither for the rest of the singer's tongue-in-cheek repertoire nor his theatrical 'voodoo' stage presentation, featuring a smoking skull named Henry and a bizarre assortment of novelty store items. Hawkins himself was not thrilled at the prospect of opening for Cave's band, despite the co-headlining status. 'I can't stand Nick Cave!' he says. 'I worked with him in 1985. They had the *audacity* to tell *me* I was going to be the opening band for Nick Cave. I said, just a minute, back up, my records were sold here before Nick Cave was born. Before he was a twinkle in his daddy's eye. Before his daddy knew how to get an erection! But I said, I tell you what, just for one night I'll open the show for Nick Cave, but you'll be sorry you did it. And I used every trick in the bag. Nick Cave could not get up on the stage. No one can get on the stage after me. You know who paid me that compliment? Nat King Cole when I was a youngster learning the business.' The relationship between Hawkins and The Bad Seeds soured rapidly throughout the tour. During the flights between gigs Cave reluctantly endured Hawkins' long monologues about how many different artists had covered 'I Put a Spell On You'. 'It was a farcical situation,' says Mick Harvey, 'because here we were making this bizarre music related to the blues, trying to reach its deepest feeling, rather than using the form *per se*, and here was this guy, a rock'n'roll cabaret act, claiming to be a genuine blues guy. Of course he played good-time music and went down a storm with the good old Aussie rock'n'roll punters. He kept making rude comments about us, like, "They wouldn't know where the seventh chord is." I had to sit next to him all the way to Perth and he was listening to Billy Joel's Greatest Hits! "Man, this stuff's great!" That sums it up for me.'

Relieved that the tour was over, the band entered Melbourne's AAV Studios to begin work on an album of cover versions, reunited with Tony Cohen after four years. 'I was stuck in Australia all this time doing silly records,' says Cohen. 'Never quite managed to make the break. I reckon they found some really great songs, they were related to a lot of his [Cave's] influences. My memory of it is a little foggy because I was pretty well off my rocker. I know they recorded so much material it was going to be a double LP. Actually it was my idea . . . "I think you'd better make it one good single album."

'Things had changed, two different bands. This was all a new experience for me, I'd never worked with anyone from another country, non-English-speaking anyway. I mean, I'd lived a sheltered little life, middle-class Melbourne was a pretty quiet sort of place. I suppose I was a little bit shocked at Blixa to start with. Here was this great, tall, skinny fella with hair sticking up six foot, wearing a codpiece and tight leather daks. Walking around Melbourne like that! I thought, What the hell have we got here? He was quite astounding, but I think we got a reasonably good rapport going early in the piece, although I didn't understand him very well. One thing I did understand was what he did in the studio was really quite interesting, his voice was great too . . . I must say I didn't feel in there with them on that one. I was just working as an engineer, quite a good engineer who they trusted.'

There were many reasons why Cave, at this stage in his career, had decided to record a covers album. The songs he chose alluded to the themes, musical genres and performers that had always influenced and inspired him: his teenage idol Alex Harvey ('The Hammer Song'); gospel (The Alabama Singers' version of the traditional gospel 'Jesus Met the Woman At the Well'); country (Johnny Cash's 'Muddy Water', 'The Singer' and 'The Long Black Veil'); blues ('Hey Joe', John Lee Hooker's 'I'm Gonna Kill That Woman', Leadbelly's 'Black Betty'); and epic sixties pop ballads (The Seekers' 'The Carnival Is Over', Tom Jones' 'Sleeping Annaleah', Roy Orbison's 'Running Scared', Gene Pitney's 'Something's Gotten Hold of My Heart', Jim Webb's 'By the Time I Get To Phoenix'). He had been working constantly on his novel for months and had not thought about songwriting, so a covers album project would allow him time to concentrate on producing his own songs.

Another inspiration for the record was Cave's admiration for a cover version album by the Australian group The Reels entitled *Beautiful*, featuring renditions of such traditional 'middle-of-the-road' material as Burt Bacharach and Hal David's 'This Guy's In Love With You'. Cave had long been impressed by the voice of their lead singer Dave Mason, and had entertained the idea of having him play Euchrid Eucrow after seeing the singer performing his own composition, 'Quasimodo's Dream', in a video. 'He's a good actor and singer,' commented Cave in 1987. 'I think the *Beautiful* record was such a magnificent mixture of bitterness and resentment, spite and hate for the whole rock industry, all wrapped up in the most awesomely, gloriously sung and performed pieces of music. It's a really nasty record and I think it has every intention of saying, "Fuck you" to a lot of people, all dressed up and very sincere.'[3]

Cave had originally considered naming his covers album *Head on a Platter* as he was convinced that the project was going to be panned by British critics, due in part to the nature of the material. After some deliberation, he decided instead upon the title *Kicking Against the Pricks*, the quote taken from Acts, Chapter 26, Verse 14, but also alluding to Samuel Beckett's appropriation of the phrase for his collection of short stories, *More Pricks Than Kicks*. For Cave, the 'Pricks' in question were the music critics. 'That was one reason why I enjoyed making that record, because I thought it would really irritate them,' he later admitted. 'It didn't have a lot of "dramatic tension" on it, and those things that our last record [*The Firstborn Is Dead*] was supposed to lack. It was basically a fuck you to all the people who thought they could tell us what we should and should not be doing.'[4]

'He was relishing the thought of a really bad critical response,' confirms Harvey, 'which shows some sort of perverse streak coming out again.' Harvey himself was initially sceptical about the merits of the project, as he would have preferred to work on original material, but when recording began his enthusiasm rapidly increased: 'The idea of grasping songs and turning some of them upside down was very attractive. Others were straight renditions. Nick had wanted to do a record featuring his all-time favourite songs but when it came to making a list of them, there weren't any. Then somehow a collection of songs got put together. When we started I liked a lot of what was there and I wanted to make it as good as possible. I started having a personal connection with it.' With a list of songs completed, The Bad Seeds quickly recorded the backing tracks, as it had been agreed that the record would be mixed in Berlin with the main vocal tracks and string arrangements to be added there.

'It was very enjoyable starting *Kicking Against the Pricks*,' says Blixa Bargeld, 'because we did six songs on the first day and another five the next day. Lots of songs were recorded but not released: The Saints' "No, Your Product"; The Loved Ones' "Everlovin' Man"; Johnny Cash's "Bullrider"; Leadbelly's "John Henry" and Harry Belafonte's "Have You Heard About Jerry?".'

After the band had completed their work on several tracks, Tracy Pew, who had all but given up music and was still studying at Melbourne's Monash University, and Hugo Race came to the studio to play on a couple of tracks, while Cave's mother Dawn played violin on 'Muddy Water'. Years later Cave would convince an American journalist that his mother was renowned as one of Australia's premier violinists, hence her presence on the album. 'We were all very well behaved when she came in,' recalls Tony Cohen, 'drinking coffee instead of beer. She was very interested in the workings of the studio. "What are these knobs for?", normal questions people ask. At least she didn't come in and say, "You must need a pilot's licence to fly that."'

Rowland Howard also later visited AAV, making contributions on guitar, organ, and a vocal track for the Velvet Underground's 'All Tomorrow's Parties'. 'I can't remember if Nick asked me in but I worked on five songs, a couple of which were eventually used,' he says. 'There were a lot of songs done, all types. Mick told me about the list of songs Nick had drawn up to cover . . . "Something" by George Harrison, that's such a horrible song . . . I think lurking in the back of Nick's brain was the idea of making a proper record that wasn't "noisy" and didn't rely on youth, but he loved the songs. I think he wanted to stop the ridiculous amount of importance that was placed upon everything he did as if it was some kind of incredible statement, a portrait of your life at that moment, rather than being a collection of songs. It was being blown out of all proportion. I know he used to listen to Tom Jones a lot, Johnny Cash and Isaac Hayes's twenty-five-minute version of "By the Time I Get To Phoenix". The record wasn't done out of a wilful sense of perversity or kitsch. All the strength it has is through its sincerity.'

For many years Cave had been increasingly exasperated with his former manager and head of Missing Link Records, Keith Glass. In Cave's eyes Glass's failure to pay what the band thought was owing to them in royalties from The Birthday Party's back catalogue was inexcusable behaviour for a former friend. The final straw had been Missing Link releasing a live album in May, *It's Still Living*, about which the band had not been consulted in any way, despite the claims of the sleeve note credits.* Cave's anger was so intense that he asked a Melbourne underworld friend to meet him at the studio to discuss obtaining the money by force. The friend dutifully arrived with a colleague who had two tattooed tears on his cheek and was clearly a little psychotic. Cave was calmly told that violence would not be necessary, just a little intimidation would 'fix his wagon'. When the tattooed associate muttered that there was always the possibility of kidnapping Glass's children, Cave told them to forget the whole thing, but he continued to nurse his bitterness.

After their work was completed, the rest of the band, apart from Cave and Harvey, returned to Europe. For a month afterwards Cave continued to work on the tracks at Richmond Recorders in Melbourne. The then head of the studio, Tim Stobart, had enticed him to work there during 'dead time' at a special reduced rate. However, Stobart would later renege on the agreement, consequently jeopardising the completion of the entire record. 'He was just interested in making money and a bit of a liar,' says Tony Cohen. 'One of those people who, when they start lying, a rash appears on their neck.'

While in Melbourne Cave also had further meetings with John Hillcoat to work on the film scripts. During the sessions it became clear to both parties that there was a gradual change of focus regarding the direction that the project was taking. 'What had evolved was a fairly sensationalist piece about hard-core prisons,' says Evan English. Hillcoat recalls: 'The film was a process of politicisation for both Evan and me in terms of the politics of prisons and institutions. Michel Foucault, who wrote *Discipline and Punish*, influenced our thinking quite a bit. Nick

* See Discography, p. 315.

was interested in the dramatic struggle of the characters and the psychological horror of what they were going through, as opposed to sociological/political aspects. This is where it started to change. What we had was a romantic vision of hell. It was indicative of white, middle-class kids who set their imaginations going from reading. It was romantic and black. The script was more in the prose poetry style of Ondaatje's *Billy The Kid*, the imagery of Victorian prisons and prison films. Evan and I started doing more research and what changed the script was when we discovered the new-generation prisons, very high tech. I'm practically obsessed with research and so is Evan. There were some characters that we both went out and talked to. Real ex-cons, maniacs, like a speed dealer that Nick knew that he introduced me to, who was actually considered for casting. He died. He had lots of tattoos, tears on his face. He embodied the disturbed psychological elements but it wasn't until we talked to brighter prisoners that we woke up.'

NOTES

1 'Nick Cave, Ten On Ten', *Juke*, 19 May 1990.
2 Paul Stewart, 'Our Wild Boy Back In Town', *Sun Leisure Supplement*, 14 November 1985.
3 Melanie Brellis, 'Nick Cave Up and Out in Melbourne and Berlin,' *Tension*, December 1987.
4 Ibid.

11

Stranger Than Kindness

In March 1986 work was meant to start again on *Kicking Against the Pricks* at Hansa Studios in West Berlin, but the master tapes were still in the possession of Tim Stobart at Richmond Recorders in Melbourne. 'The guy at the studio, who was a total arsehole, took advantage of the situation,' says Mick Harvey. 'Eventually a bill came, all Nick's "dead time" for a month was charged at the full rate. At first we refused to pay the bill, it was bloody criminal, but he had the tapes, it fucked up our whole production. It was blackmail, he said send the bill then I'll send the tapes. That's the sort of thing that can happen.' Six months later Stobart's other activities would come under close scrutiny from the Melbourne police force. 'He was a fucking joke,' says Tony Cohen. 'He needs a good ragging, that bastard, but he got his back. He sold cocaine to coppers and ended up in gaol for twenty years.' While waiting for the tapes to arrive, Cave and the band began working on three original compositions for his next LP, 'Your Funeral, My Trial'; the title track, 'Jack's Shadow', loosely based on the experiences of Jack Henry Abbott upon his release from prison ('Spat from the dirty dungeons, Into a truly different din'); and a rough unreleased version of 'Hard On For Love', the title an in-joke, appropriated from The Reals' old punk rock song.

Before mixing was scheduled to begin on *Kicking Against the Pricks*, Barry Adamson had finally decided that he had to leave The Bad Seeds and the rock world in general in order to concentrate on his own solo career, creating instrumental pieces conceptually based around imaginary cinema soundtracks. Now he found himself being drawn inexorably into the making of Cave's next LP. 'I went to have a look really,' he says. 'I didn't want to repeat myself in any way. My health was getting a bit better, a little bit. I was really enthusiastic about the whole recording session, my confidence was rising. I could see I needed to take that away with me, leave what I put in behind and carry on with my own compositions. They were surprised. I was surprised that they were surprised. I rang Nick from London after the recording session and said, "That's it for me." Now the thing that had haunted me since I was seven years old could see the light of day. I'd pushed my limits mentally, emotionally and physically in The Bad Seeds and I'd come through. I felt like what I was getting was, you've jumped ship, but I needed to change. Mick was very supportive and gave his blessing. These people never really go from inside here. If I looked back over my career I would cite Nick Cave as one of my teachers in a way to get things done. Looking back at what I'd do today I can see it was necessary to be confined in The Bad Seeds. Now I've sorted out a lot of crap around my distorted ego perceptions I can see it was a necessary thing to do.'

Cave and Harvey were startled by Adamson's decision to leave. 'He thought he was getting drawn back in so I can understand how he felt uncomfortable,' says Harvey, 'He wasn't in a good condition generally. It was the only way he could respond. He wouldn't talk about it either, he'd just clam up. He wasn't in any state of mind to deal with the personalities or things that needed to be said. He couldn't discuss it with Nick in any way at all, no comment, no discussion about the subject. Nick always takes those things very badly if someone leaves him.' Lost in his own world and preoccupations, Cave had no inkling of the extent of Adamson's problems. Harvey deeply regretted the departure of a friend and a respected fellow musician: 'A very important point to me about The Bad Seeds was Barry leaving. I think we worked together musically very well and I missed him because there was no one to take that over. It all fell on my shoulders, which I wasn't happy about. It broke up The Bad Seeds being a full band in its own right.'

Finally the tapes arrived from Melbourne, leaving only three days for the engineer, Flood, and the band to mix the record. 'We were running up and down the stairs of the studio,' Harvey continues. 'We were working on the strings downstairs while we were mixing upstairs, doing backing vocals, overdubs and even extra mixes with another engineer which were never used.' The strings were provided by the Berliner Kaffeehausmusik Ensemble whom Blixa Bargeld had seen perform one evening. The Ensemble, who had an aggregate age of over 300 years, had never had any previous involvement with rock'n'roll music and were persuaded to work on the record by Bargeld. 'You can hear on "Something's Gotten Hold of My Heart" that the cello comes in playing rhythm during the middle section and it just fades away because he couldn't keep it up after four bars,' laughs Harvey.

With *Kicking Against the Pricks* completed, Cave recommenced work on his novel, losing himself in the mythic locale he was creating, taking large quantities of speed, writing incessantly. 'He felt that doing the book was very hard on the other people in his life,' says Simon Pettifar, 'but as an artist he enjoyed the fact that he'd found a medium where he could be completely on his own and be as selfish as he wanted to be.' Throughout this period Cave was constantly reading the works of the American crime novelist Jim Thompson, which shaped the character of Euchrid Eucrow. He was enthralled by Thompson's ability to confront the reader with the schizophrenic thought processes of his protagonists in such an intense way that they began to sympathise with their psychotic logic. His other main reading matter was the Bible. 'That's the one book that I had by my side all the time, that I plagiarised completely,' he confessed to journalist Jonathan Romney. 'Each day I'd write for nine hours, and more and more I found myself writing for three and reading the Bible for six. When I began, I had a sort of intellectual relationship with it, but I don't think you can read that book for any length of time without being affected by what it's saying. I became very affected by a lot of the messages.'[1] In his cramped living conditions Cave began obsessively to create a space that he felt was somehow related to Eucrow's junkyard environment. The walls of the room were adorned with religious prints and artefacts, coupled with numerous images of naked women cut from pornographic magazines. 'I created a kind of world when I wrote this book, in a room which was quite separate from the rest of what was going on around me,' he said in July 1989. 'An obsessive and fetishistic environment which really had an influence over me. A lot of alienation, exploring the inability of a character to communicate.'[2] Early in the morning he would often be found scouring second-hand markets for trinkets and junk to adorn his room, on one occasion finding a box containing locks of a young girl's hair which he would finger while typing.

Cave's deep compulsion to work was rooted in his fear that if he stopped he would become just another ordinary person, that his work elevated him from the ordinary to the extraordinary. Having always felt dysfunctional in any form of social interaction, his writing and drugs insulated him from the outside world. 'Nick is sometimes quite hard to communicate with and he knows that,' declares Jessamy Calkin. 'You can say things to Nick and it's almost as if the words become contaminated from when you think of them when they hit the air because it seems like they're missing the target. He's always said he's had problems with personal relationships because he finds it hard to communicate. He hated that and found it a real problem. That was perpetuated through fame because it made him so self-conscious, everyone knew who he was. It's disorientating for your ego because you have no sense of yourself. Certain people admire you whatever the hell you do, play badly, you're rude to them, they still sit there with their mouths open.' The further Cave delved into Eucrow's psyche the more detached and non-communicative he became, and his relationship with Elizabeth Recker would begin to falter.

'Yes, he was locked away but I saw him often,' says Edzard Blum who, among his other activities, was now running his own bar in Berlin. 'In fact I was seeing him more often than he liked, sometimes I was too insensitive to realise that he wanted to be alone for a week to write. I'd just let him write and I'd read. It was a wild, free time, very funny and amusing, but Nick was always focused on his work and I respected that. He was very obsessed and when you take a lot of speed you become an egomaniac, that's what made me stop in the end. I was fed up with my body being in a constant state of alarm. You can't really listen to other people, you can but you're just pretending to listen. To be someone who is respected for your work means you'll always get put into roles and positions where you have to be mean and Nick, for sure, could also be a mean character. He was very self-centred and I don't think he ever trusted anyone, which is familiar to me. The lifestyle in Berlin created all this suffering, passion and obsessive behaviour which was necessary for his work. At least he used it well. Out of pain and depression comes creativity, or I should say, you can use it, other people were just worn down. Nick couldn't read newspapers, he was totally isolated, cut off from what was happening in the world.

'Elizabeth was constantly on the verge of kicking him out of her flat. Every second day you'd go in there and there'd be his suitcases already packed by the door. She couldn't cope with all that was happening. Elizabeth kept saying to me, "I just want to be a good wife for him. I want to make everything nice for him so he has everything he needs to work." She said, "Sometimes when he's on tour I just lie in bed and steam with jealousy." She'd even get annoyed when I came round: "You spend more time with Eddie than you do with me."

'Elizabeth bought an Opel Admiral which Nick called "the orgasm of the German car industry". I would always drive because Nick didn't have a licence. There was no radio in it and so Nick would often take his guitar or harmonica and play quite badly, sing and make comments in between like he was a radio announcer. One day we were coming back from scoring in Kreuzberg, driving to Elizabeth's home. Near the airport there's a huge police academy and a cop from that area sees that we are not wearing seat belts and pulls us over. I didn't have my licence and I didn't have the papers for the car, that's another story. The cop talked but I'm good at turning a situation like this to my advantage. He agreed to follow us back to Elizabeth's home where I said the driver's licence and the pink slip were for the car; I was trying to win some time in order to think. So the cop followed us and I went through a yellow light and was really surprised that he stopped because it had turned red. By now he was quite far away so I thought, this is our chance and accelerated.

'I thought in this situation it was best to park the car and leave it, sort the situation out later with a lawyer. I took a couple of quick right turns and drove the wrong way down an alley into a huge courtyard. We rushed out of the car with all the illegal things we had on us, drugs, syringes and some scales, and hid them next to the car in some bushes but we didn't look up at our surroundings. We walked down the courtyard whistling, turned right and saw a huge sign saying that the building that we had parked the car in front of was the headquarters of the Berlin police force. We completely panicked, got a taxi to drive to a phone booth to phone Elizabeth because we thought the cop would remember her address. We told her to leave the house immediately and pick up the car, to get it out of there. We stayed where we were, waited and waited, totally paranoid, but nothing happened, the cop must have just given up. We'd gone through all that for nothing! We were both very lucky during that whole period that nothing ever happened to us. I think our friendship was based on the feeling, maybe it sounds a little too much, but we were sort of outlaws and no one could touch us.'

When Cave went out at night to a bar or a club, Blum would invariably have to rescue him from unwanted attention. 'Of course the Berlin scene was very interested in what he was doing,' Blum continues. 'Nick and Blixa were the two famous characters in Berlin but at that time there were no clones running around trying to imitate him. Sometimes people would just keep staring at him and it drove him crazy, he couldn't stand it at all. In a bar Nick would get attacked by some girl who desperately wanted to talk to him and I'd go up to him and say, "But darling, I told you not to talk to girls all the time, I just won't accept it any more." We'd walk down the street arm in arm and they'd say, "What's the matter with you guys?" and we'd reply, "Don't you know we're going to get married in two weeks?" There was this French girl who was really madly in love with him. After this show at the Berlin Metropole we went to the car, got in, and she ran up behind us, opened the back door and sat down. She just wouldn't leave. He became more irritated, but she wouldn't go. Eventually we just had to pull her out. Things like that would happen often with girls.'

Cave's somewhat bitter yet humorous interpretation of Johnny Cash's 'The Singer', playing on his strained relationship with his audience and critics ('All the truths I tried to tell you were as distant to you as the moon'), was to be released as a single in June, and Christoph Dreher, who had previously directed a video for 'Tupelo', was again employed: 'That was the best video for me, that I directed. I put up three super-8 cameras from different angles. I only had one professional cameraman there, while my girlfriend and I worked the other two cameras. It was effective, very concentrated just working with Nick. We usually developed ideas together and looked for locations but when it came to shooting it was normally a rush. There was little money.' Cave obviously responded to the intimate situation and gave arguably one of his best performances to date in a promotional video, a medium in which he has often appeared ill at ease.

In London, during an endless succession of promotional interviews for *Kicking Against the Pricks*, Cave was still harbouring an intense disdain for the press. For him, revenge was a dish best served cold, as Mat Snow discovered: 'I was asked to interview Cave by the *NME*, which I had never done before. Bleddyn and I turned up at Mute's offices and we sat around there for hours. Chris Carr was there shepherding us around. Finally, four hours after the appointed time, we ended up in the same room. He'd already given me a very limp handshake and refused to make eye contact. I started asking boring questions about choice of songs and I was getting very dull, monosyllabic replies. After twenty minutes of this I asked him what was the matter, and the conversation that ensued was about how offended he'd been by that line in the Einsturzende Neubauten review and how I'd been disloyal to him. He didn't have much time for critics anyway, or so he claimed.'

Cave took great pleasure in showing Snow a journal containing writings never intended for publication, including a song entitled 'Scum', featuring Snow and Antonella Black in a vicious parody of the domestic situation during Cave's brief stay at Snow's house. 'There are some people who will take it in good part and laugh,' he told Snow, 'but I take it as a personal insult and harbour it. And then that person comes up to me and shakes my hand with a smile and says, "Hi, long time no see, burble, burble, burble." Everything that's said against me offends me, whether it's true or not. I can't fathom these people who flunked their arts courses and became rock journalists and are too goddamn ignorant about music or academic about their thoughts, or have so many hang-ups that they can't perform. Yet it is these people whose opinions are heralded and lauded as being gospel.'[3]

When Snow eventually heard the finished track 'Scum', which was distributed as a free flexi-disc with a poster sold at Bad Seeds' concerts that year, Cave could not have anticipated his reaction. 'I was so chuffed,' says Snow. 'Don Watson [then an *NME* journalist] ran into Cave and remarked in conversation how chuffed I was at the song and how it was a big ego boost. He was shocked and then he said I'm going to have to do a "Scum" for everybody that I hate in order to devalue any kudos I might perceive.' The sequel to 'Scum' was to feature Cave and Harvey's *bête noire*, *NME* journalist Amrik Rai, whom they suspected had given information to the paper's gossip column concerning Barry Adamson's mental condition in 1985. Cave's song entitled 'Snitch' was going to depict Rai furtively eavesdropping around public toilets but was never completed. One of the lines from 'Snitch' ran: 'It was about the time I wrote "The Carny", He was a Pakistani'.

As Cave was expecting, and even relishing, another critical mauling, he was taken by surprise when the album released in August received some of the best reviews of his career, as well as enjoying considerable commercial success. 'There's almost enough casual brilliance on *Kicking Against the Pricks* to totally justify Nick Cave's bloated sense of his own importance,' begrudgingly conceded Simon Reynolds in his *Melody Maker* review. This may not have been according to plan but it was obvious that Cave had successfully managed to reinvent the songs of others as if they were his own, forging a powerful statement of identity. 'It's a very revealing record,' he later admitted, 'far more revealing in a way than my own records because it tells a great deal about me, a lot more than my own writings. A lot of what I am is not presented on my other records but is on *Kicking Against the Pricks*. It's quite an honest record which also portrays a lot about what kind of atmospheres I like. That record backfired on us in a lot of ways.'[4]

That month, at the Strongroom in London, Cave, Harvey, Bargeld and Wydler recommenced recording 'Your Funeral . . . My Trial', the double EP they had begun a month previously at Hansa. The sessions were particularly painful for Wydler as he was suffering from an inflammation of the joints in his right arm, a repetitive strain injury, a common affliction for drummers. 'I was completely . . . a bad mood, depressive,' recalls Wydler. 'I came over for that one,' says engineer Tony Cohen. 'Now that's when I became a lot closer to the people in the band, particularly Nick and Mick. Coming from Australia for the first time I was depending on them quite a lot for comfort. Felt like a fish out of water. Nick and I were still running amok which disjointed things somewhat but the sessions themselves were fantastic. I was really happy with that record. I personally went through quite a bad patch, like what they went through years before, not as extreme of course. Mick helped Thomas out. I remember seeing them doing a duet on the kit.' Harvey adds: 'I ended up playing half the drums because it just wasn't physically possible for him, but we got a very tight feel out of that situation. It was very close, personal, a tightknit sound with just the four of us.'

One of the tracks recorded by the band, 'Stranger Than Kindness', featured music composed by Blixa Bargeld, stylistically echoing elements of country music, and haunting lyrics by Anita Lane in which 'the gaunt fruit of passion dies in the light'. 'It was just how I felt one day,' says Lane, 'I was grieving all the time and pining for something. I had this sadness a lot, like it was raining in my chest. We never really stopped seeing each other but we weren't together at the time. When I was young I wasn't a jealous person because I liked myself but I became more jealous as I got older. I used to see his other girlfriends as being just like me. All it meant was there was another person with whom I had something in common. Most of the people that Nick attracted were obsessive and so they were interested in me. In a way by always being involved with me somehow he never had to be committed to anybody, not even me.' Bargeld recalls: 'It wasn't very enjoyable for a lot of people, that record. Thomas was very frustrated at the time. Barry had left. He'd left after the second day. It was down to me and Mick. Mick played a big share of the music. It contains the only song that I've written [for the band], there were not so many people in the band so I had space to do something. It was just a tune that I played that Nick liked so at the end of the night I decided to put this down, six or seven layers of guitar.'

In Berlin The Bad Seeds regrouped before undertaking another long spate of touring to promote *Kicking Against the Pricks*. Although the band needed to recruit a bass player for live work the position fell by default to the versatile Mick Harvey, who was not only organising the schedule and business affairs of The Bad Seeds but also those of Crime and the City Solution. 'That's how I ended up being a drummer or playing piano and playing bass for all those years,' says Harvey. The two new members who augmented The Bad Seeds' line-up were originally considered for the role of bass player. Berliner Roland Wolf was brought in by Blixa Bargeld, with whom he had been working. Despite Wolf's protestations to the contrary his real talent lay with neither the bass nor guitar but as an accomplished pianist. Long-time friend of the band Kid Congo Powers, formerly of The Cramps and a founding member of The Gun Club with Jeffrey Lee Pierce, who was also momentarily considered for a role in The Bad Seeds, became the band's second guitarist.

'Touring was a whole new thing for me,' says Tony Cohen, who engineered The Bad Seeds' live sound for the first time on the thirteen-date European tour. 'The gigs were good, some of them great. Me and Nick were always trying to get drugs, it was really important at the time. I think Nick enjoyed the experience, got a few songs out of the damn thing, that's for sure.' Edzard Blum, taking time out from running his bar, Twilight, the new venue for Cave's marathon poker sessions, accompanied the band for the dates in Germany, beginning at Zeche in Bochum on 26 September. 'We'd been up for two or three days straight already in Berlin,' says Blum. 'We got in a tour bus and drove towards West Germany. Nick was already in a condition where he couldn't really sleep or stay awake. He was standing in the middle of the van, shaking all over his body. We'd stop at a gas station on the highway and buy a couple of porno magazines, tear them apart and glue them to the windows until they were covered with pictures of naked women so no one could look into the van. In that condition we arrived at Zeche and he had to play a show. He was just falling over on stage, tripping over the microphone cable. I even ran on stage and tried to help him because he'd caught himself up in some cables but he got really pissed off and told me to go away because he didn't really want me to help him. He was always very proud in that respect.'

By the time The Bad Seeds had performed at the Music Centrum in Utrecht on 6 October, the tour was threatening to spiral out of control. 'Nick scored in Amsterdam a really large amount of strong smack,' Cohen recalls. 'We got shit-faced. There was just too much to take. Then we had to go to France across the border. Nick had it bagged up in the seats and under the seats.' Having been subjected to a series of unsuccessful but time-consuming customs searches, the group just managed to reach the Paris Elysée Montmartre venue minutes before they were scheduled to perform. 'We get to this fucking joint and I'm going, "Jesus, the PA's not here!"' exclaims Cohen. 'The PA was the size of two little home stereo speakers. The gig erupted into violence: bouncers, blood, broken glass, people slashing each other. A group of feminists really wanted to kill Nick. The bouncers helped him get out of the back of the venue and we took off in the van to escape the riot. It was really scary, that was an intense one, Jesus, the blood. Red was the colour of that gig: the carpet, even the horrible speaker boxes they called the PA were red. I just remember these women chasing the van with broken bottles.'

Not for the first time, Cave's flippancy during an interview had led him into trouble. During the summer Glyn Brown in *Sounds* had levelled the accusation that there was a deep strain of misogyny running through his songs. Typically, rather than denying the charge, or making any attempt to elaborate on the layered lyrical themes of obsessive desire, alienation, and depiction of love as a flawed illusion of possession, Cave drily replied: 'What, a misogynist? I don't know why someone hasn't asked me that before. It's so obvious. And yet it was only a short while ago that I realised that all my songs had that kind of slant to them.'[5] After his comments were fiercely debated in the music press he perversely embraced the label and even had himself described as 'The Misogynist' in The Bad Seeds' tour brochure. As ever, in his contrary fashion, he was more than willing to act up to clichés that were applied to him, even to his own detriment.

Having played three successful UK dates, The Bad Seeds flew to Iceland to play one night at the Roxy in Reykjavik on 19 October. In the surreal surroundings of Reykjavik, with no drugs available, Cave had a couple of days to dry out before the start of the 1986 US tour beginning in Cleveland on 21 October. 'We got shit-faced drunk on the plane,' says Cohen. 'Looking out of the window there were the Northern Lights and the icebergs. Aah, it was so beautiful, I was freaking out. Then coming in to New York with Manhattan spread out below us . . . in America is where it got really weird.' From Cleveland the group travelled to New York, where they were booked to play a financially lucrative and highly prestigious media gig at the Ritz on the 23rd.

After checking into the Iroquois Hotel on West 44th Street with the rest of the band, Cave and Cohen caught a cab down to the lower east side of Manhattan to score heroin. 'Nick and I went to Alphabet City,' recalls Cohen. 'Louie, the tour manager, told us not to go there because we were white for a start. We stuck out like golf balls in that place. We went to the vacant lots, the drugs supermarket where you put the money in a bucket and the bucket goes up and comes down with whatever you want in it. I was walking twenty yards behind Nick and saw him turn a corner where he bought some syringes off some guys. A scary business, they'd just glue the lids back on and sell you used fits. We're lucky we're not dead. As soon as he'd done that the cops grabbed Nick but I didn't see them. All I knew was Nick had vanished and I was really worried. Anyway, I sat in Needle Park until the sun went down, about four hours. That was our meeting spot. When he didn't come back I started getting freaked out, sitting there in the dark, so I went back to find the others. It was about twenty-four hours until we found out what had happened to him.'

Cave was still missing on the night of the Ritz show, with the rest of the band ready to perform and still expecting his arrival. 'We were all really depressed,' Cohen continues. 'Everything was ready to go and we were still waiting. There was this guy from a music paper in Sydney, Australia, and he came into the band room. I had really long hair, I'm a skinny sort of fellow, so I put some sunglasses on and sat there and did an interview as Nick Cave. This guy was from Sydney, so no one expected to fool him, but this fucking dickhead went, "Hi, Nick," and I said, "What the fuck do you want?" He then started the interview, "Where do you get your inspiration from?" and I said, "What the fuck's it to you?" He was completely taken in! Now I think he got a little suspicious after a while when the rest of the band couldn't contain themselves any longer and were howling on the floor with laughter. Now, Nick really didn't look like he was going to show and things got more serious." Finally, after a day and a half spent phoning hospitals and police stations in New York City, Cave was eventually found by Mick Harvey.

Despite noticing that there was a police surveillance in progress at the 'drug supermarket', Cave had blithely walked in and scored. Minutes later he was grabbed and flung up against a wall with guns thrust in his face. The police asked if he was carrying drugs; he said no, but when his jacket was pulled open and three syringes were found he was handcuffed and thrown into a police bus. He then found himself in a police station, disorientated and unaware of his exact location, shoved into a wire cage holding-tank with fifty other men. To make matters worse, the only other white man in the cage turned out to be a fan, who announced loudly that seeing his idol at this close proximity had made his day. When asked if he wanted to make a telephone call, Cave replied that he could not remember the telephone number of the Iroquois Hotel where the group were staying. He asked if the officious officer could look up the number in the telephone directory, and was asked to spell the name of the hotel, which he was unable to do. Neither could the cop, and consequently Cave lost his telephone call. He spent the night in the 5th Precinct cells, sharing a one-man cell with a Hispanic junkie, the pair squabbling over who should sleep on the concrete bench. Throughout the night a black man in the next cell hurled a stream of abuse into the void, ranting and raving for hours at a time, cursing his jailers and fellow inmates, making an indelible impression upon Cave.

'I remember sitting on the steps of the venue with Mick Harvey and a couple of the others,' says Cohen. 'People were turning up and they'd spent forty-eight hours doing their hair. For Christ's sake, people with hair the size of the bloody Empire State Building, rolling up dressed in leather and chains and God knows what. We had to tell them that Nick was in jail and the gig was cancelled. Some took it well like, "Great, Nick's in jail!" The ones who'd spent forty-eight hours doing their hair were really pissed off. Did they get their money back? No. We scheduled another gig at the Ritz at the end of the tour [2 November] and about four people turned up. So it was like pretty down, getting pretty grim at that stage.'

Upon his release, Cave bought some heroin in bulk which turned out to be impure. Despite the fact that it was making him feel constantly sick, he persisted in taking the drug throughout the rest of the tour, steadily becoming sicker and having to draw on all his energies to perform. In Los Angeles, on October, after performing at the Variety Arts Theatre, he persuaded a girl to drive him to 6th and Union to try to score some more heroin but was robbed at gunpoint by a chicano junkie. After so many years it seemed to Cave that in 1986 his luck was finally running out.

The day after the US tour finished in New York, the double EP 'Your Funeral . . . My Trial' was released on Mute. The claustrophobic and fraught atmosphere in which it had been made had been channelled into creating one of the best records of Cave's solo career, restating with even greater clarity his obsessions with alienation, sexual desire, redemption, loss and despair. The records' inner sleeves, designed by Cave himself, reflected perfectly their contents. The sleeve containing the four melancholy, reflective slow ballads, 'Sad Waters', 'The Carny', 'Your Funeral . . . My Trial' and 'Stranger Than Kindness', was adorned with a print of St Veronica gazing down at the cloth with which she wiped Christ's face as he carried the cross, his image preserved on the garment. The second EP comprised three faster, aggressive sexual songs, 'Jack's Shadow', 'Hard On For Love' and 'She Fell Away', plus a cover of sixties singer/songwriter Tim Rose's remorseful murder ballad 'Long Time Man': 'Tim Rose influenced Nick immensely,' says John Hillcoat. The sleeve for this record featured a crude fifties ink-drawn pornographic print of a woman examining her genitals with a hand mirror, her downward gaze and stance similar to that of St Veronica.

While scouring a flea market in Berlin, Cave had purchased a whole set of fifties pornographic postcards and for his own amusement compiled a small black book comprising similar pairings of 'sacred' and 'profane' images: St Genevieve at the well with Christ/a man watching a woman urinate; St Teresa holding a feather/a young woman being tickled with feathers; St Rose, her hand over her heart/a naked woman clutching her breast; and so on. He joked to *NME* journalist Don Watson that the collection would be entitled *Images of Women* and would only be available as an expensive limited edition.

'Your Funeral . . . My Trial', to an even greater degree than *The Firstborn Is Dead*, reflected the themes, language and world contained within Cave's burgeoning novel, now called *And the Ass Saw the Angel*. The title, which was taken from the parable of Balaam and his ass in Numbers, Chapter 22, alluded to the novel's characters' inability to perceive the obvious. However, unlike Balaam they remain unable to do so, with tragic results.

The novel had unfolded from the script that Cave had written in Los Angeles. Euchrid Eucrow, the inbred abused mute and increasingly psychotic narrator of the novel, who hears voices and is frequently beset by visions, becomes obsessed with the valley's prostitute, Cosey Mo. Euchrid perceives Mo almost as a madonna, representing to him sexuality, womanhood and kindness. He watches Mo's near-fatal beating at the hands of an unruly mob of Ukulites, the religious sect that populates the valley. They have been whipped into a frenzy by a travelling preacher, Abie Poe; a would-be inventor and former door-to-door salesman who masks his criminal past with a fervour for purity. In Ukulore Valley he has been transformed into Prophet Poe by the credulous Ukulites. Poe leads them to believe that Mo's presence in the valley has brought divine punishment upon them in the form of a deluge of relentless rain which has lashed the area for years, devastating their livelihood, the sugar-cane crops. The viciously battered Cosey Mo is driven from the valley and Euchrid scavenges amongst the aftermath of the assault, taking items of her possessions as sacred treasures. The torrential rains continue unabated in spite of Mo's expulsion, and Poe is outcast from Ukulite society. Euchrid's intense hatred for the Ukulites and Poe ferments in his mind. The prostitute later returns to him in the form of a vision, his guardian angel.

Nine months after the beating of Cosey Mo, whilst stealing into the town square, Euchrid spies a figure '. . . like a rogue leper right off the pages of Leviticus . . .' stumbling towards the memorial statue to the valley's prophet and saint, Jonas Ukulore. The figure places a bundle at the foot of the statue. Euchrid then recognises that it is Cosey Mo. Roused by the screams emanating from the bundle, the town's physician, Doc Morrow, enters the square, but not before Cosey Mo has fled with only Euchrid having witnessed her. The abandoned infant is named Beth. As her arrival coincides with the end of the epic rains that have lashed Ukulore Valley, she is proclaimed a saint.

Unable to recognise their enclosed society's inherent paganism, the fundamentalist and self-righteous Ukulites embrace another false idol for worship. Euchrid alone knows that her mother is Cosey Mo, whom he and his father later find drowned in a ditch.

Beth's first five years in Ukulore pass without incident. Euchrid divides his time between his hideout in the swamp, where he has hidden Cosey Mo's 'treasures', and visits to the town to surreptitiously spy on Beth. In turn, the girl-child becomes besotted with her voyeur, believing that the unhinged mute is Christ. The trio of prostitute, child saint and custodial angel are inextricably bound together in Eucrow's tormented mind.

As the novel unfolds, the reader is plunged further into Euchrid's deepening insanity. Cave's great skill in relating the tale of how the mute has come to meet his death, sinking slowly in the swamp, is in stretching the reader's sympathies for his increasingly odious narrator. Euchrid witnesses his father beat his mother to death and helps him dispose of her body. In turn, he kills his father by sawing through the leg of the tower his father constructed for his captured animals to fight in. It collapses, crushing him. With this half-remembered act Euchrid descends into total madness, 'deadtime', as he calls his condition. Alone, he converts his parents' shack into his monstrous fortress, 'Doghead', which is surrounded by the wounded animals he continues to capture in his father's traps. He proclaims himself king. Flashbacks in Euchrid's distorted mind reveal how he disposed of his enemy Poe, a hobo named Kike and his mistress Queenie, and made nocturnal visits to Beth. By the novel's close Euchrid has become convinced that he must act and the voices that clamour in his head are clear and unequivocal as to what that action must be: *'Kill Beth Boom!'*

For Cave as a songwriter it had become ever more difficult to disentangle himself from the mythological environment of his novel. His mournful narration of the tale of the Carny, accompanied by Mick Harvey's eerie evocation of the ambience of a fairground, with organ, xylophone and glockenspiel, could have sprung directly from the pages of *And the Ass Saw the Angel* in its depiction of universal suffering and misery, embodied in the death of the carnival's 'bow-backed nag', Sorrow. In the novel, on the night of the 'burn-off', the celebration of the sugar-cane harvest after the years of torrential rain, Beth inadvertently frightens Sorrow, the horse of a merchant. Euchrid watches her whisper into the animal's ear, and it gallops straight into swampland, pursued by the townsfolk. Sorrow leads the people straight to Euchrid's lair, where they smash and scatter the Cosey Mo 'treasures' and the bones of his twin brother that he discovered when he buried his father's mule. Hence Euchrid is driven from his first place of sanctuary.

Similarly, Cave's use of language to invoke the lascivious desires described in 'Hard On For Love' echoed Eucrow's interior monologues: 'I am his rod and his staff, I am his sceptre and shaft, And she is Heaven and Hell, At whose gates I ain't been delivered. I'm gunna give them gates a shove'. Musically, the records illustrated how far The Bad Seeds had developed from their conception. Though Cave was now writing most of the group's music, during this period much of its execution fell to Mick Harvey. The band's considerable driving power was now marshalled to produce timeless, atmospheric and melodic compositions, such as 'Sad Waters' and the EP's title track, bearing a closer affinity to the works of Bob Dylan, Leonard Cohen and Neil Young than to The Bad Seeds' contemporaries in the post-punk rock world, or the vapid pop music scene of the mid eighties.

Unfortunately for the group, the release of 'Your Funeral . . . My Trial' was somewhat obscured by the success of *Kicking Against the Pricks* only three months previously. *Kicking Against the Pricks* had received a heavy promotional campaign, coupled with a tour after its release, which ended when the new EPs were available. Also, the unusual format of the EP, which necessitated changing the records after every two songs, caused some confusion among retailers, the general public and critics alike: 'This is a solemn and intense four sides, with only the whirling "Hard On For Love" open to misinterpretation as a kind of joke. Or at least it is, once you work out that it plays at 45 r.p.m.,' wrote Chris Roberts in his *Sounds* review.

On 7 November Cave received from Australia the devastating news that Tracy Pew had died after suffering a violent epileptic seizure, smashing his head against the bath at his girlfriend's house in Melbourne. He was only twenty-eight years old. For the past eighteen months he had been suffering from frequent fits and this condition, coupled with treatment through strong sedative medication, had meant he had had to defer completion of his course at Monash University, where he had been enjoying a very successful academic career. In the last two months of his life he had been fighting an increasingly difficult and painful battle against his illness but to no avail. He had long since abstained from alcohol but his previous years of sustained heavy drinking had taken their toll. 'When he died I got a card in the mail with an extract from Tracy's diary, which was remarkable,' says Rowland Howard. 'The gist of it was that every day when he looked in the mirror, and he looked older, it delighted him and it all took him closer to death. He was interested in pursuing some strange idea that he had.' At Pew's memorial service in Melbourne, his girlfriend Kate Jarrett picked three songs to be played in remembrance: Sam Cooke's 'Summertime', Tom Waits' 'Somewhere' and Pew's favourite Birthday Party song, 'Wild World'. 'Tracy is the one male genius I've ever met,' Cave later recalled of his friend. 'I think up until he died what was going on in his head was beyond anything anyone was capable of understanding. He was one of these characters who had such a sense of himself from as early on as I ever knew him. I never felt he was discovering himself and he seemed to be the same person when he died. It was only as I grew older that I began to understand what this guy was about.'

Cave's relationship with Elizabeth Recker had finally collapsed, due to her total exasperation at his lifestyle, and he had now moved permanently into Christoph Dreher's new two-floor apartment on Dresdener Strasse, where he would continue writing his novel and songs for his next album. 'I got along really well with him,' says Dreher. 'I can only remember two fights we had in the years he lived there, minor arguments even though it would be a pretty close situation. I worked upstairs and so did he, there were two big tables in there. There were two cubicles and he had his bed and archives there, it was a really small room. Downstairs there was a little kitchen with a shower and a larger room behind that. I didn't really want to live with anyone at all, having done that before in communes after living with my parents, but with Nick it was really different. I must say he was always very much a gentleman in a way. He generally deals with people in a well-mannered way and he is basically a very optimistic person as opposed to the general perception of Nick in the public eye. He has a good sense of humour which was very important to me. He was usually in a good mood whether he was sick or not. He's not the sort to complain like many of the junkies did when they didn't have any drugs for a while. They started to fall apart but that never happened with Nick.'

Within a week of moving into the Dresdener Strasse flat Cave met a middle-aged Greek painter named Chris who lived in the flat above Dreher's. Other tenants had lived in the building for years and had never even seen the elusive painter, who eventually invited Cave into his flat for a drink. On entering, he could barely suppress his surprise at the décor. The kitchen was festooned with all manner of Greek souvenir statues and other tourist paraphernalia. The *tour de force*, however, was the living room, which Chris had designated permanently as 'The Christmas Room'. The walls were painted red, covered with thousands of hand-made little stars cut out of paper and covered with glitter. A large nativity scene filled one corner and decorated Christmas trees were dotted around the entire room. Although he had little money Chris was a generous host to Cave, who enjoyed visiting the apartment. One evening Chris asked him to put his drink down on a glass-topped table which had Christmas decorations stuck to it. As Cave looked at the tabletop Chris turned on a light which illuminated from beneath a multitude of pictures of naked women intermingled with the Christmas decorations. Other lights around the room were brightened and 'The Christmas Room' was transformed with previously undetectable images of girls from soft-porn magazines contained within glass boxes.

Among the regular visitors to Dresdener Strasse was Tony

Cohen, who had moved to Berlin and was now living in a squat named 'the ruin'. 'We had certain common interests, wicked things,' says Cohen. 'That's the first time I really got close to Nick, I think he liked having one of his old Aussie mates around, maybe that was good for him. He was opening up a bit. If he was out of it he'd go into his shell, go into his own mind, which of course was really good for him, because that's where his creativity comes flowing forth like nobody's business. I spent most of my time sitting in his room that he had upstairs, dribbling and bothering him in the middle of the night. He was speeding and speeding, forty-eight hours, three days, solidly writing night and day. He was obsessed. He had a .45 handgun that he used to play with, rolling it round his fingers, he really was getting a bit psychotic. The novel he thought was going to be in three volumes, possibly the size of the bloody Bible. I read a lot of it, he'd give me a sheet to look at. Some of it on long flights was just stunning . . . he called me his biggest fan. It was great to read, I think I helped him with a bit of Australian slang. In the end he just banned people from coming into the room.'

'There's a line in a Neil Young song, "I need a crowd of people, But I can't stand them day to day". Key artists understand that line straightaway,' says Chris Carr. 'Nick needs people but he allows his mind to think in its own time, rather than being pressured. Nick looks a lot, observes and lives in a different frame of mind to most people. There's the sense of the loner there. He doesn't just drift from place to place, he does it for a purpose. He needed to take his art further. He started to get consumed by the book and very few people had time for it. He didn't have the confidence at the time to just let it come. Nick was able to withstand great physical pain as well as great mental torment but in the end he needed help. His relationships and his art were tormenting him.'

To score heroin Cave would have to venture out of the Dresdener Strasse apartment to the 'Rauch Haus' squat building, also located in Kreuzberg. The Rauch Haus was mostly populated with hard-core anarchist punks, who had taken the concept of 'no future' to its logical conclusion. The government had vainly tried to pacify the militant anarchists by soundproofing the basement of the building and installing amplifiers and a recording studio for their use. Disgusted with the concept of being perceived as government-funded punk rockers, the anarchists had gleefully destroyed the studio upon its completion and sold all the equipment. Although drug dealers and a few of Cave's friends lived there, the occupants of 'the rat house', as Cave called it, were generally hostile towards him because they despised heroin and heroin addicts. When going to score, Cave, wearing a suit and tie, would screech into the forecourt of the Rauch Haus in Christoph Dreher's Mercedes Benz, revelling in the cold looks from the punks that greeted his arrival.

NOTES

1 Jonathan Romney, 'Angelic Conversation', *City Limits*, 17–24 August 1989.
2 'Nick's Gospel', *Evening Standard*, Metropolis section, 17 July 1989.
3 Mat Snow, 'Prick Me Do I Not Bleed?', *NME*, 23 August 1986.
4 Melanie Brellis, 'Nick Cave Up and Out in Melbourne and Berlin', *Tension*, December 1987.
5 Glyn Brown, 'The Killer Inside Me', *Sounds*, 12 July 1986.

12

Ghosts . . . of the Civil Dead

'Nineteen eighty-seven, it was a disastrous year,' sighs Mick
Harvey, one of the few protagonists to have any clear recollection
of its events. 'Any time anything happened it was a fiasco, total
chaos.' As Cave was still working on *And the Ass Saw the Angel*,
1987 saw little activity from The Bad Seeds apart from twelve
intermittent European concert dates spread throughout the year
and sporadic bursts of recording for the group's fifth album *Tender
Prey*. This disorganised state of affairs was in no small part due to
Jeanette Bleeker, who became Cave's manager towards the end
of 1986 and for most of 1987. Bleeker had convinced him that
she had applied for a government grant which would bestow
upon him the status of artist-in-residence in the city of Berlin.
She told him about letters detailing the considerable amount
of money he would eventually receive, together with his own
apartment and donated musical instruments.

Unbeknown to Cave, Bleeker had not even contacted the Arts
Council, but with the illusory promise of the grant she managed
to bind herself to him, becoming an almost permanent presence
at Dresdener Strasse. 'She was quite a spanner in the works for a
while,' Harvey continues. 'She was Nick's manager but she only
ever did anything in Germany. She just wanted to marry him,
basically. She'd tell you euphorically about dreams she'd had
where she was dressed in white and getting married to Nick.
You were meant to keep a straight face through this. God . . .'
Though she was disliked by the majority of his colleagues and

friends, Cave stuck by Bleeker, patiently waiting for her to get her act together. Unfortunately his faith was misplaced. 'He'll often like people that other people hate and this will almost be a point of pride,' says Jessamy Calkin. 'Jeanette Bleeker wasn't popular with most people I knew but he was proud he was involved with this person. He doesn't give a shit what other people think of them but that's not necessarily to do with their good qualities, though.'

The year had begun promisingly for The Bad Seeds. In Berlin on 10 February, they were filmed performing 'The Carny' and 'From Her To Eternity' in the remaining wing of a bombed-out hotel by Wim Wenders for his forthcoming movie *Himmel Uber Berlin* (*Sky Over Berlin*), also released as *Wings of Desire*. The renowned German director was an avid rock'n'roll music fan who had first heard of Cave's group through Olivier, a friend of the band's who ran a Berlin record shop named The Gift: 'We used to hang out there in the mornings after our sleepless nights,' recalls Blixa Bargeld. 'Wim's wife, the actress in *Wings* [Solveig Donmartin] is the ex-girlfriend of Olivier. Wim used to come to the shop to buy records. He'd ask Olivier what was interesting and he'd put packages together for him, that's how he heard about us.'

Originally Wenders had wanted The Bad Seeds to compose a song for a film he had conceived as the ultimate road movie, encompassing five continents, set in thirteen countries, with different groups representing each territory. To Cave's amusement The Bad Seeds were to represent Australia. 'Alarming, at least,' he told *Waves* magazine in 1985. 'His film is quite interesting in that it's set in 1990 – so we're supposed to write a song that The Bad Seeds will be playing in 1990. I suggested a Tom Jones cover but he kind of winced at that, so we'll have to come up with something original.' However, the epic road movie which Wenders and Donmartin had written in 1984 was proving to be a Herculean undertaking, so the director decided to return to Berlin to make a smaller-budget movie and his first German-language picture in ten years, with the veteran cameraman Henri Alekan and writer Peter Handke. Wenders' object was to create a film which captured what he perceived as the real Berlin that he felt other film-makers had missed.

'It's a very intense city,' he told *Blitz* magazine, describing Berlin as an island surrounded by land with a heightened sense of freedom because its occupants realised their liberty was so fragile. 'That's why a lot of musicians have stayed here. The city constantly feeds you with the kind of energy you need to make rock'n'roll, and also to make movies, write or paint. Berlin has that quality to gather together people who wouldn't be at home anywhere else.'[1]

To offer as many insights into Berlin as possible, Wenders devised the dramatic device of having two invisible angels, played by Bruno Ganz and Otto Sander, descending upon the city. Their vision is monochrome and they cannot taste, smell or feel, but they can move wherever they wish, freely observing and listening to the city's occupants' mundane thoughts and existential yearnings. Wenders also wanted the film to be a personal love story reflecting his relationship with Donmartin: Ganz's angel falls helplessly in love with Solveig Donmartin's lonely trapeze artist, prompting the angel's longing to become human and embrace mortality.

The music of Nick Cave and The Bad Seeds finally unites the lovers. As a mortal Ganz's character dejectedly meanders through the streets of Berlin looking in vain for the girl, whose circus troupe has just left the city, he spies a poster advertising a club performance by Cave's band that night. He remembers watching her in her caravan wistfully listening to 'The Carny' and hastens to the club. She sees him for the first time and they fall in love as Cave sings 'From Her To Eternity'. 'I was really delighted with the way Wenders fitted everything together like that,' admitted Cave in 1989. 'He was taking a lot of risks by trying to incorporate our group into what is essentially a fragile movie, a very slow, moody, aesthetic work of art. To put any rock band in there was taking quite a risk. I think the movie did help to fortify some unsung areas of our music, areas that people don't seem interested in talking about. It showed some positivity in our music, that it isn't necessarily dark, negative and cynical, which I feel very uncomfortable about it being described as.'[2]

'Nick is really a part of Berlin as long as he decides to be there,' Wenders told a journalist in 1988, describing how his music seemed to emerge from the landscape of the city itself before outlining his fascination with Cave's work. 'I feel that the way Nick deals with violence, death and horror has a whole different source to something like a movie such as *Angel Heart*. Nick is dealing with his preoccupations as if he is trying to get rid of them. He's dealing with them, not just using them gratuitously, and he's almost trying to exorcise them.'[3]

Throughout 1986 and 1987 Cave was filmed for a less exalted production, Peter Sempel's avant-garde underground travelogue movie *Dandy*, in which Blixa Bargeld had also been persuaded to perform. Dieter Meier of Yello, who appeared in the film, compared Sempel's non-narrative travelogue, which was initially entitled *Five Days To Wait For Death* and featured Cave's track 'Tupelo' cut to an image of a charging rhinoceros, to a Marcel Duchamp 'ready-made'. 'If someone compares my work with Duchamp I'm very lucky,' says Sempel. 'It's the same way of going about things. You work on this idea without any grand plans then you make a big puzzle out of it, and if you're lucky something good comes out of it or it doesn't. The spectator has to see that for themselves . . . It was Blixa's idea to bring Nick in. To tell you the truth I think Nick did it because Blixa was in it. On the other hand I did give him a lot of money.' During this period Cave was still desperately short of money to buy drugs and, thinking that Sempel's movie would never be theatrically released, he eventually capitulated to the director's requests to be filmed, performing in any manner he wished for 1,000 marks for a half-hour shoot.

His main scenes for *Dandy* were shot in his room at Dresdener Strasse in front of a large, lurid, green and red portrait of a girl with her legs open which dominated the room. The artist, Fredric Wall, whose work Cave greatly admired, was one of the few people he was unable to stop entering his room when he was writing his novel in the early hours of the morning. While Cave continued working, Wall would distractedly pace the floor toying with his collection of knives. During one nocturnal visit, for no apparent reason Wall thrust a knife into one of Cave's most treasured prints, of the Madonna held aloft by cherubs. Horrified, Cave leapt from his chair, grabbed the knife, held it to Wall's throat and threatened to kill him if he ever returned. The following day Cave found the word 'sorry' scrawled in large letters across a page of text he had just written.

Cave decided to perform for Sempel's film a new song he had just written, 'City of Refuge', based upon the Texas gospel blues singer Blind Willie Johnson's 1928 recording, 'I'm Gonna Run To the City of Refuge'. Impressed by Johnson's relentless guitar rhythms and harsh, insistent voice, Cave had decided to appropriate the original chorus into his own composition. Unlike Johnson's song, Cave's 'City of Refuge' implied that the sinner would find no redemption wherever he ran: 'You will beg for the end, But there ain't gonna be one friend, For the grave will spew you out'. 'I thought it was important having Nick singing in a film with an acoustic guitar, like a real blues singer somehow,' says Sempel. 'Although it's not technically perfect, it's very strong. When he first did it he just looked to the front and sang. I said, be more dramatic, lift your head up and open your eyes, then he did it. After filming, the cameraman said, Peter I still have a minute's worth of film left. I looked at Nick and said, have you any idea what I can do with forty seconds of film? and he said, "I'll show you how I play with my revolver."'

Having recently received many impassioned long-distance telephone calls from Cave, Anita Lane finally returned to Berlin from Australia on 10 April to be reunited with him. After uprooting herself from her life and boyfriend in Australia, she was confronted with an entirely different situation upon her arrival. 'Everyone was really desperate for me to come back because he was in trouble,' she says, 'and a lot of people were really scared. They were desperate for me to be there as someone he'd listen to. I was the only person that he ever really listened to or trusted. Which was weird because I was fucked up too but I could reach his conscience or something. So I came back but during the time that he'd rung me he'd got involved with this girl Bunny. I didn't know where I stood so we wound up with this very messy triangle. She was a very, very nice girl, really beautiful, but I was a bit jealous of her.'

'I think it was difficult for everyone,' says Jessamy Calkin. 'Anita came back because Nick said he wanted her to, but when she got there, there was Bunny. Nobody knew where they were. Bunny was young, tall, athletic, blonde and incredibly beautiful. She seemed very innocent and uncorrupted at the time but in a way she was more manic than he was. Bunny was obsessed with Nick but he really liked her as well. Anita was on the edge and was really unhappy.'

In London, at Trident Studios during the first week of June, Cave and Harvey completed their work on Anita Lane's poignant first EP, 'Dirty Sings', a project which she had first conceived in 1985. 'I did tell someone once about why I made that record but they were shocked and didn't print it,' she says. 'It was to do with being really desperately unhappy and wanting to die. I knew I had something. I told Daniel [Miller] I've got this life and I don't know what to do with it, I almost don't even want it, but I'm really talented so use me. I didn't want to be on a pedestal on the record. I wanted to talk to other girls. I kind of wanted to glorify insecurity rather than being confident and successful. I wanted some kind of equality between the emotions that are raised up for people to look at, to show other emotions that are equally as valid as confidence and control. I felt that I was going to die and I wanted to leave something behind, as a suicide note I guess.'

In Hamburg in July, Cave worked very closely for three weeks with Bronwyn Adams from Crime and the City Solution, editing and writing *And the Ass Saw the Angel*. 'They were never close before but became so,' relates Jessamy Calkin. 'She was never afraid to say what she thought. When I put the book on computer there were pencil marks in the margin from Bronwyn saying, "Yeah, what do you think this is?" Bronwyn has a fine-tuned mind for that sort of thing.' Cave would admit that Adams' contribution towards shaping the novel during these intensive weeks was invaluable, and that he was ashamed that he failed to credit her in the final printed novel. 'He's always said she was very helpful,' says Simon Pettifar. 'While he was working we never communicated as much as I would have wanted. Writers work in different ways. He'd send fifty pages and I'd send four pages of notes, mostly general points. When he was in London he'd bring a new chunk with him and we'd talk about it. It was all in fits and starts so it was difficult for me to get an overall view of the story because it was going off at tangents. The language in the final book is impressive because of the richness of it, but it was more the way it was used, his capacity for understatement, irony and humour. For a long time that was present but buried in what I was seeing. You got flashes of it, something turned beneath the surface of this very impenetrable prose. You'd see it, and what was obscuring it fell away as the novel developed.' For Cave, one of the most exciting aspects of having his central protagonist a mute in the harsh environment he had created was that he could almost invent his own elaborate syntax and invective. Totally alienated and frustrated, Euchrid would draw from a variety of language styles, an assortment of arcane words from the Bible, combined with the guttural slang of the cane workers, all assimilated and filtered through the mind of the misanthropic mute.

Because of their involvement with Wim Wenders, who had recently been awarded the prize for best direction for *Wings of Desire* at the Cannes Film Festival, The Bad Seeds were invited to perform live at the Bundesfilmpreisverleihung to be held in Berlin at the Ufa Gelande on 13 June. The centrepiece of the gala film festival celebrations was to be the presentation of a special prize for *Wings of Desire*, in front of an audience comprising the upper echelons of West German society, including such dignitaries as the head of the Bundesbank and the Minister for Culture. As guest artistes at this auspicious occasion, the group were allowed to bring thirty friends to the festival, all of whom had to submit their names and passport details two weeks before the event, due to the stringent security arrangements in operation. The invitation for Cave and friends to attend was a decision the festival organisers would live to regret.

'It was sort of a pinnacle of the year's endeavours, whatever they were,' laughs Mick Harvey. 'We [the band] turned up the day before to do the sound check. There were two TV channels there to televise the event; a cable station, who actually wanted us there, who were showing a continuous live transmission, and a national station, who were presenting a condensed broadcast. They wanted us to do five songs, which we worked out. During the course of the sound check they kept coming up and saying, "I think we're only going to do three songs now." Eventually they said, "Well, we want three songs, but we want them to be soft ones." We were, once again, presented with television and television people who are just the biggest bunch of arseholes in the world. They're just idiots. So we were just taking it on the chin because there was no way to argue with them. In fact, there was no point in arguing with them because if you want to do something different you don't tell them.' The group agreed to perform 'The Singer', 'Stranger Than Kindness' and 'Your Funeral . . . My Trial', which they dutifully played to the delight of all concerned, having decided amongst themselves that the following night they were going to play 'The Singer' followed by 'From Her To Eternity' and the only ever live performance of 'Scum'.

'So all our friends turned up on the fateful 13th,' Harvey continues. 'There was a free margarita stall . . . it doesn't take much imagination to realise what happened. I was paralytic after just two margaritas. They really were very strong. I was just out cold. They got me down on to the stage and I couldn't even get up on to a chair. I was lying on the stage with my bass on saying, "Just start the song and I'll play along." Fortunately, because of the song choices I could almost just stay on one note so I was vaguely relieved about that because as I discovered while I was playing, if I did anything out of the ordinary I found myself a bar behind the rest of the band. Everyone else was totally out of it and I've no recollection of what they were doing. Alex Hacke [of Einsturzende Neubauten and Crime and the City Solution] was jumping up in front of the cameras undoing his trousers. We did "The Singer" and "From Her To Eternity" but they didn't immediately pull us off, they just decided there was going to be a ten-minute commercial break, during which Blixa gave a dissertation to the audience about something or other. Then we played "Scum", a complete fucking shambles, probably quite funny on TV. Thomas Wydler's mother was watching in Switzerland.'

After twelve hours' sleep Harvey awoke with a splitting hangover, having been dragged home by Katy Beale, and finally summoned the courage to ring Dresdener Strasse in order to try to piece together what had happened the night before. He quickly realised during his conversation with Cave that he was in fact the hero of the hour, because he had actually been able to play and his indiscretions were minor compared with those perpetrated by other revellers throughout the night. Cigarette girls dispensing sample packets of Camel had been molested and terrorised. Olivier and Alex Hacke had been running around on the dance floor with tablecloths over their heads, leaping on to diners' tables, kicking crockery in all directions, leaving patrons trembling in shock. In a desperate bid to restore order, the margarita stall had been closed and Olivier had pulled a knife on a hapless employee to negotiate its reopening. 'Olivier's a good friend of mine,' says Tony Cohen. 'I helped him on a flip-out once. We staggered out of the Ex N Pop one morning, at midday, closing time. He was locking up and there was this poor little guy that Olivier didn't like and he just went up and belted him one. "Oh! Olivier, what are you doing?" A terrible thing. He was one of those people who'd just snap. I think he's all right now, from what I've heard.'

Having already been beaten up three times that night, Olivier had dived on to the ballroom dance floor, packed with society ladies dressed in their finest evening gowns, brandishing his blade at a man whom he thought had insulted Anita Lane. Lane herself was in hospital. After returning to Dresdener Strasse she had fallen through a glass coffee table during a heated altercation with Cave at six in the morning. 'It had been a complete mess,' says Harvey. 'There were articles about it in the German national papers: "Even The Bad Seeds and their wild fans couldn't ruin the occasion," or some such shit. I mean, obviously, if you just read between the lines, we caused a lot of trouble and everyone was very upset about it because the Minister for Culture's wife doesn't normally have to put up with that sort of behaviour. I think Wim Wenders thought it was really good. He was the darling of those people, at that time, but he had a healthy disrespect for that kind of society and what they really stand for, television and the whole set-up.'

Ten days later, at the Quartierlatin on Potsdamer Strasse, Cave performed a brief fifteen-minute set consisting mostly of covers of The Carpenters' songs, at a benefit concert for Olivier's record shop The Gift. Even throughout The Birthday Party era, he had always greatly admired Karen Carpenter's work, specifically her aching voice, which he thought revealed the tension between the material she was singing and her actual feelings of suffering. His backing band for this special event featured Mick Harvey on bass, Thomas Wydler on drums and Roland Wolf at the piano. 'It would have been great,' says Harvey, 'this funny, ridiculous cabaret performance, but Nick got completely stoned beforehand and sang thoroughly flat for the entire performance. The whole effect was ruined, but never mind, that's true, he did, I'm not just picking on him, that's exactly what happened.'

On 15 August, at the Knopf Music Hall in Hamburg, Nick Cave and The Bad Seeds, together with Die Haut, Crime and the City Solution, The Swans, The Butthole Surfers and The Fall, played the first of two ill-fated concerts organised and promoted by Jeanette Bleeker under the banner 'Kings of Independence'. Though the Knopf Music Hall was only a 2,500 capacity venue, the event was oversold by 1,000-odd tick-ets. The doors to the venue were suddenly closed, barring admission to an increasingly furious crowd clutching valid tickets. The volatile atmosphere outside the hall, exacerbated by people without tickets joining the throng, soon erupted into a full-blown riot as the crowd tried to storm the building. 'It was incredible,' says Wydler. 'They were rolling burning tyres towards a gasoline station across the street. The police came. We played really late, four in the morning. I had to play with two bands. I don't remember much about it but after we finished, going to the hotel I saw all these things burning outside. Exciting.'

Mick Harvey, recalling the rioters outside the building, says: 'They were a force to be reckoned with. They set fire to the PA truck and the adjoining gasoline station. Yeah, that just went up! It was a riot. Everyone in the hall just couldn't believe it. We tried to walk out the back door: "Don't come out, there's a riot." The backstage area was just so close, the air was just thick with smoke and sweat. There was nowhere to sit down for the bands and I was thinking it's going to be another five hours before we go on. So we were just stuck. The event was so hopelessly out of control there was hardly any point feeling indignant about it, about being misrepresented this way. You couldn't even yell at the people responsible because they were having to deal with much more pressing problems than us saying, "What the fuck are you going to do!" Afterwards the venue was closed down by the police but it's since reopened.'

The chaos continued as the bands moved on to Bonn for the second 'Kings of Independence' engagement. 'It was so disorganised,' Harvey continues. 'We went on at about 5.30 in the morning, got back to the hotel at 7.30 then got up at 8.30 to go to Bonn on this big coach with all the groups, with the exception of The Butthole Surfers and The Fall, who I think were touring at the time. By the time we got to Bonn in the afternoon everyone was completely fucked, drunk from drinking the night before and whatever else they were taking. I hadn't slept and I was probably drunk again. I just remember there was this huge table with all these people sitting around it, overflowing with glasses and bottles. I just stared at it for a while, I just wanted to turn it over. There was a guy there with some of our friends who was just a slimeball drugs person who I really didn't like and I just wanted to turn the whole thing over, which I did eventually, but I didn't know that their cocaine was all over it! That's what was going on backstage in Bonn.' After the gig, the hotel where the bands were staying was raided at five in the morning by police searching for drugs, because Alex Hacke was seen casually tossing glasses into the swimming pool from the balcony of his room. After sweeping through most of the bands' rooms, they arrested Kid Congo Powers when they discovered a used syringe left in his room by another reveller. The whole contingent were finally ejected from the hotel at seven in the morning because members of The Swans were throwing raw eggs at the reception staff in the lobby. 'Everyone was in tears the next day,' says Harvey, 'the girls, I mean, I don't think the boys were crying. With our life experience at that stage we were already saying, we'll look back on this and laugh.'

On 7 September, only a few weeks after the 'Kings of Independence' débâcle, The Bad Seeds began the first of many protracted recording sessions for the *Tender Prey* LP. 'Yes, *Tender Prey* took a long time,' says Blixa Bargeld. '. . . Altogether there was a lot of wasted time and a lot of illness. I can't really remember how *Tender Prey* is.' Once again Cave had been concentrating on his novel and initially had only slow melodic instrumental pieces to present to the band. These included 'Joy Ride', 'Mercy', which eventually evolved into a song on the completed record, and 'Alice', which became 'Watching Alice'. The following day the group worked on his interpretation of 'City of Refuge' and the foreboding 'Sugar, Sugar, Sugar': 'Sugar, sugar, sugar, I can't explain, Must I kill that cocksucker everyday'.

On 18 September the sessions moved to London's Trident Studios, where Cave celebrated his thirtieth birthday on the 22nd by working on another new composition, 'The Mercy Seat', which had evolved from a series of looped tapes of a bass guitar being hit with a pair of drumsticks, recorded during the previous sessions at Hansa. The circular cacophonous noise this effect produced inspired a set of chords, which in turn evoked a melody for Cave's lyric describing a prisoner in solitary confinement on death row contemplating his crimes and three systems of judgement: society's, God's and his own. As he awaits his execution in the electric chair he steadily becomes unhinged as he weighs the worth of even inanimate objects into either good or evil. 'It was all at a peak when we started *Tender Prey*,' recalls Tony Cohen, 'really hitting it, especially the speed, which was real motherfucker. *Tender Prey* was like the end of me for a while. "The Mercy Seat" for instance knocked ten years off my lifespan, just working on it. There was so much on there, to try and make any sense out of it, which is great you know. I think we mixed it about six or eight times. The vocals were very hard, getting a good vocal sound, the difference between Nick's talking and singing. Today I could do it in five minutes. I think me being very foggy didn't help.'

Three days later the band flew to Athens to play two dates at the Club 22. Cave had been very unenthusiastic about the shows, thinking they were a pointless exercise, and had wanted to cancel them. Despite an ecstatic response from the Greek crowd after the first gig, he initially refused to return for an encore, standing at the side of the stage muttering dire recriminations against the audience and the country in general, while taking another hit of heroin. Ten long minutes later he was eventually cajoled by Harvey into performing. The band's three-song encore closed with a riotous rendition of John Lee Hooker's 'I'm Gonna Kill That Woman'. As the song crashed to a halt, the rest of The Bad Seeds walked off but Cave remained, slumped across the monitors at the front of the stage, singing again, unaccompanied, the song's final verse before finally passing out mid-line. 'The Greeks were going crazy, thinking he was such a fantastic performer,' says Harvey. 'They were touching him and pulling his hair and we were standing at the side of the stage thinking, fifteen minutes earlier he was calling them a bunch of slimeballs and now he was their complete hero. Well, that's style, you've got to give it to him. I couldn't do it, he's got it. That was a pretty intense trip, quite good concerts as I remember.'

During October Cave flew back to Melbourne to portray, in his first role as an actor, the psychotic inmate Maynard in John Hillcoat and Evan English's prison movie, *Ghosts . . . of the Civil Dead*. Since the initial drafts of the script, the film's focus had radically shifted towards a political polemic graphically portraying how prison functions to further criminalise its inhabitants, who are then released to re-offend in the 'free' world. The prison system itself produces ever-escalating crime statistics, provoking society to demand yet more draconian policing and surveillance, provided by those with a vested interest in maintaining a fearful population of subservient consumers. 'There were some great scenes that Nick wrote that were cut,' says John Hillcoat, 'outside the prison a mass murderer being shown pictures of girls. That's a preoccupation of Nick's, the victim haunting the killer. In his version of "Long Time Man" I think it's interesting that the line, "She looked up at me and began to smile" is the most intensely, emotionally sung line of the song.'

Although the emphasis of the film had drifted from Cave's existential vision of prison as a metaphor for the human condition, he still felt a strong affinity with the script and its intentions. 'My social conscience is limited in a lot of ways; there's not much I feel angry about that doesn't affect myself quite directly,' he later stated, 'but the penal system as it is, and the whole apparatus of judgement, people deciding on other people's fates . . . that does irritate and upset me quite a lot . . .'[4]

The imagery associated with old Victorian prisons had completely disappeared from the script. The new Central Industrial Prison is situated in the middle of a desert in an unspecified country. The interior, triangular in design and colour-coded in garish yellows and violets, is divided into three containment levels with inmates wearing blue and orange uniforms. In General Population, prisoners have freedom of movement, watch television and hard-core pornography, trade goods and take drugs, to which the authorities turn a blind eye as the inmates are sedated. Administrative Segregation holds high-risk inmates with limited 'privileges', while Solitary Confinement is an abyss, a dark, empty cell for prisoners who fail to adjust to the institution. The guards oversee the prison from inside observation booths, through closed-circuit television cameras.

During 1986, Hillcoat, English and the project's main screenwriter, Gene Conkie, had undertaken a tour of Marion, a 'new-generation' prison in Illinois described as 'the new Alcatraz', where the conflicting stories from inmates, guards and administrators irrevocably changed the Australians' perceptions. Hillcoat and English then read an article about David Hale, a former correctional officer at Marion, in which he stated that a 'lock-down' (confinement of all inmates and withdrawal of all privileges) at the prison, which inflamed the tensions between inmates and guards, culminating in the killing of two guards on the same day, was a deliberate move by the administration to reinforce calls for the building of a new 'super-maximum' security prison. 'When we got in touch with him [Hale] via telephone and satellite, it got more like investigative journalism as we discovered more and more,' says Hillcoat. 'Out of that came numerous plot and thematic devices that we added to what we originally had. The deliberate perpetuation of violence in order to justify the "lock-down" was based upon the events at Marion. From

outside the administrators wilfully letting the situation increase.'
An officer, David B. Yale (portrayed by Mike Bishop), based upon
Hale, was incorporated into the script to recall the preplanned
escalation of violence.

Despite the change of emphasis towards the drama-documentary
genre, key characters, situations and narrative twists that Cave
had been instrumental in developing remained in the script.
The degradation of the 'new boy' Wenzil (portrayed by Dave
Field) as he vainly tries to establish himself within the prison
originated from Cave's script, as did some of the voice-over
dialogue. Maynard, the psychotic character Cave was to portray
with his long hair cropped and 'HATE' tattooed on both sets of
knuckles, who is introduced into the Administrative Segregation
Unit to further provoke the inmates, partly originated in the
singer's interest in a notorious self-mutilator, Gary Webb, and
the prisoner who incessantly ranted obscenities during his own
incarceration in the cells of the 5th Precinct in New York.

'We put the two characters together and that's what clicked,'
says Hillcoat, 'and Maynard formed a plot basis for the manipulation that was taking place in the prison. We let Nick develop
it. Maynard's line in the film, "Officer, come here, so I can
spit in your fucking eye", was what the guy in the New York
lock-up kept screaming. You have to draw on their [the cast's]
experiences. The whole cast was in a way type-casting. That's
why Dave Mason of The Reals was cast as Lilly, to embody
gentleness. I think there is a mutual admiration between Nick
and Dave, there are similarities, a very dry, pessimistic sense
of humour. We didn't want to turn it into rock'n'roll prison,
though. We wanted to have the characters believable, although
there were inside jokes, Maynard's ranting and raving referred
back to The Birthday Party. We did individual rehearsal sessions
with Nick, preparing him for what it was going to be like on set
in advance; he could have frozen.'

'Maynard was written for Nick,' says Evan English. 'We knew
he could do it. It wasn't out of his emotional range. He knew that
person. But we put him out on a limb because his character is the
only extrovert in the whole film, in that he expresses the insanity
of the situation and just can't stop expressing it. The script just

said, "Maynard enters cage: words to be decided."' Cave himself was very apprehensive about his first film peformance, as he had assumed that he would be appearing in a small cameo role rather than a key character in the narrative's development. 'I pray that it won't appear to be a rock singer dabbling in something that's out of his depth,' he told Melanie Brellis when interviewed on the set. 'Unfortunately, no one will ever be able to read a book by me, or see me in a film, or read about me robbing a bank without seeing me first as a rock singer, which inevitably makes it weak, pretentious and egotistical.'[5]

All the interior shots of the prison were filmed on a set constructed in a disused factory in Port Melbourne. During World War II the factory had mass-produced engines for fighter planes but its layout, and even its gate entrance, resembled a prison. Cave joined the set for three days of intensive shooting after only two days' rehearsal. Of a ninety-strong cast, only twenty-two were professional actors, the rest mostly composed of ex-convicts and a few former prison guards.

Peter Milne who, together with Hillcoat's wife Polly Borland, was one of the still photographers for the film, recalls: 'It was a very tense shoot, a lot of tension between Evan and John. It was the nature of the shoot. Three months after the film was finished some of the principal non-acting members of the cast ended up in jail again.' To heighten the already fraught atmosphere on set, Hillcoat segregated the still-uniformed cast for meals so the gulf between 'prisoners' and 'guards' remained. During the breaks Cave would size up the actors he would have to abuse, thinking of insults that would provoke the most extreme reaction.

'At the time we were filming, and even when we were writing, Nick was at his lowest in terms of drugs and all that sort of stuff,' Hillcoat continues. 'That's why Maynard, at that time, was closer to his inner character. I don't think he would have survived but he was blessed with a rock-iron constitution. The reason he's so good is there's so much tension there. He was on edge. There was so much building up inside him. It was explosive. David Hale thought Nick was one of the most convincing characters in the entire film. David Hale comes from the Midwest, he doesn't even know what punk is, means, any of that. Other people on the set thought Nick had just flipped out and these were guys who'd seen quite a lot. If we'd made him memorise lines it wouldn't have worked, most of it was improvised, Gene had written some guidelines that he put into his own words. The scene where Maynard mutilates himself in the cell and the picture he draws with the blood, that was all Nick. I guided him but when we filmed I just let him go.'

After filming was completed, a wrap party was held on the prison set, where trouble quickly flared. 'Polly's younger sister and brother turned up with about fifteen or twenty friends who'd been tripping at another party,' says Peter Milne. 'I later found out I was blamed for having invited them, which definitely wasn't the case. A situation occurred that shows something about the whole myth that surrounds Nick, which isn't of his invention but is something he has to suffer. The whole impression of The Black Crow King, this dark, brooding man, that completely ignores the wit, humour, intelligence and sensitivity in so much of his work. When people discover that Nick is a polite, courteous, genuinely considerate person with a sense of humour, it's as if that's some kind of shock. It shouldn't be because he's never presented himself as anything but that. Nick like everyone else was trying to relax after a gruelling shoot. Suddenly these two guys who'd gatecrashed the party started picking on him, saying that he was responsible for the whole junkie culture in Melbourne and how dare he make heroin glamorous. I mean, that's never been the case. When Nick had a drug problem he admitted it, he certainly never glamorised it. It got to the stage where one of these guys poured beer over his head and this of course got back to the *Melbourne Truth*.' 'PUNK STAR IN PARTY PUNCH-UP', thundered the tabloid, claiming that Cave had 'traded blows with members of the cast' at the party, and attributing to him the uncharacteristic remark, 'This bloke poured a glass of beer over my head and so I decked the bastard.'

The year ended as it had begun, in chaos and confusion. In late November The Bad Seeds were booked to play three dates in Italy, beginning in Pisa on the 27th. Mick Harvey, Katy Beale, and Tony Cohen and his girlfriend drove down to Pisa planning to take a holiday after the gigs. Cave and Bleeker, who were arriving on a cheap flight from East Berlin, were scheduled to meet them at the venue in Pisa on the day of the gig. Trouble began at the first border checkpoint to enter East Berlin, when Cave realised he had lost his passport. 'I can't possibly describe to you what it means to actually get into East Berlin, to the airport, without a passport. This was the Iron Curtain,' laughs Harvey. 'Somehow, because Jeanette was such a motormouth, she actually got him through.' It was only when Cave was checking in for the flight that he was finally turned away and he and Bleeker had to dash back to West Berlin to try to book another flight. 'Everything was running terribly late,' Harvey continues. 'I went to the Pisa sports centre where we were meant to be doing this gig, sound-checked everything, went back to the hotel, and everyone was waiting outside. It's eight o'clock in the evening already and we were still getting phone calls saying Nick was on a flight. Jeanette still got him through all the borders into Italy without a passport but too late for the gig unfortunately.'

After the last show, on the 30th in Turin, Harvey and Beale had to postpone their holiday in order to drive Cave to the Australian Embassy in Milan so he could be issued with a new passport to return to Berlin. 'At the embassy they said to Nick, "Right, here we have it: 1981 passport lost, 1983 passport destroyed, 1984 passport lost, 1986 . . ." They gave him a new one and said, "Look, if this happens again you're going to get a passport that effectively says you're mentally deficient." That gave him a bit of a fright, I think. Anyway, when he got back to Berlin he found his passport under his pillow where he'd put it for safekeeping . . . Nick wasn't in a very good condition that year.'

NOTES

1 Andy Black, 'Back to Berlin', *Blitz*, May 1988.
2 Karen Schoemer, 'Get Your Wings', *Option*, May/June 1989.

3 Virginia Madsen, 'Love Minus Zero', *Follow Me Gentlemen*, September/November 1988.
4 Simon Reynolds, 'Knight of the Living Dead', *Melody Maker*, 18 June 1988.
5 Melanie Brellis, 'Nick Cave Up and Out in Melbourne and Berlin', *Tension*, December 1987.

13

New Morning

Throughout December 1987 and January 1988, at various studios in London, the *Tender Prey* sessions dragged on. During the January sessions Cave was arrested for possession of 884 milligrams of heroin. He had tried to buy some methadone from a chemist with a legitimate prescription but the staff queried its validity and called the police. He was taken to Marylebone police station where he was cleared of trying to obtain methadone illegally; however, when he was subsequently searched the police discovered heroin on his person worth around £100. He was then subjected to a 'good cop/bad cop'-style interrogation in a vain attempt to elicit information about his supplier. He was eventually released on bail, but as he had been previously convicted and fined on similar charges it looked likely that when the case came to court he would receive a prison sentence. Taking legal advice, he realised that his only choice was to present proof at his trial that he was taking steps to curb his addiction by attending a clinic, the prospect of which filled him with dread.

Cave's already depressed mood darkened further when he read music journalist Chris Roberts' account of an interview he had given to *Melody Maker* three weeks previously. A fellow *Melody Maker* critic, Simon Reynolds, was about to interview Cave for the *National Student* magazine and a forthcoming piece in the music paper when he committed the error of showing him Roberts' cover feature, entitled 'The Lizard of Oz', which had been published that day. 'He had the paper, so I read it,' Cave indignantly told *The Age* the following month. 'Here was this guy who'd come to me all sort of humble and a bit awestruck, saying, "Great" and "Ha, ha, ha." He asked me all sorts of dull, meaningless questions, I just kind of ranted on and the article is so different to the way the interview was. I mean, he just paints himself as this sort of wisecracking guy just sitting there saying, "Sure, Nick" and "Ho, ho", and it's just one funny little insult after another, capping all my answers with his own bright remarks. This other guy [Reynolds] was exactly the same. He was really nice to me, he seemed like a nice guy, but I just couldn't trust him at all. He'd ask me a question and I'd just get about four words out but I just couldn't do it. That'll be reported . . . I can't even talk to them any more. I can't even put a sentence together any more, and they consider that I'm such an emotional wreck that it's not worth their while talking to me.'[1] He was so unforthcoming during Reynolds' interview that another meeting had to be arranged.

When Cave flew to Melbourne in February to continue work on the *Tender Prey* album and to rehearse for an eight-date tour of Australia, he was grabbed at the airport by plainclothes narcotics officers. He and his mother, who had been waiting for him, were taken to a police station, where he was subjected to a rigorous search. The police found nothing. Cave had been tipped off by Tony Cohen. A week earlier, Cohen had nodded out in the toilet of a plane and when it landed in Melbourne the door had to be broken open to free him. He had told the police that he was a member of Nick Cave's entourage and that Cave himself would soon be arriving. He was released as the narcotics officers thought there would be bigger fish to fry. The incident, coupled with his bust in London, did nothing to alleviate Cave's mounting sense of paranoia.

Tempers frayed while the group were briefly working at the Studio in Richmond. 'Nick punched me on the nose during a "Mercy Seat" vocal,' says Tony Cohen. 'He kept saying, "Fuckin' headphones ain't loud enough, turn it up!" so I kept turning them up and up until the feedback must have fucking fried his brain. I'm surprised he can still hear. He just marched in and went BOFF! I stormed out in a huff. Nick and I were pretty sick. Sessions had been starting six hours late because Nick and I were so sick because we hadn't scored yet. I got a lot more of the blame for that than I think I deserved, but anyway that's my opinion. All this was putting a lot of stress on Mick Harvey. I think a lot of the time Mick was seeing his friends killing themselves and that wasn't doing him a lot of good. He's quite an organised person and he was watching this complete ratbag situation going on around him all the time. It must have been horrible for him.'

The Australian tour ended in Sydney on 3 March and the final mixing of *Tender Prey* was at last completed on the 14th after an intensive seven-day session at the Power Plant in Melbourne. 'The actual making of that record was a mess, a real fucking mess,' recalls Daniel Miller, who had been anxiously following the album's progress from London. 'It was quite difficult but I always had total faith in Mick Harvey to get whatever was necessary ultimately out of the group, in terms of getting things done and organisation. Although things were hairy for a while I never lost that trust in him because I'd seen what he'd done over the years to try and keep things going.'

Two days later, Harvey, Blixa Bargeld and Cave started recording the motion picture soundtrack for *Ghosts . . . of the Civil Dead* at a small studio on Wimbledon Street in Elwood. 'From the earliest days the music was always considered,' says John Hillcoat, 'so Nick had a feel for the film. I gave him a tape of film soundtracks I liked, *Rosemary's Baby* was one, *Badlands* was another. Blixa and Mick are obsessed with film, so's Nick. We all loved Morricone's scores.' Bargeld found inspiration for the soundtrack from a photograph of Morricone at work in a studio, surrounded by a collection of zithers, flutes, cowbells, triangles and woodblocks. 'It was like he'd constructed a soundtrack out of this bag of instruments,' recalls Bargeld. 'As I've said, I'm not that wild about playing the guitar so I thought it was a good chance to do something different,' From a very minimal collection of instruments, including tin whistles, a harmonica and the guts of a piano, the trio created the sounds and refrains that would define actual locations and characters within the confines of the prison. One of the most evocative pieces Cave wrote for the score was the melody for the title theme, 'A Prison in the Desert', sung by Anita Lane, her childlike voice emphasising the absence of the female from the brutal environment, evoking an almost incongruous fairy-tale ambience.

Back in Berlin, throughout March and April, the domestic situation at Dresdener Strasse, from where Cave had started drug-dealing, steadily deteriorated. The flat had become the local shooting gallery for all and sundry who casually strolled into the building at all hours. Christoph Dreher's tolerance of his friend's activities was wearing thin as each morning he had to contend with yet another prone figure slumped over the toilet in the stairwell he shared with Cave. There had also been complaints from the Turks in the building next door. One day, while trying to write, Cave had become so irritated by the incessant crowing of their pet rooster that he lit a six-inch Chinese firecracker, which he lobbed over the wall in the general direction of the noisy fowl. An enormous explosion was followed by an ominous silence which was interrupted a few minutes later by the irate Turkish family furiously knocking on the front door. As Cave could not understand a word they were saying he was unsure whether his firecracker had blown its intended target to pieces or if it was merely in a permanent state of shock. Either way, the boisterous rooster never crowed again.

Having been threatened by the other residents in the square with eviction, Christoph Dreher politely told Cave that he had outstayed his welcome after someone smashed down the main gate to the apartments at four in the morning frantically trying to gain entrance to his room. Cave agreed that it was time to leave. He and Anita left Berlin, but not before he had visited all his drug-dealing contacts, obtaining on credit large amounts of heroin which he had no intention of ever paying for. For Cave, Berlin had lost the romantic allure that had so captivated him during the early eighties, primarily because he had witnessed too many friends succumb to the city's increasingly drug-orientated lifestyle and the pervading atmosphere of despair that came with it. He also perhaps resented the accusations from certain quarters of the city's underground that his presence had contributed considerably to the fashionableness of heroin. 'He'd exhausted

Berlin,' says Chris Carr. 'He left debts. If they'd asked him for less or hadn't basked in his reflected glory so much they wouldn't have felt so bad when he left.'

The only viable alternative to Berlin remained the then hated city of London, from which Cave had fled years before. Fortunately the couple could seek refuge with their friend Christina Birrar, a photographer who lived with her husband and two children in a spacious converted church in Vauxhall. Birrar proved to be very hospitable and understanding, never prying into their affairs, and turning a blind eye to their frequent volatile bickering.

After a relatively long absence Cave returned to the limelight. In May, Black Spring Press published *King Ink*, a collection of his lyrics for The Birthday Party, The Bad Seeds and others, coupled with lyrics that had never been recorded, plays from *The Theatre of Revenge*, prose pieces and, perversely, a short poem he had written at the age of thirteen entitled, 'Oh I Love You Much Too Much'. 'He wanted a small book that he could try me out on and it was always the understanding that he would then do the novel,' recalls Simon Pettifar. 'He thought a lyrics book was a cash-in job, he was never interested. Then suddenly he asked, he's very shy you know, "Do you think we should publish the lyrics?" as if he hadn't been hearing me for the last two years.'

'I'm a bit disappointed with how . . . thick it is. Or rather isn't,' joked Cave when he was asked to appraise eight years' work condensed into one slim volume which resembled a prayer book more than a collection of lyrics by a rock'n'roll singer. 'I thought I'd written a lot more than that. It's kinda concise and it seems to me that I've been waffling on for years and years. Still, I guess people like Bob Dylan and so on, they've got about twenty years on me and that's why their books are so big.'[2] *King Ink* received lavish praise not only from rock critics but from other, more unexpected quarters. 'He has plundered the heritage of rock'n'roll to come up with ballads that always place drama and bravado above personal confession or threadbare machismo,' wrote the literary critic of the *Melbourne Age*, Laurence White. 'What makes many of Cave's songs so good compared to the usual slurry of pop songs is their balladry; he is a teller of stories in the style of the old rock and blues singers, and his songs seem to come from that tradition. Cave convinces us that he knows the ropes and this lends his music the glamour of authority.' The volume also enjoyed commercial success despite the misgivings of retailers. 'I didn't want it to look like it had anything to do with rock music,' says Pettifar. 'Bookshops hated it: "Why is it in hardback?", "It's an odd size", "Where do we put it, is it poetry or rock music?", "If this is a book by a rock star, why isn't there a picture of the rock star on the cover?" They thought that was the only way it would sell.'

Cave received more critical hosannas when 'The Mercy Seat' was released in early June, while his private life spiralled further out of control. Matters came to a head when The Bad Seeds started gigging again in London and during a three-date tour of Europe in July. 'Nick was running amok a bit you know, he had to slow down eventually, we all did,' says Tony Cohen. 'It was at the National Ballroom gig in London [14 July] where they finally sacked me. That was the first gig I didn't mix and Victor [Van Vugt] came in. I turned up, got to the door, didn't go in and went, "Oh fuck it." It was just after that Nick came round to where I was staying at this squat with a girl smack dealer. He'd been coming round every day. Then I'd steal smack off her and stay at his place until it ran out and go back again. Nick and I were just sitting in this room together, stoned. Then after a while Nick sort of looked up at me and said. "This is fucked." I said, "Ah, I'm sick of this." He said, "I'm going into a clinic," and I replied, "I'm going back to Australia." And that's what happened, I stayed on my folks' farm for a few years drying out. That was one of the last times I saw Nick for a long time.'

A palpable undercurrent of tension before the first gig in Holland, at the Tivoli in Utrecht on 17 July, was aggravated by the presence of a music journalist, Jack Barron. 'He was with us all the time, watching,' says Thomas Wydler. 'It was really annoying. He was even backstage. I couldn't understand why Nick said it was all right. The whole situation was quite aggressive for that tour.' Victor Van Vugt recalls: 'Jesus, he was a pain in the arse. He just kept bugging people all the time, asking them where to buy speed.' Barron had been brought over by Chris Carr, together with photographer Bleddyn Butcher, to interview Cave for an *NME* cover story, supposedly concerning his forthcoming album. The journalist had a different topic of conversation in mind. Through loose talk Barron had learnt of Cave's decision to enter a clinic and saw the trip as an opportunity to expose the extent of the singer's addiction to heroin. The fact that Cave had never made a secret of his drug consumption and that it had been snidely insinuated in numerous articles was obviously of no consequence to Barron.

The following day, in Amsterdam, after the band had played a set at the Paradiso, Barron finally started his interview with Cave in the small hours of the morning in the lounge of the Museum Hotel. Throughout the day he had been shadowing Cave's movements but Cave had still managed to evade him long enough to slip unnoticed into the red-light district to score. Cave thought the interview was going his way, having nearly convinced Barron that a new song on the album, 'Deanna', was an autobiographical tale about a childhood girlfriend with whom he committed numerous robberies until she shot and killed a couple who had abused her in a religious instruction teacher's house.

In fact the song's subject matter did bear some relation to Cave's recent past. At a club in Melbourne he had met a charismatic and precocious girl named Deanna with whom he would enjoy a passionate, intense relationship. During their brief affair Deanna would exert a powerful influence over him. The physical intensity of the couple's mutual obsession, combined with their prodigious consumption of amphetamines, led them to shun the company of outsiders in her 'house on the hill' described in detail in the song's lyrics. The song spoke of a love that validated any antisocial or criminal act beyond the law and the moral dictates of society: 'We discuss murder and the murder act, Murder takes the wheel of the Cadillac, And death climbs in the back'.

Then Barron raised the subject of 'a secret personal project concerning his [Cave's] drug problem', Mortified, Cave insisted that he did not want to discuss the subject and that if Barron was going to mention anything about it in his article he would not utter another word, even bizarrely threatening to abandon his plans to enter the clinic. Barron replied that he was sorry that he could not give such a guarantee as it would be against the grain of his journalistic integrity. Hence the interview ended.

In the morning the group travelled to Hamburg, where Chris Carr explained to Cave over dinner that Barron's piece was a major *NME* cover story which could affect the sales of the album and that he had to finish the interview, whether he liked it or not. Cave reluctantly acquiesced on the condition that Barron did not ask any more questions about drugs, or drug clinics. The second interview took place in the singer's room at the VIP Hotel on Holstenstrasse. Barron's first statement was that earlier in the day he had telephoned his girlfriend, who told him that friends of hers had become heroin addicts in an attempt to emulate Cave's lifestyle. This remark was the final straw. Cave screamed abuse at Barron, shoving him out of the room before throwing a glass at him which shattered over his head. Slamming the door after him, Cave paced the room for a few minutes, his temper steadily rising as he contemplated Barron getting away with treating him like that. He then marched downstairs to find Barron bitterly complaining to Chris Carr in the restaurant that he had thrown a glass at him. Regaining his composure Cave walked up to Barron, reassured him that he was sorry and that they should discuss the whole situation outside. Barron agreed. Once on the street Cave apologised again, then punched Barron in the face and kicked him in the groin.

Cave grabbed Barron's overnight bag, flinging its contents around as he searched for the interview tape, while the journalist offered to hand it over if it meant that much to him. Carr finally managed to intercede, admonishing Cave for his behaviour and reminding him that Barron could still write his piece from memory. 'After the whole Barron scenario I went up to his room and I embraced him [Cave] and we just fucking laughed,' says Carr. 'We knew that he [Barron] had crossed the line. He was sitting in this car fairly chastened, to say the least. I was biting the inside of my mouth trying to stop laughing.' Mat Snow remembers 'Bleddyn telling me how Jack Barron lived in fear for a long time of running into Nick Cave. Cave was rather tickled by this idea, even though he had no time for the guy. He wouldn't go to any lengths to take revenge. He'd got over that phase.'

In London, on 1 August at Great Marlborough Street magistrates' court, Cave pleaded guilty to possessing 884 milligrams of heroin. He was given a conditional discharge for eighteen months and ordered to pay £15 court costs. Brian Spiro, his solicitor, had told the court that his client was facing his drug problem and was starting on 4 August a two-month residential course for detoxification, followed by psychological counselling, at the Broadway Lodge Clinic in Weston-super-Mare, Avon. Spiro convinced the court that Cave, described as 'a musician employed by a record company and earning £5,000 a year', had previously tried to register with a doctor for treatment in the UK but had experienced problems because he had no permanent address in the country. 'It was during this difficult period that Mr Cave bought the heroin,' said Spiro. 'While he was endeavouring to legitimise his situation he was desperately in need. Mr Cave has made great inroads towards rehabilitation, but there is still a long way to go. It is going to cost him £4,000 from his own private funds to register at the clinic, and the treatment will really put him to the test.'

Now living alone in a small flat in Queensway rented by Mute, Cave was still extremely hesitant about entering the clinic, though he realised there could be no turning back. The thought of a life without drugs was completely foreign to him. The novel was uncompleted and he feared that when he eventually emerged from detoxification he might loathe the manuscript he had written. He had grave doubts as to whether his creative drive would remain intact. 'I remember going up Queensway with him,' says Jessamy Calkin, 'and every shop we went into he'd be nicking make-up for Anita and all this other stuff that he didn't actually want. I was standing twenty yards away and I could see what he was doing so I was convinced the people in the shop could too. He was just prevaricating, he was stoned and winding me up. It wasn't so literal as "I'm doing this so I'll get arrested and then I won't have to go to the drug clinic." It wasn't like that, but he was taking so many drugs at that point it was almost like he was trying to alter the course of fate in a way. He wanted to change what was inevitably going to happen to him. He was just pushing it, he was seeing how far he could go.'

On the afternoon of 3 August, Mick Harvey was patiently awaiting Cave's arrival at Mute's offices on the Harrow Road. Harvey had planned to film Cave performing against a white wall in an office in the building for a video he was directing for 'Deanna', the next Bad Seeds' single. He had hoped to use the natural daylight that streamed through the window but by the time Cave eventually staggered into Mute it was nightfall. 'He'd just been running around doing as many drugs as he could before he went into the clinic,' recalls Harvey, 'and all the natural light had gone. So he ended up looking really dark and grainy in the video because that was all the light that was left. Then I had to try and shoot everyone else the same way, which was pretty impossible to achieve. The whole exercise was fairly painless but some members were tinted a bit yellow or green, which was a bit weird.'

'Trying to get Nick into that clinic,' says Jessamy Calkin, 'my God, it was a nightmare. I'd often tried to persuade him to go into one. I'd taken it upon myself to get him on the train and into this place. He was doing a lot at the time. I thought, I've got to go to his flat this evening to make sure he gets up the next day. I got there and the light was on but no one was answering the door, I was ringing all these people up, and I kept thinking . . . Finally I managed to get in. He overdosed twice while I was there. I thought he was going to die. It was very worrying. When he came round he kept saying, "I'm all right." He was sort of enjoying that. I was in such a state but he wasn't worried at all. The next day I got him on the train and as it pulled out Nick said, "Why do I have to do this, Jessamy, why can't people like me the way I am?" It was so sad with his head poking out of the window.'

The first days at Broadway Lodge were extremely painful for Cave, who was awoken at seven each morning feeling so sick he could hardly walk. When he arrived he had been placed on an intensive methadone programme, which was curtailed after only six days and should have caused him minimal physical pain. However, he had failed to inform the clinic that he had been taking methadone for the past six months. Methadone addiction requires a longer detoxification period and Cave's detox was consequently lengthened by a further six days, a rare occurrence at Broadway Lodge where normally no pleading from a patient would change the prescribed withdrawal programme.

'I went to see him a week later and he was strutting around in his suit like he owned the place,' recalls Calkin. 'He hadn't detoxed yet, he was still taking pills. Everyone loved him and he was chatting and communicating, doing all the things he wasn't meant to do. I rang him up there once and he said we're not going to be on the phone very long. There was this guy in the background saying, "Nick, are you on the phone, are you talking?" Nick replied, "No, I'm practising, fuck off!" Nick was amazed because he'd been assigned to the counter selling books about drug abuse when the visitors came in on a Sunday. He said, "God, nobody buys any." He was sitting there, white, thin and slightly sweaty. He wasn't a very good advertisement. He adapted incredibly well in there. I was surprised because out of all the people I know I thought he'd take really badly to that environment. Although he wouldn't admit to it now, he thought it was the best thing he'd ever done, in terms of being able to stand up and communicate with people.'

Mick Harvey reflects: 'One tendency that Nick has is to rewrite history from his current perspective. He tends to describe what his motivations were then through the perspective of what his motivations are now. In 1987, during *Tender Prey*, he was getting so fucked up but now he sees it as being confused about what he wanted to do in finishing the record, recording in four countries and half a dozen studios. He can't see that his drug addiction was having an effect. At the time, in 1988, it was affecting his work, that's when it had to stop because up until then it hadn't. If that wasn't the case he'd still be using now. I think it also had a lot to do with why the book wouldn't take form, why it dragged on. Nick, you see, would argue that a lot of the creative aspects of it were inspired by it, which is valid, but it affected ordering what he had created. That was the problem. He couldn't decide whether what he was doing was good or bad and he couldn't even look at it again, or on occasion even be able to find it. It had all just turned to mayhem. A lot of people just let it take over but Nick would never let that happen.'

Jessamy Calkin continues: 'In there Nick had to get up really early and make his own bed and do menial work. It's to break down the ego and it's also to make you understand that you are powerless against the addiction, so you don't feel guilty about it. It doesn't make you morally wrong and to help you stop hating yourself which is an intrinsic part of the treatment. You're suffering from an addictive personality which you have to face. It's also to get you to admit that your life has become unmanageable and you can't cope.'

During his second week at the clinic Jack Barron's *NME* cover story, dramatically entitled 'The Trials of Nick Cave', was published, coupled with a prominent news story in the paper giving details of his trial and subsequent admission to an unnamed clinic. 'Aussie Star in Clinic After Drug Bust' ran the *Melbourne Truth*'s headline for the story, culled entirely from the *New Musical Express* piece. Barron's own depiction of events outside the hotel in Hamburg was as follows: 'I'm stunned. Reeling. "You're nothing but a shiteater," he shrieks, taking a scythe with his fist at my head. He'll never get a gardening job chopping down weeds, let alone collecting my skull. It misses.' Barron's questions ranged from 'Do you think you're lyrically funny at all?' to 'Do you feel that you are grotesque like some of your characters?' (to which Cave laconically replied, 'Well, no, I don't actually feel that'), while the double standards of the exposé were all too self-evident. 'Someone doles out that vitamin known as speed,' Barron wrote. 'I don't refuse the offer.'

For weeks after its publication the Barron article was slated on the paper's letters page by outraged readers incensed by its sensationalist style. Barron even received death threats from the more committed Cave fans. 'Well, they're my best fans, and I take this opportunity to thank them,' Cave later joked to Jonathan Romney. 'Unfortunately, I don't think any of them will ever carry it out . . .'[3]

On 19 September, *Tender Prey* was at last released and fever-ishly hailed as a masterpiece by the British music press: 'If you or I retain any doubts about Nick Cave's artistry, they should be banished forthwith. *Tender Prey* is a circumstantial classic,' wrote Chris Roberts in *Melody Maker*, while Sean O'Hagan admitted in the *NME* that, 'I once, around the time of *The Firstborn Is Dead*, called Nick Cave a miserabilist which, in retrospect, was an injustice . . . The on-going reincarnation of Saint Nick remains one of contemporary pop's most intriguing rites of passage.' In their haste to at last acknowledge his talents and perhaps make amends for their previous backlash, coupled with embarrassment over the moral concern that had been expressed about his private life, the critics' reaction to the LP overlooked the impressive body of work that Cave had already produced since 1984. 'I've come to really like it,' says Mick Harvey of the LP. 'It's like Tom Waits' *Rain Dogs* or something. It's a mixed bag, very weird.'

The album's diverse collection of songs reflected the record's erratic recording history, covering an eclectic array of musical styles, ranging from the lush Bacharach overtones of 'Slowly Goes the Night' through the bacchanalian sixties garage punk stomp 'Deanna', in part a reinterpretation of 'Oh Happy Day', to the humorous blues 'Up Jumped the Devil' with its fugi-tive protagonist 'Doomed to play the villain's part'. After the confessional despair of the ballad 'Mercy', a reworking of the John the Baptist story, and the portrait of the alienated voyeur in 'Watching Alice', it was inadvertently fitting that the album should close with the stately redemptive tones of the country gospel 'New Morning'. Cave seemed to be declaring that his indefatigable stoicism would always carry him through whatever tribulations were set before him.

Some of the songs on the album, such as 'Watching Alice' and 'New Morning', indicated that Cave was perhaps moving towards a more direct lyrical style, less rooted in narrative, in sharp contrast to his previous material. This would prove to be the case for his next album. 'All the songs that I really love by other people are just incredibly simple,' he said in 1989. 'Songs like "Bridge Over Troubled Water" or "Knocking On Heaven's Door". They're so sublime and simple. I would really like to be able to write some very simple lyrics.'[4]

On 22 September, after seven weeks at Broadway Lodge, Cave re-emerged into the world sober and somewhat frightened. The fact that he had already agreed to undertake a daunting twenty-one-date European tour to promote *Tender Prey*, beginning on 28 September in Helsinki, had caused much consternation at the clinic. Though pleased with his recovery, in the staff's eyes the rock'n'roll scene was synonymous with drug and alcohol abuse, and they were convinced that he would soon slip back into dependency if he embarked on a long tour so soon after treatment. He had been urged to listen to the advice of the other patients, his 'support system' as they were termed, who voted that he should not go. He rejected their reasoning, arguing that if other people could return to their occupations why could he not return to his? Performing and creating music was his *raison d'être* and he was not going to let anything, or anyone, stand in his way. He felt that if he remained inactive for any length of time his resolve would dissipate more quickly than if he was preoccupied. 'Me, Anita and Kid Congo picked him up from the station,' recalls Jessamy Calkin. 'It was his birthday. He appeared much more humble. He'd gone on about being brainwashed and I'd say, well, drugs are brainwashing too, it's the same, you behave differently when you're on drugs. He was still disrespectful of the norm and the way people might expect him to behave now that he was clean.'

Within three days of leaving Broadway Lodge Cave was once again facing the media. 'I thought I'd be emotionally and spiritually bankrupt after the experience,' he confessed to Nick Kent in an interview for *The Face*, 'but I actually feel much the same about most things, surprisingly enough, only mentally much clearer. My attitudes towards life haven't changed. I've just got a melancholic bent to my character.' He candidly voiced his own dissatisfaction with *Tender Prey*, which he described as 'one long cry for help', before admitting that for the past three years he had been in a narcotic-induced, emotionally somnolent state: 'I don't think I've ever been able to be honest about the way I feel about things because I've been totally numb. Best friends of mine have died and all I've felt is guilty that I couldn't feel anything. That's maybe why I wrote in the third person. Maybe all along I've been articulating how I should feel without feeling it.'[5]

For the second time in a year Cave would be the subject of a *New Musical Express* cover story interview, although the article would not be published until February 1989. On this occasion, though, he would be sharing the limelight with two of his contemporaries, his old friend Mark E. Smith of The Fall and Shane MacGowan of The Pogues. The interview, conducted by Sean O'Hagan and James Brown at the Montague Arms in south London, was the second in a series of pieces the paper had devised under the heading '*NME* Summits'. The objective in bringing together these three diverse talents for an interview seemed vague. 'The idea, I presume, was to get three very strange people, people who seem that way to the general public I might add, and see what would happen,' sniggers Shane MacGowan. 'It almost degenerated into a punch-up. There was meant to be a whole series of these *NME* Summits but I think that this one finished them off for good.'

Cave was very apprehensive about the whole affair. Understandably, there was no love lost between him and the *NME* after the paper's sensationalist coverage of his private life, and he felt that he had nothing to contribute to any discussion about contemporary music, in which he had virtually no interest and knew next to nothing about. He was still unsure of himself after his experience in the clinic and adjusting to his new hard-fought state of total sobriety. He also wondered how Mark E. Smith, with whom he had always enjoyed a volatile relationship, would react to him, as they had not seen each other for a couple of years. Against his better judgement, however, he agreed to participate in the interview as he had always wanted to meet Shane MacGowan. He was in awe of MacGowan's outstanding vocal and lyrical talents as the lead singer/songwriter and driving force behind The Pogues' spirited reinterpretation of Irish folk music combined with the energy of punk.

MacGowan himself agreed to take part in the Summit because he had always greatly admired Cave's work in The Birthday Party and The Bad Seeds, and was similarly intrigued by him. 'I hadn't met him before,' says MacGowan, 'and I was fascinated to meet him to find out what the fuck he was like. What's a person like who comes out with the kind of stuff that he writes, you know what I mean?' MacGowan had avidly followed Cave's career since 1981. 'I saw The Birthday Party in the early eighties and I was really knocked out because they were really like a mixture of The Sex Pistols and The Pop Group, two of my favourite bands who had broken up. That was just the music, then when I checked out the lyrics, with all that Catholic lunacy, that really appealed to me as an Irish Catholic. His obsession with damnation. They were on the telly a lot and I was working in a record shop so I used to get the records in, buy the lot. The guy looked and acted like he was completely insane and he was really taking rock'n'roll to its ultimate conclusion. That was the thing about Nick Cave, for me he embodied rock'n'roll and he was the only one around in the early eighties doing it. Everyone else was so fucking vapid, it was a complete and utter cultural wasteland, which is why The Pogues started.'

When Cave, Chris Carr and Bleddyn Butcher arrived at the bizarrely decorated pub, with its mock Gothic-style interior featuring skeletons astride penny farthing bicycles and stuffed animal heads adorning the walls, they were informed that MacGowan had not yet arrived. After exchanging greetings with Smith they ordered a round of drinks and awaited his arrival. When MacGowan finally appeared, he seemed a little the worse for wear. 'Shane was off his tree,' says Carr. 'He'd done some Ecstasy and had drunk a bottle of whisky on the way down. Shane had a cocktail of drugs on offer, then Nick announced that he was clean. Shane replied, "You can't do that to me, man! Not you!" and promptly disappeared into the toilet.'

When MacGowan staggered back to their table the Summit commenced. 'I was out of my brains, Cave was dead straight, drinking tea, and Mark E. Smith was pissed on bitter and very belligerent,' says MacGowan. 'It must have been really difficult for Nick but I wasn't in that position, you know what I mean.

We were ranting and raving and Nick was very quiet that day. I was amazed how together he was, considering. At the time I was really pissed off with touring and I was going on about that in the interview, and he said, "Well, why don't you just stop?" and I couldn't think of a good reason because I was on the treadmill and you can't get off it. Nick turned out to have a savage wit. He's an intense person. It was a great interview, two soul brothers and Mark E. Smith. Cave was winding both of us up, he basically instigated the fight between me and Mark Smith. He was shit-stirring, seeing how far it was going to go. Mark E. Smith was saying things to me I couldn't let him get away with, stuff about Ireland and the British Army. Sean O'Hagan went loony as well, he's from Armagh, a Catholic. Nick was enjoying it as it got more and more intense and the reporters joined in and I started going barmy.'

The *NME* summit had produced very little from its participants and had quickly degenerated into a nonsensical farce, but from that initial meeting Cave and MacGowan would steadily forge a lasting friendship which would eventually result in a successful musical collaboration. 'I like the way he's taking the piss as well, you know what I mean,' says MacGowan of Cave. 'He doesn't take himself too seriously. He's got a brilliant sense of humour and that really comes across in his lyrics. Some of them are fucking hysterical.'

After the clinic, there was a semblance of order and organisation in Cave's lifestyle and career. During his last day at the clinic Anita Lane and Kid Congo Powers had finally found an eminently suitable tour manager, Rayner Jesson, who had undergone a similar rehabilitation programme to Cave and who could empathise and help with the problems the singer would be facing performing sober on stage for the first time in his life. The redoubtable Jesson would prove to be an invaluable asset to both Cave and the group, gradually shouldering many of the organisational responsibilities that had for so long fallen solely to Mick Harvey. Cave and Lane had also been reunited, but living together in Evan English's home in Clapham, south-west London, their relationship became progressively strained, much to their dismay. The fact that Cave had been advised in rehabilitation to sever all ties with his partner – the rationale being that he might project his problems with addiction on to the relationship itself, becoming totally dependent on her – undoubtedly placed considerable pressure on the couple. 'I saw them a lot when they were living with Evan,' says Jessamy Calkin. 'Nick and Anita were very nervous. They'd had ten years together and it was very tricky for them.'

Four days after arriving back in London, Cave was back on the road with The Bad Seeds. Though anxious about the tour, he also felt exhilarated that he was returning to the stage, an arena where he now felt more confident in his ability to captivate an audience and be able to draw strength from their applause. For so long he had despised his profession, feeling guilty that he was still involved in rock'n'roll, which he considered to be on the lowest rung of his then hierarchical view of the arts. He still retained his loathing of the machinations of the music industry itself, but slowly his attitudes towards the medium of rock'n'roll music were changing. 'To go on stage and make a whole audience feel a certain way, to make them experience your emotions, the way you feel about things . . . that's pretty incredible really,' he would comment two years later.[5]

Despite the fact that he could now look at himself and his work with a degree of clarity, in some ways his life was as chaotic as it ever had been, with perhaps insurmountable problems still to be faced. 'I remember the first Berlin show [Tempodrom, 3 October] after he left the clinic,' says Edzard Blum. 'The show was brilliant but dealing with old friends he was very insecure. I was backstage and he didn't even look at me, or a lot of other people. I didn't talk to him until the end. Some guys were saying, "Hey, Nick, you still owe me two hundred marks," and other fans were saying, "Please don't ask him for this now," like they were disturbing a holy man, or something. Nick quickly became very agitated and swiftly handed out the money to the people. It was like he was telling the fans to be quiet by doing that because you could tell that he felt a bit guilty about the way he had left Berlin, but everyone has forgiven him because we know how people become when they are in that state. It doesn't count.'

NOTES

1 Gideon Flaigh, Nick Cave interview, *Melbourne Age*, February 1988.
2 Simon Reynolds, 'Knight of the Living Dead', *Melody Maker*, 18 June 1988.
3 Jonathan Romney, 'Cave Art', *City Limits*, 17–24 August 1989.
4 Karen Schoemer, 'Get Your Wings', *Option*, May/June 1989.
5 Nick Kent, 'Edge of Darkness', *The Face*, November 1988.
6 Jon Wilde, 'Nick Cave the Prodigal Son', *Melody Maker*, 17 March 1990.

14

São Paulo

Through October 1988 the European tour passed off without any serious incidents, with Cave still resolutely sober at its close on the 27th after two sold-out dates at the Town and Country Club, London. In Europe, where 'The Mercy Seat' and *Tender Prey* were proving to be The Bad Seeds' best-selling records to date, the encouraging reaction from the audiences had galvanised Cave's spirits, inspiring him to give compelling performances. 'I know now that the way I used to feel about the audience and the way I thought they felt about me was totally unrealistic,' he admitted to *Sounds'* Ann Scanlon after the Paris gig at the Elysée Montmartre, in one of the few interviews he granted to the media during the entire tour. 'It was all filtered through my own disgust with myself. A couple of arseholes shouting at the front could almost destroy an entire performance. I'd immediately feel put off by it. This audience doesn't deserve anything. Fuck this! – and I'd go and sulk up the back of the stage.' His misgivings about his previous relationship with his audience did not extend towards his relationship with the press. 'I think my feelings towards the press are completely justified. The situation has arisen where I find I can't really be honest with the press, or at least with certain papers, because the whole system of trust has broken down. And I don't know how it could possibly be repaired.'[1]

In February 1989 The Bad Seeds were back on the road again for an eighteen-date North American tour, commencing in Philadelphia at the Chestnut Cabaret on the 7th. For their most extensive tour of the continent yet undertaken they were accompanied by Uli M. Schüppel, a young German film student then studying at the German Film Academy, who wanted to make a *cinéma vérité* film of the group's progress through the United States as his final degree film. 'He had never been to America and he decided two weeks before the tour if he could make this film,' says Blixa Bargeld. 'I thought it was a bit unfair because I wanted him to do a film about a Neubauten tour. The whole idea behind it was *Don't Look Back* by D. A. Pennebaker. I showed it to Uli and I said I want this approach. Just a totally invisible camera person being around. Just backstage and sidestage and not shot from the audience. Hotel rooms.'

Mick Harvey was the co-producer of Schüppel's documentary, aptly entitled *The Road to God Knows Where*: 'Four weeks of shooting with no lighting, with a cassette player as the sound source. There was very little money. The film doesn't keep picking out the spectacular parts of the tour, which is an important point. Nick became the focus of attention, naturally, as he always has to do the chores around any tour. Uli wanted to make a film about all the characters involved but on tour a lot of the characters take a back seat. Me and Blixa were more present than some of the other people. It's good that it's not some glamorisation of the rock'n'roll lifestyle because those films usually are. That film's really the way it is, it's quite mundane. Uli found the mundane things that are interesting.

'A lot of people in Berlin when they saw the film said that Nick was aware of the camera all the time and that he wasn't being himself. They can't believe that's him, and if he's aware of the camera all the time, that's just the way he is. He's always aware of everybody around him and he's aware of being the centre of attention all the time. The camera being there had no effect on his behaviour at all, it's like having a person there that he's playing to. He was being very natural for the whole tour.'

Schüppel's black and white documentary, which received its world première at Manchester's Olympic Film Festival on 29 June 1990, captured perfectly with its long takes and slow pace the arduous drudgery involved in touring a continent which had yet to respond to The Bad Seeds with the same fervour as Europe, Australia, Israel and Japan. Rather than focusing on the brief moments of cathartic release that performing can bring to a musician on tour, Schüppel's camera unflinchingly followed Cave through a succession of amusing encounters with journalists, photographers and unhinged fans. 'One thing was clear to me from the beginning,' Schüppel has stated. 'I did not want to make one of those music films with quick rhythmic cuts from one slick scene to another, shots of monumental concerts or musicians as exaggerated mythical figures.'

Visibly still a little unsure of himself on his second 'dry' tour, Cave deals with the promotional routine with his customary caustic humour, often throwing sly, conspiratorial glances towards the camera, perhaps relishing the opportunity of presenting himself openly without the machinations of the press. In a particularly tortuous scene a young female reporter from an LA weekly conducts an awkward interview with the singer. The obviously nervous journalist's first question seems to ramble incoherently for an eternity: 'Em, seems like there's an interest in . . . I guess inspirational qualities . . . this, em, kinda like southern white trash kinda guy that goes . . . em, that kind of image of that kinda guy that so many songs are written about . . . Seems like you have that kinda, em . . . Sometimes that vein kinda comes up in different songs . . . eh, some particular . . . just one of the things you find interesting, or . . .' Cave, who has been dejectedly staring at his hotel room coffee table throughout, senses that her final pregnant pause might indicate that this is his cue to respond to her stream of semi-consciousness. 'Well, yeah, I guess I do find that interesting,' he mutters wearily, suppressing a wry smile. A portrait shot of Cave is required to accompany the article. In the hotel room Cave robotically offers his profile first to the extreme left, then right, as if he is posing for a police mug shot. The photographer, who has been setting up his equipment as if preparing for an execution and who obviously knows nothing about his subject, asks Cave if he likes being photographed.

During the preparations for a television interview the interviewer enquires of Cave if he has contributed any music to Wenders' *Wings of Desire*, because 'the music is all over the place in that thing'. At first Cave frowns with annoyance then he senses the comedic potential of the situation and informs the reporter that he and the band actually appear in the film's final reel: 'Haven't you seen the film?' he enquires with mock sincerity, luxuriating in his inquisitor's embarrassment. 'Pretend I haven't asked that question, I'll ask that again when we get rolling,' comes the reply.

Cave's temper finally snaps when for the umpteenth time a venue manager has disregarded the agreed contract and has provided substandard PA equipment. 'Well, it was OK for Devo and A Flock of Seagulls,' comes the preposterous reply from the venue manager to their enquiries. Exasperated, Cave screams, 'I don't give a fuck about that. If it doesn't get any bigger we're not playing,' and storms out of the venue. During a similar altercation concerning the PA provided at a venue in Oregon, the indomitable Blixa Bargeld is unleashed upon the unsuspecting promoters. 'They actually called me in for getting into an argument with them,' laughs Bargeld. 'They knew I was going to yell at them. It's something that happens in America all the time at about almost every gig. You do this over and over again. It's OK in LA or New York but everywhere else it's bullshit. You get there and no one cares what's in the fucking contract. They save money on your back. Once you're there, you'll play. The film actually ran out when one of the guys said to me, "You can't tell me anything. I studied music." That's when I really got angry. That was too much! . . . There was a great scene at a post-modern burger/truck stop place. Uli filmed the band's bus driver talking to his boss on the phone, saying, "They hate me! They hate me! I want to get off this job." They came out from the truck stop and said, "You can't film here, you're not going to use this." Well, this scene wasn't in the film even though it was fantastic.'

Despite *The Road to God Knows Where*'s poor recorded sound quality, which necessitated the use of subtitles, Cave was very enamoured of Schüppel's documentary. 'I actually think it's a very, very sad film, in its way,' he told *Hot Press*. 'I really like the film, and I like the bizarre communication that comes across between the group and I like its pace very much. Just how slow and tedious the whole film is reflects directly how slow and tedious that particular tour was at least. It is a very accurate document. That film was showing just what it's like for us in America. We have far less control over the quality of our performances there than we do in Europe, simply because we're more popular in Europe and we can afford to have our own PA, but in America it's all up to the gods really.'[2]

One notable episode Schüppel was unable to record on film was Cave's first Hollywood audition, for the role of a psychotic serial killer from beyond the grave, the Pentagram Killer. The movie itself was a dismal B-grade horror picture entitled *The First Power*, released the following year and starring Lou Diamond Phillips as Detective Logan, who enlists the aid of a female psychic in ridding the world of an evil immortal killer, loosely based upon LA's infamous Night Stalker, Richard Ramirez. One can only wonder why Cave decided to audition for the role, which had been offered to him. He loathed the script, written by *The First Power*'s director, Robert Resniko, yet he perversely agreed to attend a meeting with Resniko, the film's producer David Madden, and the casting agent. The part would only have reinforced every stereotypical fantasy image that had ever been projected on to him. Perhaps for this very reason, for his own amusement, he submitted himself to the supposedly informal Hollywood audition, an experience for which he was totally unprepared. Rather than enthusing wildly about the script and the merits of portraying a supernatural serial killer, he nonchalantly informed them that he could play the role if he was required but that he had been enjoying some success as a singer so it was really of little consequence to him whether he was awarded the part or not. He was as bemused by the intensity of the trio's exhortations to convince them that he was as evil as the script's character as they were by his reluctance to sell himself. He bluffed his way through before making his apologies and leaving. He did not get the part, for which he was eternally grateful when he finally saw the finished film. 'That film is so bad,' he admitted three years later. 'Lou Diamond Phillips is such a cocksucker! If I'd been in that film it would have destroyed my career.'[3]

The US tour closed with two dates at the Scream in Los Angeles on 3 and 4 March, then Cave flew back to London to work with Simon Pettifar on editing the finished draft manuscript of *And the Ass Saw the Angel*. 'A lot of things were coming together for him,' recalls Pettifar. 'He was getting a new perspective, he was getting himself sorted out personally. Whenever that happens something starts to click. I think the book was an important part of that mix. So we eventually had a draft, a beginning, a middle and an end. When Nick and I edited it we cut a bit but not that much. We had to cut out any inconsistencies very carefully because it's such a complex narrative. We sat at adjacent desks, side by side, and went through it line by line. There wasn't much rewriting to do. What surprised me was that he seemed reluctant to completely finish the book. I got the impression he wanted to finish it apart from the very last bit, for some reason. He didn't even want to write the very end. The book builds to a climax. An epilogue had never been mentioned before. I must admit I had mixed feelings about it at the time.'

Cave had written endless variations of Euchrid Eucrow's attempted slaying of the girl-child, Beth, at the foot of the town square's marble monument, revelling in the wanton brutality of the act. 'In this moment of clarity,' the insane Eucrow narrates at the close of Book Three of the novel, 'ah was struck by the effect of the new addition to the tableau and the sight of the angel and the child, and by the sublime relationship set up between the two, as if the one depended upon the other, like good and evil, heaven and hell, and indeed, life and death. Each illuminated the other by virtue of its essential difference.' Eucrow begins to weep, not tears of sadness but of pride. 'This day ah had proved mah rightful existence beyond the petty dictates of ordinary men, and ah wept proud waters, tears of greatness, rivers of salt and glory.' Now Cave wanted to compound and extend the suffering and horror he had so vividly portrayed in the novel's preceding pages. In the one-page epilogue it is revealed that Beth survives Eucrow's attack only to die months later in childbirth. The boy child is Eucrow's, conceived during one of his nocturnal visits to Beth's room; the act itself Eucrow had been unable to recollect in any detail, only in fragments. The Ukulites proclaim that deliverance is at hand from the merciless rains that once more lash Ukulore Valley and the infant is doomed to live as hellish an existence as his mother and father.

His spirits still deflated after the long US tour, Cave contemplated his future. Tired of Europe, and England in particular, he yearned once more to escape from London, its media and the music business in general, which always seemed to take up so much of his time. There remained one country which still captivated his imagination and that he had not yet visited, Brazil. His fascination with that country had been inflamed many years before by Hector Babenco's harrowing film *Pixote*, which depicted the brutal existence of a ten-year-old in the murky underworld of São Paulo. Ramos Da Silva's portrayal of the street kid who escapes from a harsh reform school only to fall into a life of drug-dealing, squalor and degradation profoundly moved Cave, to the extent that he even dedicated *Tender Prey* to Silva's memory when he learnt that he had been killed by the São Paulo police in November 1987. Cave wanted to see this beautiful yet poverty-ridden country for himself, and as usual the band presented the perfect opportunity for doing so. Three gigs were arranged, at the Scala in Rio on 12 April, followed by two dates at Projeto Sp, São Paulo. Little did Cave realise that the Brazilian tour would mark a major turning point in his life.

For the first time his high expectations of a country were actually realised. From the moment he arrived in Rio, he was swiftly smitten by Brazil, its climate, culture and spirited people. The stark living conditions of the slum dwellers in the tin shack *favelas* on the sloping hills surrounding Rio sickened him, but visually the city was the most beautiful he had ever seen. He was entranced by the vast statue of Christ the Redeemer perched atop Corcovado hill. He told friends that he thought the statue, which overlooked the entire city with its arms outstretched in welcome, was the most impressive monument he had ever seen. He was convinced that according to the weather, the time of day and the point of view from which it was perceived, the statue's countenance would appear to change. At one moment Christ the Redeemer seemed to be dispensing his blessing across Rio, the next he would appear to be an ominous figure, presiding over a crime-infested urban hell spiralling out of control.

Though the Rio concert went over well with the crowd, the reception the band received in São Paulo was rapturous, and in Cave's opinion the concerts on 14 and 15 April in the city were the best The Bad Seeds had yet performed. He was enthralled by the enormous sprawling city, Brazil's cultural centre, one of the world's largest cities with a population in excess of sixteen million and spread over 30,000 square kilometres. He might have enjoyed the rich visual vistas of Rio but São Paulo struck a deeper chord. As soon as he arrived he impulsively decided that he wanted to stay. He had been prepared for the squalor depicted in Babenco's movie and while he knew that world definitely existed, the side of São Paulo that he was seeing, with its museums, art galleries, air-conditioned shopping centres and wide variety of restaurants, was distinctly cosmopolitan and cultured. Whereas in Rio he felt he was just another 'gringo' and the object of a crime to be committed, in the streets of São Paulo he was treated with a certain amount of respect. 'The difference between Rio and São Paulo reminds me of Sydney and Melbourne,' he would later declare, 'Sydney being a beach type community. It's much more extreme in Rio . . . the sun, bodies, more emphasis on "surface" type of things. Then you go to Melbourne which seems to have more of a soul to it in a way. There's a great difference between the Rio people and the people of São Paulo. São Paulo is just huge. You go to some high point and as far as you can see in any direction is solid skyscrapers. It's not a tourist town, but it's just a great place – very chaotic.'[4]

Most important of all, in São Paulo Cave had also fallen helplessly in love. During the first gig in the city a beautiful young girl in the audience, with a radiant smile and long, flowing dark hair, had caught his eye. Throughout the set he felt almost magnetically drawn to her, shamelessly presenting his entire performance in her direction. On being formally introduced he learned that the girl's name was Viviane Carneiro, a Brazilian fashion stylist and art director. At that time Viviane spoke very little English and conversation was slow and awkward, but Cave was captivated by the way she carried herself, her elegance and the fact that she was oblivious to his celebrity. He realised that he had found the girl that he wanted to live with. He now knew that his long relationship with Anita Lane was finally over and it was time to move on. The band had left the country but Cave would stay in Brazil with Viviane Carneiro for a further ten days, at the Hotel of Angels at the idyllic coastal town of Paraty. Here their relationship would blossom. All too soon he would have to leave again for Europe to work on his forthcoming album. Amid emotional scenes he implored Carneiro to wait for him and told her that he would return to Brazil as soon as he possibly could. It would be five long months until the pair were reunited.

Anita Lane was not surprised when Cave told her that it was all over, and that he had fallen in love with Viviane Carneiro. The strains in their relationship had been all too evident to both of them for some time after he had left the clinic, but the special bond of friendship was as strong as ever. Although Anita reasoned that they had always worked best together as friends, initially their final separation still came as a tremendous blow which she would have to overcome in time. 'Anita was in quite a bad way when they split up,' says Jessamy Calkin, 'but she'd never show it. She's a very strong character. At the time when they did split up there was a certain inevitability about it, but I don't think that made it any better for Anita. I do remember that Anita had really wanted to go to Brazil and Nick wouldn't allow her to go, whereas he'd often taken her away in the past. There was a sort of finality about this and she knew that it was very significant. It wasn't such a surprise when he told her he had a new girlfriend but I think it was a terrible blow for her. I don't think anyone realised how devastating it really was. She didn't admit to that, and she probably didn't admit that to Nick. It did take her a long time to recover. I don't think Nick did it for this reason but it was a "setting free", in a way. Nick realised that something had to change and he knew that Anita wasn't going to be the one that would effect that change. The only one who could do that was him. It wasn't like they were heading for marriage and Viviane stepped in. Having said all that, I don't think it damaged their relationship now in any way. I don't think Anita bears any resentment. They were soul mates and always will be.'

Cave had a very clear conception of how he wanted his next

album to sound and the feelings he wished the songs to evoke. With the novel virtually completed, an achievement in which he took great pride, he felt a new sense of artistic freedom, enabling him to leave behind the mythic south that he had created and which had preoccupied him for so many years. As he sat down to write he found that the songs were coming to him easily. His creative powers had not evaporated into the ether as he had feared just because he had stopped taking drugs. However, he had started drinking again during his trip to Brazil. Jessamy Calkin says that Cave had a strong reaction against attending the AA meetings he was advised to attend after Broadway Lodge. 'For a while he was really drunk again. He really hated the meetings. It was meant to be anonymous and people would ask for his autograph afterwards. I can see why he hated that. He hated to be seen collaborating with something, an institution. He had to do it his way.'

The songs Cave was writing shared a seductive classic structure and a direct lyrical simplicity to express his sense of sadness at something lost never to be recaptured. The predominant themes that were emerging both in his lyrics and their musical accompaniment were those of remorse and regret. 'The Brazilians have a word for this feeling I was after,' Cave told Chris Bohn. 'When I explained to someone that what I wanted to write about was the memory of things that I thought were lost for me, I was told that the Portuguese word for this feeling was "*saudade*". It's not nostalgia but something sadder.'[5]

After a six-date tour of Greece and Italy, Cave set to work for the first time producing demos of the new material before actually recording. Now feeling much more confident in his role as a musician in the group, he wanted to exert far more creative control in the studio than he had been able to during past recordings. 'Nick had been writing a lot on the piano,' says Mick Harvey. 'Nick likes to play piano on demos because that's how he works out musical ideas. In the past he hadn't wanted the responsibility of playing the instrument for every song, which is understandable. We demoed all the songs very heavily and we were very organised before we even went into the studio. We had the string arrangements done before we went in to record the basic tracks. We tried working with Roland [Wolf] in Berlin but there were so many problems with his attitude. It just didn't fit together.' Wolf was unwilling to change his own fixed ideas about the music being presented to him and argued incessantly with Cave, who asked Wolf to stick to his conception of how he wanted his songs to be played. Wolf had also taken to shaving his head, which offended Cave's aesthetic sensibilities to such an extent that he would demand that Wolf wore a hat when in his presence. The whole situation led to an impasse to which there could only be one solution: Roland Wolf would not be accompanying the band to the studio and would leave The Bad Seeds.

Any work on the album the following month was impossible, as on 24 August the hardback edition of *And the Ass Saw the Angel* was published in the UK by Black Spring Press. Having returned to London from a six-date tour of Japan, which closed in Osaka on 28 June, for weeks before and after publication Cave was inundated with an interminable series of interviews, TV appearances, book signings and readings. On 25 August he conducted two signing sessions in London, at Waterstone's in Kensington and Compendium in Camden, followed by a reading at the Edinburgh Book Festival on the 27th. For the next four days he travelled the country from Manchester to Brighton to Newcastle promoting the novel, which was enjoying very favourable sales. The following year Simon Pettifar would sell the paperback rights to Penguin, who would issue it as a lead title in their 1990 autumn campaign, selling over 30,000 copies. Internationally the novel would be translated into German, selling over 13,000 copies in hardback, Italian, Japanese, Spanish and even Serbo-Croat and Finnish. In the spring of 1992 HarperCollins published it as a mass-market paperback in the USA, where it attained more successful sales and critical acceptance.

As Cave and Pettifar had expected, the reviews the novel received were mixed. From the UK rock press there seemed a general reluctance to acknowledge Cave's significant achievement in expanding his singular vision into a narrative novel. It was as if he had strayed from his profession into an area of the arts where he had no place, rather than viewing the novel as the natural extension of his love of narrative expressed in his songs. Many had believed that the work would never see the light of day. James Brown, in the *NME*, acknowledged that the novel was 'an impressive début' and 'clear proof for those that need it that Cave does have literary talent', but concluded that: 'The message beneath Euchrid's madness, Nick Cave's got guts. And they look and taste a lot better than Ronnie Wood's paintings or Sting's films.' Anthony Quinn, in *20/20*, deemed that 'over the length of a novel, Cave's antic, free-wheeling and undisciplined prose can get a little wearing' and that there was something 'rather disquieting about an imagination stirred to life by freakish acts of violence'. Any mention of the novel's broad humour was conspicuous by its absence.

The critical reaction from the 'straight' press, however, was far more encouraging. 'It is as if a Faulkner novel had been crossed with *Whistle Down the Wind*, and narrated by a stoned blues musician,' was the *Daily Telegraph*'s assessment of the novel, an unlikely source of praise for the 'extracurricular' activities of a rock'n'roll singer. The *Daily Mail*'s Shaun Usher pronounced that the reader would 'be startled by the scale of its originality'. Frederic Lindsay, in the *Scotsman*, appreciated the technical skill and style with which Cave had told his tale: 'Full of Biblical echoes, capable of pastiche and parody, it reads aloud wonderfully . . . Whatever the fans think, the rest of us should pay Cave the compliment his talent deserves and recognise that he has written a genuinely nasty book.'

Collectively the reviews, either good or bad, were of no consequence to Cave. His belief in his novel's worth was unshakeable. It was his personal triumph, the product of many years' diligent work and sacrifice. Nothing could detract from that. 'Nick wasn't embarrassed to ask people if they'd read the book, 'says Jessamy Calkin. 'He'd say, "Why not! What do you mean, you haven't got the time?" He wasn't bothered about being slighted. People were embarrassed that they hadn't read it because it showed them up.' Now the novel was published he felt he could finally move on, leaving behind its world of fetishes and grim obsessions. He considered that it would be a very long time indeed until he would even contemplate writing another novel because he was now all too aware of the effort involved. Though his sensibilities had not changed since its completion, the solitary existence he had led while writing had played havoc with his relationships and friendships and he desperately wanted to reacquaint himself with some semblance of a social life. 'In terms of feeling good about myself, my own sense of worth, I would like the onus to be taken off what my product is, and on to something that I feel about myself,' he admitted to Jim Shelley. 'Everything I feel good about is to do with my work and everything I feel bad about is to do with my private life, by that I mean my normal life. At the moment I use, and have used for some time, my work as a kind of convenient and happy retreat from my private life, which is something that I'm not very good at at the moment, and something I haven't been very good at, and that's not a good way to live.'⁶

On 7 September Cave gave a reading at the London Scala cinema in King's Cross after a long afternoon's signing session at the Virgin Megastore, Oxford Street. 'I had wanted him to do a reading for some time,' says the cinema's former programmer Jane Giles. 'In conjunction with it I wanted to screen two films of his choice. He had chosen a number of films, *The Karen Carpenter Story* by Todd Haines was one I remember, but I told him it had to be two feature-length films to pad the programme out. In the end he chose *Pixote* and Ted Kotcheff's *Outback* (aka *Wake In Fright*), an Australian movie which doesn't get screened here too often. The reading itself went well. Before it he was very charming and he seemed genuinely interested in the cinema. Lydia [Lunch] was here and so we went to dinner with Nick and Bleddyn. Nick came across well with Bleddyn's child so during the course of the meal the conversation turned towards the subject of children. Mischievously Nick asked Lydia when she was going to have children. She replied, "Honey, the day I have kids is the day I see you shit a watermelon."'

On 8 October Cave and The Bad Seeds began recording his sixth solo album, *The Good Son*, at Cardan Studios, São Paulo, Brazil. Cave had managed to convince Mute that recording in Brazil was both an economical proposition and an artistically stimulating environment, but in fact he desperately wanted to be reunited with Viviane Carneiro. Weeks before recording began, Cave had flown to São Paulo to be with her, and to their mutual relief the couple realised that their relationship was stronger than ever. However, for the first time in Cave's musical career the actual locale where he had been living and working would make a distinct and positive impression upon his songwriting. The most obvious manifestation of this trend would be his adaptation of the Brazilian Protestant hymn '*Foi Na Cruz*', the chorus of which translates as: 'He was on the Cross, He was on the Cross, One day, Jesus was castigated for our sins'. 'Nick loved the spontaneity of São Paulo, the people were really open,' recalls Victor Van Vugt, who engineered the sessions at Cardan Studios. 'I remember going through São Paulo and he'd be looking at these incredible baroque churches saying, "Look how they captured the suffering of Christ. His knees are torn up and bloody." He thought that was fantastic.' According to Jessamy Calkin: 'Nick is a very spiritual person, but he's also fascinated by fanaticism. I think he's almost jealous of the way people can hold these fervent beliefs. Anita told me that years ago they were coming back from Australia on the plane and Nick was sitting next to these "new" Christians. He was having really bad withdrawals and they'd tried to talk him out of how bad he felt. Then they got on to the Bible and that was it! He was correcting them on their Biblical quotations . . . Nick's really religious in a lot of ways. He's got a real Good and Bad, Right and Wrong conflict. He's very moralistic.'

The atmosphere of Brazil and São Paulo had also impinged on Cave's songwriting consciousness in a more subtle fashion. In London and Berlin he had often sat for weeks frenziedly writing and rewriting reams of song lyrics which he would then ruthlessly edit, but in Brazil, during his long walks around the city, he had composed complete songs entirely in his head. After the years of copious note-taking that had been necessary in shaping his novel, he had developed an aversion to writing on paper. He no longer felt guilty when a song presented itself to him with ease and he blessed his good fortune that they were of the calibre of the romantic ballad, 'The Ship Song' and the melancholic evocation of universal despair, 'The Weeping Song'. The latter was presented as a dialogue between father (portrayed by Bargeld) and son (Cave), in which the patriarch weeps not only with existential despair but also because of the unintentionally hurtful behaviour of the son.

Musically, Cave had not simply plundered the rich musical heritage of the country that had so inspired him but had also drawn inspiration from songwriters such as Burt Bacharach and Hal David, Simon and Garfunkel, Scott Walker and The Righteous Brothers, 'Nashville Skyline'-era Bob Dylan, and Leonard Cohen, and their direct approach to songwriting. Many of the songs he created for *The Good Son* would retain their working titles. 'The two songs that we learnt and recorded in the studio were "The Ship Song" and "The Weeping Song",' says Mick Harvey, who coordinated the string arrangements at the sessions as well as playing bass, acoustic guitar, vibraphone and percussion. 'They came together very spontaneously. There was no time to do string arrangements, we just went ahead and did them. They had a very natural feel.'

The subdued, melodious, traditional structure of many of the songs left little room for Blixa Bargeld's idiosyncratic guitar experimentation, though he displayed his unerring ability to provide exactly what was required to heighten the atmosphere of certain songs. 'My involvement on *The Good Son* was very small,' he confesses. 'I couldn't be present very much and I unfortunately had to do overdubs on songs that were full already. There wasn't much space for me. I went to Brazil on my own and they'd been in the studio for a week before I arrived. It was a no-smoking studio, no drinking or eating. It was very enjoyable working because Nick's singing was much better by then because of his health.'

'When Nick went to record *The Good Son* he was a star in Brazil,' recalls Victor Van Vugt. 'He was on the front page of the daily papers. For Nick this was incredible. The Bad Seeds were one of the first Western rock bands to record in Brazil. What's the fascination? was the question from the press . . . The demos had been done on twenty-four-track tapes in Berlin which were brought over and that was the starting block. Lyrics did change, words or lines, but it was pretty much done. Some of the songs were literally layered upon the original demos. Some of the songs had the original drums, even the drum machines, from the demos. Bad Seeds albums are always recorded very quickly. Recording was finished by 28 October, though the piano wasn't very good in the studio and some rerecording had to be done in Berlin in November with vocal overdubs. The studio was so cheap in Brazil compared to how much it costs to get seven people over to Europe and putting them in a hotel. Ten more days would have been helpful. Nick would do a piano track and then say, "I want to do a harmonica take," and I was saying, "Let me set up a microphone and listen back to that take." They do work at an incredible tempo. I remember Nick saying, "I want that really big Simon and Garfunkel snare sound." I said, "OK, let me set it up." The original took a day to set up with a drummer down a stairwell, as legend has it, because they didn't have digital reverb in those days. But Nick didn't have the patience to see it through, all the time it was, let's move on.'

Thematically the songs that comprised *The Good Son* set were amongst the most frank and personal that Cave had yet written. Couched within their narratives, including the LP's title track, were discernible autobiographical allusions intertwined with emotional evocations of lost innocence, remorse and regret. In 'The Hammer Song', the most musically aggressive track in the set, the protagonist silently leaves home while his father rages and his mother weeps, but soon longs for redemption and to return to 'home ground' as his nomadic existence has become an unbearable nightmare. The gospel-inspired 'The Witness Song' could be seen to contain veiled references to Broadway Lodge and Cave's experiences there: 'Who will be the witness, When you're all so clean and you cannot see'. The girl described in the plaintive 'Lament' bears an uncanny resemblance to Viviane Carneiro, and the ethereal presence in 'Lucy' who appears at nightfall to haunt the protagonist at 'The end of love, of misery and woe', could be Anita Lane.

In Cardan Studios Cave felt apprehensive about the new material, as the album did contain songs that marked a significant departure from his previous work, though offering no indication of the group's future direction. In a particularly candid interview with Bram Van Splunteren, conducted the following April on Dutch VPRO television, the extent of his unease during *The Good Son* sessions was revealed:

CAVE: In the studio . . . I don't know if other groups are like this, but we're not bursting with self-confidence the whole time and if you're making a record that's reasonably 'dangerous' in a way, you're taking a risk and it makes you . . .

HARVEY: The main time of doubt is after you've actually finished it. Then that's the time you wonder about what you've done.

CAVE: Well, for me it was different. Once it was finished I thought it sounded complete and I really liked it. It was while we were doing it . . . that I was very worried about it.

VAN SPLUNTEREN: Really?

CAVE: These kind of worries you can't afford to let anyone else know. You've got to pretend all the time that, 'Hey, I've got these songs, they're really good and don't worry everybody.' You can't afford to be too open with the other members, you've got to keep that surge of confidence.

HARVEY: OK, I'll let it ride.

VAN SPLUNTEREN: Come on, tell it like it is, Mick.

HARVEY: Well, I think you express a lot of . . .

CAVE: Private doubts, private doubts . . .

HARVEY: . . . about the material while we were working but it's from a particularly . . .

CAVE: Private . . .

HARVEY: Private . . .

CAVE: Something we don't discuss publicly.

VAN SPLUNTEREN: Why not?

CAVE: Because if I laid myself bare and was truly honest with you, people like you would destroy me and I'm not prepared to let that happen.

Cave delivered the final line of the interview with a knowing look, but there was perhaps more than a little truth to his statement.

NOTES

1 Ann Scanlon, 'Talk of the Devil' *Sounds*, December 24/31 1988.
2 Paul Byrne, 'Saint Nick', *Hot Press*, 23 April 1992.
3 Matthew Hall, 'Nick Cave, The Thirtysomething Years', *Puncture*, No. 24, May 1992.
4 Ibid.
5 Biba Kopf, 'Nick Cave', *The Catalogue*, No. 80, April 1990.
6 Jim Shelley, 'Angel With Dirty Pages', *NME*, 26 August 1989.

15

Henry's Dream

With the release of *The Good Son* on 16 April 1990, and the single, 'The Ship Song', which preceded it the month before, Cave reluctantly emerged from the relative seclusion of his new São Paulo home. His fears concerning the reception that would greet his new melodious and reflective LP were mostly unfounded. Awarding the album 5 out of 5, David Cavanagh in *Sounds* described it as 'a masterpiece . . . full of awe and love . . . An album with five precursors but no predecessors, a strong, sane statement of sorrow.' In the *NME*, Simon Williams observed that: 'where *Kicking Against the Pricks* was a timeless covers' paradise, this is where Cave turns the tables and creates his own potential hand-me-down classics . . . The songs are immaculately crafted, forever sympathetic to Cave's newly realised vocal capabilities.' However, there were some voices of dissent. Andy Gill, in *The Independent*, compared the string arrangements with Mantovani and complained that the record contained 'no comedy to gauge the misery against'; whilst Chris Roberts, in *Melody Maker*, deemed that it was 'a poor album from a man rich with individuality'.

More important to Cave than any critical kudos that *The Good Son* had gathered was the fact that he had proved to himself that he could still produce artistically valid work of a more overtly personal nature than he had yet created, without the aid of narcotics. *The Good Son* had also finally extricated The Bad Seeds from any trends within popular music, a long-held aim of Cave's.

He and the group now stood alone, unaffected by the vagaries of fashion. 'I think that particularly with the last record we finally "cut the strings" which hold us to any contemporary music whatsoever,' he later admitted, 'and I'm really pleased about that. I see The Bad Seeds' music just floating off somewhere by itself. We can just make our own music and anything can be happening around us and it's not going to really have much influence on us. We've finally divorced ourselves from contemporary music and in general I kind of loathe contemporary music so I'm quite happy about that. I think basically I had more confidence this time to be able to expand our musical range and to actually write more vocally challenging songs. We're getting better at what we're doing. It's just happening naturally.'[1]

Cave had also come to terms with engaging with the media in promoting *The Good Son*, according to Chris Bohn who interviewed him at this time. 'He seemed more relaxed,' says Bohn. 'He found it easier to answer questions. I think he could distance himself personally from the answers somehow. The impression I got was that he could talk about something without thinking that his whole life was on trial.'

For the video for 'The Ship Song', which depicted Cave seated at a grand piano surrounded by angelic little girls in white dresses, with The Bad Seeds providing choral accompaniment, the singer had been reunited with the *Ghosts . . . of the Civil Dead* director, John Hillcoat. 'I'm not really happy with the outcome of that clip,' admits Hillcoat. 'It's a combination of my fault and his. I have a problem working with the music industry, film gets beyond those boundaries. Video is more constrictive creatively for myself, and Nick enjoys the freedom of film, but generally with video it's back to how he looks, vanity and image. With "The Ship Song" I had trouble with the budget and working with an unknown crew in New York. Nick was very concerned with appearance and working with him on that level wasn't very rewarding. If he's self-conscious then you pick it up as well. There were really tight deadlines from the record company and I wasn't happy with the photography. I originally wanted naked cherubs running around, bumping into him and so on, but then there was the problem of nudity. He preferred the idea of little girls . . . I've noticed with his videos that he's either got to be the loud, aggressive, passionate performer, or he's got to be the ironic humorist. "In The Ghetto" and "Shivers" worked because he was more sincere and not hamming it up. There are certain faces he can project and in that one ["The Ship Song"], he couldn't pull it off. The incongruous element was there with the girls, humour was there with The Bad Seeds' choir line-up but at the same time he wanted a performance that was different, to make a break because of the song itself. Then for the next video, for "The Weeping Song" [directed by Angela Conway], he went back to the ironic humorist and the video was more successful because it worked with the obvious hammy stuff which Nick can do very well. Nick's too self-aware. I think it's something he's working on.' In February 1994, in Brazil, Cave and Hillcoat would again collaborate on a far more successful promotional video project for his single 'Do You Love Me?'.

In May 1990 Cave was once again faced with an extensive schedule to promote *The Good Son*, in all, forty-eight concerts, beginning on 13 May in Coesfeld, Germany, and ending in Los Angeles on 5 October. There were also personnel changes to be made to The Bad Seeds' line-up. It had been mutually decided that guitarist Kid Congo Powers was to leave the band due to his increasing commitments to The Gun Club, his original band, and his work on his own solo projects. 'The way The Bad Seeds is set up, the line-up shifts around,' says Powers. 'The way the music was going there was no need for wild rock guitar. Nick has always had the freedom to move in any direction he wants and I understand that. It wasn't as cut and dried as either I left the band or I was kicked out. The Gun Club is like a natural part of what I do. It's strange working with other people in a way because what I do is "Kid Congo Powers' own thing". You have to fit me into the scene. Nick follows his own path, and whatever the public makes of it is coincidental. Nick's progression is pure, I mean, I know, I worked with him for a long time. He does exactly what he wants to do. He doesn't make any concessions to "contemporary fads", or whatever. He draws on influences from years ago and makes them his own. The same with Jeffrey Lee Pierce.'

'It was very much based on practical considerations,' concurs Mick Harvey. 'A lot of problems arise out of other people's commitments outside the band. But that's the way the band works and why it works well. We couldn't expect everybody to be just involved with The Bad Seeds, there are always going to have to be clashes of interest. It couldn't be any other way. Kid had decided he was moving back to the States, the official members of The Bad Seeds all live in Berlin and Nick was in São Paulo. We couldn't have coped with The Gun Club as well. Jeffrey Lee never talks about anything he's planned. Organising Crime and the City Solution and The Bad Seeds was always very easy because I was organising both groups' timetables. I was always able to manipulate when we would be doing what. It became harder with Einsturzende Neubauten and then The Gun Club. I've opted out of that area of work now . . .'

Much to Harvey's relief he could now leave his slot as bass guitarist, that he had by default occupied for so many years, to play lead guitar. To complete the group's line-up Harvey recruited two gifted Australian musicians, bassist Martyn P. Casey, then a member of the renowned Perth band The Triffids, and organist/pianist Conway Savage, who had played with Dave Graney's Coral Snakes as well as being a solo artist in his own right. Live performances would show that the players had been chosen well. Casey and Savage's addition to The Bad Seeds made the group a real band once more, perhaps for the first time since Barry Adamson's departure in the mid eighties. Both in terms of their attitude towards music and their temperament, the new members provided the perfect foil for Cave, welding The Bad Seeds together into a cohesive unit. 'Finally I have a band that all seem to have an equal irreverence for music and performing that I have myself,' Cave later confided, '. . . I wanted a band that had the capacity to play very sentimental music if necessary, aggressive, violent music if necessary, and anything in between, and I think that's what I've finally succeeded in getting.'[2]

Throughout the 1990 tour, critics who had previously expressed indifference towards Cave's work would concur with his assessment of his new group's dexterity in marshalling their formidable power with restraint. 'This was a deep, rough, bloody cut above, gorgeous and grotesque and sublime,' wrote *Melody Maker*'s Chris Roberts of The Bad Seeds' sell-out concert at London's Brixton Academy in June. 'The selections from *The Good Son* make me feel guilty for receiving the album lukewarmly – given slack, these conventional ballads do evoke the romantic spirit they yearn for.' For the same paper, Alan Brown, reviewing the band at the Pavilion in Glasgow on 21 August was similarly impressed: 'This was a show to shame the sourest of old sceptics . . . every Roy Orbison-style military drum lick, every Hammond hop, skip and jump is gloriously in and out of place.'

In October, after having spent so much of the year on tour, Cave gratefully returned to his home on the outskirts of São Paulo, and Viviane Carneiro. During the Australian leg of the tour in July he had publicly expressed dissatisfaction with the routine involved in working within the music industry. 'The trouble is that it has to be a product,' he said of his songwriting and recording. 'My life is my work and basically it is sad that I can't spend more time building relationships with people, with places. I see my success in my product. I don't know if that's healthy. I'm constantly surprised to be able to continue being creative.'[3] He had longed for a respite from his career in order to concentrate on improving the actual quality of his life and to enjoy Viviane's company. In São Paulo he could withdraw from the rock world, reading novels voraciously, eating out at the city's restaurants, and virtually every day strolling up the steep winding road by his house to Pedro's Bar. He struck up a lasting friendship with Pedro, the proprietor of the establishment, and to view the bar as an extension of his own house. Rather than explore the country in which he had now settled, Cave was mainly content to carve a small niche for himself in São Paulo within a two-mile radius of his home.

Though limited to a small circle of English-speaking Brazilians and English expatriates, he had made strong friendships in the city and considered São Paulo home, despite his inability to learn the language. 'When I'm in Brazil I don't really do anything,' he admitted. 'I write songs and stuff, but I don't really work on things as such. We're so far away from anything here that I'm basically left alone.'[4] Perhaps here he could find the happiness and stability that had so far eluded him in Melbourne, London and Berlin. 'I was lucky enough to be at a party at his place in São Paulo,' says director Peter Sempel. 'It's a totally different lifestyle down there and he likes it very much. The people seem very lighthearted and they enjoy life.'

On 10 May 1991 Viviane Carneiro gave birth to a son, Luke, at the Adventista Hospital in Liberdade, São Paulo. Cave was overjoyed and relieved that there had been no serious complications for the Caesarean birth. He had longed for a child and had always enjoyed a strong rapport with children. 'Nick is brilliant with kids,' says Jessamy Calkin, 'and they love him as well. He'd always be playing with them in a totally unselfconscious way, whereas Blixa would be horrified if it even looked like he might actually have to hold one. In Berlin, when Nick was going out with Elizabeth Recker, he had a friend downstairs from their flat called Luke. He was six years old and didn't speak English. He and Nick were devoted to each other.' Chris Carr agrees: 'He's very good with children. He identifies with them to a certain extent.'

With Luke's birth came responsibilities that Cave had evaded throughout his life. He could no longer stand alone. In order to care for and protect his son, he had to start engaging with the outside world to impart some knowledge and guidance. Having lived the life of an alienated outsider, he now had to examine society and his relationship to it. What he saw disgusted him and his revulsion slowly seeped into his songwriting consciousness. 'He has no conception that the system that one inherits is a dictating influence about who you are,' declared Evan English in 1991. 'He believes that there is a human condition that's eternal. Love, hate, good, evil, envy, greed and so on, and to talk about economic structures is to waste your time. He believes that we've arrived at the end of history. I keep telling him to contemporise what he's doing. He likes people to contest him. I say to him, "You're a conservative fart, wake up!" He's not making enough attempts to interpret the world.' Luke's birth would steadily stimulate a degree of change in Cave's outlook. 'I now have something in my life which is without exception intrinsically innocent,' he would state the following year.[5]

In late October 1991 Cave arrived in New York City with Viviane and Luke and moved into an apartment on East 51st Street to prepare for recording a new album. While in São Paulo he had experienced great difficulty in actually writing any new material. Apart from some songs in *The Good Son* set, songwriting had generally never come easily to Cave, but in São Paulo it had proved to be a monumental task. 'When we did demos for the LP we thought it would be like the previous demo session for *The Good Son*,' recalls Victor Van Vugt, who worked on the demo session in London in August 1991. 'He said he only had a couple of songs . . . and he did. His excuse was that in his room in São Paulo the word processor and his piano were on opposite sides of the room.' The surge of confidence that Cave needed in order to write had temporarily deserted him in Brazil. He had always trusted the opinion of a select clique of friends regarding his work but in São Paulo there was no one with whom he could share his ideas, primarily due to the language barrier. With supreme effort he had persisted, breaking through his writer's block, producing reams of lyrics coupled with minimal musical accompaniment at times comprised of just two notes. His spartan musical ideas had initially confused the band. 'On occasion that was all the information the band had,' he later admitted, 'just bang on in G minor, or whatever, during the verses. Everyone sort of looked at each other and said, "That's it?" and I said, "Yeah, that's it. You do whatever you want to do."'[6] He intuitively wanted to move away from the highly structured songs of *The Good Son* towards what he would describe as 'trash-can songs', raw and aggressive acoustically based compositions into which lyrically a variety of ideas and perspectives could be unloaded during the verses, often changing viewpoint from line to line. Whereas with *The Good Son* he had wanted total control over the music's direction, with this album he was to give his musicians free rein to interpret his ideas in any manner they wished.

While in New York City Cave continued writing and rewriting lyrics. He had been inspired by the presence of Anita Lane who, together with her husband Johannes Beck and their son Raffie, stayed with Cave and Carneiro at the East 51st Street apartment. 'Anita's very impressed with Viv,' says Jessamy Calkin. 'The first time they met, Viv came over and was really friendly towards her and Anita must have seemed to be some kind of threat. Elizabeth had a lot of trouble with that because Nick and Anita will always be friends. Nick is fantastic with Anita's son.' The special friendship between Lane and Cave was as strong as ever and once again she had bolstered his spirits by approving the direction in which his songwriting was taking him and encouraging him to continue.

Many of the new narrative songs were as personal as those that comprised *The Good Son*. The chorus of 'Papa Won't Leave You, Henry' initially began as a lullaby that Cave would sing to his infant son. Henry was a name that he had considered for the child, as he thought it carried connotations of strength and courage. In the chorus's lyric the protagonist assures his weeping son that he will never abandon him, but the father is already in transit, on the road where 'many fall by the side'. Throughout, the verses alternate between the narrator's overwhelming sense of guilt and shame, in part for succumbing to intoxication ('I awoke so drunk, and full of rage, I could hardly speak'), and documenting the horrors of the world that surround him. For the first time in a Cave lyric there is overt reference to the locale where the song was written: the rainy season in Brazil is washing entire towns away, the dispossessed are 'wasting you for your money, for your clothes, and for your nothing', tin slum *favelas* explode while death squads relentlessly perform random executions. Babies are even 'being born without brains', an actual occurrence in Cubital, Brazil, which once enjoyed the dubious distinction of being the most polluted city on earth.

In 'Brother, My Cup Is Empty' the protagonist, in the throes of creative impotence and an alcoholic stupor, sits in a bar berating those who do not buy him a drink and cursing those who do, dreading the moment when he must wearily return home to his partner. He realises that he cannot 'blame it all on her' yet he has longed 'to watch her groaning in the dirt, to see her clicking tongue crack dry'. 'Jack The Ripper' humorously depicts a hapless male dominated in a domestic situation by a woman 'with an iron fist', whilst in the fatalistic ballad 'Straight To You', the narrator's perception of his loved one shifts from verse to verse; first he runs to her as a heroic protector while 'all the towers of ivory are crumbling', only to return again to suffer more punishment at her hands as 'heaven has denied us its Kingdom'. As ever in Cave's writing the lover offers both sanctuary and torment. 'When I First Came To Town', which Cave based upon the traditional ballad 'Katie Cruel', directly reflects the author's perception of his experiences in cities around the world where he was first welcomed then quickly discarded, leaving him no option but to forever wander on: 'I search the mirror, And I try to see, Why the people of this town, Have washed their hands of me'. The sense of rejection Cave felt in São Paulo was particularly acute as he had been initially smitten by the city and its people. 'After a while people stopped ringing him up,' relates Van Vugt. 'He found that very hard to handle. The novelty of his presence had worn off. He got very disillusioned and very pissed off. In the end he only had a few friends left. He was very out of touch during his last year in Brazil.'

With other new songs Cave deliberately placed himself at a distance from their subject matter. In the Latin-flavoured tale of lust, revenge and murder chronicled in 'John Finn's Wife', which could have sprung from the pages of a Sam Peckinpah script, Cave merely empathises with the narrator's lecherous desires. The story of 'Christina The Astonishing' was taken directly from Alban Butler's *Lives of the Saints*, first published in 1756. At the age of twenty-two Christina was assumed dead but during the Agnus Dei soared to the roof of the church in Liège, Belgium, to escape the smell of sinful human bodies. For the rest of her life she would flee to remote places 'to escape the stench of human corruption'. Cave would later assert that the song was in fact personal: 'I don't know if it's a metaphor for anything. I don't know how many thousands of saints you could choose from to write a song about, and obviously that one related to me in some way or I wouldn't have chosen it. She was actually physically repulsed by the smell of people, which she thought of as their mortal sin. I found that pretty interesting.'[7]

Cave had been able to devote more time to the material and to rehearse for longer than expected with the band in

Manhattan, due to the late arrival of the record's producer, David Briggs. After their unsatisfactory experiences with producers Greg Macainsh and Les Karsky during their years in The Boys Next Door, Cave and Harvey had vowed never to entrust their work to a producer again, but Mute had asked that they at least consider the possibility of using one for the forthcoming record. Rather than rejecting the idea completely they thought about the proposition, considering that the right producer could possibly bring a new approach. At the very least a name producer could bring some kudos for the band in America and they would always be in control of the situation, or so they thought. 'It wasn't suddenly "There's going to be a producer,"' insists Daniel Miller. 'When I spoke to Nick we just discussed the making of the album. I think on a number of occasions over the years I'd said, "If you want to work with a producer, consider it." Producers do lots of different things in the studio. You have a certain producer who just makes their own sound, or a producer who imposes nothing on the group's sound at all but just gets good performances out of them. For a certain type of group that's what you need.'

In London Miller and Cave had attended a meeting with the late veteran Rolling Stones producer, Jimmy Miller, but he was deemed unsuitable. Cave then consulted his record collection for inspiration and selected Neil Young's producer David Briggs because he thought Young's albums sounded as though they had not been produced at all. At the only meeting Cave had with Briggs prior to recording he told the producer this was the reason he had been picked. Rather than being offended, Briggs jovially replied, 'You hit the nail on the head. You got good ears there.' Briggs knew of The Birthday Party and was very enamoured of *The Good Son*, which he described as a delicate record, much to Cave's annoyance. Cave explained that for their new album he wanted a raw, damaged sound. Briggs replied, 'I'm the man for the job! You only have to listen to Neil's records to realise that.' Unfortunately Cave did not realise just how raw and damaged Brigg's sound would be.

Recording belatedly began in November at Dreamland Studios, Bearsville, upstate New York, but soon moved to Sound City, Van Nuys, California, until late December 1991. 'When David Briggs was overdue they were rehearsing again in Woodstock and that was really good for him,' says Victor Van Vugt, 'and that got him really together. He always works well under pressure.' At the Sound City studio, where Bob Dylan recorded his 1986 LP *Knocked Out Loaded*, relations between the band and Briggs gradually deteriorated. 'This guy [Briggs] is used to working with US rock bands touring round the track,' says Van Vugt. 'He was very good at the live stuff, getting them to deliver good performances, but when it got to the overdubbing stage I've heard it was a nightmare. At one point they were walking out to go home and Briggs was shouting, "I don't need this from any fucking Australian rock band, you bastards!" I don't think the two parties were ready for each other.'

Cave found the whole experience of working with a producer again incredibly exasperating. While the band were recording a take Briggs would dance wildly among them as they played, miming along on an imaginary guitar. Eventually Harvey asked Briggs if the band could supply him with a cardboard guitar. 'Listen, you Australians, you're funny guys,' replied Briggs. 'I'm just trying to get into it, help the mood, help the vibe. I didn't know it was sacred ground in here.' Silent glances would be exchanged between the group. They realised they were losing control of the situation but carried on regardless. At one stage Cave was told by Briggs that his voice was 'too big for these microphones' and that there was only one piece of equipment in existence that could possibly capture it, 'Poncho's mike'. Recording ground to a halt while Briggs rang Frank 'Poncho' Sampedro, Crazy Horse's guitarist, to arrange delivery of 'The Big One'.

The atmosphere in the studio became more intense as the thirteen hour-a-day sessions wore on. Cave thought that Briggs's constant domineering attitude towards the LP's engineer was despicable. If the producer's commands were not obeyed instantly, the long-suffering engineer would be banished from the studio for ten minutes to contemplate his role in the recording process, while the band sat aghast with their heads in their hands. Cave lost his temper with Briggs late one night while Conway Savage was trying to perform his vocal track on 'When I First

Came To Town', Savage, who was exhausted after a long day's session, could not complete his vocal part to his own satisfaction and kept stopping mid-tape. Briggs would offer no encouragement and merely queried in a loud voice whether the idea was worth pursuing. Cave thought that what he was hearing was brilliant and knew that with perseverance Savage would soon deliver a perfect rendition. He told Briggs to be patient and to turn the tape back on. Muttering that he was really enjoying the session, Briggs continued recording until Savage made another mistake. Finally Cave shouted that he could not endure Briggs's petty bullying any longer, that he should concentrate on the job in hand and keep his 'fuckin' mouth shut'. Briggs simply replied that he would pretend that he had not heard the remark and that he would now leave the studio for a few minutes. Cave answered that that was fine with him. Briggs would return and the cycle would start all over again.

'When he recorded Neil Young, it sounds like he just turned on a switch and then turned it off again. That works exceptionally well for Neil, but for us it didn't,' Cave later admitted. 'His philosophy is that you get a good performance, and that with every overdub you take another step away from that initial raw energy. But there are overdubs and there are overdubs. Our music requires a lot of overdubs and manipulation in the mix, because it has to do with empty spaces and sudden bursts of energy. David doesn't work well under those conditions. He calls it "overdub hell".' From the group's perspective the phrase 'overdub hell' was very apt. Cave would only have to mention that he wanted another instrument overdubbed on to a track and Briggs would start rolling his eyes towards the heavens. Long before the session ended Cave had decided that they would never again work with a producer.

Briggs had managed to generate some excitement within the band by forcing them to perform songs repeatedly for the best possible take, but while mixing the record he played back the results at maximum volume so that the group had no real conception of how the tracks would sound through an ordinary household hi-fi system. It was only after Cave had returned to Australia for Christmas that he played the LP on his mother's standard hi-fi and was shocked by what he heard. At first he was convinced that the record was substandard and that it sounded alarmingly like a basic rock record, but after listening to the tape a couple of times it began to dawn on him that the mix was the problem and that it lacked dynamics. He was reassured when he played the tape to his old friend Mick Geyer, who greatly admired the songs themselves but without prompting from Cave declared that the mixes were inadequate. Harvey and Cave realised that they would have to remix the entire record and decided to enlist the help of their old friend Tony Cohen, whom Cave had not seen for several years.

'I was on the farm and the phone rings and it was Nick,' recalls Cohen. 'He said, "It's Nick here, remember me?" I said, "Oh yeah, you're that old punk rock singer, aren't ya?" He said, "We've done this record and we've got some problems. The mixes. I've been listening to them and they don't sound very good and we were wondering if you could come in and do it." So we spent a couple of weeks in a studio in Melbourne [Metropolis Studios] fixing it all up, comparing it with the mixes that the guy in the US [Briggs] had done. In my opinion it sounded like they'd paid a lot of money for a bit of "air guitar", but anyway . . . It went really well. Nick was straight, and I was straight. We were drinking at 11 a.m., we'd go for the first fruit juice, you know, but we were totally off any drug whatsoever. It was really quick getting it together. The drug barrier wasn't there and we were having fun. There was a lot of doubt, perhaps with them at first, in particular with the record company. I'd had a fairly bad reputation two years before. It went really well and it was becoming obvious that we were back in business, particularly where Mick Harvey was concerned. He was in quality control mode quite often. You don't pay someone money to not do their job or not get good results.'

While Cave and the group had been working on the LP, now entitled *Henry's Dream*, several other projects with which they had been involved were released. In October 1991 a tribute album to Leonard Cohen, *I'm Your Fan*, featuring various artists performing the Canadian songwriter's compositions, included a contribution from The Bad Seeds. When Cave had first been approached to contribute to the record his initial reaction was that the idea was appalling and flatly refused to be involved. However, during a rehearsal in west London earlier in the year, after a prolonged drinking session in a nearby pub, the group had spontaneously started hammering out a half-remembered drunken rendition of Cohen's 'Tower of Song'. Their eighty-minute irreverent assault on the composition, which portrays the pitiful lot of the songwriter, was played by the group in every conceivable musical style and was recorded straight to DAT by engineer Victor Van Vugt. Later the track was reduced to a more conventional length in an abruptly cut-up form, to highlight the fact that The Bad Seeds in their rendition had covered every genre in rock music. Cave considered that the finished track did have some charm and decided to give the song to the album's compilers. 'Tribute albums,' says Mick Harvey, 'I think we'll have to say no to them in the future, people ask about them all the time, bloody tribute records. Certain people like it ["Tower Of Song"]. The spirit in which it was done should be fairly obvious. "Tower of Song" is a totally hilarious piece of writing. The music is so absurd.' Apart from former Go-Betweens Robert Forster and David McComb's tracks for the completed album, Cave thought that the other featured artists had failed to capture the inherent humour of Cohen's work. 'The great thing about the album as it came out is that it showed how little people understand Leonard Cohen, even his fans, even other musicians doing all these kinds of po-faced versions of his songs,' he later asserted.[9] When asked about the tribute album in an interview with *Q* magazine, Cohen himself would praise The Bad Seeds' 'really intelligent approach' to 'Tower of Song', considering that Cave had 'thought about it, and caught the spirit of the song'. Cohen was unaware of the circumstances under which it was recorded.

In December a Cave composition '(I'll Love You) Till the End of the World' was featured on the original soundtrack album to Wim Wenders' epic science fiction/road movie *Until the End of the World*. At Wenders' request Cave had specifically written the half-spoken narrative ballad for the film, which Wenders had been working on since 1985. He had provocatively entitled the song 'Until the End of the World' in the hope that the director would make it the film's title theme. Unfortunately for Cave, one of the world's most commercially successful rock groups, U2, also wrote a song with the same name, which forced Cave to amend his title. Cave would receive consolation in late autumn 1992. While working at Tower Records in New York City, his old friend Peter Sutcliffe organised a book signing by one of Cave's favourite contemporary authors, the *noir* crime novelist James Ellroy. Sutcliffe asked the writer if he could sign a copy of his latest novel, *White Jazz*, for his friend Nick Cave. Much to Sutcliffe's surprise, Ellroy, who loathes and detests rock'n'roll music, which he considers to be 'institutionalised rebellion', had heard and admired Cave's work, particularly the song featured in *Until the End of the World*. When Cave received Ellroy's novel he was thrilled when he read the author's dedication: 'Nick, feel those evil rock'n'roll chords of doom. That song in *Until the End of the World* really kicked my ass!' In subsequent interviews Cave would proudly display Ellroy's inscription at every available opportunity. 'Now, that to me, when someone you admire compliments you, that means far more than getting a good review, to be honest,' he said.[10]

On 15 November 1991, Tom DiCillo's light comedy *Johnny Suede*, starring Brad Pitt in the title role and featuring a cameo performance from Cave, received its British première at the 35th London Film Festival. Cave had agreed to appear in the film after reading DiCillo's script, based upon the director's one-man show of the same name, which charted the surreal romantic misfortunes of an innocent Ricky Nelson obsessive adrift in a contemporary urban wasteland. The hapless Johnny Suede, who sports a towering fifties-style pompadour, decides to emulate teen idol Nelson and become a pop star, his decision prompted by a pair of suede shoes dropping out of the sky on top of the telephone box he is using. With his best friend Deke (Calvin Levels) he writes preposterous ballads containing lines such as, 'I wanna meet a model who's only got one name', but is quickly reduced to painting apartments for a living. Suede finds a girlfriend, a similarly obsessed teenage queen, Darlette Fontaine (Alison Moir), whose mother has connections in the music industry. The relationship soon crumbles and Johnny finds himself dating Yvonne (Catherine Keener), a mature and independent schoolteacher who to Suede's horror does not even wear make-up. It is in this relationship that Suede belatedly grows up and faces reality. Cave's character in the film is Freak Storm, an ageing albino junkie rock star, who wears an even bigger pompadour than Johnny, together with a white rhinestone suit and pink suede boots. Though Freak Storm is a rock'n'roll joke, Cave detected sinister aspects to his character which appealed to him. Throughout, Storm offers highly dubious advice to the gullible Suede on 'chicks', bequeaths him a song entitled 'Mamma's Boy' which sounds uncannily like a parody of one of Cave's own songs from '*The Firstborn Is Dead*', and easily cons money from him under the pretence that he will secure him a record contract. Cave also enjoyed the fact that Freak Storm could have been a broad caricature of his perceived public persona during the days of The Birthday Party. The man in black would now become the man in white. Cave's friends and associates were very sceptical about the role and the film, advising him not to take it, which only heightened his interest. As ever, he was more than willing to poke fun at himself and his 'image', but there were limits. It had been suggested that his character wear transparent trousers, but he firmly vetoed this idea.

Cave found the actual shooting of the film, during a bitterly cold New York winter at the beginning of 1991, a painful experience, which reflected in his performance. The wig he had to wear caused him endless discomfort and he began to harbour grave doubts about the role. He was unhappy about the way the shoot was conducted, and throughout, tension would arise between the first-time director, who had shot Jim Jarmusch's *Stranger Than Paradise*, and the nervous singer. 'He was afraid that people would say, "Oh, that's just Nick Cave glorifying his old junkie days,"' DiCillo admitted. 'I gotta say that most of the time during shooting I was pretty much in awe of Nick . . . and a little afraid of him.'[11] One of the conditions Cave had stipulated in taking the role was that he could perform his own introductory scene. It was Cave's idea that Freak Storm would walk into a bar, order a tequila, only to be told by the bartender that there was no salt left for the drink. Storm would then grab a girl's arm, lick her armpit, down the tequila and deliver his dialogue with a slice of lemon wedged in his mouth. To placate Cave, the scene was shot but to his disappointment was cut from the completed film. *Johnny Suede* would enjoy favourable reviews when it opened in the UK in June 1992 but Cave's assessment, of both his own performance and the film, was rather dismissive: 'There are some genuinely funny moments in it, but I wouldn't do a film like that again.'[12]

The line, 'And it's into the fucking fray', from 'Papa Won't Leave You, Henry', must have seemed highly appropriate to Cave as he and the band began another extensive cycle of touring throughout 1992 to promote *Henry's Dream*, beginning with a broadcast concert at the Waterfront, Norwich, the first of fifty-four dates in various countries throughout the world. Once again Cave's work had elicited praise from the critics. The *Melody Maker* had awarded the double A-sided single 'Straight To You/Jack The Ripper' a 'Single of the Week' in March, and Gavin Martin, in the *New Musical Express*, had described the LP as 'haunted, battered, manic and exhilarating, *Henry's Dream* captures the extremes and diversity of Cave's past work while furthering his penchant for mockery and fully realised conceits'. Cave now even seemed to be actually relishing the rounds of interviews. When one journalist remarked that it was 'strange to hear this famously melancholic person chuckling', Cave, in his characteristically droll fashion, replied, 'When I'm in Australia, for instance, I laugh all the time . . . I feel I'm understood a bit more there because I have an Australian sensibility towards things. I laugh continuously there, belly laughs and stuff.' Yet his private fears would also show through: 'It was a complete and utter nightmare writing the songs for this record. It just gets harder and harder with each record. I'd like to think it was because I was becoming more and more selective, but the notion of writer's block is something that looms over me continually.'[13]

Cave now enjoyed performing more than he had ever done previously in his career, but he knew all too well the temptations and the pitfalls of the touring ordeal: 'For the road is long, And the road is hard, And many fall by the side'. His own fear of failure would keep him moving on but he longed for some stability in his still-chaotic existence.

After playing the Reading Festival, supporting Nirvana, on 30 August 1992, The Bad Seeds opened a series of charity concerts at the Town and Country Club, London, organised by the *New Musical Express* in aid of the Spastics Society. The sold-out concert was undoubtedly a high point of the group's career in live performance, with Cave energetically leading them through a summation of his music to that date. From the opening song, 'The Mercy Seat', they thrived on the ecstatic reaction that greeted them. Cave seemed to revel in the attention, posing for photographs between songs, accepting cigarettes from the audience and even welcoming the irrepressible Bingo to dance on stage with the band during 'Deanna'. 'This guy's a fireman,' Cave informed the audience about his uninvited guest, who had rolled over their heads to reach the stage. 'He saves little children.' Midway through the concert Cave announced: 'I'm going to invite one of my favourite singers to come and sing with us, if he's here, Mr Shane MacGowan.' While Cave was looking expectantly stage left MacGowan mischievously walked on behind him stage right, momentarily confusing the singer, before the pair delivered a duet of Louis Armstrong's standard 'What a Wonderful World'.

Throughout the past year the two friends had kept in touch, seeing each other socially and discussing the possibility of embarking on a collaborative project. 'We'd been planning for ages to get something together,' says MacGowan, 'but we just ended up getting pissed, you know what I mean, which was fine by me. If it happened, it happened. One idea was that he wrote a song for me and I wrote one for him.' The first time Cave had visited MacGowan's north London home he had been regaled with an impassioned and unaccompanied performance of two unrecorded MacGowan ballads, 'St John of God' and 'The Wayward Wind', delivered within inches of his face. Cave loved the songs and was amazed that they had been casually scattered about the debris in MacGowan's front room, together with other compositions, but MacGowan wanted to record the songs himself and at that time Cave had no spare songs to offer in return. Eventually it was decided that Cave would record one of his favourite Pogues songs, MacGowan's 'Rainy Night in Soho', while MacGowan would sing Cave's 'Lucy' from *The Good Son*. The A-side for the single, recorded with The Bad Seeds at Abbey Road Studios and released on 30 November 1992 was 'What a Wonderful World', a song which had always appealed to Cave. 'There's a very eerie quality to that song, it's got everything. I don't know if I'll ever be able to write a song as subtle as that,' Cave admitted earlier in the year. 'It just breaks your heart to hear that song. There's a sadness to it, but at the same time there was a person who was very successful, and by all accounts a very happy person, or someone who steeled himself against the world. It's the same way you feel when you see something that perhaps you don't have.'[14] When they promoted the single, both Cave and MacGowan were incensed that their choice of song had been viewed as ironic. MacGowan was adamant that that approach would be akin to the Pet Shop Boys 'slaughtering' 'Always On My Mind': 'That's a great Willie Nelson song, a classic version by Presley, and they took the piss. Out of the song, out of the writers, out of the people who bought it. The only people they didn't take the piss out of was themselves. The worst cover version ever. "Wonderful World" is nothing like that.'[15]

Two songs after MacGowan's departure from the stage, Cave declared that he was about to offer 'a little history lesson', whereupon he invited Rowland S. Howard to join him and Mick Harvey to play a few songs from the repertoire of 'a band we used to be in called The Birthday Party'. With Martyn P. Casey standing in on bass for the late Tracy Pew, Cave, Howard and Harvey, with a little assistance from Blixa Bargeld, delivered electrifying versions of 'Wild World', 'Dead Joe' and 'Nick The Stripper', songs that the trio had not played together for years. 'There's a few of the older folk here tonight who realise what this means close to tears,' wrote Andrew Mueller in his *Melody Maker* review of the concert. 'A full-scale Birthday Party reunion will, of course, never happen – the tackiness of such an enterprise aside, the band's defining and uniquely muscular bass-player, Tracey [*sic*] Pew, died a few years back, but for three songs tonight . . . and the Party burned again, but for that trio of bastard blues exorcisms, there wasn't a blinking eye in the house.' Songs that had been reviled in some quarters at the time of their conception were now greeted as rock classics, an irony that Tracy Pew would perhaps have appreciated.

NOTES

1 Debbie Nettleingham, 'Nick Cave', *The Beat*, July 1990.
2 Gerry McGovern, 'Always Look on the Dark Side of Life', *Hot Press*, Vol. 17, No.13, 1 December 1993.
3 Sasha Stojanovic, 'The Good Prodigal Son', *Juke*, 21 July 1990.
4 Paul Byrne, 'Saint Nick', *Hot Press*, 23 April 1992.
5 Ian Gittins, 'A Man Called Hearse', *Melody Maker*, 28 March 1992.
6 Matthew Hall, 'Nick Cave, The Thirtysomething Years', *Puncture*, No.24, May 1992.
7 Jon Selzer, 'Word For Word', *Lime Lizard*, June 1992.
8 Jon Young, 'Nick Cave: Cultivating Bad Seeds For Fun and Profit', *Cream*, June/July 1992.
9 David Quantick and Marc Pechart, 'It Takes a Nation of Brazilians', *NME*, 4 April 1992.
10 Stuart Maconie, 'A Night at the Optics', *NME*, 28 November 1992.
11 Mark Kermode, 'Retro Old 'Un Player', *NME*, 20 June 1992.
12 Matthew Hall, 'Nick Cave, The Thirtysomething Years', *Puncture*, No.24, May 1992.
13 Andy Gill, 'Titter Ye Not', *Q*, May 1992.
14 Jon Selzer, 'Word For Word', *Lime Lizard*, June 1992.
15 Stuart Maconie, 'A Night at the Optics', *NME*, 28 November 1992.

16

Let Love In

During the latter half of 1992 Cave had surprised some of his friends with the news of his intention to move to London with Viviane and Luke. He had grown disenchanted with São Paulo. 'I think they prefer their rock stars to have a little more mystery,' he confessed. 'I can't help feeling I disappointed them in some way.'[1] In late 1991 he had considered moving to America. Manhattan was out of the question because he did not want his son to grow up in a city that he considered to be a harsh and heartless environment, so he had looked north, to upstate New York. 'He toyed with the idea of moving to Woodstock,' says Victor Van Vugt, 'but one look made him realise that he's not the sort of guy who'd drive a station wagon.' While recording *Henry's Dream* Cave had become disillusioned with America and its society, which seemed to him to be spiralling out of control. The extremity that he had once found so romantic, and that had fired his imagination, now only left him with feelings of revulsion. The country's seemingly endless infatuation with death and violence appeared to him to be layered with an equally violent gross sentimentality which, in his view, seemed to permeate every other aspect of society. He was even appalled by the American use of language: 'It's the whole psychotherapeutic language they come up with. It's amazing to hear people speak about matters of the heart in a way that obviously has nothing to do with the way they feel at all. That's quite shocking, that turnaround for me, because I always found America a very fascinating place.'[2]

After much deliberation, the couple had decided to leave São Paulo for London. Cave's inability to learn Portuguese had made day-to-day life in the city increasingly exasperating for him, and though he enjoyed being left to his own devices he felt that he had been isolated from the rest of the world for far too long. Moving back to Melbourne was an attractive but unfeasible proposition because he had built his whole career in Europe. London was not the most ideal solution but because his publisher and record company were based there, it was the most practical. Yet he had hankered for the many friends he had in the city, whom he had missed while living in Brazil, and London also offered a relatively stable environment in which to raise his son. He had even grown to quite like the city that he had once so vehemently hated, because he was now immeasurably more secure financially than when he had first arrived in the capital in 1980. He could also escape the cold winter months by returning to the couple's house in Brazil, or visiting Melbourne while touring or recording.

Cave and the group began 1993 by completing their tour of Australia and performing at a series of large outdoor festival concerts around the country. Entitled 'The Big Day Out', the highly successful shows also featured Iggy Pop, Sonic Youth, Mudhoney and The Beasts Of Bourbon, artists with whom Cave shared a feeling of camaraderie, and throughout the tour he would regularly appear with most of these acts. According to David Sly, writing in the *Adelaide Advertiser* about the series' final celebratory show at the city's university on 1 February: 'It established the significance of alternative rock culture in the nineties, proved how effectively it can be organised and marshalled, and also how much simple fun it can generate. A triumph in anyone's words.'

At Atlantis Studios in Melbourne during January and February 1993, Cave and the band demoed songs that he had been working on, and mixed live tapes they had recorded at various dates in Europe and Australia. His primary reason for wanting to make a live record was to capture on stage the group's powerful interpretations of the songs on *Henry's Dream* and present them as he thought they should have sounded on the studio recordings. 'The next thing I knew they were back in Australia,' says Tony Cohen, who mixed the tapes that would comprise the CD *Live Seeds* released in September that year. 'I'd suggested this place, which was cheap and had two studios. We mixed the live stuff in the main studio at the same time as working on the demos in the smaller one. That worked out really well and it was obvious that we should really get back together as a team. Everyone's learnt a lot. It's so easy now to get the sounds and to understand what kind of sound people want.'

Cave's old friend, photographer Peter Milne, was also present at Atlantis Studios, having already accompanied the group during the 1992–3 series of tours, documenting life on the road with the band for a slim hardback book to be packaged with *Live Seeds*, and for a separate, much larger volume, *Fish in a Barrel*. 'There was a period of many, many years where I would only see them when they'd come back to Australia for the annual pilgrimage,' says Milne. 'Then I'd maybe make contact with them but in the mean time there were a whole series of divergent life experiences. But during the tours that I was working on I really got to know Nick and Mick again, perhaps more than I've ever done, and it was wonderful to see that they hadn't changed. They'd developed and matured, as I hope I have to some extent, but they're still the same people . . . In many ways Nick is still very insecure and yet, I think this is really important, he's never doubted his vision. In that respect he's still self-confident. If you have that you continue to produce and you don't get bound up with the fans, and you don't get caught up in creating what you think other people will be impressed by. You know what you want to say and you continue to say it. His insecurities are part of his greatest weakness and his greatest strength because I think that is where his genuine humility comes from. He doubts and he worries about everything, that's why he works so hard, he's a perfectionist. Sometimes it's like he works on things too much but through all that, and through his problems with drugs and so on, he's never lost that clarity of vision. I think Nick is a very complex character and there is a validity in exploring the complexities of that character, but one should be wary of being too analytical. One of the things I love and admire about Nick is that what you see is what you get. He is complex but in quite an open fashion. The complexities and apparent contradictions are there, on the surface. You don't have to dig for them. That's probably part of some people's problem with him. If you take him at face value he's honest. If you look at Nick's writing, if you look at Nick's music, I think you see Nick, all facets of his character, an accurate impression.

'I think what's changed is life is very different. Touring isn't the wild thing you might imagine. There's a fair amount of steam being let off, like you'd expect with any band, but it's not wall-to-wall groupies or anything like that. The people they tend to get in the band room are earnest young women, thrusting volumes of their poetry on them, or books that have changed their lives. There was a lot of that. At the end of some of the gigs in Europe Nick would walk away with all these books, most of which were in Greek or Italian. At the next gig he'd give them to somebody else, recycle them, saying, "This book was really important to me, you should read it." I noticed travelling with the band that it is very difficult for Nick to maintain normal relationships with people because of the position he's in. He's by no means a superstar, but he's famous enough, and the attention he attracts is very intense. It's difficult for him in public situations, a pressure he feels very acutely. You can argue that's the life he's chosen and no one's going to break down and cry about the torment of being rich and famous, but it's an additional pressure in his life. When he walks into a room when he's travelling with the band and he's got that public face on . . . there's a photo of mine from that tour where he's just sitting down having a drink and there are all these kids at his feet staring up at him expectantly. Yet in the midst of that he manages to be genuinely courteous and considerate, but it's difficult.'

In March 1993 Cave, Carneiro and Luke would move into a relatively inconspicuous-looking house in North Kensington, with a small garden containing a large shed that Cave converted into his office workspace. Not wishing to be saddled with a mortgage, he had bought the property outright for cash. Having lived a nomadic existence for most of his life, settling into a relatively domesticated situation in a street suburban in appearance would take some adjustment. His longings and experiences in this situation would inspire his lyrics for his next album, *Let Love In*, the most directly personal record he has yet produced. As ever, he would find that his songs externalised his desires and thoughts, even offering an indication of the outcome of future personal events.

Within a week of the family having moved into the property, the house was burgled while they slept upstairs, and Cave lost, amongst other items, his word processor and fax machine. The window through which the thieves had gained entry now featured a prominent Neighbourhood Watch sticker. Living in London was not going to be easy. 'I don't think it's any coincidence that a lot of the characters I write about tend to be very rootless,' Cave declared, 'always moving into or out of situations. I've enjoyed never having to be a part of society. On the other hand there's a negative side to it, which is that I don't actually feel a part of anything.'[3]

Not long after Cave had established himself in his new home, he would be writing once again at the request of Wim Wenders. Wenders was completing his sequel to *Wings of Desire*, *Faraway, So Close (In Weiter Ferne, so nah!)*, appropriately shot in the former East Zone of Berlin, since the director wanted to capture the sense of desolate disillusion that followed the euphoria of reunification in the capital. The remaining angel Cassiel (Otto Sander), like his partner Bruno Ganz in *Wings of Desire*, decides to become human, this time in order to save a girl's life when she falls from the balcony of a high-rise flat. Wenders wanted Cave to write the film's title theme and a song to accompany Cassiel's death at the hands of a ruthless gun-runner, the whole situation specifically engineered by a character who alone can drift between the world of the angels and human beings, Willem Dafoe's sinister Emit Flesti, whose name spelt backwards reads 'Time Itself'. With only a rough outline from Wenders of the plot and what he wanted from the song, together with a few rough cuts from the film, Cave set to work, enjoying the task of producing commissioned compositions to order. He would tell friends that it was almost like having a proper job. He was particularly pleased with the moving ballad, 'Cassiel's Song', recorded in London with his friend and former Bad Seed Barry Adamson playing bass, Mick Harvey providing the string arrangement and Cave himself playing the piano. 'I've always wanted to write a death song,' Cave later quipped to a journalist. 'Someone else's, of course.'[4]

In June 1993 The Bad Seeds played three European dates, in Berlin, Valencia and Barcelona, followed by two concerts at the Haifa Seaport in Israel. These were the group's first shows in the country and they were a little taken aback by the rapturous reception that greeted them, from their arrival at the airport to the concerts themselves. They were equally shocked to discover that Bad Seeds records outsold the Rolling Stones in Israel and that their performances at the Haifa Seaport, the first of which was broadcast live on Israeli radio, drew twice as many people as had Bob Dylan when he played gigs at the same venue. 'Here's another song about a guy who kills his woman,' Cave announced in a deadpan fashion to the excitable crowd midway through the first concert. 'This is a blues festival after all . . . and we feel somewhat imposters here . . . but nevertheless we will do a song by the great John Lee Hooker, "I'm Gonna Kill That Woman".' The band's encore rendition of Tim Rose's remorseful murder ballad 'Long Time Man' even eclipsed the group's own studio recording of the song on *Your Funeral . . . My Trial*, whilst a new cover song in their repertoire, Nina Simone's 'Plain Gold Ring', veering suddenly from mournful soul to an exhilarating eruption of noise, indicated the direction Cave wanted to take the band on *Let Love In*.

By mid July Cave had composed at least four songs for the new album, written mostly sitting in a bar on Portobello Road, Notting Hill. One of these compositions was a sprawling epic he had entitled 'Do You Love Me?', with its verses alternating between an almost schizophrenic description of a relationship, with the lover offering both release and torment ('She had a heartful of love and devotion, She had a mindful of tyranny and terror'), and a first-person-narrated tale of a child's first sexual experience, abused by a child molester in a darkened cinema. To clarify his concerns, Cave separated the song into two parts, which would open and close the collection of tracks, the majority of which would reflect his domestic situation. In 'Do You Love Me? (Part 2)', arguably one of his most disturbing songs, he wanted to convey the indelible intensity of an initial experience, whether good or evil, pure or immoral, and how that first sensation or violation could never be repeated. 'There was some vague idea that your first experience of love dictates the capacity you have in later years to express your emotions,' he would later admit. 'So the song was about many things – creative impotence, not being able to write, not being able to relate properly to a woman . . . I took great pains to write this song. I went through hundreds of different transformations and I hoped I maintained a mystery to the song and at the same time gave it a kind of unnerving quality.'[5]

By late summer of 1993 Cave had written a large proportion of the material for the album, and at the beginning of September the band, together with Tony Cohen co-producing, began recording for two weeks at the Townhouse III studio in south London. Both versions of 'Do You Love Me?' were recorded at these sessions, with Rowland Howard, and Tex Perkins of The Cruel Sea contributing backing vocals to the chorus of Part 1, while Katherine Blake and Donna McEvitt of Miranda Sex Garden added ethereal harmonies to Part 2. During the intensive two-week session the band also recorded Cave's 'Nobody's Baby Now', perhaps his most conventional love song, recalling a long-lost lover with a tune reminiscent of Van Morrison's 'Here Comes the Night', and 'Lay Me Low', in which Cave self-mockingly delivers his own melodramatic obituary. Beneath much of the overt humour of the funeral dirge, which depicts Cave's casket carried by a motorcade 'ten miles long', and interviews conducted with his former teachers revealing that he 'Was one of God's sorrier creatures', could be detected more serious observations: 'My friends will give up the fight, They'll see my work in a different light, When I go'. 'I Let Love In' presented another unflinching depiction of the trials and rewards to be found contained within a relationship, with the writer's perspective shifting to an ever darker mood, the lover/'tormentor' being portrayed as 'the punishment for all my former sins'. The narrative of 'Red Right Hand' obliquely warned of accepting at face value those who outwardly convey benign concern for others while masking their own selfish interests. Cave's own acute abhorrence of American television talk-show hosts who elicit lurid confessions from members of their studio audience to boost their ratings could be discerned in the lines, 'You'll see him in your head, On the TV screen, And hey buddy, I'm warning you to turn it off'.

Musically, Cave and the band, with Tony Cohen's help, were creating a full, vibrant sound which displayed many eclectic influences. 'Do You Love Me? (Part 1)' verged towards sixties Memphis soul, and 'Red Right Hand' was propelled by a taut funk riff. As ever, rather than merely mimicking soul artists that he admired, such as Isaac Hayes, Al Green and Barry White, Cave was intent on creating his own sound which carried similar associations. The rhythmic, clipped, delayed echo guitar produced by Blixa Bargeld was particularly effective in generating the ambience that he was seeking. 'During recording Blixa told me that it was the best guitar sound he'd ever had,' says Tony Cohen. 'I was very surprised at that, very unusual for him to actually say something like that.'

Recording at Townhouse III ended on 12 September, and there was a prolonged break in the album's production when The Bad Seeds went on the road for a twelve-date European tour, beginning in Prague on 21 September to promote the *Live Seeds* CD set. Cave welcomed the break from recording in order to take time to work on and revise some of the lyrics he had written, and to perform 'Do You Love Me?' and 'I Let Love In' in front of an audience to gauge how the new material worked on stage. The Bad Seeds' tour ended on 6 October in Dusseldorf, but Cave would be back on the road throughout November, participating in Die Haut's tenth anniversary tour of Europe and Brazil, along with other guests Blixa Bargeld, Anita Lane, Lydia Lunch, Kid Congo Powers, Jeffrey Lee Pierce and Alex Hacke. His contribution to the shows was to perform 'Truck Love' and 'Pleasure Is The Boss', songs that he had first sung with Die Haut in 1983 on their *Burning The Ice* album, together with an electric rendition of The Loved Ones' 'Sad Dark Eyes'.

Having worked further on embryonic ideas for songs with Victor Van Vugt and guest musicians Rowland Howard, and James Johnston of Gallon Drunk in a small rehearsal studio in west London, Cave returned in December to Australia to complete *Let Love In* with the band at Metropolis Studios in Melbourne. With recording, songwriting and mixing being simultaneously conducted at a frantic pace between two studios in the building, a process that Tony Cohen would refer to as 'the assembly line', this session would prove to be one of the most productive they had yet undertaken.

'They were pretty chaotic and intense sessions,' admits Mick Geyer, Cave's friend of many years, who was present throughout the December Metropolis sessions offering advice and encouragement. 'Nick is an obsessive type of person and maybe no more so than in the recording studio. He creates this cauldron of an environment by putting himself up against the wall with deadlines and throws himself at it with some kind of vengeance. It's the kind of challenge he relishes. In this case the record had to be completed by the time his flight was booked for Brazil.' This schedule would ensure that Cave would be occupied for sixteen or twenty hours a day, with music, lyrics or mixing.

Cave drew up a list of papers for particular songs, methodically listing all that needed to be added from the London sessions, together with detailed notes on new compositions that he intended to record. These lists can be clearly seen on the inner sleeve of *Let Love In*, splayed out all across the walls and floor of Metropolis' Studio 2, where the actual recording took place. Day by day he would mark off what had been completed. 'Nick would obsessively write them up every day,' says Mick Harvey. 'No one else could write on them because it had to be in his handwriting. If someone else wrote on them he would actually rewrite that page from the beginning and stick it back up again, because it had been polluted. He was pretty out there, I'll say that much, but he could see the funny side of it too. He'd say, "Who wrote that?" and he'd be smiling, but he'd take it down all the same. All over the piano were all the songs with his little notes, his little graphs of chord sequences, bits of lyrics.' In the first few days of the sessions Harvey was working in Studio 2, continuing to play on tracks that were still being recorded, but would soon move to the mixing room to aid Tony Cohen. As the recording of each song was finished the tapes would be delivered to Cohen for mixing in Studio 3. 'It was a very proficient way of working,' says Geyer, 'and using the two studios was fundamental in the efficiency of the process. Nick would hold court in Studio 2, while Mick Harvey would be hammering out mixes with Tony Cohen in 3.'

Concurrent with his other tasks, Cave was also engaged in completing the cover artwork for the LP. 'He had to have it done by the day the record was finished,' says Harvey. 'The release date was already set and he was going off to Brazil for six weeks, so he had to have everything finished by the start of January. So we'd be mixing, and Nick would be out there putting together all these huge sheets of paper, sticking bits of lyrics and everything all over these individual pages into a collage. It was very hard to get him to come into the studio sometimes, because he was so obsessively involved with this. He was in a pretty funny state at the time, he was kind of in extreme overdrive.'

'The time pressure really added to making the record good,' says Tony Cohen, 'because it suddenly brought it home that this record had to be done now. It crammed in a twenty-hour-a-day work load with four hours trying to recuperate. It was pretty wild. We were working like we used to, a lot of confidence seemed to be coming out of Nick at this stage, which was really good to see, and I think that spurs everybody on. If he's feeling good and confident, really enjoying it, I think everybody else does to a degree. When Nick is in frantic mode he sets up his little camp which is usually around the piano, and all the artwork started growing from around that area. He was tearing up bits of paper and making pictures on the wall, and stuff. When the pieces got too big, because they were all gaffa-taped together, he had to move out into the corridor, the walls out there, and God knows where else.'

During this session, 'Loverman', a song that had been worked upon at Townhouse III and about which Cave had expressed misgivings, finally reached fruition with the addition of two spoken passages in which Cave would literally spell out the theme of the song: 'L is for *love*, baby, O is for *only* you that I do, V is for loving *virtually* everything that you are, E is for loving almost *everything* that you do . . .' The tone of his delivery, accurately described by Chris Bohn as 'pitched somewhere between Barry White and one of Dennis Hopper's more deranged creations', united the visceral eruptions of the song's lusty chorus with the menacing soul overtures of the verses. The passages themselves had been written by Cave in the studio. 'It sounded fine to me before those two pieces were put in,' says Geyer, 'but Nick felt that the song lacked impetus. With his customary persistence he worked and reworked and hammered out those two little set pieces and sculpted them into the "vacant" passages. When it came to putting the vocal down he'd go over it time and time again until the voice itself developed patterns and rhythms in the manner of any featured instrument. He then doubled up the vocal, added some grunts and yelps for emphasis, which all lifted the song.'

In the studio Cave wrote two fast, aggressive rock'n'roll songs to give further variety to the album. 'Jangling Jack', which he later described as 'a piece of trash about the senseless, irrational and repulsive violence of America',[6] gave him ample opportunity to vent his spleen about a country he had now come to loathe. The song originated with the concept of a naive Englishman visiting New York, perhaps using England as a metaphor for an Old World colliding with the New and being overwhelmed with its violence. 'Jack' walks into a bar, raises a toast to the USA and its 'losers and winners' and is promptly shot by someone who evidently disagrees. Only in his death throes does Jack see the reality of his surroundings: 'He sees the berserk city, Sees the dead stacked in piles'.

'"Jangling Jack" was written in the studio within a day,' recalls Geyer. 'Nick wanted another rock song to add some breadth and dynamic to the record, something a little more coarse. It was originally the tale of a naive Englishman running wide-eyed into the frenetic violence of the New World in New York. The normal sort of subjects that appealed to him, that he can graft his tale on to. But by the time he'd written a few verses the original idea was immaterial. He'd write whole verses, throw them around, throw them out, invert it and write it all over again. You'd leave for half an hour and he'd still be on a single line, and then you'd leave for another half an hour and it'd all be completely different. In the end the song sits in its own mire without moralising about violence; it's comic, harsh, humorous and perverse, just like rock music.'

Though presented as an overtly humorous and disposable 'trashcan song', 'Thirsty Dog' must rank as one of the most personal songs Cave has ever written. With echoes of Leonard Cohen's depiction of love as open hostilities in 'There is a War', he delivers an incessant litany of apologies to his lover while reflecting upon his own self-destructive lifestyle: 'I was not equipped to know how to care, And on the occasions I came up for air, I saw my life and wondered what the hell I had been living'. The final rampaging verse ends with the prophetic lines, 'I'm sorry that I'm always pissed, I'm sorry that I exist, And when I look into your eyes, I can see you're sorry too'.

Throughout the Metropolis session friends and associates of the band constantly visited the studio, contributing to a perpetual party atmosphere upon which Cave seemed to thrive but which would not deflect him from concentrating solely on creating the album. 'Normally his time in Melbourne is taken up with touring and recording,' says Geyer. 'He catches up with people while he's recording. He appreciates the number of friends he has in Melbourne and he loves to work in an environment where there are a lot of people around. There were people coming in, girlfriends, children running around, but Nick was really totally oblivious to what was going on in the background. There's a particularly active musical environment in Melbourne, and there's a community of people who play music which is rather extensive and broad in its musical variety. Nick had the attitude that as these people were dropping in they be included on the album to reflect some of that camaraderie.'

Mick Harvey adds: 'It was almost like Nick would see them there, and being socially awkward as he was, because he was so completely introspective at that time, he'd just say, "Oh, well, er, you'll have to sing some backing vocal." Then this innocent visitor would be stuck in the studio, that's why there are so many different backing vocalists on the record.'

Geyer himself and mutual friend Nick S. Seferi found themselves placed alongside Bad Seeds Bargeld, Savage and Wydler to sing the 'Do da do Do da do' backing vocal on 'Jangling Jack'. 'Nick was waving his baton,' says Geyer, 'conducting as one would conduct an aggravated children's choir. The backing vocal itself was this beautifully inane and nonsensical gibberish, delivered with fervour and great enthusiasm, amongst a lot of dancing. It was very funny and a good time was had by all. More and more people arrived in the studio to witness the spectacle as it progressed, or regressed.'

David McComb of The Triffids would contribute backing vocals to 'Lay Me Low', while violinists Warren Ellis, of the instrumental group The Dirty Three, and Robin Casinader, from Dave Graney's Coral Snakes, provided the strings for Mick Harvey's arrangements of 'Do You Love Me? (Part 2)' and 'Ain't Gonna Rain Anymore', the lyrics to which Cave had completed in the studio. While writing the song he had been pondering over an appropriate metaphor for a certain woman and after much deliberation had concluded that 'rain' was apt. Once again friends and members of the band were enlisted, in this instance to help with the completion of lyrics. Cave would jokingly refer to the ensuing witty exchanges and rapport as 'thesaurus duty'. 'Any number of ideas were tossed around in the completion of lyrics,' says Geyer. 'Nick would often say, "Give me a hand with this," and you'd just throw stuff at him. Things would come up but he would be the ultimate disseminator of all this. The final word belongs to him. He's the only one with the veto power over everything.'

'He had a team of people working on words and things like that,' adds Tony Cohen. 'He often does. If he's got people around and he respects their intelligence on matters like that, he'll set them straight to work. I mean, there's no free lunch. Everybody's got to pull their bloody weight. That was all probably a hell of a lot of enjoyment for him too.'

'I think they were doing quite a lot of research,' says Mick Harvey. 'I remember them going over quite a lot of stuff out of books. I think there was a bit of "thesaurus duty", actually. I got that impression but I was in the mixing room. I can imagine Marty [Casey] shouting things out. I'm sure Blixa was involved, he comes out with some very abstract, surreal images.'

Ellis and Casinader's violins would also feature on a murder ballad that Cave had begun working on at the rehearsal studio in London in November and completed at Metropolis. 'Warren's a maniac,' says Cohen. 'He hasn't been playing that long but he's got a touch of madness that makes him really good. People often have to play the violin for years to get that good.' Entitled 'Red Right Hand II', the song took the form of a first-person narration by a schizophrenic serial killer who murders his wife and three children then changes his identity yet again to beguile another ill-fated family. This song, together with the previously recorded 'O'Mally's Bar', which relates the tale of a bloodthirsty massacre from the perpetrator's perspective, marked the beginning of Cave's next major scheme. Beginning in earnest in December 1994, he embarked on a long-held ambition to create an entire collection of murder ballads, on which Warren Ellis would be one of the many featured musicians. The project, provisionally entitled 'Murder', which will be accompanied by a film directed by John Hillcoat, will also feature a duet between Cave and Australian singer/actress Kylie Minogue on a composition entitled 'The Wild Rose'. 'Anything's possible now,' declares Tony Cohen. 'I think a good thing is that he's finding out that he doesn't have to scream and shout and bang people over the head all the time. I mean, when you get a bit older you don't have the energy to have all this anger and noise in you. I reckon that some of the best stuff is going to come out of this slightly more melodic direction. That'll be really interesting, you'll probably see a whole lot of new avenues opened.'

While recording was in progress Cave was taking time to listen to the mixes as they developed. 'Tony Cohen would be performing his wizardry,' recalls Geyer. 'Comments would fly from any of the band but primarily from Nick in a public sense, and more privately Mick with Tony Cohen. Nick wouldn't put it to committee but he'd call for comments from others on what was being done. Nick would, with really remarkable perception and recall, be able to walk into a mix after five or six hours, sit down, listen to it all and find an instrument that in the process of mixing had become inaudible. It may have been his design to use it as a primary rhythmic instrument. Finding that it was absent would mean going back and starting again. He also had the sense that if a song wasn't sufficiently dynamic then he would sit down and work out a piano piece that would subsequently be enlisted into a major role.'

'Nick always does that with the mixing,' says Mick Harvey. 'He often just lets it go for a few hours and then comes in and gets involved right at the end on details. It's always been like that, he just leaves us to it and we set it all up, getting it sounding really good overall. Then he sets about the fine details of things, which is why he was able to continue working in Studio 2. We've learnt over the years each other's strengths, that's why I'm there at the mixing desk because that's one of my jobs. It's my job to get the mix together with the engineer at that stage in the proceedings.'

'One has to insist on that after a while,' says Cohen about Harvey's assistance during mixing, 'because if there's no one there, it's very difficult to know what direction to take. There's a million ways a mix can go, and sometimes you've got to have somebody there. It was difficult. It was hard for Mick, there was a lot of work.'

'Nick always takes ideas from the floor,' continues Harvey. 'He needs the input from the band. He's kind of dependent upon it for his confidence, he's got no other feedback he can trust. Like anybody, he needs to get confirmation, he needs someone else to say, "That's really great," and then he'll feel a lot better about it. And that's what the band's there for, to make suggestions and to change things, but for these particular sessions he was a bit more cut off than usual, actually. He was difficult to communicate with because he was doing his usual thing of just getting completely obsessed with his own idea, where he was driving himself. It was a bit of a roller-coaster ride and we had to kind of just go with it. It was a very creative period.'

'Nick takes suggestions when they're good,' says Cohen. 'I'm always one to throw ideas all over the place because that's my job, and have most of them rejected, and occasionally have a good one popping through, which is exactly what has to be done. If you're too frightened to try things out with him, then you're not the sort of person that he would want to work with because it stimulates his own imagination. Overall, I think Nick was in a really good mood during the sessions. I mean, he was coping with more stuff at one time than I've ever seen done and I think he was enjoying the challenge. I remember him as being quite an inspiration. I found it hard work at the time but the final result was very enjoyable.'

The *Let Love In* sessions were concluded on 3 January 1994. 'I remember Nick having a playback after the whole thing, which is his custom,' says Cohen, 'to listen to all the mixes in the control room at a level that not very many human beings can actually stand. I remember being about halfway across the building and I could still hear it. He just stands right in the middle of it and loves it. I think that's his little sort of purge at the end of it all.' With the last track finally mixed, Cave and Harvey discussed ideas for the track order at around three o'clock in the morning. Cave then drove home, packed his bags, went to the airport and left Australia for Brazil at ten a.m. the same day.

The completed album, released on 18 April 1994, was a triumph. *Let Love In* would prove to be not only one of the most accomplished and fully realised records of Cave's entire career, but also his most commercially successful, reaching Number 12 in the national British charts. If any proof were needed of his continuing relevance and ability to create profound and authoritative lyrics welded to innovative music which spans the history of rock'n'roll, then *Let Love In* provided it with ease. The album displayed that the clarity of his unique artistic vision, and his commitment to it, had only intensified with each passing year since The Bad Seeds' conception. It also gave an unequivocal indication of the continuing ascendancy of Nick Cave and The Bad Seeds. 'The best is yet to come,' says Chris Carr.

NOTES

1 David Cavanagh, 'The Saint of the Pit', *Select*, May 1992.
2 Jon Selzer, 'Word For Word', *Lime Lizard*, June 1992.
3 Ben Thompson, 'At Last, a Comfortable Cave', *The Independent Sunday Review*, 17 April 1994.
4 Robert Yates, 'Cave Dweller', *The Wire*, Issue 123, May 1994.
5 Gavin Martin, 'From Beer to Paternity', *NME*, 2 April 1994.
6 Ibid.

DISCOGRAPHY

(With many thanks to Mick Harvey and Andrew and Lynn Trute)

THE BOYS NEXT DOOR

Lethal Weapons (Suicide VXL 4072)

LP. Various Artists. Released March 1978.

Australian punk compilation containing 3 Boys Next Door tracks, 'These Boots Are Made For Walking', 'Boy Hero' and 'Masturbation Generation'. Released on white vinyl with gatefold sleeve. Reissued on black vinyl with an inner printed sleeve. Recorded at the Media Sound Studio, Melbourne. Produced by Greg Macainsh.

'These Boots Are Made For Walking'/'Boy Hero' (Suicide 103140)

7″ single. Released March 1978.

Issued in plain paper RCA sleeve. Probably 1,500 copies.

Door Door (Mushroom L36931)

LP. Released May 1979.

Side One: 'Night Watchman', 'Brave Exhibitions', 'Friends of My World',

'The Voice', 'Roman Roman', 'Somebody's Watching'. Recorded at Alan Eaton Studios, Melbourne. Produced by Les Karsky, June 1978.
Side Two: 'After a Fashion', 'Dive Position', 'I Mistake Myself', 'Shivers'. Recorded at Richmond Recorders, January 1979. There have been 3 different pressings, the difference being label design. Recently it became available on CD. Tracks on Side One are from an album entitled *Brave Exhibitions* which was never released; this left 6 still-unreleased reject tracks. Rowland S. Howard joined the band after the recording of *Door Door*, the group scrapped half the record and rerecorded a new set of songs which comprise all of Side Two. Side Two engineered by Tony Cohen and produced by The Boys Next Door.

'Shivers'/'Dive Position' (Mushroom K-7492)

7" single. Released May 1979.

Identical versions to those on *Door Door*. No picture sleeve. Has been released several times with different label designs. The original version, by Rowland Howard's band The Young Charlatans, is available on the *Fast Forward* cassettezine (FF 004). 'Shivers' is also featured on the *Dogs In Space* soundtrack album (US-Atlantic 81789-1) and a Mute compilation entitled *The Tyranny of the Beat: Original Soundtracks From the Grey Area* (Mute A GREY 1), released in December 1991.

'Scatterbrain' (Crystal Ballroom CBR-1)

7" single. Released November 1979.

Free single distributed at the Crystal Ballroom, Melbourne, in November 1979. Has a picture sleeve. Mixed in September 1979. 'Early Morning Brain' by The Models on the other side. Recorded on a 4-track in Phill Calvert's bedroom. 'Scatterbrain' is also found on the Missing Link cassette-only release *From The Archives*. The Boys Next Door are listed as 'Torn Ox Bodies'.

'Hee Haw' (Missing Link MLEP-3)

12" EP. Released December 1979.

Side One: 'Catholic Skin', 'The Red Clock', 'Faint Heart'.

Side Two: 'Death By Drowning', 'The Hairshirt'.
All copies with printed insert. The first pressings consisted of 500 copies with the labels the wrong way around. Reissued by Missing Link in 1983, catalogue number Missing Link ING 008, with no insert. Artwork and labels are slightly different. Released on CD by 4AD on 7 August 1989 as a 13-track compilation of 'Hee Haw' and the dually named *The Boys Next Door/The Birthday Party* LP, catalogue number CAD 307 CD (see below for further details). This 13-track compilation was released on vinyl in Australia, catalogue number Virgin VOZ 2037, in 1989. Recorded July–August 1979 at Richmond Recorders. Engineered by Tony Cohen. Produced by The Boys Next Door/Keith Glass.

'Happy Birthday'/'Riddlehouse' (Missing Link MLS-16)

7" single. Released February 1980.

Free single distributed at the last Boys Next Door concert at the Crystal Ballroom, Melbourne, 16 February 1980, before they moved to England and changed their name to The Birthday Party. Exists with or without picture sleeve. Recorded at Richmond Recorders in August/September 1979 and January/February 1980. 750 copies pressed.

The Boys Next Door/The Birthday Party

A compilation LP on Missing Link (LINK 77), carrying the dual name, consisting of single and EP tracks and others. Several pressings with different artwork.
Side One: 'Mr Clarinet', 'Hats On Wrong', 'The Hairshirt', 'Guilt Parade', 'Riddle House'.
Side Two: 'The Friend Catcher', 'Waving My Arms', 'The Red Clock', 'Catman', 'Happy Birthday'.
Recorded at Richmond Records August/September 1979 and January/February 1980. Engineered by Tony Cohen. Produced by The Boys Next Door and Keith Glass. Released November 1980.

From The Archives

Cassette-only release by Missing Link containing 'Scatterbrain' and

'Enemy of the State'. The former track was originally performed by The Young Charlatans, Rowland S. Howard's previous band.

Document 82/85

UK compilation cassette released by Pleasantly Surprised. Includes 'The Hairshirt'. Released in 1983.

Unofficial bootleg recordings

Boys Next Door Live

Cassette in 6" cardboard box with a booklet. Features photographs taken by Peter Milne, originally for the fanzine *Pulp*. Limited edition of 500. Released in 1983. Live recording of their second gig at Swinburne College in Melbourne on 19 August 1977. The band were bottom of the bill. Appeared on vinyl in 1988 on False Missing Link label (Link 77). Includes cover versions and their own compositions.
Side One: 'Blitzkreig Bop', 'Ain't It Funny', 'I'm Eighteen', 'Gloria', 'Masturbation Generation', 'Who Needs You? (That Means You)', 'I Put a Spell On You', 'Commando'.
Side Two: 'My Generation', 'Big Future', 'These Boots Are Made For Walking', 'World Panic', 'Louie Louie'.

'Rye Whiskey'

7" unofficial single also contains 'These Boots Are Made For Walking', 'Boy Hero' and 'Masturbation Generation'. Incorrect recording details on sleeve. Picture sleeve. Appeared in 1990.

Cremation

Unofficial 11-track Birthday Party compilation also includes 'Death By Drowning' which was recorded at the Storey Hall, Melbourne, 3 November 1979. Clear vinyl on the Preaching Record label.

Videos

'Shivers': Band performing the song at Swinburne College, Melbourne, in a darkened television studio. Directed and produced by 'The Rich Kids', Paul Goldman and Evan English, in 1979. This video clip was later used at length in Richard Lowenstein's 1986 film *Dogs In Space* starring Michael Hutchence. Goldman and English also filmed videos for 'The Hairshirt' and 'After a Fashion', which have never been shown outside Australia.

THE BIRTHDAY PARTY

'Mr Clarinet'/'Happy Birthday' (Missing Link MLS-18)

7" single. Released July 1980.

Recorded January 1980. Same versions on the dually named *The Boys Next Door/The Birthday Party* LP. Recorded at Richmond Recorders. Picture sleeve.

'Friend Catcher'/'Waving My Arms'/'Catman' (4AD AD12)

7" single. Released October 1980.

Recorded January 1980 at Richmond Recorders. Produced by The Birthday Party. Same versions on *The Boys Next Door/The Birthday Party* LP. Picture sleeve.

The Birthday Party/Boys Next Door (Missing Link LINK 7)

LP. Released November 1980.

Recorded August/September 1979 and January/February 1980. Compilation of singles and EP tracks and others. Several pressings with different artwork. Later releases dropped the name 'The Boys Next Door' altogether.

Side One: 'Mr Clarinet', 'Hats On Wrong', 'The Hairshirt', 'Guilt Parade', 'Riddle House'.

Side Two: 'The Friend Catcher', 'Waving My Arms', 'The Red Clock', 'Catman', 'Happy Birthday'.

Recorded at Richmond Recorders.

'Nick The Stripper'/'Blundertown'/'Kathys Kisses' (Missing Link MSD 479)

12" single. Released June 1981.

Recorded at AAV Studios, Melbourne, January 1981. First 1,000 copies with pink and blue cover, later grey and black. 'Blundertown' also turns up on an Australian LP *No Worries*, containing various Australian bands in 1985 (Hot Worried 1).

'Nick The Stripper'/'Blundertown' (Missing Link MLS 32)

7" single. Released 1981/1982.

Recording details as above. Different picture sleeve from above and in black and white. There is a New Zealand version with a pink sleeve on Propellor Records.

Prayers On Fire (4AD CAD 104)

LP. Released April 1981.

Side One: 'Zoo-Music Girl', 'Cry', 'Capers', 'Nick The Stripper', 'Ho-Ho', 'Figure of Fun'.

Side Two: 'King Ink', 'A Dead Song', 'Yard', 'Dull Day', 'Just You and Me'.

Recorded December 1980 and January 1981 at AAV Studio 2, Melbourne, except 'Figure of Fun', 'Dull Day' and 'Just You and Me', which were recorded at Richmond Recorders. Engineered by Tony Cohen and produced by The Birthday Party. Released in Australia in June 1981 on the Missing Link label (LINK 14), of which the first

1,000 copies were in red vinyl. The Greek and Japanese versions also contained 'Release The Bats' and 'Blast Off'. CD version was released in April 1988 (CAD 104 CD) by 4AD, containing 2 additional tracks: 'Blundertown' and 'Kathys Kisses'. This release is also on vinyl (red) from Australia, 1988 (VOZ 2038), same tracks as CAD 104 CD.

'Release The Bats'/'Blast Off' (4AD AD 111)

7″ single. Released August 1981.

Produced by The Birthday Party and Nick Launay in London, 1981. Sleeve features stills from the 'Nick The Stripper' video. Also released on 12″ with same 2 versions in April 1983 by Missing Link (MISS 37–12) with same cover.

'Mr Clarinet'/'Happy Birthday' (4AD AD 114)

7″ single. Released October 1981.

Same sleeve and versions as the Missing Link release.

'Drunk on the Pope's Blood' (4AD JAD 202)

12″ EP. Released February 1982.

One side features Lydia Lunch performing 'The Agony is the Ecstasy', the other side entitled '16 Minutes of Sheer Hell' features The Birthday Party. Both sides were recorded at The Venue, London, on 26 November 1981.
Side One: 'Pleasureheads Must Burn', 'King Ink', 'Zoo-Music Girl' and 'Loose'. Mixed at AAV Studio 2, Melbourne, in January 1982. Not released on CD at present. Released in Australia on Missing Link (ING-004).

Junkyard (4AD CAD 207)

LP. Released July 1982.

Side One: 'She's Hit', 'Dead Joe', 'The Dim Locator', 'Hamlet (Pow, Pow, Pow)', 'Several Sins'.

Side Two: 'Big-Jesus-Trash-Can', 'Kiss Me Black', 'Six-Inch Gold Blade', 'Kewpie Doll', 'Junkyard'.
CD version released in April 1988 also includes 'Dead Joe' (different version), 'Release The Bats' and 'Blast Off' (CAD 207 CD). Released on Missing Link label in Australia (LINK-14). Release of the LP was delayed awaiting cover artwork by Ed 'Big Daddy' Roth. Barry Adamson played bass on 'Kiss Me Black' and 'Kewpie Doll' which were recorded at Matrix, London, with Richard Mazda. The rest of the LP was recorded at AAV Studios with Tony Cohen engineering in December 1981 through January 1982. A cassette version was issued, CADC 207.

'Dead Joe' (BAG 005)

7" flexidisc. Released August 1982.

One-sided single distributed free with *Masterbag* magazine. It features Barry Adamson on bass and a car crash sound effect in the middle of the track. Recorded at Matrix, London, at the same sessions that produced 'Kiss Me Black' and 'Kewpie Doll'. This track was included on the CD release *Junkyard* in 1988.

'The Bad Seed' (4AD BAD 301)

12" EP. Released February 1983.

Side One: 'Sonny's Burning', 'Wild World'.
Side Two: 'Fears of Gun', 'Deep in the Woods'.
Recorded at Hansa Studios, Berlin, October 1982. Produced by The Birthday Party. Released on CD by 4AD (CAD 301 CD) on 7 August 1989 as 'The Mutiny'/'The Bad Seed' EP. This CD features both 12" EPs with additional rough demo versions of 'Pleasure Avalanche' and 'The Six Strings That Drew Blood', which were recorded during the 'Mutiny!' sessions. The master tapes for both these 2 songs have been lost, more's the pity.

'The Birthday Party' (4AD BAD 307)

12" EP. Released 3 June 1983.

Side One: 'Release The Bats', 'Blast Off', 'The Friend Catcher'.

Side Two: 'Mr Clarinet', 'Happy Birthday'.
Compilation of singles. See above for recording details.

'Mutiny!' (Mute 12 MUTE 29)

12" EP. Released November 1983.

Side One: 'Jennifer's Veil', 'Mutiny In Heaven'.
Side Two: 'Swampland', 'Say a Spell'.
Recorded at Hansa Studios in April 1983, reworked at Britannia Row Studios, London, in August 1983. Produced by The Birthday Party. Blixa Bargeld played guitar on 'Mutiny In Heaven'. A lyric sheet was included. For CD release see 'The Bad Seed' EP.

It's Still Living (Missing Link ING 009)

LP. Released May 1985.

Side One: 'King Ink', 'Zoo-Music Girl', 'The Dim Locator', 'She's Hit', 'A Dead Song', 'Pleasureheads Must Burn'.
Side Two: 'Junkyard', 'Blast Off', 'Release The Bats', 'Nick The Stripper', 'Big-Jesus-Trash-Can', 'Dead Joe'.
12 songs (out of 13) from a concert at the Astor Theatre, Melbourne, on 15 January 1982. The missing song is 'Six-Inch Gold Blade'. Mixed at AAV Studios by Tony Cohen. Released on CD in Australia, summer 1991 (Virgin VOZ CD2048), and green vinyl (VOZ 2048). Sleeve notes stated that proceeds from the sales of this album were going to subsidise the completion of a 16mm film of The Birthday Party in concert, made by 'The Rich Kids', Paul Goldman and Evan English. This was a fallacy, as Mick Harvey relates:

'To us both these records [*It's Still Living* and *Best and Rarest*] are effectively bootleg records. It was a whole cover-up job by Keith [Glass], he just wanted to make some more money out of the material. On *It's Still Living* he put the credits on the back to make it look like we were involved and that the money was going towards finishing the film, which it wasn't at all. He pulled some sketched-out lettering, which he'd kept in his drawer, that Nick had done as a rough idea, and so he was able to put on the sleeve, "Lettering by Nick Cave". Just to make it look like Nick had done the cover design. The thing was mixed between 3 a.m. and 5 a.m. one morning, from start to finish, by Tony [Cohen] while we were practising something else out in the studio. Every so often I'd walk in and say, "Oh shit, there's backing vocals on this track," and they'd be switched on halfway through the song. That's what's on the record! He [Glass] just took those tapes. We'd mixed that way, as rough mixes, because they [Goldman and English] were going to show rushes of the film. So eventually this was released as a record. We were really pissed off about both those records. We weren't consulted about anything to do with them.'

Best and Rarest (Missing Link LINK 22)

LP. Released 1985.

Side One: 'Blast Off', 'The Hairshirt', 'King Ink', 'Junkyard', 'Big-Jesus-Trash-Can', 'Release The Bats'. Same versions as LP/singles.
Side Two: 'Blundertown', 'Kathys Kisses' (both from 'Nick The Stripper' 12"), 'Ho Ho' (unreleased take with Nick Cave on vocals), 'The Friend Catcher' (original version, previously unreleased), 'Scatterbrain' (free single), and 'The Plague' (unreleased track from 'Hee Haw' sessions July/August 1979).
According to Mick Harvey: 'Some of this material was never meant to see the light of day. It was completely Keith's idea. The cover he put together was almost like a bad joke on us, using those ridiculous old portrait photos.'

'The Peel Sessions' (Strange Fruit SFPS 020)

12" EP. Released January 1987.

Side One: 'Release The Bats', 'Rowland Around In That Stuff'.
Side Two: '(Sometimes) Pleasureheads Must Burn', 'Loose'.
Produced by Dale Griffin and recorded on 21 April 1981 at Studio 4, BBC Maida Vale studios. A CD version was also released (SFPSCD 020). This was The Birthday Party's second John Peel session.

'The Peel Sessions' (Strange Fruit SFPS 058)

12" EP. Released November 1988.

Side One: 'Big-Jesus-Trash-Can', 'She's Hit'.

Side Two: 'Bully Bones', 'Six-Inch Gold Blade'.
Produced by John Williams on 2 December 1981 at Studio 4, BBC
Maida Vale studios. A CD version was released in 1989 (SFPS 058).
This was their third John Peel session.

Hits (4AD DAD 2016)

Double LP. Released 12 October 1992.

Record One: 'The Friend Catcher', 'Happy Birthday', 'Mr Clarinet',
'Nick The Stripper', 'Zoo-Music Girl', 'King Ink', 'Release The Bats',
'Blast Off', 'She's Hit', 'Six-Inch Gold Blade'.
Record Two: 'Hamlet (Pow, Pow, Pow)', 'Dead Joe', 'Junkyard',
'Big-Jesus-Trash-Can', 'Wild World', 'Sonny's Burning', 'Deep in the
Woods', 'Swampland', 'Jennifer's Veil', 'Mutiny In Heaven'.
Available on cassette (DAD C 2016) and CD (DAD 2016 CD).
Definitive compilation of the band's recordings. Features sleeve notes
by the author.

Miscellaneous related recordings

'The Tuff Monks' (Au-Go-Go Records ANDA 22)

7″ single

'After The Fireworks'/'After, After The Fireworks'.
One-off single recorded at AAV studios in early February 1982. The
group featured Nick Cave, Mick Harvey, Grant McLellan, Robert
Forster, Rowland S. Howard and Lindy Morrison. Mixed at Richmond
Recorders in April 1982. This track was written by the Go-Betweens'
vocalists, McLellan and Forster, and was included on an Australian
compilation album entitled *No Worries* on Hot Records (WORRIED 1).
Mick Harvey recalls: 'That single was like a jam session we had in the
studio which lasted about 2 hours and that we never even finished.
When Keith got Tony to mix it somehow the whole third verse went
missing! There's a really long instrumental section, which is the third
verse. There's no singing on it! How on earth they could release it I
really don't know. It's ludicrous, a travesty. We'd even gone in and

done further overdubs on the track which didn't appear on the mix either. The whole point of the exercise was no one was meant to be credited. It was just meant to be "The Tuff Monks", no explanation, nothing. Sure enough, it was released 6 months later, without the third verse, with all our names on it. Keith Glass, again . . .'

'The Fullness of His Coming'/'I Killed It With a Shoe'

The Birthday Party (minus Phill Calvert) recorded these 2 songs with Anita Lane in May 1982. The tracks were not released at the time and the tapes lay gathering dust . . . until 'The Fullness of His Coming' finally appeared as a featured track on Anita Lane's solo LP *Dirty Pearl* in October 1993 (CDSTUMM 81).

Honeymoon In Red (Widowspeak WSP 12)

LP. Released April 1988.

Side One: 'Done Dun', 'Still Burning', 'Fields of Fire', 'Dead In the Head'.
Side Two: 'Comefall', 'So Your Heart', 'Dead River', 'Three Kings'.
Lydia Lunch with various members of The Birthday Party, Genevieve McGuckin and others, originally recorded in June 1982 in Berlin. The project was conceived as a group in itself, Honeymoon In Red, not The Birthday Party with Lydia Lunch. The label the tapes were recorded for, Rip Off, lived up to its name and had insufficient funds to release the LP at the time. An LP of the material was eventually compiled and released on Lydia Lunch's own label, Widowspeak, with the tracks completely remixed by Jim Thirlwell and Martin Bisi in May 1987. Sonic Youth's Thurston Moore was drafted in to overdub certain guitar parts at this time. Lunch maintains that Nick Cave and Mick Harvey vehemently opposed the release of the album and refused to have their names credited on the sleeve, so their contributions were credited via Lydia Lunch's imagination: 'Mick Harvey denounced it and didn't want any part of it, Nick didn't want his name used, I don't know why . . . He [Harvey] hated the notes that I wrote on it as a piece of creative writing. Nick didn't want his name used because he didn't want me to cash in on the 2 songs he sang on. I was perturbed because I didn't know what had happened to cause such a massive split, I don't know whether I'd aligned myself more with Rowland. It could have been

just a personality clash. At the time I was no angel, let's admit it, I was no angel. I wasn't the easiest person to get along with, I wasn't the saint that I am now.'

Cave and Harvey totally refute Lunch's version of events. According to Harvey: 'No, we were quite happy about them releasing the album, just as long as it didn't have our names on it. They'd gone back in and reworked the songs. We'd worked on 10 or 11 songs and the only reason 5 remained untouched was because they couldn't find the multitracks. The 6 tracks they got their hands on were completely mutilated and changed from anything vaguely resembling what we'd started doing. I didn't see any justification for putting our names on it, we had nothing to do with what had happened to the recording. As far as I'm personally concerned I had nothing to do with it at all. Lydia's initial idea was to put on the cover a sticker, "Recorded with The Birthday Party in 1982", which was untrue because it was never recorded with all the band playing, ever. There were other people involved. She wanted to exploit the name which we found pretty disgusting too. We would have been happy to have had our names on it in places, there were a couple of tracks which were fairly untouched, "Dead River" and "Done Dun", but we knew if we gave her any licence to use our names she would misuse our names.' CD version released 1989 with extra track 'Some Velvet Morning' (WSP 12 CD).

Natures Mortes (4AD CAD 117)

LP. Released November 1981.

4AD compilation for Japan. Features The Birthday Party's 'Mr Clarinet'.

Unofficial bootleg recordings

Devil in the Bottle

Unofficial 12-track compilation released on Party Records. Made in Belgium on blue vinyl in 1985. Live/studio tracks.
Side One: 'Hamlet (Pow, Pow, Pow)', 'Deep in the Woods', 'Wild World', 'Junkyard', 'Jennifer's Veil'.

Side Two: 'Scatterbrain', 'Ho Ho', 'Release The Bats', 'Little Doll', 'Cry', 'Fears of Gun', 'Catman'.

A Social Gathering For the Celebration of the Anniversary of Someone's Birth (Death Records BP 001)

LP. Released 1987.

9 tracks recorded at Aladin, Bremen on 1 July 1982, taken from a radio broadcast.
Side One: 'Big-Jesus-Trash-Can', 'Dead Joe', 'The Friend Catcher', 'A Dead Song', 'Six-Inch Gold Blade'.
Side Two: 'Junkyard', 'Hamlet (Pow, Pow, Pow)', 'Pleasureheads Must Burn', 'Fun House' (with Lydia Lunch).

Cremation

11-track unofficial compilation on the Preaching record label. Limited edition of 500 copies. Mixture of live recordings and John Peel sessions.
Side One: 'Death By Drowning', 'Figure of Fun', 'Nick The Stripper', 'A Dead Song', 'Big-Jesus-Trash-Can', 'Loose'.
Side Two: 'King Ink', 'Pleasureheads Must Burn', 'Cry', 'Sonny's Burning', 'She's Hit'.

VIDEOS

Pleasureheads Must Burn (Icon video FCL): Released 1983, rereleased 1992.

Videoed highlights from The Birthday Party's concerts at the Hacienda in Manchester on 22 July 1982 and 24 February 1983.
'Dead Joe', 'A Dead Song', 'Junkyard', 'Release The Bats', Pleasureheads', 'Big-Jesus-Trash-Can' (22/7/82).
'Hamlet', 'Pleasure Avalanche', 'Six-Inch Gold Blade', 'Wild World', 'Six Strings', 'Sonny's Burning', 'She's Hit' (24/2/83).

Also features The Rich Kids' promotional video for 'Nick The Stripper', which was also included on an *NME* compilation video.

The City: Unreleased visual documentation of the 'Mutiny!' recording sessions at Hansa Studios, April 1983. This 20-minute video graphically captures the disintegration of the band during the recording of 'Jennifer's Veil' and 'Swampland'. Directed by Heiner Muhlenbrock.

NICK CAVE AND THE BAD SEEDS

From Her To Eternity (Mute STUMM)

LP. Released 21 May 1984.

Side One: 'Avalanche', 'Cabin Fever!', 'Well of Misery', 'From Her To Eternity'. Recorded March 1984 at Trident Studios. Engineer Flood.
Side Two: 'Saint Huck', 'Wings Off Flies', 'A Box For Black Paul'. Recorded at the Garden Studios, September/October 1983. Engineer Flood.
Also released on CD (CD STUMM 17) featuring in addition 'In The Ghetto', 'The Moon Is in the Gutter', and the *Wings of Desire* version of '*From Her To Eternity*' (1987). Some LPs came with a poster.

'In The Ghetto'/'The Moon Is in the Gutter' (Mute 7 MUTE 032)

7" single. Released 18 June 1984.

Recorded at Trident Studios, London, March 1984. Engineer was Flood.

The Firstborn Is Dead (Mute STUMM 21)

LP. Released June 1985.

Side One: 'Tupelo', 'Say Goodbye to the Little Girl Tree', 'Train Long-Suffering', 'Black Crow King'.
Side Two: 'Knockin' On Joe', 'Wanted Man', 'Blind Lemon Jefferson'.
Also on CD (CD STUMM 21) with additional tracks, 'The Six Strings That Drew Blood' and 'Tupelo' (single version). Recorded November/December 1984, Hansa, Ton-Studios. Produced by The Bad Seeds and Flood.

'Tupelo'/'The Six Strings That Drew Blood' (Mute 7
MUTE 038)

7" single. Released 29 July 1985.

'Tupelo' details as above but shorter version. Recorded at Hansa Studios
and Trident Studios. Produced by The Bad Seeds and Flood.

'Tupelo'/'In The Ghetto'/'The Moon Is in the Gutter'/'The
Six Strings That Drew Blood' (Homestead HMS 029)

12" EP. Released 1985.

US release.

'The Singer' (a.k.a. 'The Folksinger')/'Running Scared'
(Mute 7 MUTE 47)

7" single. Released 9 June 1986.

Recordings engineered by Tony Cohen, mixes engineered by Flood.
Tracy Pew played bass on 'Running Scared'.

'The Singer' (a.k.a. 'The Folksinger')/'Running Scared'/
'Black Betty' (Mute 12 MUTE 47)

12" single. Released 9 June 1986.

Same as above.

Kicking Against the Pricks (Mute STUMM 28)

LP. Released 8 August 1986.

Side One: 'Muddy Water', 'I'm Gonna Kill That Woman', 'Sleeping
Anleah', 'Long Black Veil', 'Hey Joe', 'The Singer'.
Side Two: 'All Tomorrow's Parties', 'By the Time I Get to Phoenix',
'Something's Gotten Hold of My Heart', 'Jesus Met the Woman at the
Well', 'The Carnival Is Over'.
Guest musicians included Cave's mother Dawn, Hugo Race, Tracy
Pew, Rowland S. Howard, and the Berliner Kaffeehaus Musik
Ensemble. All backing tracks engineered by Tony Cohen at AAV

Studios, Melbourne, November/December 1985. Mixes engineered by Flood at Hansa Studios with Nick, Mick, Blixa and Thomas in March 1986. CD version (CD STUMM 28) also includes 'Running Scared' and 'Black Betty'. *Pricks* going to be a double LP, did record about 23 tracks.

'Your Funeral . . . My Trial' (Mute STUMM 34)

2×12" EP. Released 3 November 1986.

Side One: 'Sad Waters', 'The Carny'.
Side Two: 'Your Funeral . . . My Trial', 'Stranger Than Kindness'.
Side One: 'Jack's Shadow', 'Hard On For Love'.
Side Two: 'She Fell Away', 'Long Time Man'.
CD version (CD STUMM 34) also includes 'Scum'. Barry played bass on 'Jack's Shadow' and 'Your Funeral . . . My Trial'. Recorded at (1) Hansa Studios, July 1986, engineered by Flood, and (2) the Strongroom, London, August 1986, engineered by Tony Cohen. Mixed at the Strongroom. Co-produced by Nick Cave and The Bad Seeds, Flood and Tony Cohen.

'The Mercy Seat'/'New Day' (MUTE 52)

7" single. Released 7 June 1988.

Engineered by Tony Cohen and Flood. Mixes engineered by Tony Cohen. Produced by Nick Cave and The Bad Seeds. See *Tender Prey* for details.

'The Mercy Seat' (full length)/'New Day'/'The Mercy Seat' (video mix) (12 MUTE 52)

12" single. Released 7 June 1988.

'The Mercy Seat' (7")/'New Day'/'From Her To Eternity' (film)/'Tupelo' (7") (CD MUTE 52)

Released 7 June 1988.

'From Her To Eternity' recorded at Hansa Studios, February 1987. Engineered by Tony Cohen.

'Deanna'/'The Girl at the Bottom of My Glass' (12
MUTE 86)

12" single. Released 5 September 1988.

Recording details as for *Tender Prey*. Some copies came with a poster
and a postcard. There was also a 7" radio copy (MUTE 86).

Tender Prey (Mute STUMM 52)

LP. Released 19 September 1988.

Side One: 'The Mercy Seat', 'Up Jumped the Devil', 'Deanna',
'Watching Alice', 'Mercy'.
Side Two: 'City of Refuge', 'Slowly Goes the Night', 'Sunday's Slave',
'Sugar Sugar Sugar', 'New Morning' (identical to 'New Day').
CD Version (CD STUMM 52) also includes 'The Mercy Seat' (video
mix). Recordings engineered by Tony Cohen and Flood at Hansa Ton
Studios, Vieklang, Berlin, and the Strongroom, between August 1987
and January 1988, except 'The Mercy Seat' and 'Watching Alice' by
Chris Thompson at the Studio, Richmond, Australia. Mixes engineered
by Tony Cohen at the Strongroom, January 1988, and the Power Plant,
Carlton, Australia, in March 1988, except 'Watching Alice' mixed by
Chris Thompson at the Studio, Richmond (Australia). Produced by Nick
Cave and The Bad Seeds. The first 5,000 copies of the vinyl version came
with a 12" (P STUMM 52) limited edition of Nick Cave reading from *And
the Ass Saw the Angel*, tracks (1) 'Mah Sanctum', 'Lamentation' (2) 'One
Autumn', 'Animal Static'.

'The Ship Song'/'The Train Song' (MUTE 108)

7" single. Released 12 March 1990.

Recording details as for *The Good Son*, 12" (12 MUTE 108), CD (CD
MUTE 108).

The Good Son (STUMM 76)

LP. Released 16 April 1990.

Side One: 'Foi Na Cruz', 'The Good Son', 'Sorrow's Child', 'The
Weeping Song'.

Side Two: 'The Ship Song', 'The Hammer Song', 'Lament', 'The Witness Song', 'Lucy'. Recordings engineered by Victor Van Vugt at Cardan Studios, São Paulo, October 1989. Mixed by Flood and Gareth Jones at Tritonus, Berlin, November/December 1989. Produced by The Bad Seeds. Some LPs came with a free 7" (P STUMM 76) entitled 'Acoustic Versions', consisting of 'The Mercy Seat' (recorded May 1989, Hansa Ton Studios, by Victor Van Vugt, mixed by Gareth Jones), 'City of Refuge' and 'Deanna' (recorded 8 January 1990 at Fun City Studios, New York, by Wharton Tiers. CD version same tracks as above (P CD STUMM 76). *The Good Son* was released in Japan with the same tracks, with the addition of 'The Train Song'. US version by Mute/Elektra (60988).

'The Weeping Song'/'Cocks'n'Asses' (MUTE 118)

7" single. Released 17 September 1990.

Produced by The Bad Seeds. 'The Weeping Song' remixed by Gareth Jones at Tritonus, Berlin, May 1990. 'Cocks'n'Asses' mixed by Victor Van Vugt at Worldwide, London, June 1990. 12" same as above (12 MUTE 118).

'The Weeping Song'/'Cocks'n'Asses'/'Helpless' (CD MUTE 118)

CD. Released 17 September 1990.

'Helpless' from the Neil Young tribute LP *The Bridge*, recorded December 1988 at Worldwide Studios. Engineered by Victor Van Vugt. There is a CD release of this in US by Mute/Elektra (66605–2): 'Cocks'n'Asses' was referred to as the 'B-Side Song'. The CD also included 'The Train Song'.

'Straight To You'/'Jack the Ripper' (MUTE 140)

7" single (double A-side). Released 30 March 1992.

Produced by David Briggs, Mick Harvey, Nick Cave. Mixed by Tony Cohen, Mick Harvey, Nick Cave. See *Henry's Dream* for details. A limited edition 7" single (LMUTE140) was also issued featuring 'Straight To You' and 'Jack the Ripper' acoustic version.

'Straight To You'/'Jack the Ripper'/'Blue Bird' (12 MUTE 140)

12″ single. Released 30 March 1992.

Recording details same as above. CD single also issued (CDMUTE 140) featuring 'Blue Bird'.

Henry's Dream (STUMM 92).

LP. Released 27 April 1992.

Side One: 'Papa Won't Leave You, Henry', 'I Had a Dream', 'Joe', 'Straight To You', 'Brother, My Cup Is Empty', 'Christina the Astonishing'.
Side Two: 'When I First Came To Town', 'John Finn's Wife', 'Loom of the Land', 'Jack the Ripper'.
Produced by David Briggs. Co-produced by Mick Harvey and Nick Cave. Recorded at Sound City, Van Nuys, California, November/December 1991, except 'Christina the Astonishing' and 'Loom of the Land', recorded at Dreamland Studios, Bearsville, New York, November 1991. Mixed by Tony Cohen, Mick Harvey, Nick Cave at Metropolis Studios, Melbourne, Australia, January 1992, except 'Brother, My Cup Is Empty' and 'Christina the Astonishing', mixed by David Briggs at Indigo Ranch, California, December 1991. Engineered by Chuck Johnson (Sound City, Indigo Ranch), Tony Cohen (Metropolis), Dave Cook (Dreamland). Additional engineering assistance from Victor Van Vugt on the demos. Limited edition colour print of the cover artwork by Anton Corbijn was included with some copies. CD version same tracks as above (CD STUMM 92).

'I Had a Dream, Joe/'I Had a Dream, Joe'(live versions)/ 'The Good Son' (MUTE 148)

7″ single. Released 1 September 1992.

Limited edition 7″ single. Studio version of 'I Had a Dream, Joe', details as *Henry's Dream*. Other tracks recorded live at Paradiso, Amsterdam, on 2 and 3 June 1992 by Eurosound Mobile 3. Engineered and mixed by Victor Van Vugt at Unit 3 and Blackwing Studios, London, June 1992. Mastered at the Exchange, London.

'I Had a Dream, Joe'/'The Carny'(live versions)/'The Mercy Seat'/'The Ship Song' (12MUTE 148)

12" single. Released 1 September 1992.

Also available on CD (CDMUTE 148). Although track listing differs, recording details the same as 'I Had a Dream, Joe' 7".

Live Seeds (CD STUMM 122)

CD with accompanying photo book. Released 6 September 1993.

'The Mercy Seat', 'Deanna', 'The Ship Song', 'Papa Won't Leave You, Henry', 'Plain Gold Ring', 'John Finn's Wife', 'Tupelo', 'Brother, My Cup Is Empty', 'The Weeping Song', 'Jack the Ripper', 'The Good Son', 'From Her To Eternity', 'New Morning'.
Recorded at various concerts throughout Europe and Australia 1992/3. Mixed by Tony Cohen and The Bad Seeds at Atlantis Studios, Melbourne, Australia, January/February 1993. CD only released with photo booklet 'Nick Cave and The Bad Seeds – Live Seeds', with black and white photographs taken by Peter Milne while the group were touring Europe, Australia and Japan 1992/3. Compiled by Mick Harvey and Katy Beale. Some of the photographs included would also be featured in Milne's larger collection of photographs of the tours, *Fish in a Barrel*, published on 14 October 1993 by Tender Prey.

'Do You Love Me?' (single version)/'Cassiel's song'/'Sail Away' (MUTE 160)

Limited edition 7" single pressed on silver vinyl. Released 28 March 1994.

For recording details see *Let Love In*. 'Cassiel's Song' features Nick Cave (vocals and piano), Barry Adamson (bass and timpani), Chris Tombling, Robert Salter, Leo Payne, Sally Fenton (violins), Chris Pitsillides, Sue Dench (violas), Audrey Riley, Jane Fenton (cellos), Julia Girdwood (cor anglais). String arrangement by Mick Harvey, string conductor, Billy McGee. Produced by Nick Cave, Barry Adamson and Victor Van Vugt. Commissioned by Wim Wenders for his film *Faraway So Close*. CD single also issued (CD MUTE 160), same tracks as above. 12" vinyl single (12 MUTE 160) featured 'Do You Love Me?' (album version).

Let Love In (STUMM 123)

LP. Released 18 April 1994.

Side One: 'Do You Love Me?', 'Nobody's Baby Now', 'Loverman', 'Jangling Jack', 'Red Right Hand'.
Side Two: 'I Let Love In', 'Thirsty Dog', 'Ain't Gonna Rain Anymore', 'Lay Me Low', 'Do You Love Me? (Part 2)'.
Produced by Tony Cohen and The Bad Seeds. Recorded at Townhouse III, London, September 1993, and Metropolis, Melbourne, Australia, December 1993. Mixed at Metropolis by Tony Cohen. Sleeve design by Nick Cave and Robert Hales. Guest musicians include Rowland S. Howard and Tex Perkins of The Beasts of Bourbon and The Cruel Sea (backing vocals on 'Do You Love Me?'), Spencer P. Jones (backing vocals), Robin Casinader, Warren Ellis (violins on 'Ain't Gonna Rain Anymore' and 'Do You Love Me? (Part 2)'), David McComb of The Triffids (backing vocals on 'Lay Me Low'), Katharine Blake and Donna McKevitt of Miranda Sex Garden (backing vocals on 'Do You Love Me? (Part 2)'). CD version (CD STUMM 123) same tracks as above.

'Loverman' (single version)/'(I'll Love You) Till the End of the World' (MUTE 169)

7″ single. Released 4 July 1994.

Limited edition 'hypnotic' picture disc 7″ single, an image taken from the 'Loverman' video directed by John Hillcoat. 'Loverman' details as album Let Love In. '(I'll Love You) Till the End of the World' taken from the soundtrack to Wim Wenders' Until the End of the World. Produced by Gareth Jones and The Bad Seeds, engineered and mixed by Andre Giere and Victor Van Vugt.

'Loverman' (single version)/'B-Side' (CD MUTE 169)

CD single. Released 4 July 1994.

Also available as a 12″ single (12 MUTE 169). Same version of 'Loverman' as 7″. 'B-Side' is a 19-minute selection of 23 largely improvised, ad-libbed pieces of music recorded direct to DAT by Nick

Cave and The Bad Seeds in the past 2 years. The tune snippet titles are: 'God's Hotel', 'Do You Love Me?', 'Sugar-Coated Place Called Love', 'Kiss Me in the Morning', 'Nobody's Baby Now', 'A-Side', 'B-Side', 'C-Side', 'Loverman', 'Born To Be Your Loverman', 'Take The "O" Out Of Country', 'Jangling Jack', 'Sex Appeal', 'Where the Action Is', 'Blow That Babe Away', 'I Let Love In', 'Dadaladaladaladawn', 'Thirsty Dog', 'Man of Steel', 'It's a Crazy World', 'Ain't Gonna Rain Anymore', 'Sweet Maria', 'Lay Me Low', 'Vanilla Essence', 'Do You Love Me? (Part 2)'. 'B-Side' engineered by Victor Van Vugt, Patrick, David McCluney and Robin Mai. Edited together by Mick Harvey and David McQuarrie at EMI 301, Sydney, and Lutz at Hansa Studio, Berlin. Thanks are given to Rowland S. Howard, James Johnston and Thomas Stern for their contributions.

'Red Right Hand'/'That's What Jazz Is To Me' (MUTE 172)

7"single. Released 17 October 1994.

Limited edition of 2,000 copies printed on blood-red vinyl. Single version of 'Red Right Hand', details as *Let Love In*.

'Red Right Hand'/'That's What Jazz Is To Me'/'Where the Action Is' (CD MUTE 172)

CD single. Released 17 October 1994.

'That's What Jazz Is To Me' and 'Where the Action Is' are totally improvised compositions recorded direct to DAT by Patrick at Vielklang, Berlin, which were then edited by Mick Harvey and David McQuarrie at Studio 301, Sydney, Australia.

Miscellaneous related recordings featuring Nick Cave

Burnin' the Ice by Die Haut (Illuminated Records SUAMS 30)

LP. Released August 1983.

Nick Cave featured vocalist and lyricist on 4 tracks: 'Stow-a-way',

'Truck Love', 'Pleasure is the Boss', 'Dumb Europe'. Recorded at Studio West, Aachen, December 1982. Mixed at Studio Funk, Berlin, March 1983 by Klaus Kruger and Die Haut. As yet this album has not been reissued on CD.

The Department of Enjoyment, *NME* cassette Various Artists

Issued 12 May 1984.

Features Nick Cave and the Cavemen performing a cover of Screamin' Jay Hawkins' 'I Put a Spell On You'. The *NME* claimed the track was specifically recorded for the cassette. Highly doubtful.

'Kick-a-bye' by Annie Hogan (Double Vision DVR 9)

EP. Released June 1985.

4-track EP featuring Cave as lyricist and vocalist on 'Vixo'. Music for the track was composed by Hogan. Cave produced the track. EP recorded and mixed at Alvic in October 1983 and Wave, February 1985.

'Scum' by Nick Cave and The Bad Seeds (LYN 18038)

Sold at Bad Seeds' concerts, October 1986

Flexidisc which came with a free poster with humorous resumés of each individual band member by Jessamy Calkin.

Smack My Crack, Various Artists (Giorno Poetry Systems GPS 038)

LP. Released June 1987.

Features Cave reading 'The Atra Virago', an extract from his then forthcoming novel *And the Ass Saw the Angel*.

Gigantic, Various Artists (MM RTDO)

Cassette. Released 1987.

Features Cave reading 'One Autumn', an extract from his then forthcoming novel *And the Ass Saw the Angel*.

'Dirty Sings' by Anita Lane (12 MUTE 65)

12" EP. Released June 1988.

Features contributions by Harvey, Adamson and Cave. The track 'I'm a Believer' was co-written with Cave. All 4 tracks, 'If I Should Die', 'I'm a Believer', 'Lost in Music', 'Sugar in a Hurricane', also featured on the CD version of Anita Lane's solo LP *Dirty Pearl*.

Wings of Desire Original Soundtrack, Various Artists (IONIC2)

LP/CD. Released August 1988.

Features Nick Cave and The Bad Seeds performing 'The Carny' (same version as 'Your Funeral . . . My Trial') and 'From Her To Eternity', 'live version' engineered by Tony Cohen at Hansa Studios, Berlin, February 1987. Track co-produced by Nick Cave and The Bad Seeds, Flood and Tony Cohen.

Nick Cave The Interview

An Enigma promotional cassette of an interview conducted by Reyne Cuccuro of Rockpool in December 1988, New York City. Duration 27 minutes (E PRO - 172). Released early 1989.

Ghosts . . . of the Civil Dead, Original Soundtrack, Music composed and performed by Nick Cave, Mick Harvey, Blixa Bargeld (IONIC 3)

LP/MC/CD. Released May 1989.

'The News' (voice: Michelle Babbit), Introduction – A Prison in the Desert, David Hale – 'I've been a Prison Guard since I was eighteen years old', Glover – 'I was sixteen when they put me in prison', David Hale – 'You're danglin' us like a bunch of meat on a hook', 'Pop Mix', Glover – 'We were united once', David Hale – 'The day of the Murders', 'Lilly's Theme (A Touch of Warmth)', 'Maynard Mix', David Hale – 'What I'm tellin' is the truth', Outro – 'The Free World', Glover – 'One man released so they can imprison the rest of the world'.

Featured vocalist on theme: Anita Lane (also included on Anita Lane's solo LP *Dirty Pearl*). Original recording engineer Ted Hamilton. Album compiled by Victor Van Vugt. Voices: David Hale and Kevin Mackey as 'Glover'. Portrait photograph of David Hale by Polly Borland.

Headless Body in Topless Bar by Die Haut

LP/CD. Released May 1989.

Includes contributions by Kid Congo Powers, Mick Harvey, Anita Lane and Nick Cave. Cave is a featured vocalist on a cover of a Micky Newberry song, 'I Just Dropped In To See What My Condition Was In'. This track was also featured on a compilation LP, *Deutschland Strikes Back Vol. 1*, released in March 1989.

The Bridge, Various Artists (CAROLINE CAR LP5)

LP/CD. Released August 1989.

Neil Young tribute LP, the profits from which were to go to the Bridge School for autistic children. Features The Bad Seeds performing Neil Young's 'Helpless'.

Red Tape, Various Artists

Cassette.

Compilation tape of various Mute recording artists given away free with *Select* magazine October 1990. Features Nick Cave and The Bad Seeds performing 'Foi Na Cruz'.

The Good Songs (Mute Sonet France SA 2110)

CD. Released 1990.

5-track Cave compilation, available by subscription to the French rock magazine *Les Rockinruptibles*. Featured tracks: 'The Mercy Seat' (acoustic version), 'Rye Whiskey' (originally recorded during the *Kicking Against the Pricks* sessions and only previously available as a flexidisc with *Reflex* magazine, Vol. 1, Issue 10, 1989), 'Helpless', 'From Her To Eternity' (*Wings of Desire* version), 'The Train Song'.

International, Various Artists (CD STUMM 40)

LP/Cassette/CD. Released 1990.

Compilation of various Mute recording artists. Features Nick Cave and The Bad Seeds performing 'The Train Song'.

I'm Your Fan: The Songs of Leonard Cohen by . . . Various Artists (East West Records 9031–75598–1)

LP/Cassette/CD. Released October 1991.

Leonard Cohen tribute LP. Features Nick Cave and The Bad Seeds' unique interpretation of Cohen's 'Tower of Song', of which the songwriter was very enamoured. Engineered by Victor Van Vugt. Produced by Nick Cave and the Bad Seeds.

Until the End of the World, Original Soundtrack, Various Artists (Warner Bros. 7599 26707–2)

LP/Cassette/CD. Released December 1991.

Features Nick Cave and The Bad Seeds performing the Cave composition '(I'll Love You) Till the End of the World'. Produced by Gareth Jones and Nick Cave and The Bad Seeds.

Gas Food Lodging, Original Soundtrack, music composed by Barry Adamson and J. Mascis and Various Artists (IONIC9)

CD. Released March 1992.

Features Nick Cave and The Bad Seeds performing 'Lament' from *The Good Son*.

'What a Wonderful World' by Nick Cave and Shane MacGowan (MUTE 151)

7" single, 12" single, CD. Released November 1992.

Other tracks included Nick Cave singing MacGowan's 'Rainy Night in Soho' and MacGowan singing Cave's composition 'Lucy', the backing track of which had been recorded at Cardan Studios, São Paolo, Brazil. 'What a Wonderful World' and 'Rainy Night in Soho' were recorded at Abbey Road Studios, London, featuring all The Bad Seeds, with additional players Julia Girdwood (oboe), Chris Pitsillides (viola) and Audrey Riley (cello). Produced by Victor Van Vugt and The Bad Seeds. Strings and oboe arranged by Billy McGee and Mick Harvey. The single reached No. 1 in the National Charts in Portugal.

Viva! Eight, Various Artists (VIVA 8)

Cassette and CD. Released February 1993.

Live double LP, 110 minutes in duration, featuring highlights from 8 concerts at the Town and Country Club from 1 until 8 September 1992, arranged by the *New Musical Express* to celebrate 40 years of the paper's existence, with proceeds from the concerts and recording donated to the Spastics Society. Includes Nick Cave and The Bad Seeds performing 'Jack the Ripper' and the Cave/Howard Birthday Party composition 'Nick The Stripper' with Rowland S. Howard as lead guitarist. Recorded on 1 September 1992. (Two other Birthday Party songs were played that evening, 'Wild World' and 'Dead Joe'.) *Viva! Eight* was originally only available from the *NME* by mail order.

Faraway, So Close!, Original Soundtrack, Various Artists (EMI 8 27216 2)

LP/Cassette/CD. Released September 1993.

Features Nick Cave performing his compositions 'Faraway, So Close!' and 'Cassiel's Song'. Both songs produced by Nick Cave, Victor Van Vugt and Barry Adamson. 'Faraway, So Close!' also released as the B-side to Lou Reed's 'Why Can't I Be Good', also taken from the film soundtrack (EMI 724388080521).

Sweat by Die Haut (What's So Funny About . . . 4015698 2940–2)

CD. Released October 1993.

Features Nick Cave performing live with Die Haut at the Tempodrom, Berlin. The songs are 'Truck Love' and 'Pleasure is the Boss', first recorded by Cave and the group in December 1982. Cave also sings a cover of The Loved Ones' 'Sad Dark Eyes'.

Nick Cave and The Bad Seeds 'Stripped' (Mute Records/ Mushroom Records PRD 94/84).

CD. Released December 1994.

Bonus CD only available in Australia as a free gift with every Nick Cave and The Bad Seeds album purchased coinciding with the group's 6-date 'Let Love In' tour of the country, beginning on 9 December 1994 in Perth at the Overseas Passenger Terminal and concluding in Sydney on 17 December at the Hordern Pavilion. The 3 tracks are acoustic versions of 'The Mercy Seat', 'City of Refuge' and 'Deanna', previously released for a limited period with initial copies of *The Good Son*.

Batman Forever, Original Soundtrack, Various Artists (Atlantic 7567–82759–2)

LP/Cassette/CD. Released June 1995.

Features Nick Cave performing 'There is a Light', music by Tim Friese-Greene, lyrics by Cave. Additional guitar by James Johnston. Strings by Confederate Airforce Orchestra. Recorded at Maison Rouge and Rubbery Studios, London.

'The World's a Girl' by Anita Lane (MUTE 177)

7" single, 12" single, CD. Released June 1995.

Contains three tracks – 'The World's a Girl', 'I Love You . . . Nor Do I' and 'Bedazzled'. Cave duets with Anita Lane on 'I Love You . . . Nor Do I' (a version of Serge Gainsbourg's 'Je t'aime . . . Moi Non Plus') and on 'Bedazzled', which comes originally from the Peter Cook and Dudley Moore film of the same name.

VIDEOS

Kings of Independence, Various Arists (Studio K7 K7 001)

UK VHS video. Released 1989, rereleased 1992.

Live concert footage of Nick Cave and The Bad Seeds performing

'Stranger Than Kindness' and 'Saint Huck' at the Kings of Independence festival, Knopf Music Hall, 15 August 1987.

The Road To God Knows Where, Director: Uli M. Schüppel; Producers: Mick Harvey, Uli M. Schüppel. A co-production of Mute Films, German Film Academy, uMs-Productions 1990. (VHS Mute/BMG 790475)

Total running time: 1 hour 53 minutes. Subtitled. UK video released December 1990.

Black and white documentary of life on the road with Nick Cave and The Bad Seeds during their American tour, Chestnut Cabaret, Philadelphia, 7 February 1989 until Scream, Los Angeles, 4 March 1989. The film received its world première at the Olympic Film Festival, Manchester, 29 June 1990. Video release also included the following music videos: *In the Ghetto*, Director Evan English; *Tupelo*, *The Singer*, *The Mercy Seat*, all directed by Christoph Dreher; *Deanna*, directed by Mick Harvey. *The Road To God Knows Where* was also issued in Japan in NCTC version as a package consisting of the *King Ink* lyric book (which also includes details of *Ghosts . . . of the Civil Dead*) and a CD of the *Ghosts . . . of the Civil Dead* soundtrack, 1990.

Exhibit 1 Visible Evidence (Mute Film/BMG video 791148)

Released 1991.

Compilation of various Mute artists' videos, including Nick Cave and The Bad Seeds' 'The Weeping Song', directed by Angela Conway.

Nick Cave and the Bad Seeds Live at the Paradiso, Editor: John Hillcoat, Producer: Richard Bell, Director of Photography: John Mathieson (Mute Film/BMG Video 74321 12160 3). Running time: 57 minutes.

UK video released November 1992.

'The Mercy Seat', 'Jack the Ripper', 'The Ship Song', 'Tupelo', 'Deanna', 'The Good Son', 'The Carny', 'Papa Won't Leave You, Henry', 'The Weeping Song', 'In the Ghetto', 'From Her To Eternity', 'New Morning'. Live concert film of The Bad Seeds performing at the

Paradiso, Amsterdam, filmed over a 2-night residency, 2 and 3 June 1992, intercut with Nick Cave writing out each song title before they commence. Recorded by Victor Van Vugt.

BIBLIOGRAPHY

Nick Cave, *King Ink*, Black Spring Press Ltd., May 1988, hardback. Collection of Cave's lyrics, plays and other writings.

Nick Cave, *And the Ass Saw the Angel*, Black Spring Press Ltd., August 1988, hardback. Cave's first novel. Penguin paperback edition published August 1990.

FILMOGRAPHY

Himmel Über Berlin/Wings of Desire, Director: Wim Wenders 1987.

UK video release (Connoisseur Video CR003) Running time: 128 minutes.

Nick Cave and The Bad Seeds featured performing in a nightclub, 'The Carny' and 'From Her To Eternity'. Wenders won the prize for best direction at the Cannes Film Festival 1987.

Dandy, Director: Peter Semple, 1988. Subtitled: 'Is Valdo Kristl Right'.

Running time: 93 minutes. Shot on 16mm blown up to 35mm.

Nick Cave featured 'performer'. He also sings an acoustic rendition of 'City of Refuge'. Various Bad Seeds and Birthday Party songs included on the soundtrack. The film had its world première at The Tunnel, New York, 24 June 1988. UK première 15 June 1991 at the Scala Cinema, London, now sadly closed. Not available on video.

Ghosts . . . of the Civil Dead, Director: John Hillcoat,
Producer: Evan English, 1988. Running time: 90 minutes.

UK video release (Electric Pictures EP0022) 1993.

Nick Cave featured as an actor portraying Maynard. Also credited as
'additional writer' with Hugo Race. Cave produced original soundtrack
with Mick Harvey and Blixa Bargeld. UK première London Film
Festival, November 1988.

Johnny Suede, Director: Tom DiCillo, 1991.

Running time: 97 minutes.

Nick Cave featured as actor portraying Freak Storm. Also sings
'Freak's Mamma's Boy' written by Tom DiCillo. UK theatrical release,
June 1992.

INDEX

Individual album tracks are listed only when discussed out of context of the album on which they appear.